THE
NEW POLITICS
OF SCIENCE

DAVID DICKSON

With a New Preface

THE UNIVERSITY OF CHICAGO PRESS
Chicago & London

To Pru

The University of Chicago Press, Chicago 60637
The University of Chicago Press, Ltd., London

©1984, 1988 by David Dickson
All rights reserved. Published 1984
University of Chicago Press edition 1988
Printed in the United States of America
97 96 95 94 93   5 4 3

Published by arrangement with Pantheon Books,
a division of Random House, Inc.

Library of Congress Cataloging in Publication Data
Dickson, David, 1947–
  The new politics of science.

  Originally published: New York : Pantheon Books,
c1984.   With a new preface.
  Bibliography: p.
  Includes index.
  1. Science and state—United States.   2. Science—
Social aspects—United States.   3. Technology and
state—United States.   4. Technology—Social aspects
—United States.   I. Title.
Q127.U6D53   1988   306'.45   87-34275
ISBN 0-226-14763-0 (pbk.)

                                        CIP

CONTENTS

7

TOWARD A DEMOCRATIC STRATEGY FOR SCIENCE · 307

PREFACE, 1988

In July 1987, President Ronald Reagan announced to a meeting in Washington of the nation's top scientific, industrial, and military leaders that he had decided to launch a $150-million research and development program to investigate the potential uses of one of the most exciting scientific discoveries in recent years, "high temperature" superconductors. These ceramic materials exhibit virtually no resistance to electric currents at temperatures which, although considerably below room temperature, are still far above those close to "absolute zero" (-273 degrees centigrade) previously thought necessary to achieve such performance. The new superconductors offer the possibility of producing very high magnetic fields at relatively low cost, and thus promise to revolutionize a wide range of technologies, from high-speed trains that travel on magnetic cushions to medical scanners. Their discovery by two scientists working on what they had considered to be primarily a theoretical question epitomizes the increasingly direct linkage between basic science and high technology. Indeed, many of those attending the conference praised the speed with which the administration had moved to exploit the possibilities of a scientific breakthrough made only a few months before.

Several aspects of President Reagan's announcement, however, as well as of the way the meeting had been organized, generated widespread concern in the scientific community. One was the fact that the new research and development program was to be managed by the Department of Defense. A second was that, even though the original discovery had been made by two European scientists (later in 1987 to be awarded the Nobel prize), foreign research workers and diplomats were excluded from the meeting on the grounds that it had been organized primarily for the benefit of U.S. commercial interests. Finally, the President announced that he intended to tighten up the secrecy under which the research program would be conducted, a move which, as one physicist subsequently complained, "could strangle this infant technology in its crib."

Two weeks earlier, an equally controversial event had taken place in a London courtroom. In what was widely regarded as a test case for the biotechnology industry, a British judge overturned a patent previously awarded to the U.S.'s fastest-growing genetic engineering company, Genentech, for a process used to produce a blood clot dissolving agent known as Tissue Plasminogen Activator (TPA). The company had sought broad patent protection on a range of techniques which it had developed for inserting the gene responsible for the creation of TPA into bacteria.

The judge agreed that Genentech was entitled to limited patent protection as reward for its research efforts, but not of the scope being demanded. To grant the company the monopoly it wanted, he said, "would stop others attempting to discover alternative, possibly wholly unknown and possibly better routes to that end" and would therefore "stifle research which, in the public interest, it ought to be open to other investigators to pursue."

Between them, these two events epitomize the type of issue which has come to dominate discussion about the social dimension of science in recent years, both within and outside the U.S. scientific community. In the mid-1970s, concerns about the relationship between science and society focused primarily on the undesirable consequences of the social applications of science through technology; these ranged from the steady destruction of the natural environment to the new workplace hazards posed by science-based production techniques, such as the carcinogenic effects of synthetic chemicals. Today, the political agenda of the scientific community is filled by a very different set of topics, those raised by the implications of efforts to maximize the contribution of science to commercial and military ends. As both the Washington superconductivity meeting and the London patent decision demonstrated, many of these topics concern questions about who shall have access to and control over scientific information, the key elements making up what I describe as "the new politics of science."

This book is an attempt to explore both the origins and principal characteristics of this new politics. It was first published in 1984, and concentrates primarily on events that took place in Washington between 1978 and 1983, the period during which the new trends first emerged. Since then, these trends—and the problems that they generate—have become even more apparent. As a result, a proper understanding of the events of this period is just as important today, if not more so, than it was four years ago.

Three of the trends have remained particularly marked. The first is the financial support being given to science by an administration which is still committed to cutting back on practically every other field of public spending apart from defense. The budget for federally-funded research and development continued to grow steadily throughout the mid-1980s, and increased by 50 percent in *real* terms between 1980 and 1987. Basic research has received especially favorable treatment. Indeed, early in 1987 the National Science Foundation (NSF) claimed it had won a commitment from the administration for a succession of increases that would double its budget over the following five years.

The second trend has been the increasingly direct linkage between basic science and its commercial exploitation. "International competitiveness" has become the key motif linking ventures as different as the NSF's support for the creation of new university-based interdisciplinary research centers to a multi-billion dollar proposal to sequence the three billion amino-acid bases that make up the human genome. The private sector, too, has increasingly come to recognize that its future depends on access to basic science; according to the NSF, research grants provided by private industry to university research teams more than doubled, from $300 million to $600 million a year, between 1981 and 1986.

The third trend is the growing domination of the public funding of research by the Department of Defense. The military's share of the total federal R&D budget, having remained roughly constant (at around fifty percent) for most of the 1970s, had risen to sixty percent by 1982; in 1987, it was estimated to have reached seventy-four percent of the total. Although much of the increase was accounted for by the development costs of new weapons systems (and the figures include the research effort devoted to the Strategic Defense Initiative), basic science has not been neglected. On university campuses, military-sponsored research has almost regained the levels of the mid-1960s; at the beginning of 1986, when the Pentagon asked for bids for a new series of university research grants, it received 963 applications for only 86 awards.

From the policy point of view, therefore, the most striking aspect of the science budget since the early 1980s (i.e., since this book was written) has been its consistency. John McTague, the acting director of the Office of Science and Technology, was almost apologetic when he told a meeting organized by the American Association for the Advancement of Science in March 1986 that there was "a certain monotony" in the President's proposed R&D budget for the following year, with its demands for increases in defense R&D as well as basic research, and its emphasis on universities. But if these broad policy guidelines have remained constant, there has also been a steady increase in the tensions and conflicts resulting from the fact that science now has strategic value to both the civilian and military economies.

In the case of universities, for example, the growing presence of industrial sponsorship continues to have a major impact not only on what research is done, but on how it is done. Having initially committed themselves to remaining within the scientific community's traditional conventions of openness and academic freedom, many universities have dropped their scruples under financial pressures. Some have reversed a previous refusal to issue exclusive licenses to companies which help to pay for individual research projects. More and more university scientists are finding ways of bending the rules of publication. Some insert fabricated data into published research papers as a substitute for what companies want to keep secret; others, in the words of one West Coast university vice-chancellor, have hinted that their research results "have simply not appeared on library shelves." A study carried out at Harvard University in 1986 showed that university scientists who worked with industry funds were four times as likely to keep their research secret as their colleagues; two-thirds of them felt they were being pressured to spend too much of their time on commercial activities.

Other tensions have grown around the dominance of the military in research funding. In 1985, partly under the pressures from the academic community described in chapter 3 of this book, the Department of Defense agreed that it would not censor the basic research which it supports in universities. But its influence is still keenly felt in other ways. At the insistence of the Pentagon, foreign scientists have been excluded from an increasing number of scientific conferences; in 1985, fifty papers were summarily withdrawn, at the Pentagon's insistence, from a meeting organized by the Society of Photo-Optical Instrumentation Engineers, and the twenty-two which were eventually delivered (after the appropriate censorship) had to be presented at a session from which most foreign participants were excluded. The Pentagon has also tried to prevent scientists accepting DoD funding from expressing their personal views about its policies; Donald A. Hicks, the undersecretary of defense for research and engineering, said in an interview in *Science* in 1986 that he felt no such funds should be given to any scientist openly criticizing the Strategic Defense Initiative.

Finally, the past four years have also seen the expanding importance of the issues raised in this book in the international arena. Science has found renewed political support in virtually every nation in the world; perhaps the most notable example is the Soviet Union. Not only has leader Mikhail Gorbachev described scientific and technical progress as "the main lever for the solution of all economic and social issues," but the policy of *glasnost* originated, according to several observers, in discussions about how to stimulate the nation's scientific base.

It is therefore not surprising that the international tensions surrounding science have also expanded. NSF director Erich Bloch has expressed his belief that science, as "a highly competitive field," is "no more international than commerce is"—thus reinforcing the view of knowledge as a commodity described in chapter 2. Conversely, U.S. attempts to control access to its science are being viewed increasingly harshly by foreign countries. The British computer manufacturer ICL complained of "growing technological imperialism by the United States" after it had been required to obtain an export license for the knowledge contained in the heads of some American computer scientists that it had recruited. And political support in Europe for EUREKA, a major program of collaborative technology projects, has been partly the result of a backlash against the increasingly restrictive terms being imposed on foreign participants in major U.S. technology ventures, ranging from the SDI research program to the space station being planned by the National Aeronautics and Space Administration.

The original text of the 1984 edition of this book has not been altered for this paperback edition. Like any author, I might have chosen to express myself differently in some passages, with the benefit of hindsight—particularly in those which have given rise to misunderstanding. I might not, for example, have been as harsh in my remarks about the ideological basis of attempts to expand the teaching of science in public schools, since I accept that this is a necessary component of even a critical appreciation of science. Similarly my comments on creationism, which have been picked up by several reviewers, were in no way meant to imply support for what I consider to be a dangerously reactionary social movement, but were merely to illustrate my argument that the dominant perception of science need not always be the one handed down by an intellectual elite. There are also some serious omissions, of a detailed discussion of the feminist perspective on science (touched upon too briefly in the final chapter) or of alternative scientific strategies available to the Third World countries, among others.

Despite these weaknesses, I hope the events that have taken place since 1984, some of which have been referred to above, illustrate the continuing relevance of the book's major themes. I hope, too, that the appearance of this paperback edition will help to stimulate wider public appreciation and discussion of these themes than have perhaps existed up to now.

ACKNOWLEDGMENTS

To Jan Annerstedt, Rosemary Chalk, Dan Greenberg, Carol MacLennan, Colin Norman, Bob Ubell, Susan Wright, and especially David Noble and Bob Young, for perceptive and (usually) encouraging comments on draft material.

To many others, including Karim Ahmed, Bob Alvarez, Gene Frankel, Richard Grossman, John Holmfeld, Richard Kazis, Jonathan King, Charlie Komanoff, Les Levidow, Al Meyerhoff, Ward Morehouse, Dorothy Nelkin, Francisco Sagasti, Jean-Jacques Salomon, Jacob Sherr, Margaret Seminario, Nicholas Wade, Christopher Wright, and Burke Zimmerman for helping me to develop my ideas about American science policy, even though they may not always agree with the result.

To those in Washington who have generously given their time to provide me with information on and insights into the formal and informal operations of the policy-making machinery.

To the Department of Technology and Social Change, University of Linkoping, Sweden, for six weeks' hospitality in the spring of 1982, when chapters two and three were written.

To David (Dai) Davies, who, as then editor of *Nature*, sent me to Washington in 1978, and to John Maddox, who kept me there.

To Wendy Goldwyn of Pantheon, for everything one could wish in a publisher's editor.

To Pru, for unfailing support in countless ways; and to Catherine and Christopher, for their confidence that one day "the book" would be finished and there would be time for other things.

Gif-sur-Yvette, France
DECEMBER 1983.

THE
NEW POLITICS
OF SCIENCE

INTRODUCTION

WHO WILL DETERMINE THE SHAPE OF THE FUTURE? AND HOW WILL IT BE done? Until relatively recently, the single most important factor allowing an individual, group, or social class to mold the lives of others was access to superior force, whether military or civilian. Today that force is being replaced by science. Over the forty years since the end of the Second World War, advanced technology has become the key to both economic and military power. And over the same period science has become the key to advanced technology. Access to, and control over, the scientific knowledge produced in the nation's universities and its government and industrial laboratories has become central to control of the economy—and thus ultimately of the nation's future itself.

The last few years have seen the reemergence in the U.S. of an almost religious belief—dormant for much of the 1970s—in the powers of science-based technology. Industrial leaders argue that only scientific and technological supremacy over the rest of the world will allow the country to prosper economically.[1] Military leaders claim that only a rapidly increasing military research budget, feeding directly into ever more sophisticated weapons of mass destruction, will ensure a stable peace. Politicians have picked up and faithfully amplified both refrains. President Reagan's State of the Union address at the beginning of 1983 was largely a hymn of praise to the cornucopia of technological promise, and he approved substantial increases in the basic science budget to under-score this faith. Meanwhile each of the potential Democratic candidates for the 1984 presidential race was trying to demonstrate how his own brand of technology policy and support for science would help to "reindustrialize" America faster and more effectively than the proposals of his rivals.

Seldom discussed in these debates, however, are the forms of political control that new technologies—whether promoted by Republicans or Democrats—bring with them. The more an individual becomes depen-dent on a commodity owned and controlled by others, the more vulner-able he or she becomes to the ends that others seek to achieve through that ownership. Science is no exception. It is noticeable that the renewed enthusiasm for science on the part of industrial, military, and political leaders has occurred at the same time as a major tightening of control over science by private decision-makers summed up in the headline to a recent article by a senior official with the National Academy of Sciences: "Knowledge as Real Estate."[2] This in turn has provided new opportuni-ties for ensuring that the applications of science through technology respond first to the pressures of private profit rather than social need. Science then comes to reinforce the power of those who own or have access to capital (and thus profit directly from its increase in value) over those who do not.

The patterns of influence and control that permeate American science and its applications have worldwide implications. Almost half of the Western world's research and development is carried out in the United States, which, with an estimated research and development budget of $86 billion in 1983, spends more money on science than Japan and the industrialized nations of Europe combined. America's continued supe-riority in virtually all fields of science allows it to determine the terms on which other countries will be given access to its technological fruits. Scientific collaboration is offered to some (such as China, Japan, or India) in return for political and economic favors and denied to others (such as the Soviet Union) as punishment for unacceptable behavior. Both developed and developing countries alike are promised access to the science that they lack facilities or resources to produce themselves on condition that they open up their internal markets to American capi-tal and refrain from anti-American policies. Science, in this sense, has become a currency for diplomatic barter—with the U.S. holding the bank.

The purpose of this book is to outline the network of political relation-ships, both domestic and international, that are increasingly expressed through science and technology. It is not my intention to try to evaluate the overall performance of science as such; it goes without saying that scientific research has made substantial contributions to increasing the material welfare of mankind, and promises to continue to do so at an accelerating rate. Given this positive side of the equation, however, criticism of modern science and technology is usually limited to its "abuses" (such as military technology, particularly nuclear weapons) or its "side effects" (such as environmental pollution or new workplace hazards). I intend to go beyond these critiques, to look at how the patterns of control over science reinforce and reproduce basic patterns of political control that operate in society. For the increasingly central *economic* importance of science gives it a *political* significance that is often lost in debates that focus on how it is applied to socially desirable or undesirable ends.

What I have tried to show in this book is that decisions ranging from the broad allocation of scientific resources among competing areas of basic science, to the detailed application of scientific results to market-determined needs, are increasingly concentrated in the hands of a class of corporate, banking, and military leaders, assisted by those in other sectors, such as universities, whose political allegiance lies with this class in practice, if not in principle. I also hope to demonstrate how this process has been actively encouraged by the "science policy" of recent U.S. administrations. The measures by which this is being done do not show up in the research budget as such. Rather, they are to be found in the details of the institutional and legislative evolution that has taken place over the past few years in order, it is claimed, to improve the environment for rapid technological innovation and reduce the weight of social controls on new technologies. These steps include increased tax incentives at the expense of direct federal support (shifting leverage over research funds from public to private hands); patent reform (tying up scientific knowledge as a form of private property subject to monopolistic exclusive control); revisions to anti-trust legislation (justifying anti-competitive business practices in the name of international competitiveness); incentives for closer links between universities and business (giving the corporate community the first bite at the fruits of university research); tighter control over the transfer of scientific knowledge to other countries (using science as a tool of foreign policy); and so on. The result is that fundamental decisions concerning the directions of the nation's scientific enterprise are being steadily removed from the domain of active public decision-making, despite the fact that a high proportion of the research on which today's (and tomorrow's) high technology is based has been paid for out of public funds, and that this research is supported largely on promises of its contribution to public welfare.

My approach has goals at two levels. The first is to describe the major elements of this new era in science policy, which started in the mid-1970s under President Gerald Ford, accelerated under President Jimmy Carter, and took off under President Ronald Reagan. The situation we currently face had its origins in the immediate postwar period, a boom time for science, when political enthusiasm, grounded in the success of the Manhattan Project, spurred by the shock of the Russian Sputnik, and reaching its apogee during the Kennedy administration, provided scientists with both lavish financial support and high social status. This period was followed, from the mid-1960s, by a stage of questioning and doubt, when more direct payoffs were asked of the scientific community. Today we are in the middle of what I would characterize as the third phase of postwar science policy. Once again budgets are moving rapidly upwards (see Figure 1), and the dominant credo again follows Vannevar Bush's *Science: The Endless Frontier*—written in the wake of science's wartime successes, endorsed as the philosophy of the first phase, but harshly criticized in the second.

At the second level, my goal is to explore the political roots—and consequences—of this scientific renaissance. One of its main functions, I suggest, has been to counteract the surge of "grass-roots democracy" that swept the U.S. in the 1970s, originating in the civil rights and anti-war protests of the previous decade, subsequently embracing a broad-based critique of modern technology generated by the environmental movement and labor union struggles over occupational health and safety. These movements threatened the traditional power bases of American society not only directly but—often more successfully—by questioning the cultural assumptions (such as the identity between science and progress) on which this power rested. In an attempt to head off the social disruption that these movements portended if carried to their full conclusion, Congress and the administration passed a series of laws aimed at limiting the undesirable consequences of science and technology through social regulation. In doing so, however, the government was implicitly endorsing the legitimacy of public demands for direct social control over the way science was produced and applied. As the nation's economic problems worsened toward the end of the decade, the corporate sector used them as an excuse to counterattack and to reestablish its claim to keep decision-making over science—the key to the development of the forces of production—in private hands.

Just as a decade ago critics challenged the cultural assumptions of government and corporate leaders and their attitudes toward science in order to help open decision-making to public scrutiny, so today the corporate community is using the same tactic in reverse. Stiff environmental controls on chemical processes are criticized as being "unscientific"; those who reject science as the core of modern education—and yet continue to criticize its social effects—are described as "technologically illiterate"; critics of the technological choices of corporate America are labeled "anti-science" (a bit like calling an art critic "anti-art"). In many such ways the image of science as a positive social force is being used to mask efforts to make the practice of science, and its applications through technology, less susceptible to direct democratic control.

The dialectic between the material and the ideological roles played by science is a constant theme running through my analysis. The balance

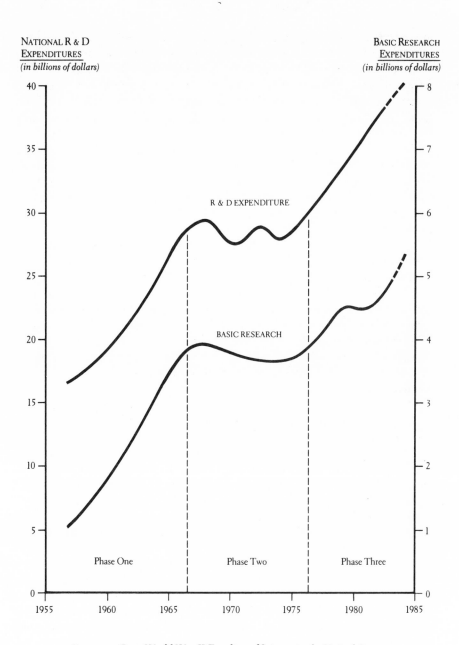

NATIONAL R & D
EXPENDITURES
(in billions of dollars)

BASIC RESEARCH
EXPENDITURES
(in billions of dollars)

R & D EXPENDITURE

BASIC RESEARCH

Phase One

Phase Two

Phase Three

FIGURE 1: *Post–World War II Funding of Science in the United States*

The funding of U.S. science after world War II can be divided into three periods. The first two decades were a period of unprecedented growth, dominated by federal funds. The next decade saw stagnant budgets and a broad questioning of science. Since the late 1970s, support for science has taken off again—this time largely spurred by the private sector. All figures are expressed in constant 1972 dollars.

in emphasis, however, varies throughout the book. In the first four chapters I describe the main characteristics of what I call "the new politics of science" by exploring its manifestations in separately identifiable (but frequently overlapping) domains: government science policy, the relationship between universities and the corporate community, the relationship between the scientific community and the military, and finally the use of science to achieve foreign-policy objectives. In each instance I have tried to show how a renewed interest in basic science—justified primarily as a necessary component in advanced technology (itself justified as crucial to economic or military strength)—has been accompanied by efforts to focus control over this science in the hands of private decision-makers, and to use this control to achieve political as well as economic objectives.

The next two chapters look in detail at the broader political context in which this process has taken place. Chapter Five describes the successful containment of demands for greater direct public control of both science and technology, illustrated respectively by the debates over controlling the hazards of recombinant DNA research and the evolution of the Office of Technology Assessment. Chapter Six looks at efforts to head off the indirect exercise of this control by reducing the impact of social constraints on private decision-makers and encouraging the stepping up of unfettered technological innovation, both endorsed in the name of science and progress.

The final chapter attempts briefly to synthesize the themes emerging from the previous analysis. It puts them in a historical context by showing how the projection of confidence in science and scientific "progress" as a cultural belief has, at various strategic points in both European and American history, been used to help secure the structural changes that capitalist society has periodically undergone to escape economic collapse, while masking the social costs that these structural changes have imposed. In the past these costs included the imposition of new forms of wage labor, the introduction of assembly-line disciplines, and so on; today they range from the relaxation of health, safety, and environmental regulation to wide-scale unemployment that could well be caused by the replacement of human labor by machines. The chapter ends with some thoughts about the implications of my analysis for future political action. It suggests issues that need to be attached to the agenda of political movements that seek to contest the growing control of America's corporations over its political life, pointing the way toward a system that will promote science and technology in harmony with the goals and values of democracy, not in conflict with them.

Most of the material for this book was gathered during the four years I spent in Washington covering developments in American science policy for the British weekly science magazine *Nature*. This has resulted in two limitations. First, it means that I lean heavily on issues that became public controversies during this period—such as the regulation of recombinant DNA research or the growth of the biotechnology industry—rather than others which, though perhaps equally significant, lay relatively dormant. The second limitation is a tendency to accept Washington's definitions of "significant political issues," definitions that do not always coincide, as I found in several trips around the U.S., with the issues faced "on the ground." Yet I would suggest that, from a long-term perspective, many of the most significant issues of any particular era tend to be those that either surface as major controversies in the mass media or are brought to Washington by the protagonists to be resolved. It is around these issues, and with the limitations of selectiveness in mind, that I have tried to weave my analysis, at the same time attempting to stand back a little from their internal dynamics—and the language in which they tend to be conducted—to demonstrate how they form part of a broader political pattern of events in a way that the participants may often be unaware of.

In part this aim has meant focusing more than is conventional in discussions of science policy on the individuals engaged in such controversies, concentrating both on their institutional affiliations and on the power groups to which they belong (by which I mean those groups that have a significant impact on Washington policy-making). One of my biggest surprises on arriving as a British journalist in Washington was the strength of the belief that politics was made essentially by the decisions of individuals (from "the President has decided . . ." downwards), an impression frequently used to mask the fact that American politics, perhaps even more than in Europe, is based on the building of coalitions and the exercise of pressure-group power. Indeed, in practice the merits of a political position tend to be measured more by the weight of the coalition supporting it than by any inherent value it may possess. Take, for example, the successive volumes of reports by "ad hoc committees" and "special commissions" on "what's wrong with American technology" —most of which do little more than repeat the findings (and usually the empirical data, what little there is of it) of preceding reports. In dutifully ploughing through these reports, it is difficult to avoid the conclusion that their role is merely to enlarge the power base of the coalition in favor of particular political objectives (such as greater tax incentives for corporate research and development, or a more "benign" patent policy), not to add to the stock of public knowledge. It is for this reason, rather than a desire for historical accuracy in itself, that I have emphasized the institutional connections of individuals making public statements about science policy, for in terms of political analysis these are often as significant as—if not more so than—the content of the statements themselves.

Finally, a word about my purpose in writing this book. It is a political book, written for an avowedly political purpose: to describe how the control of science has become a key element in the control of American society, what is wrong with the way that this control is currently exercised, and how things might be improved. In writing the book, I do not apologize for appearing to depart from the traditional "neutrality" of journalism, since I do not believe that such neutrality exists; if there is any change from conventional journalistic practice, it is merely in making more explicit the political assumptions contained in even the most innocent-looking news story. I do not pretend, or expect, that everyone who reads this book will share the perspective from which it is written; nor that the reader will agree with all the interpretations placed on the events that I have tried, as accurately as possible, to describe. What I do hope, however, is that those who are already concerned about some of the topics I cover will find their understanding broadened and deepened about why things happen in the way that they do—and about what the alternatives might be. It is through such an enlarged understanding of the political functions of modern science, combined with the will to formulate the necessary changes and explore ways of putting them into effect, that the validity of my analysis will be put to its proper test.

1

THE
NEW POLITICS
OF SCIENCE

IN PRESENTING HIS ANNUAL REPORT TO THE LEADERS OF THE SCIENTIFIC community at the end of April 1983, Frank Press, president of the National Academy of Sciences, opened on a confident note. "My report to the members this year must be made in the context of a new mood in the country," he said, "one that looks to science and technology for economic progress and national security to an extent that may be unprecedented."[1] Press was not overstating his case, for the prospects facing American science were brighter than at virtually any point in the previous twenty years. With enthusiastic backing from both the administration and Congress, federal support for science was at an all-time high; when combined with the contribution from the private sector, total funding for research and development in 1983 was expected to reach 2.7 percent of the gross national product—greater than in any other Western nation—compared to 2.2 percent only six years earlier.

There were other indications of this new enthusiasm. The two branches of government, for example, were falling over each other in their eagerness to provide more money for science education in schools. Science, which had been scrabbling for both funds and respectability in Washington only five years earlier, was now definitely "in." As William Carey, executive officer of the American Association for the Advancement of Science, expressed it in an editorial in the magazine *Science:*

"With such blessings from both the executive and legislative heavens arriving in profusion after years of dwindling rations, scientists and educators alike could be pardoned for pinching themselves."[2]

The reasons for this shift were not entirely mysterious. Faced with an economic crisis to which traditional economics seemed unable to provide an effective solution, politicians of both parties clutched eagerly at the mystical promise of high technology as a cure for the nation's ills. Between January and March 1983, the first three months of the 98th Congress, over 200 separate bills introduced in either the Senate or the House of Representatives suggested ways of improving the country's capacity for technological innovation. Virtually every city and state in the nation developed plans for attracting high technology industries as the solution to their economic problems, with many, such as New York and Chicago, setting up their own "science and technology foundations" to provide funds for such initiatives.[3] Wall Street twitched with the same nervous enthusiasm. Announcing that "we have reached a pivotal moment in the history of science and technology," investment analysts Merrill Lynch launched, with Japanese and European partners, a new high technology fund known as SCI/TECH Holdings, which pledged to put at least 80 percent of its assets into science and technology industries. For its inauguration in March 1983, it raised over $800 million in capital, apparently the largest initial endowment of any mutual fund in history. "We are in the midst of a science-technology craze," the chief investment strategist for Morgan, Stanley and Co., Barton M. Biggs, told his company's elite clientele.[4]

Beneath the general euphoria, a few voices of dissent could be heard. Some pointed out that the promise of high technology was, indeed, no more than that, and it could prove inflated—perhaps even creating the same backlash that had occurred in the late 1960s. Biggs himself went on to warn his investors of "a few incipient signs of a world-class bubble in the blowing"[5]—a warning reinforced later in the year when some of the high-tech stocks began to drop in value as rapidly as they had earlier increased. Others pointed to the unequal distribution of the rewards that high technology offered. One survey from the Bureau of Labor Statistics predicted that high technology would, directly and indirectly, create a million new jobs in the next ten years, but contrasted this to the two million that had been lost through plant closings in the previous three. High technology was already beginning to reinforce traditional class divisions; at the high school level, for example, a gap was widening between those schools that could afford access to computers and those that could not.[6] Finally, it began to be pointed out that the military's new interest in science-based technology coincided with an increasingly aggressive stance toward the Soviet Union, a stance many feared only increased the risk of nuclear war.

As far as the Reagan administration was concerned, however, few doubts were allowed. Indeed, in many ways the administration's arrival in Washington at the beginning of 1981 had formally raised the curtain on this new era in postwar U.S. science and technology policy. Two predictable themes, both reflecting broad commitments from Ronald Reagan's pre-election manifesto, dominated the new administration's thinking about science, and each was soon expressed in budget recommendations presented to Congress. In line with promises to reduce government's role in civilian activities, federal support for applying science directly to social needs—for example, through the development of new energy technologies—was substantially reduced on the grounds that private corporations should be left to decide whether or not to fund such activities, using the criterion of commercial profitability. At the same time, reflecting a commitment to increased military spending, there was a shift in emphasis of government support from civilian to military research. The budget proposals presented to Congress at the beginning of 1981, and passed virtually intact later in the year, included an increase of more than 20 percent for military research spending, while funds for civilian research were kept almost level with the previous year—a pattern that was maintained in subsequent years.[7]

Such a shift in priorities had been generally anticipated by the scientific community. So, too, had the second thrust represented by the budget proposals—even if its initial virulence was unexpected (and the damage caused was largely rectified two years later). This was a direct ideological attack on federal funding of various aspects of science, in particular science education and social science research, which had previously been the target of vociferous criticism from the conservative wing of the Republican party.[8] Many scientists were upset to discover, for example, that a congressional aide who had been responsible for outspoken criticism of the National Science Foundation (NSF) in the mid-1970s, arguing that its science education programs had been used to propagate a liberal, anti-religious ideology in the nation's public schools, was placed on the transition team responsible for establishing the new administration's priorities for the agency. Concern changed to dismay when, in its first budget proposals, the administration proposed eliminating all support for science education (already suffering a decline) from the NSF budget, and reducing funding for the social sciences by half. Both cuts were bitterly contested; to many scientists, they seemed to confirm their worst fears that a new wave of conservative anti-intellectualism was imminent.

The most significant aspect of the new administration's attitude toward science, however, lay—like Sherlock Holmes's dog—in what it did not do. In a budget marked by major reductions in virtually all areas of social spending, from food stamps to environmental protection, the research budget was singled out—second only to defense—for favored treatment, remaining a top priority for continued investment of public funds. In the words of a budget document published by the Office of Management and Budget: "One area of traditional federal responsibility that has been protected from severe reductions in the revised 1982 budget is support of basic research."[9] In budget proposals submitted to Congress for each of the three years 1982, 1983, and 1984, increases for spending on basic science were requested that were several percentage points above the anticipated level of inflation. The effect of these proposals—in each case supported eagerly, although with some shift in emphasis, by Congress— was to secure an estimated (real) increase of 7.8 percent in federal funding for research and development over the first three years of the Reagan administration, at a time when virtually all other areas of federal support were being drastically pruned. As the London-based *Economist* described it in a news item commenting on the record federal research and development budget request of $447.8 billion for 1984: "The arts of science now seem to rank next to the arts of war among Mr. Reagan's priorities."[10]

Initially the scientific community was thrown into confusion, for it had a long history of distrusting conservative Republicans. In 1964, 50,000 scientists across the country organized themselves in what science journalist Daniel Greenberg described as "a successful political baptism" —campaigning to help defeat Republican presidential candidate Barry Goldwater (Reagan's spiritual predecessor) by painting him as incompetent to administer a complex technological society.[11] Four years later their worst fears seemed confirmed when, despite the campaign efforts of "Scientists and Engineers for Humphrey," Richard Nixon was elected President and proceeded not only to impose the biggest cuts in the science budget since the end of the Second World War, but also to sweep scientists from the corridors of power they had confidently patrolled for the previous two decades. Not surprisingly, there was little enthusiasm among scientists for candidate Reagan and his conservative views during the 1980 election campaign.

This distrust spilled over into the post-election period. At a meeting held at the National Academy of Sciences in October 1981—shortly after the science budget had, in common with all other federal expenditures, been threatened with a 12 percent across-the-board cut—the Reagan administration's policies toward science were widely criticized by leading members of the scientific community. Paul Gray, president of the Massachusetts Institute of Technology, complained that the cuts, even if later reversed, showed a lack of comprehension of the way that science worked, since they reflected a mismatch between the time scales of government decision-making and the cycles of scientific discovery. Physicist Alan Bromley, president of the American Association for the Advancement of Science, claimed that "guerrilla warfare" had already broken out among scientists who found themselves competing for limited research funds. And the meeting agreed to a "consensus statement" which warned that the effects of the administration's policies could inflict "irreversible damage" on the nation's scientific community.[12]

Two years later, however, the scientific community was singing a different tune. There was undeniable budgetary confirmation of the Reagan administration's claims that science had been singled out for favored treatment. Overall support for science was increasing even faster than it had under the Carter administration—including a proposed 17.4 percent budget increase for the National Science Foundation, over 10 percent higher than the anticipated rate of inflation. Thus, little criticism was now heard. Indeed, the President's science adviser, forty-three-year-old Los Alamos physicist George A. Keyworth II, who had been the target of fierce attack at the 1981 academy meeting, was now hailed as a hero. The largest increases were still concentrated on research linked to military and high technology objectives. But there were significant increases for areas of basic science from high energy physics to astronomy. The administration even seemed to have reversed its previous antipathy toward the social sciences and science education, committing itself to a significant increase in NSF funding for both subjects.

It wasn't only a question of money. The whole thrust of the administration's approach to science rapidly began to generate a groundswell of support within the scientific community, for it coincided closely with this community's own ideas about how science should be run. On the one hand, Reagan and his officials were pushing for more status and prestige for science and scientific expertise. On the other, they were supporting scientists' demands for greater autonomy and freedom from direct social controls (described by one prominent Reagan science adviser, Edward David, president of Exxon Research and Engineering, as "the privilege of decision in R&D"[13]). Both had been severely challenged over the previous decade; both were now being resanctioned by an administration that openly spoke not only of the essential function of science in an advanced industrialized economy, but also of the need to allow the scientific community to choose (within preselected areas of priority) its own research projects relatively unhampered by explicit social commitments, by using excellence in research rather than social relevance as the principal criterion of merit, and thus as a guide to those projects most worthy of support.

The changes had admittedly been building up over the previous several years. Science's return to political favor, after its period in the wilderness during the Nixon presidency, had started in the mid-1970s under President Gerald Ford and had rapidly gathered some steam under President Jimmy Carter. Indeed, many of the Carter administration's ideas and initiatives were built on directly by the Reagan administration. Immediately after the 1980 election, one science adviser explained that "the science and technology field is not one in which there are radically different views on different issues."[14] A year later a report from the

American Association for the Advancement of Science pointed out that "the most striking feature is the degree of similarity in the stated policies affecting R&D of this and previous administrations."[15]

Yet the *political* endorsement by the Reagan administration carried an added significance. Both of its predecessors had supported science as one area of public spending among many deserving greater support; in contrast, science's success in its "survival of the fittest" battle against the Reagan budget ax augmented its privileged status in the eyes of Washington, even in those conservative circles that disapproved in principle of public funding of all but a few selected social activities. In an editorial in *Science* Keyworth emphasized that federal research dollars were "not an entitlement"; the administration was increasing funds for research, not because it felt it had a moral obligation to do so, but because it was convinced that "our leadership in the international marketplace is at stake."[16]

Whatever the motivation, the increases came as welcome news to the leaders of the scientific community. Frank Press, previously President Carter's science advisor, had as the new president of the National Academy of Sciences been responsible for the October 1981 meeting in which the scientific establishment had let off its collective steam in the direction of the White House. Yet when Press later appeared before a congressional committee he had primarily words of support for the new administration, choosing to stress how U.S. scientific institutions needed to adapt to the "new political realities" they faced, and to emphasize the willingness of the scientific establishment to enter negotiations over how it should absorb the changes.[17] A year after that he was describing the budget increases for science being sought by the Reagan administration as "very innovative" and "highly laudable."[18]

Both Keyworth and Press were, in their different ways, commenting on the fact that a major transformation was taking place in Washington in terms of the attitudes of the nation's policy-makers toward science. Its endorsement by the Reagan administration has appeared to make the transformation a reflection of partisan politics. But as the initiatives already taken by the Carter administration together with Press's personal acquiescence in and enthusiasm for his successor's policies indicate, the roots of the revolution transcend simple partisan distinctions. Rather, they reach to the base of the U.S. political economy, reflecting in particular the close-knit connections between basic science and those advanced technologies being pushed to the center of the industrial, economic, and political stage. It is these connections that are likely to determine the basic framework of public policies toward science for the next decades—regardless of the political complexion of the administration occupying the White House.

The transformation in science policy has created a new agenda for the research community. In the postwar decades, support for science was based directly on its potential contributions to the government's major technological endeavors. Initially this meant meeting military requirements and promoting the development of nuclear power; subsequently support was expanded to include efforts to exploit the civilian and military uses of space. There followed a decade in which the principal thrust was to make science directly relevant to social needs—for example, in tackling health problems such as cancer and heart disease, in developing new energy sources to substitute for oil and nuclear fission, and in protecting the environment.

The focus has now shifted again. This time the contribution of science to the competitive strength of American industry and to military technology has risen to the top of the priority list. At the end of 1982, Keyworth justified the proposed hefty increases in the research budget, and its particular emphasis on the physical sciences and engineering, on the grounds of a year-long study in the White House of "the competitiveness of those industries that either produce high technology products or depend on high technology for manufacture,"[19] confirming his earlier conclusion that "basic research is America's ace-in-the-hole."[20] Later he made it clear that the extra funding being granted to basic research in universities was intended for a purpose: "It's a *challenge* to the universities to assume a greater role in helping us regain our momentum in world technological leadership."[21]

Complementing the new agenda has, just as significantly, been the creation of new political coalitions controlling how funds for basic research should be allocated. For the first three postwar decades, the private sector took a relatively back seat in influencing the choice of priorities and the shape of federal research programs. Industry's rediscovered enthusiasm for basic science, however, has brought it back to a dominant role exerted from the front ranks of scientific decision-making. Government research priorities are now strongly influenced by the directions suggested by the private sector; universities are renewing ties with private corporations that have not flourished as healthily since the 1930s; states are eagerly acting as marriage brokers to such alliances, keen to promote high technology solutions to local development problems and to accept whatever conditions the private sector lays down for its cooperation. As Edward David of Exxon puts it: "Autonomy is giving way in industry, government, and academia alike to a close integration with the innovation system."[22] It is a system in which private capital rules. And through a myriad of institutional realignments—some dramatic (such as the doubling in corporate support for university basic research), some incremental (such as the appointment of industry representatives to government advisory boards)—control over science is being steadily concentrated in capital's domain.

In the light of such developments, the current revolution in science policy contains both new promises and new threats. The experience of the past thirty years has demonstrated that there is no simple, automatic connection between expenditure on science and economic and social progress. The economy did not respond automatically, as some had predicted, either to the "science push" policies of the postwar period or to the "demand pull" policies that succeeded them. Current policies simultaneously reflect an understanding of the importance of science and an awareness of the complexities of applying it successfully to social goals, whatever the dominant political system.

The new threats, however, are equally significant. If the Reagan administration has infused a new vitality into the research community, it has also exacted a heavy price. The implication of the new agenda, placing military strength and international competitiveness in high technology at the top of the priority list, is that planning for science is now almost exclusively based—whether in the short, the medium, or the long term—on the needs of the military and the marketplace; social objectives (such as protection of health or the natural environment) have been displaced as the principal focuses of research planning and are accepted only to the extent that they are compatible with increased military strength or commercial profits.

Furthermore, the new political partnerships have resulted in patterns of control over science that directly conflict with conventional notions of democracy. The postwar period saw decision-making over the allocation of funds for science largely dominated by scientific, military, and corporate elites, defined by C. Wright Mills as "an intricate set of overlapping cliques [sharing] decisions having at least national consequences."[23] At the time, however, the rapid expansion of the nation's research budget maintained enough pluralism to avoid an excessive concentration of research funds and to support a steady expansion of the whole research agenda. In the late 1960s and early 1970s, the domination of these three groups was challenged (with varying degrees of success); attempts were made to democratize science policy by opening it up to a wide range of new inputs. Now, waving the banner of social efficiency and international competition, and with the direct encouragement of Washington, these three elites are reestablishing their alliances. Democracy, it is argued—particularly in science—must be sacrificed in the interests of a healthy economy; technological progress is again being interpreted to mean primarily high profitability in private corporations, rather than full employment or the most socially desirable forms of economic growth.

Those most directly affected by the set of principles and decisions lumped together as "science policy" are the members of what is loosely identified as the scientific community. According to definitions used by the National Science Foundation, there are currently about 700,000 scientists employed in research and development work in the United States —in other words, one for every 160 members of the working population.[24] The density of scientists in the U.S. is higher than in any other country in the world. It compares with one scientist for every 250 workers in other industrialized nations, and one for every 2,000 or more in Third World countries.

Reflecting the growing centrality of science to the modern economy, the number of scientists has increased almost six times since the Second World War, far more than any other professional group. The period of most rapid growth was during the 1950s and early 1960s, when the total number of scientists in the population grew at an annual rate of over 7 percent. A decline in research budgets caused by reductions in military and space research during the early 1970s took its toll, although its major impact was on research engineers. Employment for scientists increased steadily at a rate of about 4 percent a year between 1970 and 1980, the largest increase occurring in business and industry, where employment of scientists increased by 58 percent over the decade (compared with a 37 percent increase in universities and other educational institutions, and a 12 percent increase in the federal government). Despite a decade of equal rights legislation and attempts to attract women and minorities, science remains essentially a white, male preserve. Women, for example, account for less than one-tenth of all engineering and scientific workers (compared with two-fifths of the professional and technical work force taken as a whole), and they have higher rates of unemployment and underemployment than their male counterparts. Racial minorities make up even less (one-twentieth of scientists and engineers; one-tenth of the professional and technical work force).[25]

In its broadest sense, "science" can be defined as the activity of those who define themselves as research scientists. In 1983 the United States spent an estimated $86.5 billion from both public and private sources on activities that come under the broad heading of research and development (R&D), which includes both basic research and investigation of the ways that the results of this research can be applied to new products and processes. This formidable sum is more than that in all other industrialized Western nations and Japan combined, and about one-third of the world's total. In the postwar period most of this money came from the government. Industry, however, has been steadily increasing its research budgets. Thus, whereas in 1968 industry was spending only half as much as the government on R&D, in 1980 for the first time since the 1930s it spent more. Figures increased rapidly as research spending—as in the federal budget—seemed to defy the recession. According to a survey by McGraw-Hill, the private sector increased its R&D spending in 1981 by almost 20 percent over the previous year, the most rapid increases coming in the fields of information processing (34 percent increase), electronics (21 percent), chemicals (21 percent), and telecommunications (20 percent)—all areas defined as "high technology" on the basis of their R&D intensity.[26]

Not surprisingly, given this trend, the bulk of the nation's research and development (74 percent in 1983) is now carried out in industrial laboratories, even though about one-third is paid for by the federal government. As far as basic research is concerned, universities and colleges are the highest performers (estimated $4.97 billion, or 47.5 percent of the total, in 1983), followed by industrial laboratories (19.4 percent), and the government's own research laboratories (15.3 percent). A further 9.1 percent of the nation's basic research is carried out in R&D centers administered by universities (such as the astronomy centers run for the National Science Foundation, or the high energy physics laboratories funded by the Department of Energy); the remaining 8.6 percent is performed in other independent research centers.[27]

The heavy spending on R&D has helped to put the U.S. in a dominant international position in the creation of new technologies. As a top Commerce Department official put it at the beginning of 1983: "The U.S. has by far the world's most advanced technology in almost every area of interest."[28] The same dominance is also reflected in spending on so-called basic science—research carried out with no specific application in mind, but which is nevertheless "the principal mode for developing the knowledge base necessary for future science and technological breakthroughs," according to the National Science Board.[29] In 1981 the U.S. spent a total of $9 billion on basic research, again higher than almost all its Western partners combined. Two-thirds of this support ($5.9 billion in 1981) comes from the federal government, on the grounds that the research is of such a long-term, risky nature that individual companies would not be prepared to support it.

One of the principal concerns of science policy is to decide the criteria according to which federal funds are divided among different groups of scientists. In countries with a centralized ministry or department of science or research (such as France), the process of selecting priorities is relatively straightforward. The U.S., however, has adopted a pluralistic approach to the funding of science, so that a scientist can—in principle —apply for support to a wide variety of government agencies, each of which has been allocated its own research budget. A university physicist, for example, might apply to the National Science Foundation, the Department of Energy (which, for historical reasons related to the emergence of major research facilities at national laboratories, is responsible for high energy and nuclear physics), the Department of Defense, or even—if appropriate—one of the smaller agencies, such as the Department of Commerce.

This pluralistic approach means that there is no single "science budget" prepared by a small group of government officials, proposed by the administration, and voted on by Congress. Rather, the total amount of money spent on science is calculated by adding together the research budgets of all the separate agencies, each of which has to be negotiated with Congress separately. The lion's share of the research and development budget goes to military projects, primarily funded by the Department of Defense (47 percent in 1980, rising to a predicted 70 percent in 1984, according to the Reagan administration's proposals). Three mission agencies—the Department of Energy, the National Aeronautics and Space Administration (NASA), and the Department of Health and Human Services—each now has an R&D budget roughly one-third that of the Pentagon's. Other agencies, such as the Department of the Interior, the Environmental Protection Agency, the Department of Agriculture, and the Development of Commerce, each has an R&D budget about an order of magnitude lower—but still far from insignificant. (See Figure 2 for a plan of the organization of American science.)

The biggest supporter of basic science is the Department of Health and Human Services, which, through the National Institutes of Health, provides the bulk of funding for biomedical research in the nation's universities and medical schools, with an estimated basic research budget of $2.24 billion in 1983. Second to this is the National Science Foundation, created shortly after the war to channel federal support to university research in nonmedical fields. In addition, each government department supports an increasing amount of basic science out of its own research budget. NASA, for example, spent $605 million on basic research in 1983, about 18 percent of its total R&D budget. The Defense Department and the Department of Energy jointly spent $788 million on military-related basic research, with the Department of Energy spending a further $844 million on basic research related to energy needs. Other agencies spend smaller but often still significant sums. The U.S. Department of Agriculture, for example, had a basic research budget of $263 million in 1982, the Department of the Interior $86 million, and the Environmental Protection Agency $20 million.[30]

The simplest indicator of an administration's attitude toward science lies in the budget proposals it submits to Congress at the beginning of every year, indicating which budgets it wants to increase and which to cut back. Over the preceding eighteen months, each individual agency works out what research it would like to carry out or support in the following fiscal year (which begins on October 1) and how much it is likely to cost. These estimates are then submitted to the Office of Management and Budget, and a lengthy series of negotiations begins, in which the White House seeks to insert its own preferences and goals into the budgets of different agencies, while the agencies try to defend their own priorities and pet projects. The outcome of these negotiations is the President's budget submission to Congress in January, accompanied by a statement setting out the broad principles on which the proposals have been based.[31]

Budgets for each of the separate agencies are then closely scrutinized by two parallel sets of committees in the House of Representatives and

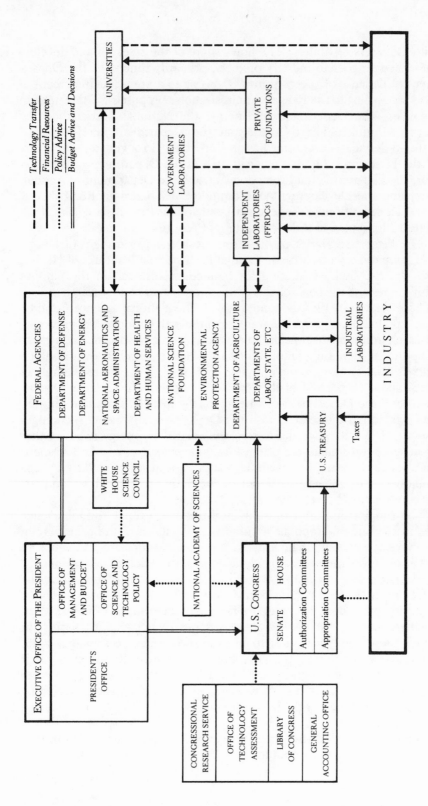

FIGURE 2: *The Organization of United States Science*

FIGURE 2: (facing page) *This schematic representation shows the process by which the resources the U.S. devotes to research and development (estimated at $86 billion in 1983) are allocated among the different sponsors and performers of research. Just under half of this money is provided by the federal government, and is spent according to priorities endorsed by the congressional budget process. Government-sponsored research is carried out in four principal sectors: university laboratories; independent laboratories or research centers (often run by a university or a consortium of universities, and known collectively as federally funded research and development centers [FFRDCs]); the government's own laboratories; and research laboratories of private corporations.*

Industry spends most of the money it allocates to R&D (estimated at $44 billion in 1983, or 51 percent of the nation's total R&D budget) in its own laboratories, and the rest in independent research centers and universities. Industry also receives substantial research contracts from the federal government (particularly in fields such as defense) and provides advice to Congress on how the federal research budget should be allocated. In addition to federal and corporate money, as well as funds from their own endowments, universities receive a significant proportion of their research funding from private trusts and foundations (which in turn are usually supported directly or indirectly by grants or investment income from private corporations).

Other groups that can influence the allocation of R&D resources include the National Academy of Sciences (which provides advice to government agencies, Congress, and the White House) and the various advisory institutions attached to the U.S. Congress (the Office of Technology Assessment, Congressional Research Service, and Congressional Budget Office). In addition, congressional committees hold a series of public hearings on both authorization and appropriations bills at which the administration justifies its proposed expenditure and outside groups can express their approval or disapproval of the President's budget recommendations. At a later date, Congress's General Accounting Office can check whether the money has been spent in the way that Congress intended.

This formal description of the process should be taken only as an approximation. It does not take into account the continuous feedback mechanisms at work, such as the two-way dialogue between agencies and the Office of Management and Budget in preparing their budget requests, with the President occasionally being called in to adjudicate. Nor does it adequately express the many informal mechanisms through which advice is given to the government—for example, through coalitions of university and industry representatives, or the more broad-based activities of groups such as the American Association for the Advancement of Science. For a more detailed description of the way the budget process works, see the annual R&D reviews published by the AAAS. The 1982 version, analyzing the budget for Fiscal Year 1983, contains a concise summary of the process prepared by Willis Shapley et al., identifying 160 steps that a budget proposal goes through before any money is actually spent. (Willis H. Shapley et al., Research and Development; AAAS Report VII, Federal Budget—FY 1983. [Washington, D.C.: American Association for the Advancement of Science, 1982]).

the Senate. Authorization committees in both legislative houses discuss whether in principle Congress should endorse the projects on which the agencies (backed by the White House) want to spend money and approve their price tags, deleting and amending projects as they see fit and placing a ceiling on total expenditure. Appropriations committees discuss how much money in practice Congress should grant for the various projects, adding—or more usually deleting—funds from the administration's request and from the proposals passed to them by the authorization committees and as a result wielding, in practice, greater control over science policy. Once a single figure for each project has been agreed on by both houses, usually the result of compromises reached in joint meetings between members of all the relevant committees, the resulting bill—either authorizing or appropriating funds for the project—is passed to the President, who signs it if he accepts the outcome or sends it back to Congress for a new round of negotiations if he does not.

The above description may sound relatively mechanical, but the length and complexity of the budget process provide ample scope for political maneuvering.* Playing to the public gallery, for example, Congress each year likes to be seen increasing funds for biomedical research; the administration's request therefore always comes to Congress looking smaller than the White House really wants, in anticipation of the inevitable increases that will take place in committee. Conversely, knowing that the defense research budget will probably be cut back, the administration tends to come in with a request significantly higher than it expects Congress to approve. Furthermore, like any other special interest group, the scientific community tends to develop a close working relationship with the two committees that are in the strongest position to defend and promote its interests, namely the House Committee on Science and Technology, or the science and technology subcommittee of the Senate Committee on Commerce, Science, and Technology. Conversely, the power and prestige of both these committees in Congress, neither of which has a "natural" political constituency, depend largely on the extent to which their actions generate support and approval from the scientific community.

Such maneuvering comes as a surprise only to those who believe the scientists' plea that their craft is above politics. Yet it does not take much observation of science in practice to discover that the scientific community has its own internal power structures, its elites, its hierarchies, its ideologies, its sanctioned norms of social behavior, and its dissenting groups.[33] And the more science, as a social practice, forms an integral part of the economic structures of the society in which it is embedded, the more the boundaries and differences between the two dissolve.

---

* Willis Shapley has identified 160 separate steps through which the budget has to pass before any money can be spent.[32]

Groups inside the scientific community, for example, will use groups outside the community—and vice versa—to achieve their own political ends. Dissenting groups within and outside the academic world have turned increasingly to political dissenters (such as Senator Edward Kennedy of Massachusetts) to strengthen their cause. Similarly the leaders of the scientific establishment, including both its corporate and academic elites, have seldom been shy to seek support, endorsement, and protection from their own political counterparts.

This mutual reinforcement between groups inside and outside the scientific community can take many forms. At one level it is relatively pragmatic, as when the military provides funds to support university scientists, and these scientists in return provide knowledge that can be used to generate insights into potential future weapons systems. But it can have an important political dimension, as when groups on one side of the barrier support claims to power and legitimacy made by those on the other. This support can again be practical, as when one group persuades its supporters in Congress to take up the case of another (for instance, when the Defense Department lobbies against tight federal regulations on university research). Alternatively, it can display a strong ideological component, as when university scientists legitimize the complaints of private corporations over excessive government regulation by describing the regulations as "unscientific," while the corporations in return promote the interests of these institutions through heavily subsidized advertising campaigns with the message that "science is good for you." Taken together, this broad system of mutual reinforcement defines the framework through which the politics of science operates.

The origins of contemporary science policy, as well as the political principles on which it is based, lie in the arrangements established during the 1940s for mobilizing the scientific community in support of the war effort. Vannevar Bush, president of the Carnegie Institution in Washington and a former dean of engineering at the Massachusetts Institute of Technology, persuaded President Franklin Roosevelt in the summer of 1940 that, despite their apparent remoteness from practicality, scientists working in university laboratories could produce the new military technologies needed to defeat both Germany (the U.S.'s scientific superior in the 1930s) and Japan. Bush also convinced the President that this could be done most effectively if, once provided with adequate financial support from the government, scientists were left to decide for themselves how this support should be distributed, and how their efforts should be organized. The result was the creation of the National Defense Research Committee, superseded a year later by the Office of Scientific Research and Development. Although most of the funding came from the Army, these were the organizations through which government support was channeled to, among other projects, radar research at the MIT

Radiation Laboratory and the development of the atomic bomb at Los Alamos. They were also the organizations which guaranteed that political controls over science would be exercised only at arm's length.[34]

After the war ended, the government needed little convincing that substantial federal support for academic science, previously considered virtually taboo on both sides, promised a path to civilian prosperity. The dominant question, however, was the political arrangement under which this should be carried out. Many members of Congress, although accepting the principle of public funding, argued that research should be carried out within the conventional framework of public accountability and scrutiny for the way that the money was used. In particular, Senator Harley M. Kilgore of West Virginia had introduced a bill into Congress during the war proposing the postwar creation of an Office of Science and Technology Mobilization. Science would be developed as a public resource committed to "the betterment of humanity." All patents resulting from publicly funded research would be publicly owned; research funds would be distributed to the scientific community by a board with representatives from all social groups, including consumers and small business. Kilgore's bill, described by Assistant Attorney General Thurman Arnold as a type of Magna Carta of science, envisaged a scientific establishment directly responsive to democratic procedures.[35]

The notion struck horror in the heart of the scientific community. The war had convinced scientists that their contribution to technological progress was indispensable; but it had also convinced them that this success would not have been achieved in wartime if the scientific community, once provided with adequate funding, had not been allowed to run its own affairs. Kilgore's proposals for a peacetime institutionalization of government support combined with direct democratic control were firmly resisted. Bush complained that it would "hold grave dangers for the full development of science."[36]

In response, Bush headed a panel of scientific colleagues—mainly physicists—whose report, under the evocative title *Science: The Endless Frontier*, set out the terms under which the scientific community was prepared to enter a peacetime contract with the state. The report spoke in fulsome Baconian language of the promises that science offered: "Science has been in the wings. It should be brought to the center of the stage—for in it lies most of our hope for the future." It accepted that "since health, well-being, and security are proper concerns of government, scientific progress is, and must be, of vital interest to the government." But it laid out a set of "basic principles" in which Bush insisted that, even though any agency created to finance research should be administratively and fiscally responsible to the President and Congress, it was "of the utmost importance" that support of basic research in universities, colleges, and research institutes "leave the internal control of policy, personnel, and the method and scope of the research to the institutions themselves."[37]

The scientific community's plea for public support yet political autonomy generated considerable opposition. Even some scientists saw the demands as audacious. In 1947 President Harry Truman vetoed a bill, passed by Congress, which would have set up a National Science Agency along the lines proposed by Bush, arguing that the proposed arrangement would be "divorced from control by the people to an extent that implies a distinct lack of faith in the democratic process."[38] Yet slowly Bush's principles, endorsed by the scientific establishment through the National Academy of Sciences, as well as by the corporate sector through the National Association of Manufacturers, won the day. Kilgore's proposals for direct social control over science were quietly shelved. In 1950, with Truman now preoccupied with the Korean War, the National Science Foundation was finally established. Admittedly, its initial funds were meager. But the political arrangements, with NSF activities being made responsible to an independent committee of scientists (the National Science Board), were in principle—although it later turned out differently in practice—a clear victory for the scientific establishment against direct social control of science.[39]

Federal research budgets grew steadily during the 1950s, rising from $920 million (0.3 percent of the gross national product) in 1946 to $3.45 billion (0.8 percent of the GNP) a decade later. During most of this period the main focus of government policy was on ways of using science to achieve military objectives. In 1955, for example, almost four-fifths of the federal government's expenditure on R&D was going to the Department of Defense, just over a tenth to the Atomic Energy Commission, one-fiftieth to the Department of Health, Education, and Welfare, and a mere 0.1 percent to the National Science Foundation, still languishing in relative obscurity. By the mid-1950s, however, even the Pentagon's enthusiasm for science was beginning to wane; in 1957 a tremor was sent through the university research community by a rumor that Defense Department support for basic science was about to be reduced by 10 percent.

The turning point came with the launching of the Russian Sputnik at the end of 1957. Caught embarrassingly unawares by what proved to be both a major technological feat and a successful propaganda coup by the Soviet Union, the United States was shaken out of its previous complacency and agreed to a full-scale mobilization of the scientific and technological community. Its first response was to accelerate its own space efforts, substantially increasing the funds for satellite research and, in 1958, creating the National Aeronautics and Space Administration. More important, however, the scientific community was able to use Sputnik to establish its vital presence at the heart of government.

Ten days after the Sputnik launch, President Dwight D. Eisenhower invited the members of his Science Advisory Committee to the White House. The scientists did not waste the opportunity. They warned Eisenhower that although the Russian success in space was relatively insignificant in technical terms, it could signal much larger problems five or ten years down the road, since the Soviet Union could no longer be treated as technologically backward, and Russian politicians appeared to be consciously setting out to challenge the technical superiority of the West. The challenge was urgent, yet the U.S. was not equipped to meet it. In particular, the scientists told the President that there was an insufficient flow of scientific advice into the administration, and suggested that a new mechanism was needed to bring the "voice of science" to the highest level of the executive branch.[40]

Eisenhower's reaction was swift. A few days later, James Killian, then president of MIT, was invited to Washington and offered the new post of special assistant to the President for science and technology. The Science Advisory Committee, which had previously met only twice a year and had reported to the President through the Office of Defense Mobilization (a compromise reached with the Bureau of the Budget), was raised in status and given direct access to the Oval Office. The next year, a full-scale program of federal support for science education in the nation's schools was put into effect through the cleverly named National Defense Education Act.

The Sputnik episode was therefore a key turning point in postwar U.S. science policy from two points of view. Fears of Soviet supremacy in science and technology—whether or not they were legitimate—were used to justify an increased commitment of federal funds to civilian research, which rose dramatically in the years that followed. At the same time, it marked the full acceptance of the scientific community in the corridors of Washington.

Both tendencies, whose seeds had been sown during the Second World War and had been slowly gestating for the following decade, emerged into full bloom in the hothouse atmosphere of John F. Kennedy's administration. The new President, as well as the nation whose vigor and optimism he appeared to represent, fell into a virtual "love affair" with science. After Sputnik, scientists were given, in Killian's words, "a flabbergasting array of responsibilities." The columnist Meg Greenfield reported at the time that scientists were "looked upon by the White House and by many in Congress as saviors and miracle workers."[41] President Kennedy—spurred on by his ambitious science adviser, Jerome Wiesner, a previous director of the MIT Radiation Laboratory—was full of ideas about how a massive expenditure in science would boost the civilian economy. Science was to be put to work on the New Frontier, solving the problems of urban renewal, of weather control, of exploiting the oceans—and of placing man on the moon.

Both basic and applied research benefited from this new enthusiasm. The science budget started on an upward trajectory that was to continue for several years. Total federal spending on R&D increased by 42 percent in real terms between 1960 and 1968, an average expansion of almost 5 percent a year. Support for basic science, although a relatively small proportion of the total R&D budget, rose even faster, more than doubling over the same period. The main recipients of this public largesse were the nation's research universities, institutions that had rejected almost all public funding before the war; their basic research expenditures tripled, rising from $433 million in 1960 to $1,649 million by 1968.

Inside the corridors of power, scientists wielded more influence than they had ever done before—and perhaps since. At the center was Wiesner, who orchestrated a network of advisory committees producing reports on subjects that ranged from oceanography to consumer protection, and whose staff had been consolidated in 1962 into a new Office of Science Policy. Not everyone appreciated Wiesner's activities. Philip Abelson, editor of *Science* and a strong critic of the concentration of authority in the White House and the Executive Office, wrote that "Dr. Wiesner has accumulated and exercised more visible and invisible power than any scientist in the peacetime history of this country."[42] Others, describing Wiesner as a self-appointed "czar of American science," complained of his arrogance and authoritarian methods. Yet for once scientists relished being not just on tap but on top. In January 1961 *Time* magazine selected fifteen prominent scientists as its collective men of the year, stating that "statesmen and savants are their servants . . . science is at the apogee of its power."[43]

It was too good to last. Within only a few years, President Lyndon Johnson, waving the umbrella of his Great Society, was suggesting that the time had come to start looking for a payoff and directing science to more mundane social issues such as highway safety, crime, poverty, and urban decay. In June 1966 the White House issued a statement in which Johnson suggested that "a great deal of basic research has been done. I have been participating in the appropriations for years in this field. But I think the time has now come to zero in on the targets by trying to get our knowledge fully applied." The biomedical community was invited "to determine whether too much energy was being spent on basic research and not enough on translating laboratory findings into tangible benefits for the American people."[44]

It was during the Nixon administration, however, that the reaction set in most thoroughly. Basic research dropped to the bottom of the political priority list; after its heady growth in the 1960s, federal support for basic research fell by over 10 percent in real terms between 1968 and 1971, and stayed virtually constant for the next four years. In cutting back the basic science budget, Nixon, like his predecessor Johnson, argued that the principal task now facing government was not to discover more new knowledge, but to find ways of putting what already existed to good use. After Kennedy's New Frontier and Johnson's Great Society, Nixon chipped in with his own New Technology Opportunities Program. Top research priorities, it was announced, would include clean energy, the control of natural disasters, transportation, emergency health care, and drug control. Symbolic of the whole approach was Nixon's announcement of the inauguration of a ten-year "war on cancer," an effort which, he confidently announced, would show that man was capable of using the same scientific skills that had taken him to the moon to come up with a cure for the most threatening of all human diseases.[45]

External pressures on the administration played an important role in the shift. The mid-1960s had seen a vociferous critique of the social consequences of unfettered technological development, ranging from the environmental damage caused by the side effects of modern science-based production processes to the use of sophisticated electronics in the war in Vietnam. Encouraging the application of science to socially desirable ends was seen as one response to this challenge. It would also, the White House hoped, mop up many of the unemployed scientists and engineers who had lost their jobs when the Apollo program had successfully reached its goal of landing man on the moon by the end of the 1960s.

The shift in emphasis from basic to applied research also reflected growing disenchantment within Congress about the return the government was getting on its investment in science, as few of the promises that scientists had rashly made at the beginning of the 1960s appeared to be bearing fruit. In the case of Defense Department spending on research, for example, this disenchantment was reflected in the so-called Mansfield Amendment to the Pentagon's budget for 1970, which explicitly stated that research should be supported only if it could demonstrate direct relevance to some military need. (For further discussion of the Mansfield Amendment, and its impact—often overstated—on the research budget, see Chapter Three.)

Behind this, however, lay what was perhaps the most significant factor in explaining the administration's reduced enthusiasm for science. This was the change of heart in the private sector. In the postwar decade, American industry had expanded rapidly, based largely on scientific discoveries such as synthetic chemicals and computers, which had been made in the 1920s and 1930s. In this period innovation seemed justified for its own sake, and profits could be made merely by following in the footsteps of such technological leaders as IBM, du Pont, or General Electric. By the end of the 1960s, however, the field was becoming saturated, and there were fewer quick gains to be made from jumping on the innovation bandwagon. Profits were now to be sought elsewhere, primarily by reducing the costs of production. Emphasis shifted from product to process innovation, and from capacity expansion to the rationalization of existing production techniques. As a result, research and development became less attractive as an investment compared with other ways of meeting the bottom line.

Reflecting this disenchantment, basic research performed by industry dropped off even more sharply than that by the government, falling in real terms by 37 percent between 1966 and 1972. A survey carried out by the Industrial Research Institute revealed that one of the most important reasons for this decline was an increasing concern for short-term profitability, with corporate research efforts coming under strong, centralized control in an attempt to secure an immediate payoff.[46] Like the Department of Defense, industry became reluctant to support research that promised only long-term rewards—rewards which might never come.

As the fortunes of science dropped, so too did the political influence of the scientific community. In January 1973, shortly after his reelection, President Nixon announced the dismantling of the scientific advisory apparatus that had been built up over the previous decade and had acted as the visible embodiment of the scientific community's leverage in Washington. The post of President's science adviser, which had been filled for the first time in 1970 by an industrial scientist, Edward David of the Bell Telephone Laboratories, was abolished completely, and the responsibilities of the Office of Science Policy were transferred to the National Science Foundation. Also eliminated at the same time was the President's Science Advisory Committee (PSAC).

The scientists' demise is often blamed on the personal antagonism of Richard Nixon. Certainly a major factor in his decision to abolish PSAC was the fact that several of its members had gone public with criticism of administration policies, in particular over plans to site anti-ballistic missiles and construct a supersonic aircraft (finally shot down by Congress after a bitter fight). Nixon had also been alienated from the academic community by the bitter demonstrations—often led by scientists—which had taken place on campuses across the nation in protest at the Vietnam War.

Yet the seeds of the political counterrevolution against science and scientists had been circulating for some time. If President Johnson's remarks about making science relevant to social needs had already shown that the scientific community could no longer expect privileged treatment from the federal government for their own projects, it also meant that scientists could no longer expect privileged access to the levers of power. Johnson is said to have been particularly critical of what he saw as PSAC's failure to make a substantial contribution to his Great Society scheme.

Faced with what appeared to be a political threat to its very survival, the scientific community picked up the challenge of making its work address social needs directly. "We must try to reverse the disillusionment with science of the American public," Glenn Seaborg, president-elect of the American Association for the Advancement of Science, told the association's annual meeting at the end of 1970. "And we're going to have to make science more relevant to human problems than we have in the past."[47] Yet the transformation was a reluctant and painful one, not the least because it appeared to scientists that they were no longer going to enjoy the autonomy to determine their own research programs, but would be forced to admit greater social participation in the affairs of the scientific community. And this development, it was feared, would undermine the whole basis on which the postwar expansion of science had been built. One scientist reported that his colleagues "very nearly panicked" when they were told by Johnson that they had done enough basic research and should now start working on its applications.[48]

The period in the political wilderness did not last long, even though the institutional changes introduced by Nixon took some time to reverse (since they required a new act of Congress). This time, the initial trigger for science's return to political favor was the economic recession that gripped the U.S. in 1973 and 1974. What emerged was a gradual awareness in political circles that U.S. private corporations could no longer expect to dominate world trade as easily as they had done before—or to remain immune from global economic trends. Searching for clues to the U.S.'s poor economic performance, attention soon turned to the relationship between research spending and commercial success. The theory that began to emerge was that, in the long run, the economy would remain healthy only through a continuous infusion of new technological innovations—and that this could be assured only by continued support for basic science.

The precise relationship between science and economic growth is highly controversial; indeed, economists differed substantially on the precise size of the contribution of technical change—and hence indirectly of R&D spending—to productivity growth. But there was soon little disagreement that the most dynamic sectors of the U.S. economy were those, such as microelectronics and pharmaceuticals, in which spending on research had been relatively high. Two economists with Data Resources Inc. have estimated that in the three postwar decades, high technology industries produced a compound growth of 6.7 percent, compared with a 2.6 percent expansion in the low technology industries.[49] Other statistics demonstrate how the science-based industries have come to play a central role in maintaining a competitive position for the U.S. in international trade. R&D-intensive manufactured goods are now the principal means by which the U.S. is able to maintain a positive trade balance in the international marketplace. Between 1970 and 1976 the balance of trade surplus in such goods, covering products such as machinery, chemicals (including pharmaceuticals), aircraft, and instruments, rose from $11.7 million to $29.0 billion; over the same period the deficit in non-R&D-intensive goods widened from $8.3 million to $16.5 billion.[50]

Reinforcing the same message, the economist Edwin Mansfield demonstrated how those U.S. industries that spend relatively high amounts of money on research and development are also the leading industries in manufactured exports, foreign direct investment, and licensing; he calculated that in a selected sample of companies 30 percent of the expected return on R&D expenditures came from some form of technology transfer.[51] Individual companies came to realize that, as the ex-chairman of Dow Chemical, Carl A. Gerstacker, has put it, "the importance of research and development to U.S. . . . . producers will be basic as competition for world markets intensifies."[52]

Thus, although no one can give precise figures, it is now generally accepted that research and development in general—and basic research in particular—make a fundamental contribution to the expansion of capital, in particular by being used to produce new products and as the basis of new production processes. As such, science has come to play an important strategic role for U.S. corporations and the U.S. economy. More collectively, a report from the Organization for Economic Cooperation and Development (OECD) has described how "intellectual capital—scientific resources and the aptitude for technological innovation—constitutes the major asset of industrialized nations in the new modes of international competition and interdependence."[53] (The international implications of this are explored more fully in Chapter Four.)

As the OECD's choice of language indicates, the increasingly important role of science and technology in both the domestic and the international economy has changed the way that science is *characterized* in the context of economic decision-making. The same view can be found in President Carter's frequent assertion that money spent on science should be considered an "investment" rather than an overhead. And this, in turn, has had important implications at the level of the research laboratory—and for public debates over the control of science and its applications—as the results of research come to be treated as what GE's Arthur Bueche has described as "knowledge capital."[54]

The semantics are significant. Science as an essentially undirected activity, even if carried out with the promise of long-term technological spin-off, fit easily within traditional concepts of academic scholarship, requiring, for example, the complete freedom of scientific communication and exchange for the growth of scientific knowledge. Science as an economic commodity, however, has very different implications. The language itself is the language of the boardroom and corporate investment planning. As "knowledge capital," research is expected to generate an appropriate return, since business firms undertake R&D primarily to enhance their future profits. "Aside from the form of the income-earning property that is acquired, R&D expenditures are conceptually like other kinds of business investment," says economist George N. Carlson.[55] Control of knowledge becomes a vital weapon in the corporate armory—and thus a crucial factor in determining the form of the new politics of science.

From the mid-1970s, the newly recognized strategic importance of investment in research and the development of new technologies began to produce a decisive shift in the corporate sector's definition of the appropriate role of the federal government in supporting research. The corporate community rejected the Nixon administration's approach to direct federal intervention in stimulating new technologies, but it revived the idea that economic prosperity could not be secured without substantial investment in basic research—and that responsibility for funding this should lie primarily with the public purse. It thus sought to persuade the administration to bury its previous hesitations and go back to substantial funding for basic science.

Scientists themselves, still smarting after their enforced exit from the President's inner circle, were already regrouping their forces for a counterattack. If the demand for social relevance posed a political threat to the internal organization of the scientific community and its control of scientific resources, it was a threat that could be met only through coordinated action. As a report for the Paris-based Organization for Economic Cooperation and Development, largely written by Harvard professor Harvey Brooks, pointed out: "New socially oriented goals are coming to the fore while long-term emphasis on space, defense, and atomic energy has begun to recede visibly. This has produced severe strains and dislocations in the American scientific establishment, which have led the scientific and technological community to look with greater favor on more centralized models of science policy."[56]

Scientists' initial response to their ouster from the White House was to seek to establish a new power base in Congress. Leaders of the scientific establishment such as Brooks and Wiesner lobbied hard for the creation of the Office of Technology Assessment (OTA), which many saw not only as a mechanism for providing the same synthesis of scientific advice on political issues that had previously been the responsibility of the President's Science Advisory Committee, but also as a vehicle through which scientists could maintain their access to the levers of power. As we shall see in a later chapter, such ambitions successfully prevented the OTA from delivering the full-scale critique of the social impact of scientific discoveries that many had expected from it, particularly when this critique focused on the way that science itself was organized and controlled.

But the OTA was only half a step in the desired direction. Ambitions for a full return to presidential favor remained close to the surface. In April 1974, less than eighteen months after the Office of Science Policy had been abolished by Nixon, a select committee of the National Academy of Sciences produced a report recommending "a scientific and technological presence" in the White House.[57] The conclusions were hardly surprising, given the fact that the committee's chairman (James Killian), most of its members, and its executive assistant (David Beckler) had been heavily involved in the activities of the President's Science Advisory Committee. Perhaps more surprising was the fact that the report spoke of the potential of science almost entirely in glowing terms, with no reference to the broad public debates then current about the less desirable social aspects of science.

The academy's proposals—like those for the Office of Technology Assessment—were eagerly picked up by the science committees in Congress, whose own power and prestige had suffered in direct proportion to the reduction in the science budget. Even more important, however, they now struck a responsive chord in the private sector, reinforcing its own ideas about the importance of research-based industries. Industry was eager to see renewed growth in the research budget. It was equally keen to reduce social and political controls over the applications of research results, controls that directly challenged its domination of technological choices through the marketplace and thus challenged the political relationships on which the marketplace depends. Industry therefore shared the scientific community's desire to remove the shackles meant to produce "relevance" in research, and to restore to science its previous autonomy from direct accountability and social direction.

A key figure in coaxing government blessing for a new alliance between science and the corporate sector was Gerald Ford's Vice-President, Nelson Rockefeller. Squarely placed in the center of America's corporate elite, Rockefeller appreciated both the economic contributions of science to the nation's industrial base and the political value of scientific advice at the top levels of government. Early in 1976 he told the annual meeting of the American Association for the Advancement of Science—rejecting the arguments of critics of the nation's nuclear energy program—that mechanisms were needed for "bringing into focus the facts and informed, mature, objective judgments of the scientific community."[58] He was also an enthusiastic supporter of the science court idea, which sought to reduce social conflicts to conflicting testimony between scientific experts. But most important, Rockefeller realized that science must be put back at the center of the political and economic stage.

Rockefeller was the principal administration architect of Ford's proposal to Congress on June 9, 1975, to reestablish the Office of Science Policy (renamed the Office of Science and Technology Policy) in the Executive Office of the President—a move widely applauded both by the scientific community and by its corresponding committees in Congress. The proposal was passed into law on May 11, 1976, when Ford signed the National Science and Technology Policy, Organization, and Priorities Act. Ford described it as reflecting "a renewed recognition of the importance of scientific, engineering, and technological contributions," and symbolizing "the confidence we Americans have in our ability to improve our way of life and to find better solutions to the problems of the future."[59]

Under the patronage of Rockefeller, the leaders of the scientific community slipped back into positions of influence in Washington. Largely at Rockefeller's initiative, an informal group of prominent industrial and university scientists had already been assembled to advise the administration. In preparation for the new Office of Science and Technology Policy (OSTP), Ford gave Rockefeller and National Science Foundation director Guyford Stever responsibility for organizing two expert groups to provide "advice on scientific and technical aspects of issues and policies that must be addressed at the highest level of the government."[60] Both groups were chaired by leading members of the corporate research community who had long been friends of Rockefeller. Simon Ramo, vice-chairman of TRW Inc., chaired a committee given the job of looking at "the contribution of technology to economic strength." The other committee, under William O. Baker, president of Bell Laboratories, was to look at anticipated advances in science and technology and their national policy implications. The members of the panels emerged from a day-long meeting with Rockefeller organized by Ramo and attended by many members of the Commission on Critical Choices for America (including John W. Foster, of the Lawrence Livermore Laboratory, and Edward Teller), which Rockefeller had organized before becoming Vice-President.

Both advisory groups were made up of prominent members of the research and corporate establishments, many with strong links to the defense and intelligence communities. The Ramo panel included senior executives from IBM, General Electric, Texas Instruments, and the Polaroid Corporation, together with scientists from New York University, Stanford, Princeton, and MIT. Arthur Bueche of GE was given responsibility for a study on the effects of federal regulation on science. Even after OSTP had been reestablished, and Stever had officially been appointed the new science adviser, the advisory apparatus was kept intact. In October 1976, a few days before the election, Ford announced the creation of a "President's Committee on Science and Technology," with Ramo and Baker as chairman and vice-chairman respectively.

The restoration of the scientific community to political favor continued under President Carter. Carter's connections with the East Coast liberal corporate establishment (for example, through his membership on the Trilateral Commission) had made him aware, like Rockefeller, of the extent to which those companies saw their future in the promotion of high technology—and the important contribution basic science could make toward this goal.[61] During the 1976 election campaign, Carter's chief adviser on scientific issues was Lewis Branscomb, previously director of the National Bureau of Standards, subsequently appointed vice-president and chief scientist of IBM. Other close advisers—such as Zbigniew Brzezinski, soon to become National Security Adviser—described to Carter the value of science in both domestic and international affairs.

Once installed in Washington, Carter soon showed himself to be sympathetic to demands from the corporate and research communities for greater support for basic research. Although the decline of the early

1970s had soon flattened out, basic research spending did not begin to expand significantly until the end of the Ford administration, rising 2 percent between 1975 and 1976, and 4.5 percent the following year. In the 1978 budget, reflecting a combination of administration and congressional enthusiasm, funding for basic science rose by 8.6 percent in real terms (or 16.0 percent in current dollars), the highest increase since the early 1960s.[62] This early start was maintained during the remainder of Carter's term of office. In the four years of the Carter administration, the research budget rose by 18.8 percent (76.6 percent in current dollars), according to statistics from the American Association for the Advancement of Science (AAAS).[63]

Reinstating the political influence of the scientific community was less straightforward. Carter's election commitment to reducing the federal payroll and the network of government advisory committees extended to an initial desire to dismantle the science advisory apparatus that had only just been re-created. Seeing the danger that its hard-won success might slip through its fingers, the scientific community—backed by its corporate allies—lobbied strongly for it to be retained.[64] And in May 1977, Carter announced as his science adviser and the new director of OSTP Frank Press, Institute Professor of Geology at MIT and a past member of Ford's advisory committee chaired by William Baker.

During his four years in the White House, Carter worked hard with Press to give his administration a strong pro–science and technology image. In March 1979, for example, Carter presented the outlines of his science and technology policy to Congress in a statement that criticized the declining support for basic science in the 1960s and early 1970s; he emphasized that he had "sought to reverse these trends" by redirecting attention toward the nation's long-range needs, and concluded that "prudent planning for the future demands a deliberate and continued commitment to basic research."[65]

From the corporate sector's point of view, however, Carter's attitude toward science and research remained hampered by his administration's commitments to the various social groups—environmentalists, labor unions, minorities, etc.—that made up the increasingly fragile Democratic coalition. These were the groups that still demanded "social relevance" in research programs, firm controls on potentially hazardous research and its applications, the use of federal research funds to achieve social objectives only indirectly related to science (such as equal opportunities for women and minorities, or an equitable regional distribution of federal funds), tight constraints on "giving away public property" by weakening the patent laws, and a strong federal role in developing technologies ignored by the marketplace.

Such commitments limited the pace at which the Carter administration was able to move its science policy in the direction the corporate research community wanted. Carter's science adviser, Frank Press, for example, found it difficult to hide his distaste for the administration's decision to support an ambitious solar energy demonstration program. He argued that the pace of movement in this direction—however desirable—should be dictated by a careful balancing of scientific discovery and market demand, not through heavy federal subsidies. Yet his views were overshadowed by those of the Council on Environmental Quality, whose members contended that only a program of massive federal investment could help the infant solar industry over the threshold at which its activities would become self-sustaining.

It was the same story with technological innovation. Two goals were pushed strongly by the private corporate community as government steps that would speed up technological innovation: the liberalization of patent legislation and significant tax breaks for research expenditures. Neither, however, figured prominently in the proposals the administration produced after an eighteen-month Domestic Policy Review, suggested by Press at the prompting of the corporate research community, and carried out by the Department of Commerce. (The fate of the Domestic Policy Review is discussed in Chapter Six).

As we have already seen, the Reagan administration showed soon after its arrival in Washington in 1981 that it shared the willingness of its predecessor to continue support for basic science. Reagan himself, although expressing many of the conservative political views of his ideological cousin, Barry Goldwater, had few doubts about the economic importance of high technology industries, if for no other reason than that these provide the backbone of the economy of the State of California, of which he was governor from 1967 to 1975.

It might have been otherwise. Some conservative economists had challenged the fundamental idea that it was appropriate for the federal government to be supporting basic research at all without an explicit mandate to do so. The argument was put forward most forcefully by the Nobel-prize-winning economist and guru of monetarist theory, Milton Friedman. Friedman suggested that both the National Science Foundation and tax subsidies to higher education were "undesirable and should be terminated."[66] In an open letter to the late president of the National Academy of Sciences, Philip Handler, Friedman explained that he could not add his support to complaints by his fellow economists about cuts in funding for economic research at the National Science Foundation, even though he had benefited from such funding in the past. "I favor major cuts in NSF grants as a step toward the abolition of the NSF," he wrote provocatively. "What ethical justification is there for imposing taxes on people to finance scientific research for which they would not voluntarily contribute?" he asked, arguing that "the burden of proof that the benefits of government financing exceed the costs surely rests on those who support such financing."[67]

Even fellow conservative economists, who might fully support such arguments applied to the arts, found the asceticism of Friedman's position difficult to accept—although it was later endorsed by a coalition known as the National Conservative Political Action Committee. The Heritage Foundation, in its *Agenda for Progress* presented to the incoming Reagan administration soon after the 1980 election, began its analysis of federal support for science by stating that "in a study filled with accounts of federal program failures, it is refreshing to find an area filled with spectacular successes—space and general science."[68] Written by Richard Speier, a former staff member of the Office of Management and Budget specializing in major science facilities, the report gave both economic and cultural reasons for supporting basic science. On the one hand, it said, science provided the knowledge necessary for long-term economic growth; on the other, "research with no foreseeable commercial applications could be abandoned entirely, but it would not be in the interests of modern civilization to do so."[69]

During the 1980 election campaign, similar ideas had been presented to Reagan by Simon Ramo, who set out his views about the economic and political importance of science in *America's Technology Slip*, a book that encapsulated much of the thinking then popular in the corporate community. The book aimed a direct attack at what Ramo and others identified as the "anti-science" movement and those who considered all advanced technology to be "evil."* Pointing to "a severe mismatch . . . between the high potential of technological advance and the low rate of scientific-political progress," Ramo contrasted those who "want less technological development and more rules to regulate and minimize it" with those who were "agonizing over evidence that America has developed a serious technology slip." The government should be kept out of those activities where the free enterprise system could do a better job; although it has to be a permanent factor in setting the climate for technological innovation, the government "has little to offer in *directing the technological and scientific effort*" (italics added), according to Ramo, since "most of the experts are to be found in private industry and the universities." At the same time the government should provide generous support for university research, but "with a minimum of administrative burdens." As for applied research, "the market will make the best decisions as to what R&D should be accomplished and what products represent success in that area of technology." In Ramo's words, for such technology, the government is at best an "incompetent third party."[70]

Despite Friedman's suggestions, then, the dominant question facing the science policy-makers of the Reagan administration has been not how to get the government *out* of funding basic research, but how to get

---

* Significantly, the "anti-science" label was never used by the groups Ramo was implicitly criticizing. It was not science as such that these groups attacked; rather, it was the material and ideological use of science by American capitalism—a different target.

the private sector *in*. The specific interests of the corporate community in research were identified by a science transition team set up to advise Reagan shortly after his election victory and headed by two prominent members of President Ford's advisory committee, Ramo and Bueche. (Both were tapped as potential science advisers to Reagan, but are said in turn to have turned down the offer, as did several other members of the corporate research establishment.) The task force included many other members of the Republican science establishment, among them Baker, David, Stever, and Teller. Others were prominent individuals from the worlds of industrial and military research with Republican connections.*

Four key issues identified by the task force were to form the initial framework for thinking about science in the Reagan administration, and largely explain the form adopted by the administration's subsequent science policies. Topping the priority list was the need to emphasize the importance of R&D in stimulating economic growth, an item that had already been at the top of the Carter administration's science policy agenda. Second was the need to enhance the role of the research community in strengthening the nation's military technology. Next came the need to reduce the impact of social controls on research by reducing accountability requirements for federally supported R&D. Finally, the task force underlined the need to improve scientific consultation with the White House—in other words, to give scientists back some of the political power they had lost in the late 1960s and the 1970s. Scientists and engineers, it said, should be allowed to play a more constructive role in formulating policy on a wide range of issues, such as foreign trade, industrial strategy, national security, innovation, productivity, and unemployment.

The scientific community could not have asked for a better expression of its own wish-list. And the task force's acknowledgment of the central importance of science to all areas of federal policy was symbolized by its endorsement of the appointment of a science adviser to the President. On entering office, the Reagan administration had seemed to share much of Carter's initial hesitation about whether a presidential science adviser was really needed. But after prompting by the task force, by the

---

* Task force members included Harold M. Agnew, president of General Atomic Co. and previously director of the Los Alamos National Laboratory; Franklin Murphy, chairman of the board of the Times Mirror Company of Los Angeles; William A. Nierenberg, director of the Scripps Institute of Oceanography; Lewis H. Sarett, senior vice-president for science and technology with the pharmaceutical firm Merck and Co.; Bernard Schriever, retired general of the U.S. Air Force; Frederick Seitz, former president of the National Academy of Sciences and of Rockefeller University in New York; Wilson K. Talley, professor of applied science at the University of California at Davis; Teddy F. Walkowicz, president of the National Aviation and Technology Corporation of New York; and Albert D. Wheelon, vice-president and group executive of the Hughes Aircraft Corporation.

scientific community, and by the community's supporters in both Congress and the press, the White House began a search for a successor to Press.

It took some months to fill the post, partly because of the difficulty in finding an individual who was of sufficient stature to be acceptable to the scientific community, yet prepared both to accept a government position whose status was still ambiguous and to identify closely with the social, economic, and military programs of the new administration. After a search lasting several months, the White House announced that it had picked George Keyworth, a physicist who had spent virtually all his professional career at the Los Alamos National Laboratory. Keyworth fit the White House's needs well. Scientifically, he had a respectable, if relatively undistinguished, career as a laser physicist. Politically, he had no ax to grind on behalf of the scientific community. Furthermore, describing himself as a converted Republican, Keyworth had few reservations about supporting the administration's commitment to strengthening the nation's military technology, of shifting major responsibilities for research and development to the private sector. His appointment is said to have been strongly endorsed by Edward Teller, the so-called father of the hydrogen bomb, a staunch critic of the Soviet Union, and a senior science adviser to Reagan when he was governor of California. Keyworth himself later claimed, "My number one job is being sensitive to the President's philosophy."[71]

Because he was relatively unknown in science policy circles (unlike most of his predecessors, he had virtually no experience in Washington), Keyworth's appointment raised concerns in the scientific community when it was first announced. These concerns were heightened by Keyworth's first public statements on science policy, in which he suggested that the U.S. could no longer expect to be at the forefront of all branches of science, and that scientists would have to become more selective about which fields they supported.[72] Yet Republicans soon closed ranks behind him. When some of Keyworth's public remarks justifying cuts in parts of the research budget raised questions about the suitability of his appointment, leading members of the Republican scientific establishment came to his defense. "In this era of changing public policy, candid words from authoritative sources are even more appropriate than usual. So we are fortunate to have Keyworth in position," Edward David wrote in response to an interview published by the Scientists' Institute for Public Information.[73]

Keyworth's appointment was not the only controversial one. Although the White House, like the previous administration, decided against recreating a full-scale President's Science Advisory Committee, Keyworth himself appointed a White House Science Council to advise him on specific policy issues. Keyworth insisted that the members of the committee had been selected as individuals, not as representing any particular viewpoint or discipline. Yet the makeup of the committee provided a microcosm of the administration's perspective on science. All the members were male, all were white, and there were no social scientists. The majority of members were physicists, mostly with considerable experience in working on military-related problems, with members such as David Packard (chairman of the board of Hewlett-Packard and Deputy Director of Defense under President Nixon) and chairman Solomon Buchsbaum (executive vice-president of Bell Laboratories) emphasizing the link to high technology corporations.[74]

The administration put its stamp on other scientific appointments, too, including some that had traditionally been considered "nonpolitical." For the head of the National Science Foundation it selected Edward A. Knapp, like Keyworth a former physicist at the Los Alamos National Laboratory, where he had been head of the accelerator technology division. Keyworth had previously made it clear that, although the administration was looking for a scientist of "excellence," at the same time, "ultimately we will choose a person whose philosophy is compatible with the President."[75]

Knapp's arrival at the NSF in the fall of 1982 precipitated further controversial changes within the agency, since he moved quickly to fill other top positions with Reagan appointees. He demanded the resignation of the NSF's deputy director, physicist Donald Langenberg, who had been appointed by Carter (and had spent some time as acting director) as well as that of one of the agency's assistant directors. Although the firings seem to have been the result of political naiveté rather than a cold-blooded plot, to some, the general message seemed to be that, in return for giving the foundation a substantial budget boost, the White House was demanding its pound of flesh in terms of greater control over the activities of the agency by making its own appointments of senior staff. "The nonpartisanship is breaking up," an NSF employee complained to one reporter.[76] Knapp and the White House both denied the charges, but many were not entirely convinced.

It was the same story with the government's scientific advisory boards. The *Washington Post* reported in June 1982 that political referrals were being used to fill vacancies on expert advisory committees to the Food and Drug Administration.[77] Similarly, the Department of Agriculture was found to be using tests of political allegiance for candidates to its scientific peer review panels, while the Department of the Interior admitted that names of potential members of its science advisory committees were routinely submitted to the Republican National Committee for approval (and, as has been pointed out elsewhere, only those approved tended to be nominated).[78] Echoing Keyworth's words, department officials admitted that, faced with a choice between two scientists with comparable qualifications, preference would be given to the one who was "philosophically compatible" with the political priorities of the Reagan administration.[79]

The use of political criteria to make scientific appointments appeared to conflict directly with the supposed neutrality of scientific advice to government. In proposing the creation of the National Science Foundation after the war, Vannevar Bush had stressed that "the agency to administer such funds should be composed of citizens selected only on the basis of their interest in and capacity to promote the work of the agency."[80] The tradition of nonpartisanship ran deep. After disclosure by *Science* early in 1982 of the Agriculture Department's political vetting of its scientific appointments, the Secretary of Agriculture, John R. Block, hurriedly announced that the procedure was being discontinued, claiming that the checks had been demanded by the White House through the Office of Management and Budget (OMB).[81]

What was remarkable, however, about the Reagan administration's moves—or at least Keyworth's defense of these moves—was the open admission that political compatibility was a legitimate demand to make of scientific appointees. In the late 1950s, when President Eisenhower had asked his science adviser George Kistiakowsky to support the presidential candidacy of Richard Nixon in the forthcoming election, Kistiakowsky (who had no great liking for Nixon anyway) declined on the basis that it was important for scientists to remain nonpartisan. He also refused to exclude Wiesner from PSAC meetings even after the latter had become Democratic candidate John Kennedy's science adviser.[82] Even in the political campaigns of the 1960s, scientists had primarily stressed their support for candidates' views about scientific and technical topics. Yet in defending the Reagan administration's political vetting, Keyworth made no claims to impartiality or objectivity on the part of scientific advisers. It was "eminently reasonable," he said, for the administration to seek scientific panels at all levels that shared—as did he—the political philosophy of the President. There were not many panels that tackled issues that were 100 percent scientific and technological, said Keyworth, citing examples from abortion to industrial innovation. The government's need was for "competent scientists who understand what President Reagan perceives as the role of government."[*83]

Keyworth went further. The Reagan administration, he said, faced the task—and the opportunity—of forging a coherent science policy for the first time since Vannevar Bush in the period immediately following the Second World War. Keyworth quoted with approval the words of his predecessor, Frank Press, that there had been no such coherent policy in the U.S. since that time. "I am perfectly prepared to define and justify our science policy," he confidently added.[85]

The claim was somewhat exaggerated. No administration since Eisenhower, the first President to appoint a full-time science adviser, had

---

* Even Frank Press, as president of the National Academy of Sciences, was forced to warn of "the destructive results of applying political criteria when competence and dedication to national needs should be the determining factors."[84]

denied having a science policy. In defining the administration's ideas about science as a new policy, Keyworth was essentially doing little more than legitimizing the redefinition of science policy in terms compatible with the political philosophy of the new Republican administration.

This is not to underestimate the significance of what Keyworth himself characterized as a "third generation of the postwar enterprise of science."[86] What is signaled is a reinjection of the spirit of free enterprise into science, and a direct challenge to any effort to subject science to social control.

What have been the principal characteristics of this new form of science policy? The first is that it seeks explicitly to recognize the dominant role of the private sector in setting the agenda for the public funding of science. Support for basic science is channeled into those areas that in the long term are expected to make industry more competitive in the global marketplace, such as advanced computers, biotechnology, and materials research (a goal Keyworth describes as "pragmatic"[87]). In allocating major increases in the basic research budget in its budget proposals for 1984, the Office of Management and Budget placed particular emphasis on research in the physical sciences (illustrated by a 15.9 percent increase in basic research funded by the Department of Energy) and mathematics (increased by 21.6 percent at the National Science Foundation). The OMB was explicit about its motivation: "Advances in these fields are keys to future national defense and the long-term competitiveness of the U.S. economy, particularly in high technology industries."[88]

The second characteristic of Reagan's science policy is that the application of the results of this research to civilian needs is to be left to the private sector and the profit motive. Previous administrations, Keyworth told a meeting of the American Association for the Advancement of Science in June 1982, had promoted R&D policies "predicated on the wishful thinking that government could somehow operate independent of market forces." In contrast, the Reagan administration was now pulling back from areas such as solar energy, with the intention of creating "a clear-cut and predictable distinction between what should be public-sector and what should be private-sector responsibilities."[89]

This philosophy was perhaps most clearly revealed in the new instructions given to the Department of Energy for deciding the type of research it should support in its own laboratories. In the mid-1970s the department had spearheaded government efforts to cushion the impact of escalating oil prices by promoting intensive research programs into new energy sources. The justification was that many of these new technologies, such as those exploiting solar and wind energy or conservation techniques, were receiving little attention from the private sector since their benefits were long-term and often difficult to characterize solely in economic terms (for example, by appealing to the security advantages of reducing dependence on foreign energy suppliers). The result was a major expansion in research in these areas during the 1970s. Much of it was concentrated in the national research centers such as the Oak Ridge National Laboratory in Tennessee and the University of California's Lawrence Livermore Laboratory, which were encouraged to diversify away from their previously almost exclusive interest in the military and civilian uses of nuclear energy.

The interventionist role of federal government symbolized by these programs became an early target of the Reagan administration. Transition task force co-chairman Arthur Bueche had little hesitation in identifying energy research as an area in which the government was not only unfairly competing with, but indeed subverting by its very presence, the private sector. Addressing a congressional committee in June 1981 on the future of the national laboratories, he suggested that the time had come to "begin to think about transferring the work and people to the university campuses and industry where we can produce more of the people we need and where the work can be more expeditiously commercialized."[90] Conversely, when AAAS executive officer William Carey suggested to a Department of Energy advisory committee that its report on the laboratories include the recommendation for a study of their transfer to a public corporation such as the Tennessee Valley Authority —a proposal that was opposed by Roland W. Schmitt, Bueche's successor at GE and on the panel—the suggestion was discreetly dropped on the grounds that it might be picked up by the press and used against the administration's plans for "privatizing" the work of the laboratories.[91]

This shift from applied back to basic research occurred across the whole spectrum of federal research, and it has become a key feature of the new era of science policy. A report published by the Center for Science and Technology Policy of New York University underlined the broad significance of the change. It identified President Nixon's use of federal R&D support in the early 1970s to stimulate the economy by sponsoring research in socially relevant areas such as transportation, housing, communications, and energy as a "tangible divider" between two previous eras of science policy—signaling "the ideological victory within the Republican administration of the proposition that civilian-sector R&D is a lever that, in the hands of the government, can affect the macroeconomic problems of productivity and international trade." In contrast, ten years later, the question of whether federal activity was called for *at all* preceded the question of which activities would be the most effective under what conditions. The result was "the beginning of a reversal in the postwar trend toward civilian-sector research."[92]

The new spirit of free-enterprise science has not stopped with the choice of research projects or the new division of responsibilities between the public and the private sectors. The third goal the Reagan administration has sought to achieve through its science policy is a fundamental change in attitude on the part of the scientific community. The notion of scientists as independent scholars, motivated solely by a thirst for knowledge and unconcerned about the eventual utility of their results, has been banished for good (even if it only half-existed in practice). Basic scientists—like company managers—are now clearly expected to keep their eyes on the bottom line; the only difference is of time scale.

Keyworth outlined what he described as "the new reality" facing scientists in a number of speeches. "The research community has an important role to play in this country's future, but it *has* to come to grips with the realities of the 1980s," he warned.[93] The good news was that science was back in political favor, and furthermore that the Reagan administration was prepared to accept scientific excellence as the dominant criterion by which the extra money was to be allocated within fields selected for priority funding. All scientists had to do was demonstrate that they could get together relatively amicably and present the government with an agreed list of scientific priorities and the best facilities to tackle them. "Those disciplines that present well-considered, unified agendas for research have the best chance of getting support for their programs," Keyworth explained. But if they failed to do this, they should not be surprised if "outsiders"—i.e., politicians—tried to make the decisions for them.[94]*

In principle, reintroducing excellence as the main criterion for research funding had the reasonable goal of making sure that research funds were concentrated in those areas of science likely to be the most productive. In practice, however, it also meant reinforcing traditional definitions of research topics and techniques, definitions that had been expanded by the requirements on scientists to engage in interdisciplinary research, or that specifically aimed at producing solutions to identified social problems. This in turn reinforced the traditional hierarchical structures of the scientific community, which justified their existence by the need to maintain excellence in research. (These structures had themselves been threatened by the imposition of "social" objectives, since this was not a dimension in which they could claim any particular expertise.)

Furthermore, in return for this extra funding and relative autonomy, the members of the scientific community had to fall in line with the administration's more general philosophy toward science. This meant a greater willingness to welcome industrial representatives into their labo-

* Ironically, this is just what happened when the White House, without consulting the scientific community, inserted funds for a new advanced materials research facility at the University of California's Lawrence Berkeley Laboratory. Congress, citing the lack of peer review, dropped the project from its budget request—and immediately replaced it with projects of its own for physics facilities at two less prominent universities but with powerful political supporters, without any prior consultation with the scientific community.[95]

ratories and to push their discoveries into the commercial marketplace —i.e., to recognize that science was no longer to be treated as a public good but as a private commodity. The extra money for basic research, said Keyworth, was only half of the administration's strategy. "What we are counting on is the payoffs from new perspectives, from imparting a better sense of reality and stimulation of the marketplace to a basic research community that has become increasingly isolated from it over the decades."[96]

In raising the level of federal support for selected areas of basic research while reducing the external controls over the way research money was spent, Keyworth was in many ways reinstating the social contract between government, industry, and the research community forged at the end of the Second World War, according to the principles drawn up by Vannevar Bush and his scientific colleagues. Their idea was that, with industry's support, large-scale funding for science should be provided out of the public purse. *Financial* accountability would still be required —if applied less rigorously than in the immediate past—for the way the money was spent, but the scientific community would be freed of all direct democratic involvement in the choice of research topics.

This arrangement was unique in the history of public administration. In 1962 Don K. Price of Harvard University wrote that science had become "the only set of institutions for which tax funds are appropriated almost on faith, and under concordats which protect the autonomy, if not the cloistered calm, of the laboratory."[97] The questioning of science that came from virtually all points on the political compass from the end of the 1960s to the middle of the 1970s, however, put this social contract in question. Complaints focused on frustrated expectations of payoffs from research programs, on the occasional blatant misuse of federal funds (for example, to pay vacation expenses), on the apparent frivolity of some research projects (particularly in the social sciences), and on the way research often seemed to be conducted with little concern for its social consequences.

Two principles were frequently invoked as ways of making the substance of science as democratically accountable as its funding. One was that constraints should be placed on which questions about nature (and society) it was legitimate for science to ask (such as whether one social group had an innate ability to perform better on intelligence tests than another); the second was that all publicly funded research should be shown to have a relevance to some immediate (and democratically sanctioned) social goal. Both principles found ready advocates in Congress, as well as the wider public. Caught in the grip of demands that could be enforced through the threatened withdrawal of their lifeblood, namely federal research funds, the scientific community expressed resignation. "Very reluctantly I have concluded that the supporting society will, increasingly, insist not only that the uses of science be democratically accountable, but that the conduct of science be accountable as well—however uncomfortable that may make scientists," wrote Philip Handler, president of the National Academy of Sciences, in 1980. "For better or worse, the terms of a new social contract between the scientific community and the larger society are now being forged."[98]

Handler need not have worried. At the prompting of its corporate backers, the Reagan administration has now successfully reinstated the original contract, as scientists had been suggesting—usually implicitly, sometimes explicitly—for several years.[99] Indeed, it has succeeded in going even further than Bush and his colleagues were ever able to do in shifting the control of science and scientific results from the public domain, where it can be democratically controlled and applied directly to social needs, to the private sphere, where public control can be exercised only through the indirect mechanisms of the marketplace.

Bush, for example, had strongly argued that patents arising from publicly funded research should remain the property of the scientist who made the discovery and his (or her) institution. His report proposed that "there should certainly *not* be any absolute requirement that all rights in [discoveries resulting from publicly funded research] should be assigned to the government."[100] At the time, Congress had other ideas. The results of public research, it was argued, were public property; to leave the patent with the scientist, who could then profit a second time from its exploitation, meant that the public would be paying twice for the same service.

The argument prevailed until the 1980s, when it was pinpointed by the corporate community (and the academic world) as one of the supposed causes for America's loss of technological leadership. Patent reform became one of the goals of the Carter administration's efforts to boost technological innovation. Consistently thwarted in Congress, where the idea of altering the laws was described by Senator Russell Long as "a giant public giveaway,"[101] the corporate research community finally managed to secure an amendment to the Patents and Trademarks Act which would allow universities and small businesses to keep the patent rights on federally sponsored research. Even the Carter administration seemed to share some of Long's scruples, suggesting (in a proposal rapidly dismissed by the corporate community and its supporters in Congress) that patents be permitted only for certain pre-agreed uses. And with continued opposition in Congress, it took an order from President Reagan directly to government agencies, requiring them to offer patent rights to all performers of federally sponsored research (regardless of size), to complete the transformation and achieve a goal that had consistently eluded Bush and his successors for the previous thirty years. (See the next chapter for further discussion of changes in patent legislation.)

It was the same story with tax policy. Industry had long argued that it should be allowed a tax break on its research and development expenditures as a way of encouraging additional investment in research. Since 1954, companies have been allowed to deduct all R&D costs as expenditures, yet they have continuously sought more than this, namely that R&D expenditures be given an extra credit against profits. Washington, however, consistently showed reluctance to grant what many feared would become a convenient tax-dodging device. During the Nixon administration, for example, George Shultz, director of the Office of Management and Budget, decided after a meeting with the National Commission on Productivity not to award companies tax credits for R&D expenditures, arguing that these were a very costly way of achieving relatively small results; instead he proposed an 8.5 percent increase in the federal R&D budget.

The corporate community had more luck with President Carter, who, although dropping proposals for such a tax break in his innovation initiatives announced in November 1979, introduced the following year a bill that would allow a limited credit on an individual company's *additional* R&D expenditures over the previous year. Again, however, it was under the Reagan administration that the idea of substantial tax credit found virtually all the support it needed from the White House. Corporate executives such as Bueche of General Electric had long suggested that a tax credit would be the single most effective way of stimulating more corporate research. In the summer of 1981, with full administration support, Congress passed an omnibus tax bill that included a 25 percent tax credit on increases in R&D expenditures and an accelerated depreciation of R&D equipment, as well as increased tax deductions for research equipment donated to universities.

Calculations about the beneficial financial impact of the tax cuts, despite their apparent precision, were often highly (and sometimes purposely) misleading. Indeed, it was ironic that the administration was prepared to support policy recommendations based on calculations whose dubiousness would have caused them to be thrown rapidly out the window had they addressed the reason for tough controls on a new chemical pesticide. Furthermore, they were opposed by some prominent economists. Joseph Pechman of the Brookings Institution in Washington, for example, told a meeting of the AAAS in 1980 that the existing full deduction for R&D outlays was about as far as the tax law should go: "If we are to spend federal funds to promote research and development, we should make an effort to maximize the return on our money. In general, tax deductions or tax credits are difficult to limit and usually turn out to be wasteful." Pechman said that some economists tended to exaggerate the positive effect of tax incentives on investment; the expected payoff was only "modest." Public support for R&D should thus be restricted primarily to direct outlays, and administered by agencies that "can distinguish useful projects."[102] Pechman's criticisms were borne out later when the Reagan administration admitted that those who had benefited from its newly introduced tax breaks on research included fast-food restaurants and movie producers.[103]

Yet the financial benefits of the tax break were secondary to their main purpose, namely to give industry a greater stake in—and hence greater control over—the totality of U.S. R&D expenditures. As economist Edwin Mansfield pointed out, addressing a meeting organized by the National Science Foundation on April 24, 1981: "Perhaps the most important advantage of such tax credits is that they involve less direct government control than many alternative devices to stimulate additional R&D."[104] This was precisely the strategy that Pechman had warned against. But it was what the Reagan administration wanted, since, despite the public subsidy that the tax breaks represented, they provided one more mechanism for concentrating control of research in the private domain.

The science policy of the Reagan administration, therefore, has had two clear beneficiaries. The first has been the corporate community, which has successfully achieved a fundamental redefinition of the responsibilities of the federal government for civilian science. Today there are few echoes of the calls for relevance to social—as opposed to military and industrial—needs in federal research programs that were heard so loudly, and raised so much disquiet in the scientific community, a decade ago.[105] The principal task of government science policy, as far as the private sector—and the Reagan administration—sees it, is to create an environment that provides the maximum encouragement, and the minimum obstruction, to their own research and development programs. The benefit to private corporations is double. On the one hand, they obtain privileged access to the results of publicly funded basic research through the provision of exclusive licensing agreements made possible by recent changes in patent legislation; on the other, their own research is subsidized through tax breaks, government subsidies, and the publicly funded training of their research workers.

The second beneficiary has been the scientific community, which has seen its financial budget expand rapidly, and has also been given back much of the power and prestige it enjoyed in the 1950s and early 1960s. In its budget request submitted to Congress at the beginning of 1983, the Reagan administration suggested increasing funding for university research by 17.8 percent (13.8 percent in real terms) between 1983 and 1984—more than any period since the boom years of the 1960s.[106] In the process, universities, too, have been absolved from the responsibility of pursuing "socially relevant" research, since they have been told that questions of social desirability can now be safely left to the marketplace, and this is where their first allegiance must lie.

What have been the costs to the rest of us? The first has been the increasing exclusion of social criteria from decisions about how research is conducted and how the results of research are put to use. Placing the market and the corporate community squarely back in control of decisions about the civilian applications of scientific knowledge has meant that the sole criterion used to decide on such applications is private profit. Environmental, social, and ethical questions surrounding the conduct of research and its implications are once again being relegated to the sidelines; "getting the economy back on its feet" has become the supreme goal to which science is being committed.

One area where this has had an important impact is employment. If profit is the dominant criterion used to direct technological innovation, then any unemployment created by the innovation will be disregarded as an unfortunate but unavoidable by-product. In the past, fears that rapid technological innovation would lead to widespread unemployment as machines take over the work of men and women proved unfounded, since the parallel expansion of the service sector was able to absorb many of those losing their jobs. Today, however, there are no alternative jobs opening up. In Europe unemployment is currently over 11 percent—the highest level since the depression of the 1930s—and in the United States it is not far below this level. It would be misleading to blame this unemployment directly on technological change as such; in most cases, unemployment has been caused by wider economic factors leading to the closing of factories and, frequently, threats to complete industries.[107] However, what is obvious is that the job opportunities in the new high technology industries are far from adequate to absorb the large pool of unemployed labor. One computer scientist from Carnegie-Mellon University has predicted that by the year 2010 the number of people employed in manufacturing in the United States will drop from 26 million to 3 million, yet he adds that no one in power "understands what's happening or grasps the extent of what's coming."[108] If left to market forces alone, however, there is no incentive for corporations to base new investment plans primarily on the number of new jobs they create.

The same goes for energy and environmental factors. Stressing the logic of market choice alone necessarily eliminates nonmarket criteria, such as the security of energy supply or the social desirability of one form of energy over another. Nuclear energy is the most obvious case in point. The nuclear industry continues to argue—although with decreasing conviction—that nuclear power could still be the cheapest source of energy in the twenty-first century, even when the necessary measures have been taken to ensure human and environmental protection. Yet the social consequences of a heavy dependence on nuclear energy— such as the threat of the diversion of plutonium fuel obtained from reprocessing or from the products of fast breeder reactors, or more broadly the inevitable links between the civilian and the military uses of nuclear power—make this option unacceptable to many people, even at the lower cost.

In the university laboratory (as we shall see in greater detail in the next chapter), the new pressure to treat scientific knowledge as a private commodity rather than a public good has had its own insidious consequences. Scientists who once shared their ideas and results freely with colleagues, confident that the social norms of the scientific community were sufficiently strong to ensure that they would eventually receive full credit, now guard the same information jealously, since it could prove commercially valuable. Fears of being ripped off escalate each time a report is published of one scientist trying to claim credit for a money-spinning discovery that another scientist claims was originally his or hers.

On the other side of the coin, relying on market forces to determine research and development priorities can skew such priorities away from areas where, although the social needs are pressing, the economic incentives to tackle those needs are weak. One example might be research into the application of genetic engineering techniques to the needs of small-scale farmers and cultivators, often very different from the needs of the large agribusiness corporations, whose principal interest lies in the amount of profit they can squeeze out of the land, not the maximum employment or social cohesion they can provide. Another is research into new techniques for applying microelectronics to the specific needs of the disabled. Often such projects do not qualify as "basic" research, yet neither are they the types of projects to which private companies are prepared to devote large sums of money, since the financial payoff is likely to be low.

Many of these social research priorities, of course, could be attacked with the funds currently being applied to military research. It would be utopian to believe that any major nation in the modern world can be persuaded to give up all claims to military power, that this power should not be based largely on the effectiveness of its military technology, or that this technology should not be consistently improved through programs of research. To accept the need for such research, however, is not the same as endorsing the massive expansion of Pentagon-supported science now taking place in the nation's research laboratories. Nor does it mean supporting the degree of control which, as we shall see in Chapter Three, is now being given to military and national security agencies over the way in which the results of this research are disseminated.

Beyond the question of research priorities, the resanctification of science creates less tangible political threats. One is the scientistic tendency to pretend that difficult political choices can be reduced to a neatly quantifiable cost-benefit analysis. The attractions of moving in this direction are obvious, not merely because it appears to offer a more "rational" form of decision-making (as we shall see in Chapter Five), or even because it presents social data in a form that can be easily assimilated into the technocratic administrative procedures of a complex industrial society, but because the apparent certainty of hard numbers provides a powerful defense of political actions.*

In the same vein, there are intrinsic dangers in the reinstatement of the prestige of the scientific expert. Public pronouncements by scientists are frequently used to defend (and attack) policy decisions. The Reagan administration, for example, used Keyworth to brief the press on its MX missile and proposals for a new anti-ballistic missile defense system, despite his lack of direct involvement in either situation—provoking one observer to comment that "they seem to think there is a political advantage in deploying the President's science adviser on behalf of politically controversial issues."[110] Yet the scope of such pronouncements frequently goes far beyond the expertise claimed by the individual concerned. In such circumstances the role of the scientist is frequently to legitimate decisions that have been made on the basis not of science but of economic and political factors. Statements by experts have their proper place—most often in pointing out the technical or logical fallacies in arguments being put forward by others. They are seldom valid as a basis for either making or justifying social and political decisions.

There is also a threat coming from the opposite direction, namely that, based on the professional, technical judgment of its science advisers, the government will be tempted to pursue what is "technologically sweet"— to use Robert Oppenheimer's description of the hydrogen bomb—rather than what is morally acceptable, socially desirable, or even economically sound. A case in point is the proposed funding of a manned space station, long sought by scientists from the National Aeronautics and Space Administration, initially opposed by Keyworth as an extravagant waste of money at a time of budget stringency, later supported by him as an appeal to the "national spirit" which could lead to a series of ambitious new space missions, perhaps even eventually a manned landing on Mars.[111] Similar ideas lay behind Reagan's demand for a massive satellite-based laser missile protection system. The ultimate logical conclusion of these arguments, as David Joravsky has written, is "that leaders will feel encouraged to some 'rational' use of nuclear weapons by scientific advisers whose function it is to tell what is technically feasible, not what is humanly right."[112]

Perhaps the greatest threat of the new science policy is the extent to which it reinforces the unequal distribution of social power and, at the same time, masks its political effects by cloaking them in an apparent cover of pragmatism and neutrality. "Scientific" thinking about policy issues has supported a shift in federal priorities away from *social equality*

* The power of numbers used in this way, for example, was not lost on Reagan's budget director, David Stockman, who admitted in an unguarded magazine interview that when a White House computer had not given him the answers he needed to defend a particular round of budget cuts before a congressional committee, he had merely adjusted the computer's instructions to obtain the answers he wanted.[109]

—a concept foreign to the discourse of science—and toward *social efficiency*, to which science has had lengthy experience in contributing. In the process, it has contributed directly to the undermining of democracy and to cutting back on many of the gains made by this democracy in the 1970s.

The shift in concern from equality to efficiency has not been accidental. Rather, it has followed widespread fears expressed during the 1970s about an "excess of democracy" that was spreading through the United States, making the country (it was claimed) both economically weak and politically ungovernable. This excess of democracy seemed a direct threat to the orderly social system that many senior scientists in important advisory positions seemed to yearn for. Jerome Wiesner, science adviser to President Kennedy and subsequently president of MIT, said in an interview with *U.S. New and World Report* that "our problem at the present time is not that the world has become more complex, but that we have become a society in which we have let a lot more people have a voice without at the same time figuring out a way of keeping the system operating. . . . This leads to a paralysis of decision-making. What is needed is the reestablishment of a governmental mechanism to end the paralysis."[113] Carter adviser and NAS president Frank Press has called for more centralized control in government, quoting a report prepared by the NAS that had drawn attention to "incoherent and even chaotic decision-making by a dozen federal agencies" on policies affecting technological innovation,[114] and suggesting that "the nation deserves a process of assessment, and coordinated policy-making at the level of the President and his Cabinet in this important area."[115] Reagan adviser Simon Ramo describes the principal political need as being not more democracy but more systems analysis, since the more precisely a system can be modeled, the more easily it can be controlled from the top.[116]

Describing the choice as being between democracy and efficiency, however, is itself misleading. Rather than opting for a tightening of authority in the name of technological progress, it should be possible to select a different route, one that achieves greater efficiency in the use of scientific knowledge and technical resources through greater democracy and participation, instead of at their expense. To do this will involve stepping outside the agenda for technological progress as it is framed by the major corporations, with the implicit support of the scientific community, and experimenting with new ways of subordinating economic activity to desirable social goals.

A necessary component in this solution will be greater participation by the community in decisions about the allocation of scientific and technical resources, rather than confining these decisions to the leaders of the scientific and the corporate communities, as is presently the case. Already some labor leaders have recognized the challenge to which they need to respond. Writing in a recent issue of *Technology Review*, William

Winpisinger, president of the International Association of Machinists and Aerospace Workers, expressed it as follows: "The real problem of technological innovation is that its contribution is totally controlled by what we in the machinists' union have come to call the 'corporate state.' That phrase connotes the tremendous success of the corporate sector in harnessing our public institutions to private corporate ends. But it also connotes the corporate control of the total resource base—not only raw materials and direct production labor, but the intellectual and scientific communities as well."[117] Tony Mazzochi, of the Oil, Chemical and Atomic Workers, speaks similarly of the value of using scientists, employed directly by workers, to carry out genetic screening programs and other projects on workers' health. "We all have to understand the politics of science in the workplace; that is the first step," says Mazzochi. "Secondly, we should begin a political discussion about the need for workers to control scientific capabilities so that ultimately we can legislate this concept into reality."[118]

Some suggestions about how a truly democratic science policy could work will be discussed in the final chapter of this book. Any such efforts, however, face some formidable obstacles. In the next three chapters we shall see in detail how the new directions in science policy are being promoted by powerful political coalitions, each dedicated to private— rather than public—control of knowledge and its applications. The first is the coalition between the nation's private research universities and corporations. The second, the renewed set of links being established between the scientific community and the military establishment. The third is the control that multinational corporations are able to exercise over the flow of U.S. science and technology to Third World countries. Science, each of these power groups argues, is not only too important to be left to the scientists, it is also too important to be left to politicians— or to the public. It is a formula with many dangerous implications, not least for the future of democracy itself.

2

UNIVERSITIES AND INDUSTRY: KNOWLEDGE AS COMMODITY

EARLY IN 1975, A GROUP OF SCIENTISTS GATHERED AT THE WEST COAST resort of Asilomar to address the rising concern both within and outside the scientific community about some of the potential dangers of recombinant DNA research. Almost seven years later, a second meeting on the hazards of this research was held in another conference center on the same stretch of California coast. In both cases the purpose of the meeting was to discuss how scientists engaged in such research should behave. The "hazards" under consideration, however, were very different. The first meeting concentrated on threats to human health and the natural environment that might inadvertently arise from experimental manipulation by scientists of the genetic material of living organisms. In contrast, "Asilomar 2," as it came to be widely dubbed, was called to discuss growing tensions in the scientific and academic communities caused by the eruption of commercial interest in the same techniques during the period between the two meetings.

The participants, too, were different. The 1975 discussions were organized and conducted largely by practicing scientists, with the participation of some invited lawyers, philosophers, and other academics. The talks were set up as a forum open to selected members of the press. At the second meeting. held in the resort of Pajaro Dunes, it was the turn of university administrators and the business community. The meeting

—this time closed—was organized by the president of Stanford University, Donald Kennedy, and co-hosted by four other top research universities, whose presidents were also present: the University of California, the California Institute of Technology, Harvard University, and the Massachusetts Institute of Technology. Each president had in turn been asked to invite one senior university administrator, two university scientists, and two representatives from companies with which the university had contacts. As a result, the participants included senior executives from some of the largest companies in the country, including not only those most closely identified with the growth of the genetic engineering industry, such as Eli Lilly, Cetus, and Genentech, but also Damon Corporation, Cabot Corporation, Gillette, and Syntex Pharmaceuticals.

The roots of the meeting lay in growing concern on university campuses and among a wider public about the effects of commercial interest and involvement in research at the frontiers of molecular biology. This interest had brought lucrative dividends to many university scientists, but it also threatened the integrity of university research—for example, by raising barriers to the open exchange of information, stimulating conflicts of interest and loyalty between a scientist's commercial and academic commitments, and disrupting the social relations of the laboratory. Stanford president Donald Kennedy had previously told a congressional hearing that although "basic research in universities on behalf of both Stanford and the Association of American Universities [needed] more, not less, relationship to industry," the danger was real that there would be "some contamination of the basic research enterprise in the university by a new set of values and new objectives."[1]

Although the specific subject area addressed at the Pajaro Dunes meeting was molecular biology and biotechnology, the implications were much broader. "Neither the opportunities nor the problems are, of course, confined to biotechnology. Some have arisen earlier, in other technology; and we shall no doubt face all of them again," said a prospectus sent out by Stanford. Biotechnology was a useful place to start. "The contemporary state of genetics and molecular biology presents us with so many of the central issues in paradigmatic form that it will, in our judgment, be wisest to concentrate our considerations on it—seeking whenever possible to illuminate by comparison." But the prospectus described how any conclusions reached would be equally relevant to all those research areas in which the private sector was showing an increasing interest. Not only other scientific disciplines but, given the interest in cultural programming and the cable television phenomenon, even the humanities were "likely to follow," Stanford warned.[2]

If the substance of the Pajaro Dunes meeting was representative of issues emerging across a spectrum of academic disciplines, equally symptomatic was the way the meeting was organized. Unlike the earlier conference at Asilomar—and despite concerns, expressed privately by even some of the participants, that the result would be to diminish the public credibility of its conclusions—the meeting was not open to the press, on the grounds that this would inhibit open discussion. (One university public relations officer later compared it to a political caucus, asking whether Democrats would invite Republicans to such a meeting.) Publicity was confined to a press conference on the last day, at which the conclusions were announced in the form of an eleven-page statement, largely prepared before the meeting began. A public interest group, the Natural Resources Defense Council (NRDC), had demanded access to the meeting, since at least one of the participants—the University of California—was a public institution and its affairs should therefore be open to public scrutiny; the request was turned down by UC president David Saxon, who pointed out that the meeting, sponsored by the Henry J. Kaiser Foundation, was a private one.

There was a logic behind the decision to hold a closed meeting, even beyond the fact that some participants felt public discussion would be an obstacle to frank debate. The meeting provided an opportunity for both sides to exchange views and feelings. But it also had a political function, for it was intended to act as a forum for moving toward a consensus on both goals and strategy for the different groups involved, namely the university and corporate leadership. Faced with growing public concern about the consequences of closer university-industry links, universities were moving quickly to respond—and they wanted to work out the best way to do it, in a way that would not cut them off from a potentially rich source of funding.

Donald Kennedy, at a 1981 congressional hearing, claimed that the relationship between universities and industry must be "carefully structured" if a "highly evolved and highly efficient mechanism for doing basic research is not to be unwittingly damaged."[3] The question was: Who was to do the restructuring? As in the earlier meeting at Asilomar, the participants feared that unless universities (this time in explicit collaboration with industry) developed their own guidelines, regulations would be imposed on them from the outside—as a state commission had already done in the case of the University of California. Additional regulations, universities complained, not only would interfere with the work of scientists, but would also stand in the way of closer links with outside companies. "We're fighting against moving too quickly and developing something that will impede relations with the private sector," said Dean Charles Hess of the College of Agricultural and Environmental Sciences at the University of California's Davis campus, where fierce controversy had arisen over the commercial links of some of its plant geneticists.[4]

Not surprisingly, given this political function, there was a considerable difference of interpretation of the meeting's conclusions between those who attended and those who were not admitted. No specific recommendations emerged; the participants emphasized in their final statement that it was up to each university to decide individually on the precise form in which any guidelines should be put into practice. Nevertheless, they were able to "get some principles on the table," in the words of Donald Kennedy, and "set an agenda for future discussions of the issue."[5] This in itself meant to the administrators that the Pajaro Dunes meeting was a successful first step in dealing with the rising tensions in universities. To critics such as the NRDC, however, the fact that this agenda had essentially been negotiated by top university administrators, faculty members often connected with outside companies, and senior executives of some of the companies themselves, with no participation by representatives of other groups such as laboratory workers, labor unions, or consumer representatives, symbolized the political dangers which, they claimed, could arise from the universities' growing involvement in the process of transforming public knowledge into a private commodity.

The massive federal investment in universities since World War II, they argued, meant that university research should be seen as a vast *public* resource, one that was now in danger of being auctioned off to the highest bidder. Shortly before the final press conference at which the meeting's conclusions were announced, the NRDC released a letter outlining its concerns. The letter's signatories include twenty-five scientists from universities across the country, including those represented at the official meeting. It ended by quoting President Eisenhower's warning that "in holding scientific research and discovery in respect, as we should, we must be alert to the equal and possibly opposite danger that public policy could itself become the captive of a scientific-technological elite."[6] The implication was that the universities were in even greater danger of falling under the control of this elite in rushing to help beat off "Japan Inc." than they had been in the 1950s when they were drafted to meet the needs of the "military-industrial complex" in facing the Soviet military challenge (something that Eisenhower had first drawn attention to in the same speech).

The NRDC's complaints about exclusion from the Pajaro Dunes meeting came at a time when rapidly tightening links between the academic and the corporate communities were signaling what Donald Kennedy of Stanford described as "a new era in university-industry relationships."[7] The dangers contained in these new relationships are usually described in terms of the threats they present to traditional academic values, such as academic freedom and objectivity. To characterize the dangers in this way, however, frequently diverts attention from the broader political implications of these moves, namely the way that they reinforce the power of the corporate-academic-military elite identified by Eisenhower. This trend has, to be sure, serious implications for universities, ranging from the marginalization of subjects that do not contribute directly to rapid technological growth, to a reduction in the intellectual space available for critical reflection on contemporary social trends. But it has even more serious implications for the community outside the university, since, by strengthening a key link in the contemporary science-power relationship, it reinforces the general concentration of power in the hands of the corporate community.

In principle, of course, there is little new about U.S. universities maintaining close links with private corporations. Indeed, the U.S. educational system has long prided itself on the emphasis placed on the functional role of universities in society, frequently compared favorably to the more distant relationship between the academic and corporate worlds which has traditionally existed in some countries in Europe. University presidents sit on the boards of major corporations, and company executives in turn act as university trustees. University researchers tend to be more willing to work on applied problems than European scientists. A report from the Organization for Economic Cooperation and Development, for instance, claims that France, the United Kingdom, and Germany each "still looks with something approaching envy at the U.S."[8]

What is new, however, is the depth and intensity that corporate interest in university research has recently acquired, in particular the new stress being placed on the potential value to industry of *basic*, rather than *applied*, research. This interest is a direct result of the close link between basic research and high technology industries such as biotechnology and microelectronics. As a report presented to President Reagan by the National Science Board in 1982 pointed out, interest in university-industry research relationships is becoming more intense because of the growing perception that industrial products and services are increasingly dependent on fundamental scientific understanding. "With this dependency the distinction between basic and applied work often disappears. Fundamental ideas and approaches become a necessity and they are used in both universities and industry."[9]

This trend is blurring traditional lines of responsibility and giving the corporate community a greater interest in the content of universities' basic research agendas. During the massive buildup of university research facilities in the postwar period, industry took a relatively back seat, tacitly endorsing federal policy, but leaving research priorities to be negotiated between the universities and the government. Now the political relationships are changing. Even though the federal government's contribution remains dominant in financial terms, social priorities and objectives are being relegated to a subordinate position as universities' basic research efforts are increasingly molded to meet corporate needs.

Tensions have inevitably arisen from the conflicting social norms and values of the academic and corporate worlds. The conflict has been put succinctly by Leon Wofsy, professor of immunology at the University of California, Berkeley: "The business of business is to make money . . .

and the mode is secrecy, a proprietary control of information and the fruits of research. The motive force of the universities is the pursuit of knowledge and the mode is open exchange of ideas and the unrestricted publication of results and research."[10]

Some of these tensions are the straightforward results of an inevitable difference in operating styles. Others, however, have political roots. Claiming the commercial competitiveness of American industry as their overriding goal, universities and industry have teamed up to challenge the democratic control of knowledge and to argue that the social applications of such knowledge should primarily be achieved through the marketplace. A straightforward division of labor has been negotiated. The universities will be responsible for generating this knowledge free from direct government or public interference; companies will be responsible for applying it to commercial products and processes. As a research manager at Rockwell International puts it: "Breakthroughs take the brain power of universities and the management of industry."[11] Both sides are now collaborating to engineer not only the research conditions but also the social and political environment to encourage any such breakthrough that promises to make a commercial profit. Although federal funds are still the principal source of research support, universities and industry have combined to reduce control by democratic institutions on either side.

Such developments represent the opening of a new phase in the history of American universities and their relationship to the corporate community. Linkages between the two stretch back to the early nineteenth century. Many started with the agricultural industry, which has always enjoyed a close relationship with state universities. This was formalized in the Morrill Act of 1862, which set up the system of land-grant colleges under which federal funds were distributed to states explicitly to support the efforts of colleges in sustaining local agricultural industries. The terms of the act were clear: colleges were required to "teach such branches of learning as are related to agriculture and the mechanical arts" in order to qualify for federal funds.

Industrial links were also established through university staff who were employed by private corporations, primarily as consultants, to advise on problems such as the chemical aspects of textile manufacturing or the analysis of crude oil. Soon these links, too, began to be formalized, often based on observation of the success of German industry in linking its activities to those of university research laboratories.[12] The ties are vividly illustrated in the histories of several of the largest private research universities. Perhaps the most obvious example is the Massachusetts Institute of Technology, whose charter, when it was licensed by the Commonwealth of Massachusetts in 1861, specified that the new institute should generally aid "by suitable means the advancement, development, and practical applications of science in connection with arts, agriculture, manufactures, and commerce." According to one senior MIT administrator, the result has been the creation of a "cooperative, mutually supportive, and interactive relationship with industry as an integral part of its mission in teaching and research.[13] MIT president Paul Gray has put it more bluntly: "Our academic roots are in American industry."[14]

The relationship, as David Noble has shown in *America by Design*, drew increasingly close during the second half of the nineteenth century.[15] This was the period that saw the first emergence of science-based production, primarily in the electrical and chemical industries, with companies such as General Electric, Westinghouse, AT&T, Dow, and du Pont quickly establishing their dominance through the products of their research laboratories. Both industries depended, from an early stage, on the commercial application of knowledge generated in the laboratory. Furthermore, building on the successful formula developed by Thomas Edison, both industries were quick to realize the value of large research empires on the grounds that, as Elihu Root was later to claim, "the prizes of industrial and commercial leadership will fall to the nation which organizes its scientific forces most effectively."[16] This meant concentrating on both applied and basic research. By the 1930s, for example, the Bell Laboratories were carrying out more basic research than any university in the United States.

The industrial interest in science also meant drawing universities even more closely into the corporate sphere of influence, since they were soon recognized as offering the most likely source of ideas required for innovative products and processes. In a report prepared for the recently established National Research Council in 1918, Henry Pritchett, president of the Carnegie Foundation for the Advancement of Teaching, commented that, as had been the case for some time in Germany, "it is today part of our plan for progress for the future to establish such relations that the investigator and the manufacturer shall understand each other and shall cooperate for the promotion of science and industry."[17] William Wickenden wrote that "the existence of the great research programs of industry is predicated upon the existence of a vast army of free, disinterested and even impractical researchers at work in the laboratories of colleges and universities."[18] Not only did industry recognize the value of the research results that the universities produced, but it also acknowledged the important role of universities as a training ground for future industry scientists. By the end of the 1930s, a range of relationships had been established between the universities and the private sector, including the use of university scientists as consultants, the sponsoring of university fellowships, the sharing of expensive equipment, and a limited amount of direct sponsorship of research to supplement endowment funds and foundation grants (which provided the bulk of research support).

In contrast, there was an inherent distrust of any government involvement in university research. Many individuals in the academic and the political communities argued that this could create an unwarranted interference with free enterprise, both commercial and intellectual. Indeed, there was a general feeling that government grants to private universities were "improper, if not unconstitutional."[19] A study of the fifteen members of the Science Advisory Board established by President Roosevelt in the 1930s to look at possible federal sponsorship of university research found that two-thirds feared political involvement more than they wished to involve science in society, while only three or four felt that the risk of political control was worth taking in almost every case—a feeling shared by the National Academy of Sciences as well as many members of Congress.[20] Significantly, no provisions for increased R&D spending were included in any of President Roosevelt's plans to deal with the economic depression of the mid-1930s.

All this was changed by World War II, which opened the second major stage in the evolution of the university-industry relationship. Vannevar Bush's report *Science: The Endless Frontier* described the mutual benefits which, it was claimed, would flow from a close relationship between government and private universities, based on the then radical proposition that private funds were inadequate to meet the nation's anticipated research needs. The principal beneficiaries of Bush's proposals were intended to be the research laboratories of the nation's colleges and universities. Together with the nonprofit research institutes, wrote Bush, "these provide the environment which is most conducive to the creation of new scientific knowledge and least under pressure for immediate, tangible results."[21]

If universities were to meet the rapidly growing demands of industry and government for new scientific knowledge, "their basic research should be strengthened by use of public funds." Under the organizational framework proposed by Bush, which led directly to the creation of the National Science Foundation, support for research in universities and colleges rose from $31 million from all sources in 1940 to $3.4 billion by 1975—two-thirds of it provided by the federal government. Even allowing for inflation, this represents a real increase of about 25-fold, significantly higher than that for the research budget as a whole.

The private sector also benefited directly from the growth of federal research funding. Not only was it able to use results emerging from the university research laboratories, but it also received its own share of the increased federal funds. The late 1940s and early 1950s were halcyon days for U.S. science, when universities and industry worked closely together toward common research objectives, both drawing heavily on the federal purse. In financial terms, industry's contributions to university research budgets remained, at least in the 1950s and early 1960s, relatively constant (doubling in value between 1953 and 1966). However, in contrast to those who claim there was a deterioration in the relationship over this period, a recent National Science Board report points out that "there are many indications that such relationships remained both vigorous and varied."[22]

Despite their initial common interests, however, the paths of universities and industry had already begun to diverge. Various political factors are occasionally cited to explain this. One familiar target has been government intervention in the universities, based on the argument that federal support per se has deliberately weaned universities away from attending to the needs of the private sector. Others, placing a later date on the split, have been tempted to blame it on the hostility toward industry on university campuses that developed during the student anti-war protests of the 1960s.

In practice, however, the reason for the divergent paths seems to have been more structural than deliberate. A principal cause was the fact that federal support for education and research increased in the 1950s and 1960s much faster than that for industry. As a result, even though industry sponsorship of research continued to grow significantly in absolute terms, as a *proportion* of academic research funding it dropped precipitously—from 10 percent of the total in 1955 to 5 percent in 1960, and less than 3 percent in 1970.

As Bruce Smith and Joseph Karlesky have shown in *The State of Academic Science*, this imbalance in itself had a number of implications for the university-industry relationship.[23] For example, as university research departments expanded, the growth in demand for teaching and research staff meant that graduates no longer thought of industry as the principal source of their future employment; as a result, research students showed less interest in industrial topics while at college, and graduate training programs became more oriented toward careers in academic science.

Equally important was a growing divergence between the self-perceived research needs of government and of industry. The main concern of the government in supporting university research—particularly in the period immediately following the launch of the Russian Sputnik—was to stimulate the science and technology required for national defense. University research scientists were, as a result, encouraged to think in terms of developing increasingly sophisticated technologies to meet the needs of the nation's defense and space programs and to carry out basic research related to these goals. Yet this was very different from the direction in which industry wanted to go. The generous support offered by the defense and space agencies attracted university researchers, particularly in engineering departments, toward high technology problems that were not always the most important from industry's point of view, and indeed often had little in common with the foremost industrial needs. "Defense and space research focused on *performance* improvements while other industrial R&D continued to emphasize cost improvements as well. There was no question that the former seemed the more interesting direction for university engineering faculty to pursue," writes Walter S. Baer.[24]

In contrast, industry found that basic research did not contain the quick fix to its technical promise that science had appeared to offer immediately after the war. Reacting to a growing feeling that science had been oversold, by both scientists and the federal government, industrial companies cut back significantly both on their own activities in basic research (many closed laboratories that had been opened in the immediate postwar euphoria!) and on their basic research support to universities.

What I have characterized as the second phase of university-industry relations was therefore marked by a growing distance between the two, with the university carrying out basic research for its public sponsors, and industry increasingly seeking short-term gains from its own internal research programs. Various efforts were made in the early 1970s to bring the two sides closer together—in particular, through schemes developed, initially at the prompting of the Nixon administration, by the National Science Foundation. Yet there was little active enthusiasm from either side, and collaboration remained at a relatively low level. Industry's share of total academic R&D expenditures dropped from over 6 percent in 1960 to 2.8 percent in 1975, and increased little over the next few years.[25]

In the late 1970s, however, all this began to change yet again. As basic research moved to the center of the civilian economy, industry became more and more aware of its need to keep up with developments at the frontiers of science (a strategy that some companies, such as AT&T with its Bell Laboratories, had been doing all along). No longer was it content merely to wait at the laboratory door for the results of research programs to emerge at a leisurely pace. Now it needed to know what was going on in the laboratory as it happened—and, if possible, before it happened.

As a result of the new growth in demand for corporate access to basic research, pressure for the reestablishment of alliances between industry and the universities began to grow, eagerly promoted by industry-based lobby groups such as the Committee for Economic Development and the Industrial Research Institute.[26] Edward David, previously science adviser to President Nixon, fleshed out the philosophy that was reemerging in his presidential address to the American Association for the Advancement of Science at the beginning of 1979. He claimed that "the time has come for a closer and more intimate relation between industry and academia." David's agenda was explicitly political. Coupled with industry's need for new technologies based on science was a desire to counter "tendencies at the national level to deemphasize pluralism, competitiveness based on technical excellence, and dependence on high achievers." Together, he said, these all implied the need—and indeed even supplied "a driving force"—for "a new synergistic relationship between the scientific community and industry—the industrial connection."[27]

The new industrial connection has, as David predicted, been receiving increasing attention from government, industry, and university policymakers, each committed to the idea that it forms an essential component of any strategy to increase the international competitiveness of American industry. The connection has taken a variety of forms. The most significant characteristic common to many of the new arrangements has been the emergent collaboration in basic research between universities and industry, with no federal involvement. One of the first—and in some ways the most controversial, since it broke new ground in defining the terms under which privately sponsored basic research would be carried out—was a $23 million, ten-year agreement signed in 1975 between the chemical firm Monsanto and the Harvard Medical School to support the work of two faculty members, Judah Folkman and Burt Vallee. Monsanto's appetite seems to have been whetted by the potential development of an anti-tumor agent from Folkman's research on what he described as a "tumor angiogenesis factor." Formally, however, the arrangement between the company and the medical school left it up to the scientists to determine—with the company's approval—which avenues of research should be pursued (a relatively novel arrangement since traditionally companies had contracted specific research projects from university scientists, with a clear idea of the results they were hoping to achieve). In return for this freedom, Monsanto received first pick of any patentable results to emerge from the research. In other words, the university scientists would direct the research phase, while the company would take over the task of developing and commercializing any potential products arising from the research.[28]

The Harvard-Monsanto deal pointed the way for a succession of bilateral university-industry arrangements. MIT, for example, announced in April 1980 that it had reached a ten-year agreement with Exxon Research and Engineering Company to provide between $7 and $8 million for research into combustion science. The agreement was described as "one of the largest and longest in duration of its kind between a university and a corporation," according to an MIT press release.[29] This was dwarfed later in the same year, however, by the Massachusetts General Hospital —the major teaching hospital linked to Harvard Medical School—which announced a $50 million deal with the German pharmaceutical manufacturer Hoechst, under which the company has established a complete new department of molecular biology. Monsanto itself announced in May 1982 that it had agreed to a five-year, $23 million program of collaborative basic research with Washington University in St. Louis. Other arrangements, though less significant in financial terms, have nevertheless continued to receive wide publicity. Yale University, for example, announced a three-year, $1.1 million grant from Celanese Corporation for research into the use of enzymes in chemical and textile production. Washington University entered into a three-year agreement for research into the commercial development of monoclonal antibodies with the Mallinckrodt company. Rockefeller University in New York received a $4 million contract from Monsanto to support research on the structure and regulation of plant genes. MIT received a $100 million grant from industrialist John Whitehead to establish a new institute for biomedical research. And the chemical empire of du Pont has committed $6 million over five years to fund research in a new genetics department at Harvard Medical School.

Not all support has been provided on a one-to-one basis. The growing number of bilateral agreements has been complemented by multilateral arrangements set up to collect funds from various corporate sponsors and distribute them to university research projects. A Semiconductor Research Cooperative has been established under the auspices of the Semiconductor Industry Association—initially suggested by executives from IBM—to promote the development of university basic research programs in integrated circuits. Originating in California but based in South Carolina, the cooperative raised $5 million in research funds in 1983 from companies that included most of the major ones in the field, such as IBM, Advanced Micro Devices, Signetics, Fairchild, Motorola, Control Data Corporation (CDC), and Rockwell. The goal of the organization is to fund "centers of excellence" in eight to ten universities known for their work in key areas of computer science. Specific research projects are selected by the cooperative, and the member companies will share the technical information that comes from them; total research funds distributed in this way are expected to reach $40 million a year by 1986. The first grants were made in November 1982, when $3 million was shared between the University of California at Berkeley, Carnegie-Mellon University, and eight other universities to support research on integrated circuits. In 1983 this was supplemented by funding for microstructure science at Cornell, and plans for comparable facilities at other universities, both public and private, were well advanced.

A similar initiative was launched in 1981 by a number of major chemical companies through a group known as the Council for Chemical Research, whose primary purpose is to boost the industry's financial support for academic research in chemistry and chemical engineering. First suggested in 1979 by M. E. (Mac) Pruitt, then head of research for Dow Chemical, the council set itself the goal of enrolling forty companies and a hundred universities. The council distributes funds raised from individual companies through a general Chemical Science and Engineering Fund, hoping eventually to raise between $8 million and $10 million a year for university chemistry research.

Although no comparable cooperative research arrangement has yet been worked out for biotechnology—largely because in the initial stages of commercial interest there was little shortage of research funds from the venture capital market—several smaller cooperative funding agreements have been established. For example, the New York investment company E. F. Hutton set up an affiliate, DNA Sciences, to raise money on the venture capital market and distribute it both to university research groups and to the small entrepreneurial research companies that these groups have frequently spawned. Similarly, on the West Coast, Stanford University and the University of California combined to set up a company, Engenics, which raised venture capital from six major chemical engineering and biotechnology companies—General Foods, Koppers, Mead, Bendix, Maclaren Power, and Elf—and distributed these funds to research scientists at the two universities. And in April 1983, Cornell University announced it was setting up, with the help of the state of New York, a new Biotechnology Institute to which three major companies— Union Carbide, Eastman Kodak, and Corning Glass—had pledged to provide up to $2.5 million annually over the following six years.

Close ties between universities and industry have been enthusiastically endorsed by political leaders. During the Carter administration, for example, the Domestic Policy Review of Industrial Innovation expressed concern that "there has been an ever-widening gap between the university and the industrial communities and as a result this key national source of new technological knowledge is not being adequately tapped for its innovative potential by the private sector."[30] Two staff members of the Office of Science and Technology Policy, in a paper written after a meeting between President Carter's science adviser, Frank Press, and leading industry research executives, suggested that "the time appears to be ripe for major improvements in university-industry relationships"[31]— an assessment based on extensive discussion in the White House with corporate research executives and university administrators, and reflected in various initiatives supported by the administration.

Even though funding for many of these initiatives was dropped by the Reagan administration, the concept continued to receive strong support from the White House. Greater collaboration "promises to reestablish the strong academic-industry linkages which existed prior to the rapid growth of federal funding in the 1950s and 1960s." And "the continued financial health of the universities will require that they develop a greater receptivity to working with industry," suggested Reagan's science adviser, George Keyworth, in one of his first public speeches. Keyworth made it clear that, as far as the details of new relationships were concerned—and in contrast to some previous government policies—Washington was not going to get involved, since "government should stand back and let good things happen."[32] Yet indirectly—for example, by promoting changes in tax and patent policy (described in more detail later)—it has given such cooperation its enthusiastic support.

Congress, too, has been keen to promote the "industrial connection" through federal agencies. Largely as a result of congressional pressure, the National Science Foundation began to offer support for research by private companies, previously considered taboo unless the research was judged to be nationally significant. In January 1978 the National Science Board agreed to change the guidelines for research grants awarded by the NSF to permit funding of cooperative research projects involving both universities and industry—a compromise solution agreed to after several individual university members of the board had objected to open funding of corporate research as unfair competition.[33]

The cooperative research program, whose initial budget was set by Congress at $4.7 million, rapidly became popular. A year later, NSF director Richard Atkinson presented Congress with a long list of research projects that were being funded. "Now that the program is becoming known, the size of the response is exceeding our expectations and out-pacing the funds that were budgeted," he announced.[34] Industrial sponsors, who were required to provide some of their own money in addition to the NSF funds, included many leading names in U.S. industry. Thus the foundation found itself supporting research into thermal cavities being carried out jointly by Bell Laboratories and Lehigh University; into digital signal processing between Raytheon and the University of Rhode Island; into robot manipulation between Westinghouse and the University of Florida; and into new types of metal catalysts between du Pont and the University of Delaware.

Another approach developed through the NSF was the creation of joint university-industry research centers, each designed to meet the needs of a particular industry or group of companies. The NSF characterized its role in such collaborations as a catalyst. It used a system of funding by which, although providing the initial seed money for such centers, its contribution steadily decreased over a period of five years, during which time the center and its sponsoring university were responsible for finding alternative support from the private sector.

The most successful of these centers has been the Polymer Research Center established at MIT in 1973, where small-, medium-, and large-scale firms support research into mathematical modeling of injection molding and improving the impact resistance of fiber-reinforced polyester. By 1978 industrial support for the center had increased to about $500,000 a year, and the NSF was able to drop out of the picture, leaving the center self-sustaining on industry funds alone.[35] Based on the success of these centers, a similar program for the support of "centers for research into generic technology" (COGENT) was suggested by the Department of Commerce under the Carter administration as part of its Domestic Policy Review of Industrial Innovation in 1979. As a result of the review, the Carter administration proposed establishing three such centers, the first one to focus on welding and joining. The scheme was eliminated, however, in the early weeks of the Reagan administration on the grounds that it represented an illegitimate interference with the market economy.

Using federal grants as a source of seed money—or, as NSF director Atkinson described it, of "pre-venture capital"—various universities have been able to develop research facilities directly tuned to the needs of industry. One of the largest single amounts of NSF support has gone to the National Research and Resource Facility for Submicron Structures at Cornell University, which won a $5 million grant in open competition with forty other research institutions. As with the NSF's joint university-industry centers, industry participation has been built in from the earliest stages. Of the eight members of the facility's policy board, four come from major telecommunications and computer companies, namely Bell Laboratories, IBM, Hewlett-Packard, and Intel Corporation. Other companies with which the facility has established links through its affiliates program include Eastman Kodak, General Electric, Hughes Research, Rockwell International, Texas Instruments, and the Xerox Corporation. The initial NSF grant has now been supplemented by a major grant from the Semiconductor Research Association.

A similar initiative taken independently by Stanford University has led to the creation of a Center for Integrated Systems. The purpose here has been to integrate research and fabrication on the one side with systems architecture on the other, a form of vertical integration from materials through devices and components to complete systems. The new center has been partly financed by seventeen companies, each of which agreed to contribute $250,000 a year for an initial three-year period, in this case supplemented by a grant of $8 million from the Pentagon's Defense Applied Research Projects Agency. The committee that liaises between Stanford and the corporate sponsors is chaired by the president of Hewlett-Packard (itself largely a creation of Stanford alumni), and includes top executives of several local advanced technology companies, including Intel, TRW, and Xerox. Among the companies that have agreed to sponsor the center are General Electric, Fairchild, Hewlett-Packard, Honeywell, IBM, Northrop, Tektronix, Texas Instruments, TRW, and Xerox.[36]

Cornell and Stanford are not alone in using federal funds to catalyze a close collaboration with high technology companies. At Rensselaer Polytechnic in New York State similar research on large-scale integrated circuits is being conducted at a new Center for Integrated Electronics—the "most expensive program ever undertaken by the university," according to the center's director, Andrew J. Steckl.[37] MIT has formed a Microsystems Industrial Group to expand its work in very large-scale integrated circuits, with $8 million in federal funding and several $250,000 a year commitments from industry, aimed at creating a tighter bond with industry through linking the design and fabrication of microsystem components. And similar schemes are springing up in virtually all universities in the U.S. in an attempt to exploit the recent surge of interest in high technology.

Overall, the result of these various collaborative schemes both with and without government support has been, as *Business Week* described it at the end of 1982, that "the trickle of industrial support of science at universities a few years ago is turning into a torrent."[38] According to figures from the National Science Foundation, industry spending on universities increased almost fourfold between 1972 and 1982, reaching a total of $400 million. Where industry funding in 1978 amounted to less than 3 percent of the total university research budget, by 1982, suggested the NSF, it had risen to between 6 and 7 percent of university R&D.[39] Exxon's Edward David suggests that an "absolute minimum target" for direct industrial support should be 10 to 15 percent, a figure that would return the ratio of industry's support to the level of the early 1950s.[40]

For individual universities the increases have been significant. MIT claimed in 1981 that research support from industry had tripled from $6 million to $18 million, now constituting 10 percent of the institute's total research budget. A $3 million contribution from the Control Data Corporation to support research at Purdue University, together with other business arrangements, helped raise the industrial support of Purdue's research budget from 5 to 12 percent. Rensselaer Polytechnic claims that, with the funds it has raised for its new Center for Integrated Electronics, almost 20 percent of its research was funded by industry in 1981. The figures could go considerably higher. Rensselaer dean of engineering George A. Ansell says, "We hope to end up with 40 percent."[41]

Reflecting this growing collaboration, data from the NSF demonstrate the fruits of increasing cooperation between university and company scientists in producing scientific research. Between 1973 and 1979 the NSF reports a growth from 19 to 31 percent in the number of scientific papers produced by industry scientists with university-based collaborators; in physics the growth was from 13 to 17 percent, in engineering and technology from 9 to 12 percent, and in mathematics from 28 to 37 percent.[42]

Just as important as the size of the contributions or the increase in collaboration, however, is the degree of leverage over the universities' basic research agenda that the new linkages are providing to corporate sponsors. Industry executives frequently emphasize that they have no desire to impose directions on research, leaving it to the curiosity of the individual research scientist to decide the most promising areas of study and lines of attack. "We want [scientists] to work on their own ideas and to come up with something brand new," says Mac Pruitt of Dow.[43] Even if demands for specific research results are not made, however, the pressures remain in the form of preference for one field or area of basic research over another. A report from New York University's Center for

Science and Technology Policy indicates that industry would like to see a change in traditional university procedures so that "university basic research can be planned with at least a knowledge of those areas of science in which industry can identify a need for more effort."[44] Kenneth Smith, associate provost at MIT, admits that, even in providing funding for basic science, "funding sources almost always carry subtle incentives in the direction of what research should be carried out."[45] Pruitt himself goes on to acknowledge that universities receiving funding from Dow for basic research "would have to understand Dow's needs."[46]

However low-key, industry's interest in basic research is inevitably encouraging universities to select areas of research that promise an eventual chance of commercial profit; indeed, this has been the principal goal of corporate policies in this area. Even the federal government, previously the champion of academic freedom, has acknowledged that corporate interests should be allowed to dominate decisions about what research should be done. According to Richard Atkinson, one important key to the success of centers funded by the NSF—and an indicator of the way the agency saw its federal role—was the dominant position given to the private sector in determining research priorities. "The government should provide guidance and direction to the participants but not control the agenda," he told a congressional subcommittee.[47] Although initial funding for Cornell's microstructure facility was provided by the NSF, "research emphasis and policy for the facility are being set or strongly influenced by industry," admits the director of the new center, Edward D. Wolf.[48] It is an objective which, not surprisingly, has been warmly endorsed by the Reagan administration.

Industry funding also favors a broader form of selection, namely that the areas of science receiving increased funding—such as mathematics and physics, rather than psychology or ecology—are those that feed directly into "high technology" areas such as semiconductors, microelectronics, catalysis, automation, and biotechnology, rather than being evenly distributed across all fields of science. Indeed, the link to high technology seems to provide the key to the success of collaborative industry-university ventures. In contrast to the success of the Polymer Research Center at MIT, for example, the NSF failed to generate sufficient industry interest in two other centers launched at the same time: one based at North Carolina State University, engaged in furniture research; the other operated by the Mitre Corporation in New England, where it has been hoped that a university-based center would help promote energy research in universities in accord with the needs of local power utilities. NSF director Atkinson put it straightforwardly when he addressed a congressional subcommittee in 1979: "A crucial point we have learned is that the projects are most successful when high technology industries—such as electronics, chemicals, aerospace, and pharmaceuticals—are involved. These industries possess the requisite capability to convert today's basic science into tomorrow's applied research and technology."[49]

Yet the interest of high technology companies in university research cannot be measured solely in terms of the results that emerge—patentable or otherwise. Because of its critical contribution to high technology, knowledge about basic research has itself generated a new strategic value. Many companies consider that an equally important result of their collaboration with university scientists is that it provides them with a foot in the academic research community and a way of keeping abreast of developments at the frontiers of science, giving them access to new ideas that are evolving in the laboratories often long before such ideas have made their way into print.

This early-warning system provides information that can have an important strategic value to multinational companies working in a highly competitive economic environment. As Christopher Freeman of the University of Sussex's Science Policy Research Unit puts it: "The advance of scientific research in many different fields is constantly throwing up new technical possibilities, which are to a large extent independent of any particular market pressure. If a firm, or a country, can monitor this advancing frontier, by one means or another, it may be able to gain both a technological and a market lead over its competitors by the speed of its response."[50]

Asked to explain what Hoechst was getting for its money from the Massachusetts General Hospital if the research was not going to be kept secret, the director of the hospital's research, Ronald Lamont Havers, replied that the company was mainly interested in access to new knowledge: "They are not primarily concerned with the development of patents or new products. These they can take and develop in their own laboratories. If that's what they wanted, they've got their own in-house laboratories which would do that for them."[51] Monsanto's director of research, Monte Throdahl, claims that the main value of the $23 million deal with Harvard Medical School is that it gives the company "a window on the new biology."[52] John Linvill, the director of Stanford's Center for Integrated Systems, uses the same metaphor, saying that he is offering companies a "very good window" on the more than $12 million a year research program in microelectronics being carried out at the university. "What they get can be encapsulated best by the words 'lead time.' They will get lead time on research being done here, they will have first access to it, and deeper access to it," he explains.[53] Robert J. Erra, vice-president for finance at the Scripps Clinic and Research Foundation, indicates that companies such as Eli Lilly and Johnson and Johnson that are investing in work at Scripps are building a quick way to find out about new technology. "That's really what they're buying: a chance to get know-how ahead of their competitors."[54]

What is therefore motivating companies to build close links to universities is not so much the specific results of the research they are sponsoring as the *strategic* advantage that such knowledge provides them in maintaining their competitive position in the international market. The most important information relates not so much to specific products as to broad lines of future product development. Scientists engaged as consultants are asked to perform as guides to directions that product lines may take in future, either those produced by the company itself or those of its commercial competitors; the researchers provide data for a sort of scientific commodity futures market in the same way that a satellite flying over another country can be used to predict the size of its agricultural crops—and hence the likely trends in international commodity prices that tell U.S. farmers whether or not it will be profitable to plant a certain crop.

Thus the new shape of international high technology competition has placed universities in a situation that is significantly different from before. The gap between basic research and commercial interest has been dramatically narrowed. Previously, knowledge represented economic power primarily in its applied form, i.e., through its application to specific products and the control over those products generated through the patent system. But the dynamics of the international marketplace have given Bacon's claim that knowledge is power a new twist: scientific knowledge has become a strategic tool for company planners, a way of guiding them toward future products and markets, if possible ahead of rival companies—and countries. The results have been dramatic. As one Stanford professor of medicine expressed it during a meeting of the university's research committee, "I don't think there has ever been a time when an intellectual pursuit could give as much simultaneous reward academically as well as financially. When people begin to measure their success in terms of millions of dollars [in terms of equity value] brought about by thirteen days of consultancy work every quarter [the maximum permitted under Stanford's conflict-of-interest rules], it has a very different implication than it did when it brought in only a fraction of their university income."[55]

The full impact of industry's current interest in basic science in universities does not therefore stem merely from its desire to apply the fruits of university research to new products. Rather, the significance comes from the *structural* shift in the relationship between the industrial and the academic research communities. For most of the postwar period, the two were connected through what might be described as a "series" relationship; basic research (in contrast to applied research) was usually characterized as research whose benefits (in terms of new products) were by definition "long-term," the two adjectives being used almost interchangeably. The strategic value of scientific knowledge in the marketplace, however—and particularly the value that possession of such knowledge acquires in the equity market—has given rise to a new form of relationship, one in which industrial and academic scientists are working on parallel tracks. Often the knowledge of whether a certain experiment works—for example, whether a particular gene is able to express itself within a foreign organism—can simultaneously have both a scientific and a commercial value (in one case helping to increase the amount of fundamental knowledge about basic living processes, in the other providing clues to the potential viability of new production techniques). The same is true for the close relationship between fundamental discoveries in materials science and the needs of semiconductor manufacturers; in both cases research workers find themselves focusing on the same microphenomena. Indeed, such research is often referred to as "strategic research," and although this term is intended primarily as a technical description, the research, as we have seen, has commercial and, ultimately, political significance as well.[56]

Universities have obviously benefited, both financially and intellectually, from the overlapping and intersecting interests in basic research that they now share with the corporate community. "There were parallel lines of interest between what we were doing and what Celanese wanted to do," explains Charles K. Boeckelman, deputy provost of Yale, in describing the origins of the research agreement between the company and the university. "It is an honest confluence of interests."[57] But the new values that have been given to basic science have had several less desirable implications for universities. Some of the most heavily publicized have arisen as a result of the inevitable temptation to university scientists to capitalize on their "insider" knowledge, either by establishing small research companies or by licensing this knowledge to private corporations as consultants. As Nobel laureate Arthur Kornberg remarks: "Understandably the scientists who provided the ideas, techniques, and practitioners of genetic chemistry are reluctant to be excluded from its financial rewards by entrepreneurs and venture capitalists."[58]

The opportunities have been many. One hundred fifty small biotechnology companies sprang up in the period from 1979 to 1981, a large proportion established by such individuals, sometimes in a glare of national publicity, most often through low-key negotiations with private bankers and venture capitalists. One of the first to travel this path was Herbert Boyer, professor of biochemistry at the University of California, San Francisco, who established Genentech with entrepreneur Robert Swanson in 1976; with a few thousand dollars, they created a company with a book value of several hundred million, even before it had developed a single marketable product. Another was Walter Gilbert, professor of molecular biology at Harvard University, who resigned his university post (although remaining a "senior associate") in February 1982 in order to work full-time as chief executive of Biogen, a private company he had established with several other university scientists in 1978.

The mushrooming of these small biotechnology companies, along with the rapidly growing interest of major chemical and pharmaceutical manufacturers in the academic aspects of genetic engineering, has created lucrative opportunities for faculty scientists to spend a considerable amount of time acting as private consultants, often on a profit-sharing basis. At UC Davis, six faculty members are now acting as consultants for Calgene, a company set up under the guidance of professor of plant biology Ray Valentine; they help to steer the company's research programs toward the most potentially fruitful directions. According to Harvard president Derek Bok, the number of faculty members with private consultancy arrangements rose from "a handful" to between forty and fifty within a couple of years.[59] Similarly, Donald Kennedy reported that in 1981 Stanford had "perhaps two dozen or more" faculty members who had made personal arrangements with mostly small biotechnology companies, many paid for their services with a share of the equity of the company to which they were providing advice.[60] In both cases the figures are now undoubtedly significantly higher than when they were announced. The science correspondent of the *Washington Post* found that in the case of molecular biology, every senior research worker of note in the U.S. had an agreement with some company interested in the commercial aspects of biotechnology[61]—a situation that has led another observer to comment that "the stage has perhaps been reached at which almost every biological advance discovered in American universities is made by, or made known before publication to, someone who has a possible commercial interest in keeping it secret."[62]

Universities themselves have been quick to exploit the same opportunities. Seeing their faculty members suddenly generate substantial additional income by putting their academic experience up for bid on the open market tempted many universities to follow the same path. Administrators soon began to investigate ways in which the research environment could be given a cash value, often claiming that if they did not seek profits from the exploitation of their research, others—possibly less scrupulous—might not hesitate to do so. "One worry is that industry will skim the cream off for a small amount of money," said James McKalvey, dean of engineering at Washington University, soon after the deal with Mallinckrodt had been announced.[63] Professor Wiliam F. Massey, vice-president for business and finance at Stanford University, told a meeting of the university's faculty that many felt the "natural income of the fruits of research" accruing to the university through patents and licensing fees was not commensurate with the true value of the research, and that "windfall profits" might therefore be going to others. He went on to explain that he was talking about the value that Stanford as an institution created through providing the environment for research, the facilities for research, the critical mass of scientists, the stability, management, peer groups, and so on. "It's important that we find means by which the university can participate in the entrepreneurial returns that come from those things that we create here," he concluded.[64]

All such activity, however, has raised serious questions about its impact on traditional academic procedures. One problem area has been growing secrecy, both in scientific laboratories, where scientists are increasingly reluctant to discuss their work openly with colleagues, and in scientific meetings, where important details may be withheld from discussion on the grounds that this could prejudice the chances of obtaining patent protection at a later stage. This secrecy has generated strong feelings in the scientific community, traditionally accustomed to unrestricted discussion of new ideas. At a meeting of the American Society for Microbiology in Dallas in early 1981, a lawyer from Exxon suggested that before coming to a scientific meeting to present a paper, scientists should have their proposed remarks notarized, giving details of when and where they came up with their ideas and where they were going to discuss them. "I was chilled by that," reports Jonathan King, a scientist who attended the meeting. "A few of my colleagues said it is a total change in the canon of what is proper scientific ethics and how science works."[65]

Several incidents have been reported in which scientists, having delivered research papers at an open meeting, have subsequently refused to divulge details of the techniques used on the grounds that this was proprietary information. To many scientists, this strikes at the integrity of the whole scientific method, whose lifeblood depends on open communication of ideas. "I think the temple is being taken over by the moneylenders," says Edward Garvin, associate professor of physics at Stanford. "It is absolutely unethical for people who are employed academically in the university to put themselves in the position where they cannot speak about a major thrust or development of their research freely to their cohorts. That isn't much different from some of us who've done classified research."[66]

Increased secrecy does not merely act as a barrier to open communication; it also interferes with the social processes used to guarantee the quality of scientific research in other ways, such as the peer review process. In most cases where industry has sponsored a university basic research project, the content of the research has been endorsed not by the traditional peer review system, but merely by agreement between the company and the scientists involved. The research director of du Pont says that he discourages company scientists from reviewing NSF grant proposals because "people could say we saw something in an application and then acted on it, when we might have been working on it already."[67] One scientist worked for several months on a problem before he discovered that Monsanto had already successfully carried out the same research, but had never published it.[68]

Equally important has been the disruptive effect on relationships among individual research workers. In 1980, for example, the University of California filed a complaint against Genentech and Hoffman-La Roche claiming that a cell line that had been passed from a university scientist to the company through a third party, and was subsequently used as the basis for a method of producing human interferon patented by the two companies, was legally the property of the university. The case was settled out of court at the beginning of 1983, when the company agreed to pay the university an undisclosed sum for the use of the cells, thus implicitly acknowledging the university's proprietary rights. The litigation was dropped.[69] However, the experience has already made many university scientists wary of some of the traditional means of communication, whether the exchange of ideas or of materials developed within the laboratory. A committee set up by UC San Francisco to look at the research agreement between the university and Genentech found that, with one exception, those interviewed believed that the manner in which the contract was being carried out—with results from the university laboratory subsequently being transferred to Genentech for commercial exploitation—had led to "serious disruption" within the department. "A recurrent theme was that people were loath to ask questions and give suggestions in seminars or across the bench, for there was a feeling that someone might make money from someone else," the committee reported.[70]

Particular problems have been created for postdoctoral students, who usually work on scientific topics and problems identified by their research supervisors; indeed, frequently both graduate and postdoctoral students are used to carry out parts of a broader research program being conducted by more senior staff in the laboratory. The danger here is that if the senior research staff have commitments to outside companies, these commitments may—consciously or unconsciously—influence the subjects selected for the graduate students to work on.

A reporter from *Chemical and Engineering News* encountered numerous complaints from postdoctoral students about the commercialization of research. One said a professor in his department had offered him a job in a company the professor worked for as a consultant—but had not offered the student any help in finding an academic position, which was what he was seeking. Another claimed that a professor had suggested a group discussion of "practical projects" without telling the laboratory staff that he was employed as a consultant for a private company that might have benefited from some of the ideas thrown out.[71]

Some students have been sworn to secrecy about their work, even though it is conducted in a university laboratory. Others have complained that their ideas have been transmitted without their knowledge to outside companies for whom their supervisor works. A graduate student at Stanford University, for example, complained to the university that her faculty adviser had informed a company for whom he consulted of her work, and the company had subsequently put a team on the problem and solved it before she was able to.[72] A professor of zoology at UC Davis pointed out that Calgene research workers planned to initiate a research project that directly competed with the research objectives of one of his own graduate students. "I view this situation as an infringement of academic freedom and potentially harmful to graduate education in general," he complained.[73] The Harvard conflict-of-interest guidelines now state explicitly that potential conflicts could be generated if a member of the faculty "directs students into a research area from which a member hopes to realize financial gain."[74]

Another problem created by the parallel relationship between university and industry research interests—one that even industry has become concerned about—is the growing brain-drain caused by university faculty members who leave their academic laboratories to pursue identical research in a commercial setting, benefiting from higher salaries, more generous technical support, and more modern research equipment. Such a trend inevitably decreases the ability of universities to train a new generation of research workers. By sacrificing long-term viability for short-term gains, warn both universities and industry, the nation may be consuming its scientific seed corn, drawing young scientists away from academia as a career, and even from advanced degrees. Investigators from the Office of Technology Assessment found that in molecular plant genetics there were already so few experts available that virtually all had been drawn away from the campus by industry. "As a result there is no generation of scientists left to train the next generation of plant molecular biologists. This is a great fear now in plant molecular genetics," one OTA staff member reported.[75]

Finally, there is the constant concern that greater industry funding of university research will create a growing threat to dissent on university campuses. Although the level of corporate funding is likely to remain substantially less than federal funding, the leverage provided by the increased support—in terms of a greater willingness by universities to support industry-promoted programs of research and education—will inevitably affect the general university environment, since academic research carried out with industrial objectives has an influence on students, faculty, and industrial workers out of all proportion to the funds actually spent.

Presented with this list of real or potential hazards, faculty members have not always agreed that all schemes to exploit university research are desirable. Many have expressed particular opposition to proposals to make an equity investment by the university in companies set up to exploit such research, arguing that it is important to maintain a sharp distinction between the spheres of academia and commerce. In the fall of 1980, for example, the faculty of Harvard University derailed a proposal that had been put together by the university administration to share in the equity of Genetics Institute, a company being set up by one of its professors of molecular biology, Mark Ptashne. The university, like others in the academic community, had been mesmerized by the enormous values placed on small biotechnology companies that had decided to go public. Genentech, for example, had seen its shares rocket from $35 to $80 on the first day of Wall Street trading, giving the company a value of several hundred million dollars almost overnight; a few months later, Cetus, a company set up in the early 1970s by entrepreneur Peter Farley in collaboration with scientists from Stanford and UC Berkeley, raised over $100 million in its first public offering, the largest sum ever raised by a new issue on Wall Street.

Such events spurred Harvard to consider the Genetics Institute proposal. (It had already discussed—but rejected—a similar deal to commercialize its research in computer software several years earlier.) Under the proposal, Harvard would receive a 10 percent share of the equity in Genetics Institute, which Ptashne was setting up with privately raised venture capital. In return the company would be given exclusive rights to any patents that emerged from Ptashne's research at the university. As Harvard counsel Dan Steiner, one of the principal architects of the idea, later explained: "What attracted us? Very simply, the apple . . . looked very big and very shiny. The chances of very large and significant financial return to support future research at the university was there."[76]

Many faculty members gave the proposal enthusiastic support. Henry Rosovsky, the dean of the college of arts and sciences, suggested that universities had to consider alternative sources of income, and that "this is one of a series of areas that we have to explore."[77] Others, however, expressed serious reservations about the impact an equity relationship with faculty members might have on the university, claiming that it could create undesirable secrecy in the laboratories, influence academic appointments, and eventually undermine public credibility in the university. One biologist, for example, complained that "the whole matter violates the role of the university in our society so extensively and so terribly that I don't see how anything can come of it. . . . It would mean that in everything we do, in our laboratories, in our scholarship, we are joining with the university to make a profit."[78] Equally significant, there was also skepticism on Wall Street about such an explicit attempt to merge the worlds of science and commerce. "I wouldn't put a penny on it," said an analyst with the brokerage firm Eberstadt and Company, which had helped raise venture capital for a number of small biotechnology companies.[79]

The criticism, both internal and external, soon took its toll. After the proposal had been discussed informally at a meeting of the university faculty, it became obvious that over half the faculty were opposed to the idea. A few days later, Harvard president Derek Bok announced that the university was not—for the time being—planning to take an equity share in any company set up to commercialize the work of faculty members.

As he later explained it in his annual report to the university's trustees: "All in all, the financial advantages to the university appear more speculative than we have supposed heretofore, while the dangers to academic science seem real and severe."[80]

Harvard's conclusions appeared to be shared by other members of the university community. MIT, for example, had tried in the early 1970s to launch a development company, known as the MIT Development Foundation, to exploit university invention generated by NSF funds in fields such as metallurgy and electronics. However, the venture was terminated six years later, partly because it was discovered that the potential conflicts of interest were greater than had been initially realized.[81] Stanford explained that it, too, had at one point considered—and rejected— the idea of direct equity involvement by the university in a company run by its scientists. At the Pajaro Dunes meeting, the participants agreed in their concluding statement that "it is not advisable for universities to make such investments unless . . . there are sufficient safeguards to avoid adverse effects on the morale of the institution."[82]

Out of the public eye, however, universities have been continuing to pursue this theme. The University of Michigan has established the Michigan Development Corporation to develop the commercial potential of university-based discoveries in biotechnology, microcomputers, and robotics. In California, Stanford and UC Berkeley have combined to set up a company, Engenics; 35 percent of the equity in the company is owned by the two universities, 30 percent by a research foundation known as the Center for Biotechnology Research, and 35 percent was sold, at a cost of $7.5 million, to six major chemical and biotechnology companies. Stanford claimed that it had managed to avoid the problems that had plagued the Harvard proposal by setting up the company as a "buffer corporation" and channeling the research funds through the nonprofit center. Others, however, felt that the differences were largely cosmetic, and that the arrangement merely disguised the relationship between the various parties. "There is more smoke there, but it is essentially the same idea [we] decided against," said a patent licensing officer at Stanford's rival university, Harvard.[83]

The closer the worlds of academe and high finance move together, the more acute has become the danger that split loyalties between academic and commercial responsibilities could influence decisions made in the academic sphere, such as decisions about the nature and scope of research projects. Such conflicts have always been present whenever universities have sought funds from industry.* Yet the conflicts have grown

---

* According to California Rural Legal Assistance in San Francisco, in one instance a research project at UC San Francisco into the health effects of the pesticide DBCP was terminated shortly after the university department received a $400,000 grant from a major chemical company that produced the pesticide. In another case, research at MIT into the use of methanol as a substitute fuel for automobiles was terminated shortly before the department received grants from the Ford Motor Company and from Exxon.[84]

as individual faculty members have increased their personal stake in outside commercial ventures. At the UC Davis campus, the multinational fertilizer company Allied Chemicals made an investment in Calgene shortly after the same company had also agreed to finance a $2.3 million university-based research project through the university's Experimental Station on the mechanics of nitrogen fixation in plants. A series of complaints followed from other members of the faculty, pointing out that the stated objectives of Calgene were virtually indistinguishable from those of the Experimental Station, and claiming that granting permission for the research projects was "a serious error portending grave consequences to the university."[85] Dean Charles Hess told Ray Valentine, who was both the principal investigator on the university grant and a major equity holder in Calgene, that he would have to choose between one or the other. Valentine chose Calgene, and agreed to withdraw from the university project (which had previously been financed by the National Science Foundation).[86]

Following this experience, UC Davis introduced new rules covering potential conflicts of interest, since, in the words of Hess, "current university policy is not definitive in dealing with the type of apparent or potential conflict of interest" that occurred in the Allied Chemicals case.[87] Other universities have been doing the same. Harvard University agreed to a new set of rules in October 1981. These now explicitly state, for example, that research contracts cannot be accepted from outside corporations if there is a ban on the publication of research results, or if researchers are required to develop marketable products.[88]

The scientific community liked to present these attempts to provide new conflict-of-interest rules as evidence of a sense of social responsibility. Often, however, they were more the direct result of external pressure, either real or threatened. Spurred by complaints about Valentine's activities at Calgene—as well as Boyer's involvement with Genentech—the State of California's Fair Political Practices Commission (FPPC) reversed a position it adopted in the early 1970s that university scientists should be exempt from the strict conflict-of-interest regulations applied to other state officials. Previously, faculty members had argued successfully for such an exemption on the grounds that the new regulations, introduced in the aftermath of the Watergate scandal, would create an unacceptable threat to academic freedom. Early in 1982, however, the members of the FPPC decided, by a three-to-two majority, that "academic freedom" was no longer a sufficient defense for nondisclosure. They adopted a recommendation that all university faculty members should be required to divulge their financial interest in any company sponsoring their work at the university.[89]

The recommendation did not go as far as some critics had wanted. California Rural Legal Assistance, which had for several years been waging a court battle against the university for its support of research into labor-saving agricultural equipment, had demanded that scientists be required to disclose all their outside financial interests. However, the universities had hoped they could resolve the issue through internal checks, and had strongly resisted pressure for greater public oversight.

Even with its more limited role, the FPPC has demonstrated its value. Early in 1983, when it presented its first annual report on filings made by University of California staff, the committee reported 100 cases in which there was a significant relationship between a researcher receiving funds and his or her interest in the source of the funds. In three cases, changes were demanded in research contracts. One professor with several research contracts with mining companies was told that he could no longer keep secret the computer codes used in his research, even if the companies demanded it; in another case, a professor of plant pathology was not permitted to accept a grant from a company in which he held substantial stock. Admittedly, the changes required for compliance with the FPPC requirements have been relatively minor (in the latter case, the professor merely arranged for the funds to be given to someone else in his laboratory). Moreover, some faculty members have complained about the paperwork involved. But as an editorial in the journal *Nature* put it: "The system works; fairness and academic freedom have been served and research support has not ultimately suffered."[90]

Keen to demonstrate to the public that they were aware of the dangers raised by closer links to the academic world, several leaders of the scientific community provided warnings of the pitfalls that lay in their path—provoking the comment from one Harvard administrator that universities were trying "to get pregnant without losing [their] virginity."[91] At the same time, however, optimism was invariably expressed that none of the problems were insuperable, nor should they be considered as major obstacles to enhanced university-industry collaboration. Each, it was confidently asserted, could be negotiated to a satisfactory outcome. Tensions, it was claimed, were largely the result of "misunderstanding and mistrust among members of industry, university students and faculty, and the general public"; they merely required greater discussion and enhanced credibility. "Hazards to university academic freedom from university-industry research relationships are manageable," asserted a report prepared by the National Commission on Research. "It appears to be possible to plan a program of high-quality university-industry cooperative research fully consistent with the academic environment."[92]

The reasons for such confidence are not difficult to discern. As basic research carried out by universities comes to play a greater and greater role in the civilian economy, access to such knowledge, as I have already argued, grows correspondingly in importance for the private sector. To the extent that universities stand to benefit directly from this interest, no one is anxious to suggest that the two groups' priorities and procedures may be incompatible—and both are keen to reach accommodation. The result is that universities have expressed few complaints about being drawn ever more closely into the service of international capital. And arguments about academic freedom or values that might conflict with this goal, even if offered lip service, are seldom given dominance over more pragmatic considerations. Conflicts of interest, added secrecy at scientific meetings, the disruption of social relationships in the scientific community, excessive industry control of research strategies, and so on, all are deplored. Yet actions are always taken within limits; for the disruption that each causes is accepted as a symptom of the larger political strategy, namely to grant private corporations greater access to and control over scientific knowledge. And the strategy itself has become so important that dissenters in the research community can rarely be afforded much influence on its outcome.

Each of these developments, however undesirable, is justified by the need to increase the international competitiveness of U.S. industry. The National Commission on Research report legitimates its recommendations by placing them in this wider context, suggesting that enhanced linkages "could make a significant contribution toward improving the climate for innovation in the United States," and citing "widespread and serious concern among leaders in government, the universities, and industry over the erosion of U.S. hegemony in science, technology, and the rate of productivity."[93] Jerome Wiesner of MIT suggests that "universities can, and must, play a pivotal role in achieving and maintaining a highly competitive national position."[94] Andrew J. Steckl, director of Rensselaer Polytechnic's new Center for Integrated Electronics, claims that since Japan's industry-university coalition pulls together in the same direction, "we have no choice but to follow that example."[95]

The direction in which universities are told that they have "no choice but to follow" is one that increasingly seeks to implant the values of private commerce on what had previously been the domain, to use physicist John Ziman's phrase, of "public knowledge."[96] The switch is not absolute; many universities, particularly those with close links to industry such as MIT and Cal Tech, have, as we have seen, always acknowledged the importance of these values. The danger is that what was previously a dialogue is now becoming a single field of discourse. In order to exploit industry's interest in basic research, universities are learning that entering the business world means "gearing yourself to playing by industry's rules," as one research management consultant told a workshop organized by the National Science Foundation in 1983.[97] A professor of chemical engineering suggests that this includes listening to and copying "the way people in industry talk."[98] It is through such changes that not only the goals but also the means of academic research are being remodeled to meet the needs of capital.

In many cases these changes are reinforced by local efforts to bring universities and industry together. At the urging of local industrialists, many states have supported closer links between universities and local industry, arguing in particular that this could help catalyze the growth of high technology companies on which many claim their economic future depends. Reference is frequently made to the role played by MIT in shifting the industrial base of Massachusetts from its dependence on shipbuilding and textiles, helping it to become one of the country's major centers for microelectronics and computers. In the period immediately after the Second World War, for example, MIT president Karl Compton personally guaranteed bank loans needed to keep from bankruptcy the small high technology companies that had sprung up along the famous Route 128. Others recall how Frank Terman, professor of engineering at Stanford, virtually single-handedly created Silicon Valley when he persuaded the university to establish a research park where many small companies formed by the university's engineering graduates were able to set up shop. More recently, Stanford has acted as a catalyst for the growth of a clutch of small biotechnology firms in the same area. If MIT could do it for Massachusetts, and Stanford for California, why can't we find a way of doing the same in our own locality? companies across the nation began to ask.

Indeed, those in the corporate world who had long viewed universities with a mixture of apprehension and distrust—but now observed that the relocation of high technology companies frequently occurred around academic communities—began to look at them in a new light. Universities were seen as devices for promoting regional prosperity, as well as their own company profits. Arguing that high technology has a better chance of success if it is carried out next to a university, the state legislature of Michigan has established a nonprofit Industrial Technology Institute in Ann Arbor that will build a robotics research park to feed ideas to local entrepreneurs. "We think that the University of Michigan is a tremendous unused resource both in this area and in Michigan as a whole," comments one local industrialist. "There's just a fantastic desire in industry to gain access to univeristy expertise," says another.[99] The vice-president of a local computer control company, William Ince, chaired a joint "technology-based industry-university committee" to explore how links could be improved. Plans have been drawn up to use the university to spearhead a major shift in Michigan's industrial base, moving it from basic manufacturing—including transportation and automobile production—into high technology areas such as robotics and biotechnology. Corporate executives admit that close linkages with the academic community itself have a commercial value, since they tend to enhance a company's high technology image. "I think the university's charisma alone is an important factor to us in technology businesses," asserts chairman Ince.[100]

Michigan's efforts are but one example of a strategy now being pursued by virtually every state in the nation. The idea is to exploit the existence of basic research facilities in the universities to attract high technology companies to the region as a basis for economic growth. "The university environment is the engine of technology and the driving force behind bringing technology into an area," says the president of a Cincinnati computer software company.[101] Local universities have been the center of high-tech development strategies in cities as different as Minneapolis, Austin, Denver, and Philadelphia. Pennsylvania has created a Ben Franklin Partnership between state government, universities, and business to support research and "turn scientists into businessmen."[102] New Jersey followed this model with plans for a Thomas Edison Foundation to pursue the same goals.

It is uncertain how many of these development plans will be successful. Certainly the demand for high technology companies is likely to exceed supply, for the near term at least. And even those states that do attract such companies are unlikely to find that they make much difference to the social problems, in particular mass unemployment, associated with the decline of the so-called smokestack industries; indeed, many industry-university ventures in robotics, such as those at the University of Michigan and a joint project between Westinghouse and Carnegie-Mellon University in Pittsburgh, are designed specifically to displace workers. What is certain, however, is that by recruiting universities into their development plans, many states are rapidly assisting—often deliberately—a major shift in the dominant values of academic life, a shift that merely accentuates the increasing control of the corporate sector over all aspects of higher education and research.

The increasingly close link between industries and universities has pragmatic advantages for both sides, namely more research money for universities and higher profits for companies. But it is important to recognize the extent to which these are complemented by a growing *political* unity between the two sets of institutions. Both have lobbied in favor of more government funding of basic science and the university infrastructures needed to perform it. But in addition, through united efforts on issues such as patent and tax reform, both have joined forces in helping to concentrate ultimate control of science and its applications in the hands of private capital, and to fight off all claims for the social control of knowledge, whether at its point of production or application. In doing so, the coalition has frequently acted as part of a broader political realignment aimed at stemming what are often described as the "excesses of democracy" of the 1970s, and reinforcing the control of social elites through science, as described in Chapter One.

Universities often argue that the principal reason for encouraging greater industry sponsorship of university research is precisely the fact that it would reduce the degree of government control over the research agenda—indeed, over higher education in general. Richard Lyman, president of Stanford, warned that "the closer the federal government gets to direct funding of the core of our activities, the greater the danger that we shall become inescapably dependent on that support, in which case our capacity to fight back when the regulatory going gets tough will be minimal." [103] And the National Commission on Research suggests that a reliance on government funding of university research is a trend that may be "detrimental to the long-term interest of this country." [104] Corporations share this concern. "Probably . . . the main reason that corporations continue to give money [to institutions of higher education] is the fear that, if their contributions were to be halted, the financing gap would be filled by the federal government," says an article in the *New York Times*. [105]

This common political interest in opposing social control on the production and application of scientific knowledge, whatever their purpose, has given rise to common lobbying efforts in support of such a goal. In waging disputes with the federal government, many academics soon discovered substantial advantages in linking their protests to those of private corporations. As Stanford's Lyman put it: "We must learn to make alliances in politics. There are faint stirrings of greater cooperation between business and higher education. Such cooperation will not always be possible, nor in our interest. But we ought not to imagine that we can win many battles by being above them." [106]

One organization that took the lead in cultivating this political alignment was the American Council on Education (ACE). The council was established in 1918 as a central agency representing the nation's largest educational associations. From its earliest years, it has seen one of its principal functions as being to bridge the gap between higher education and industry. By the late 1970s, when industry decided once again that it needed to cooperate with higher education (and vice versa), the ACE stood ready to respond. In 1978 council president J. W. Peltason established a Business–Higher Education Forum "dedicated to closer understanding and cooperation between business and higher education on problems of mutual and national concern." Attending the first meeting of the new forum were representatives from thirteen major corporations, including Rockwell International, Ford Motor Company, General Motors, the Bank of America, Continental Groups, Pfizer, AT&T, General Electric, and Procter and Gamble. The presidents of seventeen higher education institutions also attended, including Princeton, the University of California, the University of Pittsburgh, Georgetown University, the University of Pennsylvania, and Radcliffe College.

Peltason had high ambitions for the forum. Not only was it going to be an "exclusive personal contact point for the highest ranking leaders of corporate America and American higher education," aimed at facilitating "understanding of corporate America on the campuses of the nation's universities," but it would also be a highly visible focal point where "mutual appreciation of problems and needs [would] be advanced; thus the forum could well become a national center for nongovernmental leadership."[107] In other words, the forum was intended to cement a political partnership between the leaders of the business and the academic communities, one in which they could generate a common consensus to ward off political opponents such as labor unions, consumer and environmentalist groups, or prying congressmen—in fact, anyone who challenged their conceptions of the nation's problems and how they should be solved. "We're going to zero in on those places where the universities and corporations can work on the problems more effectively together," Peltason explained.[108] High on the agenda of the first meeting were the problems of productivity in industry.

Strengthening research links between industry and universities soon became one of the forum's priorities. At a meeting in May 1980 the forum agreed that it should lobby in favor of laws and regulations supportive of cooperative research.[109] A further meeting at Harvard University the following year laid the groundwork for establishing a task force to look at ways of boosting corporate support for basic research. Dealing primarily with university administrators rather than bench scientists, the ACE has found that they have much in common with corporate executives. "It's not like apples and oranges—more like tangerines and oranges," explained the forum's staff director, Tom Stauffer.[110]

Another cooperative effort was the creation of the National Commission on Research, established in 1978 specifically to prepare a series of reports on the state of the nation's research facilities, and "to examine the process by which the federal government supports academic research and to propose changes designed to improve that process."[111] The commission was formally created by six separate professional societies: the National Academy of Sciences, the Association of American Universities, the American Council on Education, the Social Sciences Research Council, the National Association of Land Grant Universities and Colleges, and the American Council of Learned Societies. Primarily an academic group, it also had as members several representatives of the corporate world, such as Edward David of Exxon and Monte Throdahl of Monsanto. Although it was partly supported by government grants, three-quarters of its funding came from private foundations with strong links to the corporate community, including the Exxon Education Foundation, the Ford Foundation, and the William and Flora Hewlett Foundation. Its main function was to collect information on various aspects of government policy affecting the research universities, and to catalyze debate on particular themes. Its political function, like the Business–Higher Education Forum, was to reinforce the coalition between the university and the corporate sectors, in particular by arming both sides with legitimation, through a series of reports, of their demands for changes in government policy to reduce social controls on science.

One area where universities and private corporations collaborated to mutual advantage was the reform of patent legislation, a campaign that culminated in 1980 with the amendments to the Patents and Trademarks Act automatically giving universities (and small businesses) the rights to any patents arising from research funded by the federal government. In pushing for the new legislation, universities argued strongly that patents could generate a source of much-needed income. But the incentive was not only money; equally important was the fact that the new patent laws allowed them to parcel up the results of research programs into a form over which private companies could exert direct—and usually exclusive—control, an essential step in securing scientific knowledge for the private marketplace. The new law has thus become one of the cornerstones of the burst of university-industry cooperation that followed its signing by President Carter in 1980.[112] It has also helped tighten corporate access to the results of scientific research.

Patents represent knowledge in pure commodity form. Equally important, patents represent knowledge as private property, property that someone else can use only on your terms. The idea that inventors should be rewarded with a period of time in which no one else may copy or use their invention without permission is enshrined in the U.S. Constitution. Indeed, the Constitution's only reference to science is in the context of a discussion of patents; Article 1, Section 8, directs Congress to "promote the progress of science and the useful arts by securing for limited terms to authors and inventors the exclusive right to their respective writings and discoveries." The writers of the Constitution intended primarily to reward individuals for their skill and imagination; since then, however, patents and patent protection have become key weapons in the corporate armory in a way that few of the Founding Fathers could have anticipated.

Although some universities have always collaborated enthusiastically in industry's search for patents, most have in the past stayed aloof, contending that it was against the public interest to restrict access to the fruits of scientific research—particularly since the need for a financial return on the invention (the initial reason for the patent law) was not relevant in the case of scientists whose research costs had already been paid by the federal government or some other sponsor. As one Patent Office official has admitted, until relatively recently many universities viewed patents as "sort of immoral and not in keeping with their role in society."[113] In 1934, for example, the president and fellows of Harvard University adopted a policy statement that "no patents primarily concerned with therapeutics or public health may be taken out by any member of the university, except with the consent of the president and fellows; nor will such patents be taken out by the university itself except for dedication to the public."[114] The fellows even agreed to provide legal advice to any faculty members who wished to prevent outsiders from patenting their discoveries or inventions. Robert Merton, a sociologist of science, argued in the 1940s that one of the norms of the scientific community might be thought of as "communism," since all intellectual property was held in common, and "the scientist's claim to 'his' intellectual property is limited to that of recognition and esteem."[115]

Under pressure from the private sector to gain exclusive control over scientific discoveries, many universities (including Harvard) have had a change of heart. The commercial attractions have been obvious. University administrators have looked with envy at those of their colleagues who have been able to come up with commercial winners such as the stannous fluoride toothpaste discovered by the University of Indiana (and licensed to Procter and Gamble for marketing as Crest), and the drink Gatorade, developed in the laboratories of the University of Florida. Perhaps the most successful organization has been the Wisconsin Alumni Research Foundation (WARF), set up in 1925 by alumni from the University of Wisconsin in Madison in protest at the university regents' decision not to accept gifts from outside incorporated educational endowments. Their licensing of profitable research has provided over $100 million in extra funds to the university. Two lucrative patents made over to WARF by faculty members were a method for activating vitamin D in milk and the anticoagulant coumarin, a potent rat poison commonly known as warfarin.

Faced with such examples of successful entrepreneurship, as well as the sight of venture capital companies waiting at the laboratory gate, checkbooks in hand, universities buried their previous scruples and started to develop mechanisms for exploiting scientific discoveries in the marketplace. Licensing officers began to walk the corridors of science laboratories, asking scientists whether they were working on anything that had potential commercial value—and waving the examples of warfarin, Gatorade, and Crest toothpaste in front of their eyes. Many universities revised their rules on the publication of research results to make patenting easier. Harvard, for example, agreed in 1975 that it would no longer be "institutionally inactive" in transferring the results of research to the marketplace.[116] Referring to WARF as the "paradigm" case, Harvard president Derek Bok told the university's trustees in 1980 that patents offered an incentive to search more vigorously for patentable discoveries in their laboratories.[117]

Although not all patents become money-spinners, some universities have struck it rich. Stanford claimed to have received over $1 million in the first year of licensing the basic techniques of genetic engineering developed by Stanley Cohen and Herbert Boyer, moving it immediately to the top of the university league from its previous position as an also-ran. Some private estimates suggested that, if the patent claim withstood later legal challenges, it could reap up to $1 billion for the university during its lifetime.[118] However, apart from isolated instances such as

Wisconsin, Florida, and Indiana, or Professor Jay Forrester's invention of the magnetic core memory at MIT (which brought the institute over $19 million in royalties), few universities have made, or expected to make, substantial fortunes out of their patents. Indeed, many have even lost money; a survey carried out by the Association of American Universities (AAU) revealed that twelve out of thirty-five universities approached showed a net deficit of between $500 and $60,000 a year. Even in those that made money the revenue was relatively small compared with the overall budget. The University of California, for example, generated $1.25 million in patent royalties in 1980, compared with a net operating budget for the university of $2.3 billion.[119]

An incentive whose importance equals that of money is that an enhanced patent program is a means of strengthening links with private companies. Speaking on behalf of both the AAU and the ACE, Tom Jones, vice-president for research at MIT, told a congressional hearing on patent regulation in 1978 that universities generally supported new patent arrangements "not because of potential financial return (which is minimal) but because of their value as effective instruments for technology transfer." Jones estimated that U.S. universities, in total, had probably earned no more than $9 million in patent royalties the previous year; the real value of university licensing programs was that they helped "to build a bridge with industry."[120]

The message that Jones and other university leaders brought to Congress was that knowledge could be exploited through the marketplace if, and only if, it was turned into the appropriate commodity form—in other words, into private property. Monopoly control, it was claimed, was necessary for companies to regain the costs involved in turning the idea into a marketable product. In particular, this required that companies be permitted exclusive licenses on scientific ideas, since only this would give them the lead time necessary to prevent competitors from capitalizing on their development efforts. Monsanto's demands for exclusive patent rights to any useful discoveries before it would agree to its $23 million grant to the university was Harvard's principal reason for changing its patent rules in 1975. "Patents are a must," an executive from Johnson and Johnson told the annual meeting of the Association of American Medical Colleges in 1982, describing the idea that open and unregulated scientific publication should be the first priority as a "narrow viewpoint."[121]

This desire for exclusive licensing, despite its apparently undemocratic nature,* is a characteristic that distinguishes high technology companies from some of their predecessors. When Senator Russell Long, the powerful chairman of the Senate Finance Committee, stated in a Senate

---

* Indeed, exclusive licenses on government patents had been declared unconstitutional by an assistant attorney general in the Department of Justice in 1974.

debate on the proposed reforms that U.S. agriculture was the most efficient in the world largely because of federal support for agricultural research provided to land-grant colleges through the Morrill Act—and that none of this had been achieved through patent protection for research results—Senator Adlai Stevenson, Jr., one of the keenest promoters of the reforms, dismissed the parallel as irrelevant. The production of soybeans "is a little different from the production of computers, let alone the most advanced aircraft, let alone the genetic engineering which could do more than anything that has already been done to increase agriculture production," Stevenson suggested.[122]

The existence of exclusive licensing agreements also constituted one of the more controversial aspects of agreements between universities and individual companies to sponsor programs of basic research. Many scientists felt that they were essentially undemocratic, in that they restricted the opportunity for anyone apart from the sponsor to seek ways of applying the results of such research to social goals. The companies, however, have generally insisted on first refusal on exclusive licensing arrangements as a necessary condition for their support—terms most universities have eventually been prepared to accept as the inevitable price of agreeing to corporate funding of basic research.

Demands from universities and their industrial supporters, such as the Pharmaceutical Manufacturers Association, that research contractors be automatically awarded the rights on federally funded research and allowed to grant them on an exclusive basis to private corporations were embodied in almost all the many proposals for patent law reform introduced into the Senate and the House of Representatives in the late 1970s. The main thrust of most of these was to extend to all federal agencies a system of "institutional patent agreements" (IPAs), developed experimentally by the National Institutes of Health and the National Science Foundation in the early 1970s. Any university that had signed an IPA was automatically awarded all patent rights to research funded by the federal agency, provided it was able to demonstrate that it had adequate administrative apparatus to ensure that licensing of the patent was actively pursued.

Such proposals to change the patent rules generated strong opposition. Critics both inside and outside Congress claimed that by automatically awarding patent rights to institutions that had already been paid once for carrying out the research, the public was being asked to pay twice for the same results, once in the laboratory and the second time in the store when they bought the final product. Consumer activist Ralph Nader wrote to Jay Solomon, head of the General Services Administration, claiming the IPAs represented a "massive giveaway" of government property and suggesting—on the basis of previous court decisions—that they were unconstitutional and "contrary to the public interest."[123] Nader quoted a decision by Judge Barrington D. Parker in a District of Columbia court in 1974 that the granting of exclusive licenses to patents owned by the U.S. was unconstitutional—a decision that was vacated on appeal on technical grounds, but was never contradicted. Michael Pertschuk, chairman of the Federal Trade Commission, told Senator Gaylord Nelson's Small Business Committee that there was "no factual basis" for claims by both universities and industry that giving away title to private contractors promoted the commercialization of government-financed inventions. Indeed, he stated, "the available evidence shows just the opposite." [124] Senator Russell Long described one version of the patent reform bill as one of "the most radical and far-reaching giveaways I have ever seen in the many years I have served in the United States Senate." [125]

Some university scientists shared the reservations. Accepting the argument that more active efforts were required if research were to reach the marketplace, but reluctant to see individuals and institutions profiting excessively from the procedures adopted, they proposed alternative arrangements. Joshua Lederberg, professor of genetics at Stanford University—and currently president of Rockefeller University in New York—suggested to Senator Nelson that all government-owned patents should be passed to a national, not-for-profit R&D foundation, perhaps modeled on Britain's National Research and Development Corporation. This foundation would use any profits to fund grants and contracts for further research. "Universities should not share in the license fees *except* to the extent of their cost-sharing in the research that led to an invention," wrote Lederberg. Individuals should not, in principle, be rewarded for the results of work for which they were already receiving an academic salary, since this could "distort their academic functions." [126]

Yet the stakes were too high. Prominent spokesmen for the corporate community contended that if patent rights were not granted to universities, giving them the right to issue exclusive licenses to private companies, the companies would refuse to invest in the development efforts needed to turn the research results into useful products. Despite the continued opposition of the Department of Justice—which, like the Federal Trade Commission, argued that there was no reason to change existing arrangements—both universities and industry found powerful supporters within the federal government. Changes in the patent laws were finally passed by Congress in the closing weeks of the Carter administration.

Of course, companies were correct to argue that, without strict patent protection, they were unwilling to invest in the development work needed to bring new products to market, and that patents, as a form of publication, were a way of avoiding excessive trade secrecy. But the importance placed on the form in which knowledge could be transferred from the laboratory to the marketplace underlines the extent to which patent laws explicitly reflect the economic and political assumptions of U.S. capitalism, namely that the private property relationship should dominate all other considerations. If other countries chose to do things differently, it was argued, then this was because they had different political systems to which alternative arrangements might be more appropriate. When Tom Jones of MIT referred the Small Business Committee to the words of the Constitution, he suggested that they represented explicit recognition by the Founding Fathers of the role of the profit motive as an essential ingredient in the effective transfer of technology from the laboratory to the community.

The recent changes in the patent law must therefore be seen in their full political perspective. The debate over the reforms illustrates not only three of the principal themes of the new thrust for closer links between universities and industry, but also the way that these reinforce the general concentration of control over science in the hands of a corporate class. First, the need for patent reform was justified largely in terms of the dynamics of international competition, rather than any internal or social logic; legislative endorsement of the commodity form of the results of university basic research was a direct recognition of the growing importance of high technology within both the domestic and the international community. Second, the form of collaboration was designed to recognize the laws of free enterprise by encouraging the transfer of scientific knowledge to the public through the market rather than by other means, such as federal or state procurement policies, where it might meet social needs that the market is not equipped to address. Third, Congress was persuaded to endorse the idea that knowledge had to be transferred as private property to provide corporations with monopolistic control over its use—a decision that implicitly discriminates against other ways in which the same knowledge could be applied, ways that do not depend on the logic of private profit.

Another focus of the alliance between academic and corporate leaders was a concerted campaign to reduce social controls on research and its applications. There were several pragmatic reasons for such a coalition. Industry, in particular, provided universities with the political leverage they needed in Washington to oppose regulations imposed in the 1960s and early 1970s, leverage they would have lacked if they had tried to fight the battles on their own. In return, universities, when they made public statements about how regulation was supposed to be shackling the economy and retarding technological progress, were legitimizing the demands of industry by cloaking them in an aura of academic and scientific respectability.

There was also a close ideological affinity between the two sectors, which found a common interest in characterizing social controls on their activities as unwarranted interference, either with academic freedom or with free enterprise. MIT's Jerome Wiesner warned of the danger of putting "too many shackles on those elements of society—universities, business, and even some parts of government—that have made our tech-

nological achievements possible."[127] Industrial leaders have complemented Wiesner's argument, similarly linking their fate to that of the
universities. Robert Hatfield—chairman and chief executive officer of
the Continental Group, a director of Johnson and Johnson and the New
York Stock Exchange, and a trustee of both the Committee for Economic Development and the Conference Board—told his fellow businessmen that it was important for them to become central spokesmen in
the debate about federal regulation of the universities. He explained:
"The reason is that reducing the regulatory pressures on colleges and
universities will reduce the general government tendency to regulate.
When business speaks for higher education, therefore, they will also be
speaking for business."[128] And Wiesner was widely applauded when he
suggested that "what [universities] need, and what the country needs, is
regulation of regulation."[129]

As the presidents of Yale and Harvard had warned their alumni, federal patronage appeared to be becoming "one of the most serious threats
of the next several decades," wrote Caspar Weinberger, previously Secretary of Health, Education, and Welfare, at the time chief vice-president and general counsel to the Bechtel Group of companies, and later
Secretary of Defense in the Reagan administration. "What we are witnessing now," he continued, "is a political phenomenon in which government regulation expands to control the decision-making processes of
private institutions."[130] In the process of their rapid postwar expansion,
universities had become part of a larger blurring between the public and
the private sectors. Now they were experiencing the reverse trend, part
of a broad movement to eliminate social control from "private" activities
in general.

Some of the biggest battles between the universities and the government, in which industry soon participated, took place over regulations
drawn up by the Office of Management and Budget setting out the accounting procedures that universities should use to demonstrate that
federal research money had been used in the way Congress intended.
OMB officials pointed out that the accounting guidelines, contained in
a document known as Circular A-21, were merely intended to improve
the effectiveness of such procedures. (Each university is audited by a
single agency, whichever provides the largest source of research funds.)
Universities, however, represented the new rules as a sign of excessive
social demands. Special criticism was leveled at the requirement that any
scientist receiving a federal grant should list how his or her time had
been divided, on a day-to-day basis, among teaching, research, administration, and other activities. OMB, supported by several members of
Congress, claimed this was necessary to determine how much of the
academics' time should be allocated to different sources of founding.
Many scientists, however, described the reporting requirements as a
form of inquisition that challenged their right to autonomy.

Tensions between universities and government auditors had their roots back in the social contract negotiated between science and the state after the Second World War. In supporting science primarily through a system of "project grants," the government had at the time agreed to leave decisions about the allocation of funds, and the scientific assessment of their use, in the hands of the scientific community, operating primarily through the peer review process. In return for abrogating this scientific accountability, however, it required strict fiscal accountability for the way the money was spent. (The alternative, full-cost reimbursement, would have required the government to specify in advance the research results it expected, a demand that the community claimed might be appropriate for conventional contractors but was unrealistic for basic science.) Congress indicated that universities should "maintain adequate records to demonstrate that the funds intended for a particular project are used only for that project, as designated by the funding agency, and for no other purpose, however meritorious."[131]

Initially both sides had little difficulty in making the system work satisfactorily. Both the public and the politicians had a broad trust in the scientific community, and raised few questions about how it decided to spend the money allocated to it from the public purse. Gradually, however, as budgets increased, so did demands for greater accountability. By the early 1970s, when spending on science was no longer the sacred cow it had been in the post-Sputnik years, the science budget had lost much of its protected status and began to be treated by federal auditors much as any other type of expenditure. Universities had become "too large, too expensive, and too important to be left undisturbed."[132]

Accountability demands were reinforced by a growing distrust of scientists at the individual level. In one instance, it was discovered that the director of the National Institute of Neurological Diseases and Stroke had directed his institute for two summer months from a holiday house on Cape Cod, claiming the official $25-a-day government travel allowance. In another, the director of the National Institutes of Health told the intergovernmental relations subcommittee of the House Government Operations Committee that NIH's primary concern was arranging for research to be conducted rather than accounting for the money spent; he later acknowledged that NIH does have such a continuous management responsibility. By raising questions about the way research funds were being spent, and opening the daily affairs of scientists to public scrutiny, the subcommittee, under its chairman, Representative L. H. Fountain, challenged the traditional view that the internal checks and balances within the academic community provided an adequate guarantee of ethical conduct that required no outside surveillance or control. The significance of this move has been described by Daniel Greenberg as leading to "a new politics of science, a politics characterized by a diminution of *de facto* sovereignty that pure science had nurtured during the postwar period."[133]

Responding to Fountain and other members of Congress, the federal government tightented up its accounting rules and procedures. Misuses of research funds, however, continued to come to light. In 1975 a research scientist at Harvard's School of Public Health, having refused to sign blank expense claim forms, discovered the university was improperly transferring money allocated by the federal government for research to other purposes. Investigation turned up a memorandum from the assistant dean for financial affairs describing how the school benefited financially "from less than-federally-intended diversion of federal funds," since "a certain proportion of the salaries and fringe benefits of faculty supported by the federal research funds is, in fact, diverted into the teaching programs."[134] (Harvard later agreed to repay the federal government $4.6 million improperly charged to research grants.) In another case, a graduate researcher lost his job at Johns Hopkins University after publicizing the fact that his department head was moving research funds from one project to another without informing his federal sponsors.

In themselves, such practices were seldom particularly serious. Most universities have informal mechanisms for adding flexibility to the way research funds are distributed, claiming this is necessary to guarantee the continuity of research projects. Yet the social contract with the scientific community was based almost entirely on trust, and the incidents were sufficient to fan the flames of public—and congressional—disapproval. At hearings of the Fountain committee in 1979, government auditors claimed diversion of funds was "widespread" in the nation's universities (although adding that "in some cases the dollar amounts were admittedly limited"). Moreover, they complained that in many universities accounting practices were inadequate for them to certify that funds had been used for their intended purposes.[135] At one university it was discovered that equipment was being bought at cost price, then being charged to federal research grants at retail value. In the case of Harvard, a close audit of the School of Public Health concluded that $2.4 million had been wrongfully spent on consultants' fees, indirect costs, and fringe benefits, and that a considerably greater sum could not be properly accounted for. Both figures were strongly contested by Harvard, as was a later reassessment, made in 1982, claiming that $1.7 million should be repaid to the government for improper charges made between 1975 and 1977. Nevertheless, charges like these received wide publicity. "The Colleges' Big Con Game with U.S. Grants," starkly proclaimed a headline in *Business Week*.[136]

Even where they accepted occasional transgressions, universities bridled when these were used as the basis for the stringent new accounting requirements contained in Circular A-21. Eventually they decided to fight back. Circular A-21 was only one of many federal regulations introduced over the previous decade defining how universities should conduct their affairs if they wished to continue to receive federal funding. Other social demands made of universities ranged from equal rights legislation to detailed steps necessary to make college facilities available to the handicapped. In financial terms, many of these other regulations had a considerably greater impact, but A-21 generated the most heat, since it struck at the heart of the academic community's desire for independence from social controls.

The warnings about its impact were easily hyped up. "The basic federal-academic relationship, after nearly three decades of the most fruitful partnership, is floundering," warned Jerome Wiesner in a heavily publicized speech in 1978.[137] Less extremely but equally directly, the Sloan Commission on Government and Higher Education, a private study by a select group of leaders of the business and academic communities, criticized the government's "lack of perspective" in its relationship with universities.[138] Similar complaints came from the National Commission on Research in its various reports on the government-industry relationship. Critics of university regulation linked their demands for relief to the broader argument that federal controls on the private sector were sapping the nation's economy. According to the National Commission on Research: "As the United States comes to depend more heavily on high technology exports and upon skilled scientists and technicians to develop and manage their technologies, it will depend more than ever on the research universities. . . . The public demand for accountability must, then, consider seriously the potential and actual role of the universities in meeting vital public needs."[139]

During the Carter administration, the fight between government auditors and university scientists over Circular A-21, and particularly the demand for so-called time-and-effort reporting, quickly made its way to the top of the executive branch. The president's science adviser, Frank Press, and the executive director of OMB, Bowman Cutter, were called in to mediate. The universities' efforts to curb regulation had received various types of support from the private sector. A case in point involved the remarks of A. Bartlett Giamatti, president of Yale, to university alumni. In his words, the first time he heard of A-21 he "thought it was a vitamin." Giamatti went on to warn that "never have I seen the lash of federal regulations applied to a crucial area of the nation's intellectual life with such seeming indifference to financial and human consequences."[140] The corporate community, already rehearsed in their own objections to federal regulations, applauded warmly. "Furor over a nonvitamin" announced a full-page advertisement taken out in the nation's top scientific and technical journals by United Technologies. The ad claimed that the A-21 controversy showed how Washington's tentacles were spreading on campus, "threatening academic freedom and scientific inquiry."

Press and Cutter persuaded OMB officials to soften some of the harsher requirements of A-21. With the arrival of the avowedly anti-regulation Reagan administration in Washington in January 1981, the academic community expected a more sympathetic hearing. Initially they were disappointed, even though industry had gone in to bat on the universities' side. Soon after Vice-President George Bush was appointed head of a task force to look at ways of reducing the impact of regulations on the private sector, he was presented with a statement by the ACE's Business–Higher Education Forum, pleading for "more systematic, rational national policy on regulation." The complaints of universities and industry were laid out side by side. Neither party did much to hide their political objectives. "The most important of regulation's effects is the growing and unwelcome degree to which government intrudes in business, labor, academic institutions, and elsewhere," the statement said.[141] When the ACE was asked by Bush to suggest where reform was needed, it proposed seventy rules affecting colleges and universities be scratched, shelved, or overhauled. The list was presented to Bush by a small delegation that included the chairman of Rockwell International, Paul Rockwell, and the chairman of United Technologies, Paul Henson. At the top came OMB's Circular A-21.*

The administration's response, however, was less enthusiastic than anticipated. Even Republican bureaucrats, it appeared, felt that accountability was a good thing; when federal spending was being reduced, it was even more important to check that money was being spent in the proper way. When later in the year the Bush task force produced a list of regulations that needed the most urgent attention, it included several affecting universities, such as the requirement that equal support be provided for men's and women's sports. But no mention was made of A-21. OMB officials claimed that universities had informed them that "everything was going well." Glen Schleede, executive associate director of OMB, told congressmen that accountability was still an important requirement. "As long as tax dollars paid by our citizens and other public revenues are being used, those of us who have all or part of our salaries paid from these sources will bear a special responsibility to account for the use of those funds," Schleede wrote in a letter.[142]

The academic community was less than delighted. "They simply have not delivered," complained Sheldon E. Steinbach, general counsel of the ACE.[143] Universities, their corporate allies at their side, stepped up the pressure. When new revisions were published in 1982, it appeared that the lobbying had paid off, for OMB had made several of the changes the universities had been proposing. Further revision, this time apparently under pressure from the White House, came in 1983. In particular, the Department of Health and Human Services provided twenty-two universities with funds to try an experimental auditing technique using

* By this time the forum's membership had increased to include Shell Oil, Exxon, Monsanto, United Telecommunications, TRW, Armco, and Mobil.

private auditors, helped by the universities' own auditing staff.[144] There were still conflicts. Federal auditors, for example, threatened to demand repayment of over $1 million from the University of California at San Francisco after failing to find full information provided by faculty members on the way they had divided their time between teaching and research.[145] In general, however, the universities felt that the tide was turning in their direction, and that this had in no little part been the result of the extra muscle the corporate community had given their lobbying efforts in Washington.

If the corporate community has needed little prompting to help universities in their fight against social regulation, universities have not been slow to return the favor. The use of university scientists by industry in public policy debates stretches back as far as the earliest collaboration between the two sectors. Whenever industry has been accused of antisocial practices—such as polluting streams or exposing workers to occupational hazards—there have been scientists willing to challenge the evidence and attempt to discredit charges on the grounds that they are "unscientific." Indeed, during the Santa Barbara oil spill in the late 1960s, the state of California was unable to find a local scientist with the appropriate expertise willing to give evidence against the oil companies, because all those contacted were already receiving research grants from the same companies.[146] Two authors, Bruce Owen and Ronald Brautigan, put it explicitly in a book called *The Regulation Game*. In a chapter headed "Co-opting the Experts," they suggested that this is most effectively done either by hiring scientists as consultants or providing them with research grants: "This activity requires a modicum of finesse; it must not be too blatant, for the experts themselves must not realize that they have lost their objectivity and freedom of action. At a minimum a program of this kind reduces the threat that the leading experts will be available to testify against the interests of the regulated firms."[147]

As individual battles against particular regulations broadened into a general counterattack, so industry turned increasingly to the academic community to support its case. The more scientists were prepared to speak out against the burden of regulation, the more legitimacy was attached to industry's complaints. The National Commission on Research suggested that "the participation of a presumed neutral third party, such as the university researchers, would add to the credibility of industry intentions"[148] and could play an important role in enhancing the ultimate credibility of regulatory decisions in the eyes of the public. Frequently the pitch was blatant, as industry leaders encouraged university scientists to use their social prestige to promote the case against federal involvement. When Mac Pruitt, research director at Dow Chemical, invited the heads of university chemistry departments to a company-sponsored conference in 1979 to discuss plans for a scheme to funnel corporate funds to university laboratories, the conference opened with a presentation by Dow officials strongly criticizing the "overregulation" of the chemical industry, and urging scientists to speak out in elaborating on this argument. "Some of the academics quietly wondered what they had let themselves in for by attending the gathering," noted one observer.[149] The previous December, the president of du Pont, Edward Kane, made a similar pitch at a symposium to mark the seventy-fifth anniversary of MIT's laboratory of physical chemistry. "People in academic life have considerable leverage in our society . . . they carry high credibility in their contacts with the media and with government," Kane told his audience. "You in universities are in a good position to present that argument and point the policy-makers toward sensible decisions."[150]

Leaders of the academic community were quick to oblige. Repeating a litany of increasingly familiar complaints from the corporate sector, they began to highlight the problems in their public speeches. When Paul Gray was appointed president of MIT in 1979, he used the opportunity to warn that the U.S. had "lost a certain edge in technological innovation," to complain of "excessive regulation" of both technology and research, and to suggest that even if technology had been the cause of many of today's social and political problems, the solution lay in more technology, not more regulation. "New President Is Chosen at MIT; He Warns of U.S. Technology Lag," the *New York Times* dutifully reported in a front-page story the following day.[151]

Up the road at Harvard there was similar endorsement of industry's complaints against the government. In July of the same year, a meeting was jointly hosted by the university with the Senate subcommittee on international trade and the New York Stock Exchange. Again the participants hammered away at the same themes, although this time the organizers paid for their own publicity in the *New York Times* with a full-page advertisement proclaiming, "The United States *Must* Strengthen Its Competitiveness." With Harvard's name prominently displayed below the headline, the statement emphasized that "regulation should not be allowed to stifle our competitiveness."[152]

Many universities freely laid their credibility on the line to support such arguments. Academic researchers, they argued, offered just the skills and expertise needed for an "objective" analysis of important policy questions raised by the interaction of science, technology, and public policy. Assessment studies undertaken in universities would be characterized by "unbiased analyses which can clarify competing alternatives for the decision-maker," suggested Wiesner of MIT. In contrast, he said, technology assessments presented in the political arena "seem too often designed to justify a single course of action and fog over the merits of competing alternatives"[153]—an ironic statement considering the fact that Wiesner had himself been one of the strongest lobbyists for the creation of Congress's Office of Technology Assessment.

However questionable the assumed objectivity, industry was quick to take up the offer. Both MIT and Stanford were approached by major chemical corporations early in 1978 about setting up discussions on the risk and regulation of chemicals. At MIT the eventual result was a joint program with Harvard on the impact on human health and the environment, formally unveiled by Wiesner in October 1979. At Harvard, Christopher DeMuth, director of the Kennedy School Project on Regulation —and subsequently drafted to help direct the Reagan administration's attack on regulation—claimed there existed "well nigh growing agreement among scholars that the process of adversarial regulation suffers from inherent shortcomings." These included "a disregard of fundamental economic aspects of regulation and a well nigh universal suppression of innovation and competition," as well as "protracted and unnecessary disputes between government and business over information disclosures, plant inspections, etc."[154] Funding for the joint program soon materialized from major chemical companies and their organizations, including the Chemical Manufacturers Association, DOW, Monsanto, Exxon, and du Pont. Officials from MIT—an institution that prides itself on having its "academic roots" in American industry—promoted the value of the research that would be carried out by a new institution "whose competence, objectivity, and integrity would be unquestioned."[155]

Perhaps the most aggressive use of the prestige of American universities to promote the political programs of its private corporations came in a report presented to President Reagan in April 1983 by the ACE's Business–Higher Education Forum under the title *America's Competitive Challenge*. The report was prepared by a task force chaired by R. Anderson (chairman and chief executive officer of Rockwell International) and David Saxon (president of the University of California).* It made clear its political intent by arguing that meeting the challenge of international competition required "a shift in public attitudes about national priorities." In addition to making familiar statements about the need to ensure that regulatory statutes "are compatible with the needs of our economy to remain competitive," the academic leaders endorsed the corporate world's opposition to "national economic planning, income redistribution, and plant-closing restrictions," each of which, they argued, was "counterproductive to achieving economic revitalization."[156] Although providing nothing in terms of additional insights into the problems it addressed, the report was one more brick in the university-industry coalition that helped ensure a unity of political outlook, and a powerful justification of attempts to combat "increased government intervention

---

* Other members were the presidents or chancellors of seven leading public and private universities and colleges (Harvard, Carnegie-Mellon, Notre Dame, Radcliffe, the University of Florida, the University of Pittsburgh, and the State University of New York) and top executives from six leading corporations (GE, Ford, Air Products and Chemicals, United Telecommunications, Pfizer, and AT&T).

into private-sector activities"—i.e., to make the corporate sector directly responsive to democratic demands.

Clark Kerr once described the university as a public utility, an institution whose principal purpose is to serve the public good rather than any particular segment of the community.[157] This is even more true of the university as a research community than of the university as an educational institution, particularly of private universities which have received little federal support for teaching programs, yet where most of the government's research support is concentrated. The result of massive postwar investment in basic research, as Dael Wolfle, a former editor of *Science*, has put it, is that such universities have become "public institutions doing public business."[158]

By increasing links to the private sector, however, the public resources that universities now represent have been placed directly at the service of private corporations. It is not merely the research results that companies desire privileged access to—results which could often, as has been pointed out, be obtained within their own laboratories—but the skills, experience, knowledge, and insight of the scientific community (again, properties that have been built up through heavy public subsidies). Asked what Hoechst expected to get out of the agreement with the Massachusetts General Hospital, Ronald Lamont Havers, the hospital's director of research, claimed its principal desire was to tap all aspects of the research environment. "We had discussions last week with an American company and they thought that Hoechst was getting a very good deal relatively cheaply, not from the patents, not from the people, but from the fact that America in this area of science is ahead, and they have the opportunity to train people who will go back and start probably an in-house laboratory within Germany. I think that is where they are going to get their payoff," he told a congressional subcommittee in June 1981.[159]

The benefits to corporations are significantly greater than the products of isolated research contracts. They are reflected in the broader leverage that these contracts, together with developments such as the changes in patent policy and the broader evolution of the academic ethos, provide over the whole university research enterprise. Both supporters and critics of this trend agree that industry has done well out of the deal. The director of research administration at Case Western Reserve University writes that "university-industry partnerships in research and development are a bargain for industry," since although a company pays for the direct costs of research, plus some overhead, "the almost priceless infrastructure of the university comes without cost."[160] Two critics, David Noble and Nancy Pfund, point out that this "priceless infrastructure" has usually been built out of public funds. They argue that bilateral deals between universities and private corporations have "in essence transformed a part of the public-sector social resource into a private-sector preserve," since companies have been provided with access to "a resource they could not have created with many times" the amount of the research agreements involved.[161]

The process of devoting public facilities to the increase of private profit, as well as the general tightening of "the industrial connection," has led to a fundamental redefinition of the desirable "social relevance" of university research. In the late 1960s and early 1970s, when universities were accused of scholasticism and indifference to social needs, the response to direct public pressure was to encourage the growth of "relevant" research in areas such as energy, health, and the environment, and to stress the broad relationships between science and society. The reasoning behind government support for these initiatives was that the private sector would not, for various reasons, support the necessary research.

The social responsibilities of scientists, however, have recently been given a new interpretation; they are now defined as the need to help private corporations achieve their economic and political objectives. The commercialization of research results—including acquiescence in changes in the patent system—is portrayed as a public responsibility. "Academic scientists often believe that their ideas, having been discovered in the spirit of freedom, ought to be freely available," complains one administrator at the University of Michigan, as if such attitudes displayed the height of naiveté.[162] Paul Gray, president of MIT, told a congressional subcommittee that the universities had a "responsibility" to make their research innovations available to the public through commercialization by the private sector.[163] The National Commission on Research states that universities, through close collaboration with industry, stand to gain "enhanced public credibility for service to society."[164]

Thus, at the same time that the direct imposition of social controls, through the actions of the federal government, are seen as a major threat to university independence, direction from the corporate sector toward the needs of the market is welcomed by both universities and their corporate sponsors as a breath of freedom and fresh air, and an act of social responsibility. As already suggested, this paradoxical position becomes less enigmatic when viewed as part of a broader picture. Close links between universities and industry are merely the reflection within the research community of a broader strategy adopted by U.S. capital, namely its effort to tighten control over access to the results of scientific research. Since scientific knowledge has become a crucial factor determining both new high technology products and new high technology production processes, universities—the most productive source of this knowledge—have become increasingly swept up in a strategy whose overt objective is to maintain hegemony in the global marketplace, yet whose hidden agenda is greater corporate control of the whole of U.S.

society.* These are the dominant pressures that have structured the new university-industry partnerships that have emerged in the past few years.

From the universities' point of view, next to the obvious financial advantages lie the broader questions of the impact that close linkages with the private sector through the research community could have on the other essential roles the universities are expected to play. Karl Marx, in a much-quoted passage, summarized his view that it was important to see the ideas of men as molded by the demands placed on them by external social, economic, and political forces, rather than looking on such forces as the product of the ideas of individuals. "The mode of production of material life," he wrote, "conditions the general process of social, political, and intellectual life. It is not the consciousness of men that determines their existence but their social existence that determines their consciousness."[166] The same perspective might be applied to the institutions that are supposed to represent a nation's consciousness, namely its universities, as external pressures mold the internal contents of teaching courses and research programs.

Recent statements by the Association of American Universities, the leaders of the nation's research universities, the Business–Higher Education Forum, the National Commission on Research, and other similar bodies should be read not as internally generated expressions of autonomous desires, but as institutional responses to external demands. "The new partnerships illustrate the pragmatic ability of higher education and industry to adapt to changing times," says one professor from the University of Michigan.[167] They express, in ideological form, the material needs that industry now expects universities to fulfill. This has profound implications. Eric Ashby, former vice-chancellor of Cambridge University in England, has described the universities in the modern world as "a bastion of pluralism, humanism, tolerance, openness to alternative truths, and ability to separate prejudice from error."[168] In contrast, a report for the Carnegie Foundation has recently warned of the dangers of turning universities into "academic supermarkets."[169] Already the president of the University of Colorado, Arnold W. Weber, complains that "it's difficult to retain a commitment to the humanities when the hot ticket is science and technology."[170]

The price is paid at the intellectual level. Industry's desire to control the products of university research laboratories—and its need to develop mechanisms to allow this control to be exercised—presents a direct chal-

---

* More corporate control of the national economy and less democracy seem the implicit message of the Business–Higher Education Forum report to President Reagan. It states that "public policy-making affecting U.S. competitiveness is disordered and fragmented—creating a climate of uncertainty, instability, and recurring boomlets and declines for the private sector." The report also complains of "the ad hoc process by which fiscal, monetary, trade, investment, regulatory, anti-trust, human resource, and other policies are considered."[165]

lenge to the democratic traditions on which the academic community has traditionally prided itself. Faculty democracy remains a cornerstone of university life; at Stanford, a debate over how far the university should become involved in the commercialization of research results ended with a strong plea from professor of medicine Halsted Holman that, whatever happened, decisions had to remain in the hands of faculty members: "The buck stops here. We as the faculty say what we are and behave that way or we capitulate and say that all we are here is an arm of the rest of society, in which people are not behaving by any particular code but are rather engaged in personal profit maximization by whatever mechanisms the results will allow them to get away with—which is a way I would not like to define the university."[171] Yet often university scientists feel that the industrial connection is putting such democracy at risk. At MIT, for example, faculty members wrote to President Gray objecting to arrangements under which research funds donated by multimillionaire John Whitehead for a new biomedical research institute were to remain formally under the control of a family trust, on which the university had minority representation. "This plan threatens to change the nature of higher education," complained one faculty member. "We lose control over our faculty appointments, we lose control over our graduate students, we lose control over the direction of our research."[172] At Washington University in St. Louis, one scientist claimed that an arrangement by which basic research projects funded by Monsanto would have to be approved by a panel of eight scientists, half from the company, was "far too close control for my taste."[173]

University administrators insist that many of the fears are exaggerated. The Pajaro Dunes meeting emphasized, in its final statement, that having established the broad outlines of détente between the corporate and the university communities, it remained up to individual universities to decide how to put these into practice. Yet the amount of autonomy left to universities, faced with both economic and political pressures to conform to the dominant ideology, is already circumscribed. If the Pajaro Dunes meeting could take place only outside the sphere of public debate, then the same threats to democracy are likely to be repeated on individual campuses around the country. Democracy in the university, as in other institutions, will have been sacrificed in the name of progress and high technology to the concentration of economic and political power in the hands of the multinational corporations and academic elites. "The control over science by scientists—the hallmark of the postwar pattern —is increasingly becoming the control over science by the science-based corporations that scientists serve, and sometimes own or direct," writes historian David Noble. "The issue here has little to do with the fanciful contrast between 'basic' and 'applied' research, and even less with the struggle to defend 'pure' research against external controls. The issue, rather, has always been—and continues to be—control by whom, and to what end?"[174]

3

SCIENCE AND
THE MILITARY:
KNOWLEDGE AS
POWER

FROM ITS EARLIEST ORIGINS IN ANCIENT GREECE, WESTERN SCIENCE HAS enjoyed a close and productive relationship to military power. This relationship has intensified in the forty years since the Second World War, a period in which, building on the experiences of that war, the rapid escalation of military force in both East and West has been grounded increasingly on the applications of advanced scientific knowledge to weapons of mass destruction. Science has done well out of its role, for the rise to positions of influence and favor of the scientific establishments in both hemispheres has been largely due to the contribution science has been able to make to new military technologies. Since 1960, for example, more than twenty U.S. Nobel prize winners have drawn direct support from the Department of Defense. Indeed, the rapid buildup of U.S. science over this period has been as much the result of a largely accidental spin-off from the arms race as a reflection of a conscious political desire to promote science for its own (or society's) sake.

The other side to this coin, however, is that there are today almost as many American scientists and engineers helping, directly or indirectly, to develop new ways of destroying life as there are trying to improve it. The United States government spends twice as much on military research and development as it does on R&D devoted to all other social goals put together, and three times as much on its military research and development programs as it does on aid to developing nations. The phenomenon is not confined to the U.S. According to calculations by Colin Norman, then at the Worldwatch Institute in Washington, D.C., almost half a million scientists and engineers are engaged in military R&D projects consuming one quarter of the global R&D budget.[1] As Ruth Szilard writes: "Military R&D is able to attract a share of scientists and engineers far out of proportion to the military component of the world's product. The market for which they work is unlimited in its ability to absorb the newest that brainpower and technology can produce at no matter what cost.[2]

For most of the 1970s, the situation seemed to be improving, as the U.S.—together with other Western nations—reacted to social pressures resulting partly, although not entirely, from criticism of the role of the research community in supporting military efforts in the Vietnam War. Attention shifted to the research needed to address social problems such as health, energy, and protection of the environment. Now, however, the pendulum is swinging back again. A rapidly growing proportion of the federal research budget is again being devoted, directly or indirectly, to military ends such as development of the "smart" weapons which use sophisticated technology to balance the superior numerical weight of Soviet weapons. Whereas military research and development expenditures had absorbed approximately 47 percent of the total federal R&D budget in 1980, by 1983 budget proposals submitted to Congress by the Reagan administration suggested that for the fiscal year 1984 the proportion should be 70 percent; between 1983 and 1984 alone, the administration recommended an increase in military R&D 24 percent above the expected rate of inflation, almost the largest increase of any single item in the entire federal budget (and the major contributor to an overall R&D increase of 13.3 percent). Congressional reaction to the growing budget deficit, due largely to high general military expenditures, was expected to reduce this slightly. Nevertheless, between 1980 and 1983, federal spending on defense-related R&D increased by 22.3 percent *in real terms*; in contrast, federally supported civilian R&D *decreased* by 30 percent over the same period.[3]

The balance in federal funding for basic research has shifted in the same direction. Between 1980 and 1983, support for basic research funded by the Department of Defense (DoD) increased in real terms by 28.4 percent; in contrast, support for basic research from all other federal agencies increased by only 4.5 percent. Within the total picture, the Pentagon's share of the basic research budget increased from 11.1 to 13.1 percent. This does not sound too dramatic when compared with the overall R&D figures (in which the increases are largely accounted for by development work on large-scale projects such as the MX missile and the B1B bomber); but the Reagan administration has also made it clear that the significant increases secured, with congressional blessing, in the basic research budget of other agencies—in particular the National Science Foundation—have been targeted in areas such as mathematics, physics, and engineering partly on the extent to which these subjects contribute toward strengthening the nation's military technology.*

Among the principal beneficiaries of this increase in Pentagon funding for science have been the nation's universities and colleges. The Department of Defense carries out most of its R&D work either in its own laboratories or under contract to industrial corporations. When it comes to basic research, however, a significant—and growing—proportion of this is contracted to university scientists, usually in relatively small project grants provided under the same terms and conditions as they would be by any other government agency. Furthermore, as research money from other agencies becomes more difficult to obtain, universities are turning increasingly to the Pentagon to make up for the loss. As a result of these two trends, military funding for research increased from 10.8 to 16.4 percent of the total research budget of U.S. colleges and universities between 1980 and 1983, rising in current dollars from $455 million to $813 million over the three-year period. In constant (i.e., inflation-adjusted) dollars, this was an increase of almost 50 percent over a period in which federal support for university research as a whole dropped by 3.3 percent.[5]

Reactions to this trend have predictably been mixed. Many scientists who previously might have had qualms about receiving research support from the military felt they had little alternative if they were to keep their research teams together. As one professor of public health, who had applied for Pentagon funding in anticipation of cuts from the National Institutes of Health, put it: "I have forty people working for me. I can't wait until a disaster occurs to look for other sources of funding."[6] The Defense Department has found substantial demand for its research money particularly where this promised to make up for the increasing difficulty in raising support from civilian agencies; over 2,500 applications, for example, were received for 200 awards offered under a scheme introduced in 1983 to provide DoD funding for university research equipment for which the principal source of support had previously been the National Science Foundation. Pentagon chiefs had few doubts that the tightness of the general funding for university science was contributing directly to this enthusiasm. Richard D. Delauer, Under Secretary of Defense for Research and Engineering, told a congressional committee in April 1983 that one significant reason for this enthusiasm was "the

---

* According to George A. Keyworth, President Reagan's science adviser: "Basically, we look to science and technology to provide us with technological superiority in defense. . . . To pursue this objective we must support programs and institutions that seek, nurture, and capitalize on the kind of new knowledge that supports development of new technologies. We will continue to evaluate our overall science and technology program—both civilian and military—to make sure that the flow of both knowledge and personnel is adequate to meet future defense needs."[4]

depression out there, the fact that other elements of funding [have] slowed down. And it's surprising how many converts that makes."[7]

The revitalization of DoD sponsorship of basic research, however, has also aroused growing opposition on university campuses. After the student protest movements of the late 1960s and early 1970s, one of whose main targets had been military-sponsored research in the universities, the issue of scientific links to the military lay relatively dormant for most of the 1970s. The new Pentagon funding for university research has revived intense memories of the not-too-distant past. "It looks like a return to the 1950s, when much of the expansion of universities was based on military support for research," commented linguist Noam Chomsky of MIT, one of the most outspoken critics of university involvement in the Vietnam War. "We'd be in a much more healthy society if the Pentagon had no role whatsoever in supporting research in universities."[8] For the 1982 meeting of the American Association for the Advancement of Science, the radical group Science for the People, which had dropped the military issue for most of the 1970s, published a pamphlet containing echoes of past militancy. It urged "that scientists again join the struggle against the militarization of the nation and the university."[9] Student protests against the military sponsorship of university research, frequently linked to demonstrations against the proliferation of nuclear weapons, took place at such campuses as the University of Michigan, the University of Wisconsin, the University of Rochester, and the University of California, each of which had been the site of violent confrontations in the late 1960s.[10]

The protesters reiterated a litany of complaints familiar from the earlier protest movements. They pointed out the extent to which the demands of military technology skew research from other social priorities, on both the national and the international levels. According to calculations made by Colin Norman of the Worldwatch Institute in Washington, 24 percent of R&D efforts of the governments of the world goes to defense, compared with 8 percent to space, 8 percent to energy, 7 percent to health, 5 percent to transportation, and 3 percent to agriculture and food production.[11] Commenting on the balance of priorities in the Reagan R&D budget, Science for the People complained that "the new DoD policy is creating a narrow pattern of research interests. Funds that might have enhanced the lives of the weak and the poor are being diverted to study war."[12] Others raised the moral question of whether it was right for universities to be heavily involved in weapons research. The Senate Assembly at the University of Michigan, whose research support from DoD had been growing rapidly, passed a resolution, later rejected by the university regents, calling on university departments to establish a mechanism that would bar any research "a substantial purpose of which is to destroy or permanently incapacitate human beings."[13]

In addition to these complaints, however, a new element has crept into university protests. There is concern about the tightening control the military is demanding over the scientific knowledge universities produce—even knowledge that may emerge from unclassified research, or from projects the military itself has not funded. The main emphasis of the Pentagon's increases in university funding has been on basic research programs, and in line with conventional practice scientists are told that in principle they are free to publish their results in the open scientific literature and to continue as active members of the public research community. This apparent openness, however, has been accompanied by growing attempts to place controls on access to and dissemination of basic research results in the name of national security, controls which universities have frequently been prepared to accept as the price of increased DoD funding of research.

As with the corporate sector's demands described in the previous chapter, the military's growing interest in controlling the results of research is directly linked to the increasing importance these results play in the development of new military technologies. It is the fact that the work of basic scientists is directly relevant to advances in fields with obvious military applications—such as lasers, cryptography, microcomputers, materials science, and even various types of manufacturing processes— that has stimulated much of the military's renewed interest in university-based research. But it is also this same fact that has made for the military's desire to prevent the results of such research from falling into the hands of other, potentially hostile, countries. This is the root of a new Faustian bargain being offered to universities: more funding for basic science provided they are prepared to accept more controls on the findings of their scientists.

The offer has placed universities in a dilemma. Although they are keen for the extra research support, the additional controls directly undermine the traditional norms and values of the scientific community, which include complete openness in scientific publication and in the international exchange of ideas. There have been some vigorous protests. When in April 1982 President Reagan signed a new executive order expanding the criteria by which the results of scientific research could be classified as secret, a report from the American Association of University Professors countered that the new rules posed "an unwarranted threat to academic freedom and hence to scientific progress," that they required "drastic revision in order to be tolerable to a community of scholars committed to free inquiry."[14]

University administrators, while frequently just as outspoken in public, have nevertheless tempered their opposition and stretched their principles when it has come to negotiating for the new research funds. Two areas have been unaffected: there has been no difficulty in reaching agreement either on the conditions covering basic research contracts of no immediate relevance to military technologies (carried out, as before,

with complete openness of publication) or on research which is sufficiently sensitive that the military has declared it classified from the start
(and which, as a result of their experiences in the 1960s, many universities now have rules against accepting). The difficulty lies in what both
sides admit is a growing "gray area" in the middle, an area where the
work is sufficiently broad or long-term in application not to be declared
classified but, equally, has sufficient possible implications to make the
military reluctant to grant the traditional open exchange of ideas.[15]

It is in this gray area that universities, although continuing to protest
some of the more extreme demands being made on them by hard-liners
in the Pentagon, have nevertheless agreed to accept an unprecedented
degree of control over basic research. For example, while accepting that
some universities may find some of the suggested procedures "objectionable," the Corson Report—prepared by a committee of the National
Academy of Sciences and written largely by members of the academic
and corporate research communities—acknowledged the existence of
areas for which "limited restrictions short of classification are appropriate." * Reflecting the increased strategic importance of basic science in
these areas, one of the criteria for such limited restrictions, the report
argued, is that the research involves a technology that "is developing
rapidly, and the time from basic science to application is short."[17] Building on the Corson Report's recommendations, a separate forum of DoD
and university officials, established primarily to discuss the tensions created by the demands for new controls, endorsed a statement that unclassified but "sensitive" fields of research identified by a DoD-established
committee "would be subject to controls," such as barring the participation of foreign research workers.[18]

Although the university community, in line with the Corson Report,
insisted that this gray area was small, it is likely to grow as more and
more areas of "basic" science appear to have a direct relevance to military
technology. Furthermore, the compromise academic leaders told the
Pentagon they were prepared to accept was significant. For it represented
endorsement of the principle that even in peacetime, the government is
entitled to place controls on the conduct of unclassified research and the
dissemination of its results on grounds of national security—a principle
in direct conflict with the traditional notion that no restrictions of any
kind should be placed on basic research. Even the Defense Department

---

* The report is usually called the Corson Report, after the chairman of the committee that
prepared it: Dale Corson, professor emeritus at Cornell University. The statement about
"objectionable" procedures referred to a proposal that universities might have to accept
responsibility for policing the activities of foreign scientists prohibited from access to certain
facilities or research activities. In such cases, said the report, "it is not inappropriate for
government-university contracts to permit the government to ask a university to report
those instances coming to the university's attention in which the stipulated foreign nationals
seek participation in any such activities, however supported."[16]

acknowledged the importance of the move. Edith Martin, Deputy Under Secretary for Research and Advanced Technology, claimed that it was evidence of a "phenomenal" change of attitude by many members of the scientific community.[19] An article in *Business Week* described the Corson Report's recommendations as a "capitulation" by academics which, it said, heightened concern in industry that it too might have to come to the same sort of compromise.[20]

Yet the academic community had several reasons for reaching such a compromise. The most obvious was money. If these were the most liberal terms on which the Department of Defense could be persuaded to put money into basic research—and if the controls looked as if they were likely to have only a minor impact on that research, at least to the extent that the majority of university scientists could be persuaded to accept them—then in practice they might turn out to be a small price to pay for increased government support of university science.

Beyond this, however, there was a deeper reason for reaching a compromise. Military support for university research is not only financial; it also has an important political dimension. Both the academic and the military communities have historically shared a distrust of any direct social involvement in the way they run their affairs—and both have tended to acknowledge with approval this characteristic in the other. Many scientists looked back with nostalgia at the postwar period when, taking their lead from the organization of the wartime Manhattan Project, agencies such as the Office of Naval Research provided generous funding for universities with virtually no strings attached.* This approach is compared unfavorably with the many social demands on the research community introduced in the late 1960s and 1970s—in particular, the demand for direct social accountability (illustrated, in the case of military research, by the requirements of the Mansfield Amendment, described below).

One of the attractions of military support for research at present is that the military has been able to reinforce the universities' own attempts to reject direct democratic control over the contents of their research programs (even if this means substitution of control by military authorities). The Defense Department has willingly assisted universities in their fight against federal regulations, such as those contained in OMB's Circular A-21. It has argued against an excessively rigid interpretation of the Mansfield Amendment, allowing university scientists to select their own research topics within fields considered broadly relevant to military needs. And it has actively encouraged private companies to tighten their links with the university research community, in particular by making

---

* As one historian of science has put it: "In the initial postwar years, scientists feared that government support of science would distort the direction and purposes of science. But when the military's research support seemed free of these consequences, scientists became the leading advocates of increased public investments in academic science."[21]

more of their funds available for undirected basic research and offering bonuses to companies that subcontract some of their work to university scientists.[22]

In this context, there is a rapprochement between the university and military establishments—at least those parts of the military establishment most sensitive to the academic community's complaints, usually those with direct responsibility for managing the Pentagon's research efforts. They find themselves not adversaries but allies in seeking to isolate discussion about particular research programs and their full implications from the arena of public debate and democratic control. Included in this alliance are many of the largest high technology corporations in the U.S. —companies which have profited directly from the universities' pursuit of basic science as well as the military's enthusiasm for high technology, but which also want to remain as free as possible to sell their products in international markets.

Such an alliance may help to ward off the more extreme demands made by Pentagon hard-liners for direct control over science (often imposed in the name of the Export Administration Act of 1979, which permits the government to control unclassified scientific information where this can be described as "technical data"). But in broad terms, the result is to contribute to the general separation of science from the democratic process.

More particularly, it holds specific dangers of fueling the arms race between the two major superpowers. For example, much of the basic research that the Pentagon currently supports in the universities, such as microcomputer theory and materials science, is explicitly aimed at keeping U.S. military technology between five and ten years ahead of the Soviet Union. Indeed, it is those fighting hardest against social controls on science who often cite the fact that the U.S. is now ahead of the Soviet Union in "nineteen out of twenty leading military technologies" as evidence of the advantage of letting scientists get on with the job, free of outside interference.[23] Yet it is precisely this type of thinking that inevitably fuels an escalating arms race and continuously (indeed often consciously) undermines any effort at arms control, since even if restrictions are agreed on for one generation of weapons, the next generation, often even more powerful and potentially destructive, always remains waiting in the wings. To quote Rute Szilard again: "R&D is the quintessential instrument through which antagonistic cooperation between the leading adversaries ensures a never-ending spiral in weapons technology."[24]

Furthermore, from the universities' point of view, the new pact with the Pentagon has reinforced what might be described as "the permanent mobilization of science"—a characteristic that appeared to diminish in the late 1960s and early 1970s, but is once again beginning to flourish. Military support for basic research must inevitably be committed on a long-term basis if it is to achieve significant results. For universities, this has the advantage of providing a stable base for future planning. At the same time, however, it builds them into the structure of a weapons economy that they have an active interest in helping to maintain and expand.

Finally, at the political level, decisions made away from public scrutiny (with conclusions subsequently offered for public acceptance) often tend to concentrate on "worst-case" scenarios (such as the supposed "missile gap" of the 1960s). An apparently logical response to these scenarios may then be the rapid development of new military technologies—another argument in favor of more military funding of university research, but a further built-in bias against attempts at arms limitation. There is also a tendency to go uncritically for the "technical fix" to complex military and diplomatic problems. One such example was President Reagan's proposal for a space-based anti-ballistic missile system using the latest developments in laser technology. The proposal was put forward against the recommendations of many of his close advisers, was viewed skeptically by many in the scientific community, and was seen in Europe as an implicit weakening of the U.S. commitment to NATO and as destabilizing arms control negotiations. But it was promoted by science adviser George Keyworth as a challenge to the ingenuity of the nation's scientists, and was accompanied with the promise of generous funding for any university scientist prepared to take it up.[25]

By contributing to such overall strategies, military-sponsored basic research, fueled by dreams of technological power and free of direct democratic controls, can itself become a threat to world peace. "No element in contemporary armaments dynamics has assumed such a central position, with such a profound impact on the arms race, as military R&D— the core and nerve center of the race in technology," writes Marek Thee of the International Peace Research Institute in Oslo. "It operates in a way which makes armaments dynamics organically tied to structures in economy and production, to the military establishment, the state bureaucracy, and the scientific-technological innovative adventure of the second technological revolution. . . . Military R&D steers clear of social control and tends to become ungovernable."[26]

To put recent events in perspective, it is important to understand the extent to which military support of science has been used throughout the modern history of the United States as a weapon against demands for direct social accountability for the way in which public money is spent on research. The government has long acknowledged the value of publicly funded science to its military forces. This goes back to 1804, when, in one of the first government-sponsored research programs, the War Department, at the request of Thomas Jefferson, agreed to provide support for the Lewis and Clark expedition. Sixty years later the National

Academy of Sciences (NAS) was chartered by Abraham Lincoln at the height of the Civil War to provide consultation and advice on scientific and military questions.

In both cases, science was given access to valuable new resources. But scientists were also quick to explore ways in which the military's need for science could be used to pursue political goals as well, namely to limit the degree of control the government required in return for its support. If the National Academy of Sciences was expected to fulfill the military's needs, so—at least the scientists who created it hoped—the government should respect and assist their own aspirations for the academy, namely that it should provide a mechanism for centralizing and consolidating control within the U.S. scientific community (i.e., reinforce its own power base in order to strengthen its political leverage).[27]

This goal was thwarted during the second half of the nineteenth century as the federal government established its own network of scientific advisory bureaus, while large corporations began to create their own research organizations. Both steps diffused the scientific enterprise to such an extent that central control became difficult to justify. War came to the scientists' rescue, the trigger being U.S. entry into World War I in 1917. The president of the National Academy of Sciences, George Ellery Hale, had long been trying to raise the academy's status—and political influence—by using it to coordinate centrally the work of the nation's scientists. Previously his efforts had met with little success. During the war, however, faced with the need to mobilize scientists to meet the German threat, President Woodrow Wilson eventually agreed to endorse Hale's ideas and establish the National Research Council (NRC) as a clearinghouse for research projects and scientific information. Universities such as MIT and Throop College—later transformed by Hale into the California Institute of Technology—quickly pledged their support, marking the beginning of a long and fruitful partnership between university scientists and the military. (Sixty-four years later, President Reagan's science adviser, George Keyworth, pointed out almost offhandedly at a congressional hearing that "MIT and Cal Tech were built largely with DoD funds."[28])

An unexpectedly early armistice cut short the opportunity for much detailed work to be carried through by the NRC. However, the apparatus had been established for the centralized control of science by the scientific community—a goal long sought by Hale, and the origins of what Don Price was later to refer to as the "scientific estate."[29] This apparatus survived intact, partly because of substantial support from the corporate sector. In its new peacetime guise, the NRC successfully shifted its focus from military to industrial research needs. It argued that the war had demonstrated the value of organizing the community in a collaborative effort—and had also shown that the scientific community could qualify for government support while keeping its affairs within its own hands and free of government intervention.

The scientific community's political status remained low in the postwar period, during which the most powerful organization, largely because of its links to industry, was not the academy but the American Chemical Society. In addition, relationships between the military and the scientific community lapsed. Partly this was due to a continuing distrust on the part of many university scientists of accepting any federal funds. But in addition, many scientists were morally reluctant to work toward military goals. In turn, military authorities saw little value in basic science, arguing that most of the technical knowledge it needed to improve its weapons could be generated within its own research laboratories. Budget requests for the technical bureaus of the armed services were frequently cut back by the President or senior military officers, and Congress showed little inclination to challenge their decisions. Shortly before the Second World War, as Hunter Dupree has pointed out, the Army reduced its R&D budget on the grounds that "the crisis was too serious to wait for research," preferring to allocate the funds to the purchase of new equipment.[30] Even as late as 1940, Navy spending on all forms of R&D was only $8.9 million.

Once again war changed fundamental attitudes, not only toward science but to the way it should be governed. Previously, one reason for the gulf between the military and the civilian scientific community had been a dominant military conviction that civilian scientists and engineers could contribute to useful military R&D only if directed and controlled by armed services officers. Soon after the outbreak of war, Vannevar Bush—working with James B. Conant, MIT president Karl T. Compton, and NAS president Frank Jewett (director of the Bell Laboratories)—convinced President Roosevelt not only of the potential importance of an organized defense research effort, but also that this would not be effective if carried out under military (or government) control. He therefore proceeded to mobilize civilian scientists, first through the National Defense Research Committee (NDRC), subsequently through its offspring the enlarged Office of Scientific Research and Development (OSRD), an independent federal agency established on the orders of President Roosevelt and reporting directly to him.[31] Although operating under governmental auspices, the link remained loose. The NDRC bypassed the existing agencies responsible for the support of science, and Bush spent much of his time heading off the ambitions of potential rivals, many with active congressional backing.[32] OSRD worked through providing research contracts to academic and industrial laboratories, an arrangement which not only reassured the scientists in these institutions that they were not going to be recruited into new institutions, but also placed civilians in a commanding rather than a subordinate role in organizing and carrying out military research. In this way, scientists were able to serve the war effort while maintaining their independence from outside control. In the words of Gerald Piel, editor of *Scientific American*, while "the universities transformed themselves into vast weapons development laboratories," they and their scientists also dealt with the military "not as contractors, but as privateers, bringing along their own novel weapons systems."[33] And Daniel Greenberg comments that, although the arrangement negotiated by Bush "was intended to reconcile freedom with accountability, it was clearly weighted toward freedom."[34]

As the war was coming to an end, Bush successfully parlayed science's military successes into obtaining commitments to increased federal funding for science, without direct accountability, for its continued, peacetime support. Both Congress and the federal government started to explore ways of bringing the military research apparatus that the scientific community had established within the normal framework of democratic controls. Reacting against these proposals—just as he had opposed plans for Senator Harley Kilgore's Office of Technological Mobilization (see Chapter One)—Bush and his colleagues backed plans to establish a Research Board for National Security (RBNS) under the National Academy of Sciences to investigate the more fundamental scientific aspects of defense technology. This proposal, however, received equally strong criticism from the executive branch. President Roosevelt's budget chief, Harold D. Smith, argued that it was important for defense research— indeed for all research—to be subjected to "the same democratic control as any other activity of the government."[35] Both sides stood firm, and attempts to reach a compromise failed. Truman, when he took over the presidency on Roosevelt's death in June 1945, backed Smith's position, reportedly saying of the academy: "We cannot let this outfit run the government."*[36]

At the urging of Bush, Truman permitted the RBNS to remain under the academy as a temporary expedient, while attention shifted to the larger issue of who should control funds for scientific research in general. Plans for the academy-run board collapsed, but both army and navy technical bureaus started to grant funds to university researchers on the principles pushed by Bush, with the Office of Naval Research (ONR) being established in 1946. Although intended purely as an interim arrangement, this system remained intact during the protracted negotiations leading to the establishment of the National Science Foundation (NSF), and eventually became permanent almost by default. By 1950 the ONR had already provided research contracts to 200 universities for 1,200 separate research contracts. In the first postwar decades it financed

---

* Historian Daniel Kevles suggests that an autonomous RBNS could have operated as an independent source of advice to the President on defense technology (a function filled later by the President's Science Advisory Committee). As such, it would have been a counterbalance to the military's newfound enthusiasm for innovation in weaponry. By throwing his influence behind the academy scheme opposed by President Roosevelt, Bush, together with his colleagues in the scientific establishment such as Compton and NAS president Jewett, "contributed substantially to the failure of civilian control of postwar defense research."[37]

about half the students taking doctorates in the physical sciences and sponsored much subsequent basic research in areas ranging from high energy physics to X-ray astronomy. During the Korean War, scientists who had worked in military research and subsequently returned to universities enthusiastically signed up for reenlistment and were given influential positions, particularly in the U.S. Air Force.

In the postwar decade the scientific community flourished under the terms of the contract Bush had negotiated—with generous public funding, and minimal public accountability for its use. Both principles became threatened, however, as the military's enthusiasm for science began to wane in the mid-1950s, just as it had done twenty years earlier. DoD funding for basic science remained almost constant between 1952 and 1957, leading to a drop of about 25 percent in real terms because of the impact of inflation. In the summer of 1957, faced with the need to economize after the Office of Management and Budget had placed a stringent budget ceiling on the Pentagon, DoD suddenly announced it was cutting its research budget by 10 percent—an announcement that caused the abrupt termination of numerous university research programs, many of which had come to depend almost entirely on the Pentagon as their largest provider of research funds. The result was immediate panic in the scientific community.[38]

Relief came sooner than expected. On October 4 the Soviet Union launched the first Sputnik, catalyzing a new national enthusiasm for basic science, and DoD funds for universities soon began to flow liberally again. As part of a general renaissance in enthusiasm for science, fanned by new fears of Soviet technological dominance, a memorandum from Defense Secretary Neil McElroy set out DoD's new belief that basic research, an essential ingredient in what he called "potential military power" as opposed to "military power in being," thrived on steady support rather than crash programs.[39] It was a message that the university community had long waited to hear, and it responded with enthusiasm. Scientists also lost no time in exploiting the opportunity to reestablish their position in Washington with a full-time presidential science adviser, and the creation of the President's Science Advisory Committee (PSAC), largely devoted in its early years to providing the President with advice on defense technologies.

Military support for university science was facilitated by the fact that the Pentagon reorganized internally, giving those sympathetic to the scientific community's demands for relative autonomy considerably more power than before. The Defense Reorganization Act of 1958 created a single office of Director of Defense Research and Engineering (DDR&E), who had direct authority to approve or disapprove all DoD research programs, and became both the chief spokesman for a strong military research budget and a buffer between the scientific community and its military customers. The same act created the Advanced Research

Projects Agency (ARPA), placed under the authority of the DDR&E; it has been one of the principal sources of university research support. Indeed, both the DDR&E and ARPA (now known as DARPA) remain the principal focal points for DoD support of basic research.

The military's enthusiasm for science was maintained and expanded by McElroy's successor: President Kennedy's Defense Secretary, Robert McNamara. Close links with university scientists were strengthened by the new DDR&E physicist Harold Brown (ex-director of the Lawrence Livermore Laboratory and later President Carter's Secretary of Defense), as well as by Kennedy's science adviser, Jerome Wiesner (postwar director of the MIT Radiation Laboratory and previously a member of PSAC). The links were based on the emerging philosophy that advanced technology in all military fields, rather than brute force—i.e., technological quality, rather than quantity—was the principal means by which the U.S. should maintain its military superiority over other nations, in particular the Soviet Union. Basic science, it was held, made a fundamental contribution to this strategy.

Universities were soon coopted into working on projects such as the intercontinental ballistic missile (ICBM), nuclear-powered strategic submarines, supersonic bombers, and high-speed reentry vehicles. McNamara tends to be remembered best for the systems analysts and their budgeting techniques that he introduced to the Pentagon; yet their long-term significance was much less than those whom James Fallows describes as "the impresarios of high technology." With McNamara's blessing, they "made their research and engineering division of the Pentagon the power center for decisions about new weapons, and . . . used the analysts' economic calculations as cloaks for each new project they proposed."[40]

Within a few years, however, the cosy relationship between the universities and the military ran into a new set of problems, this time related to the lack of direct accountability on both sides. Military research became the focus of student protests over U.S. involvement in the Vietnam War and, as such, a symbol of academic collaboration with U.S. imperialism. Campuses rang with demands for "no more war research," and saw bloody demonstrations against the "war machine" and the "knowledge factories" that fueled it. Student activists characterized the university laboratories and research institutes that constituted the military research network as a "fourth armed service, as crucial to the national defense as the three conventional services."[41] Attitudes shifted dramatically. In 1961, John S. Hannah, then president of Michigan State University, had told a parents' convocation: "Our colleges and universities must be regarded as bastions of our defense, as essential to the preservation of our country and our way of life as supersonic bombers, nuclear-powered submarines, and intercontinental bombers."[42] In contrast, eight years later, scientists across the nation were holding a symbolic one-day strike to protest U.S. policy in Vietnam and the way universities, with their links to the military through sponsored research, were implicitly endorsing this policy.[43]

Scientists, having successfully argued after the war that a free science was an essential component of democracy, were now told that a free science had become a threat to that same democracy. "The universities might have formed an effective counterweight to the military-industrial complex by strengthening their emphasis on traditional values of our democracy, but many of our leading universities have instead joined the monolith, adding greatly to its power and influence," Senator J. William Fulbright complained in a major Senate speech in December 1967.[44]

The direct response of many universities to these protests was to ban any connection with classified research. In several cases this meant separating off the contract research centers they had previously operated for the Defense Department. Stanford University, for example, split off the Stanford Research Institute, which became a separate contract research company. MIT's Instrumentation Laboratory changed its name to the Charles Stark Draper Laboratory and shifted its focus from military guidance to space, air transportation, and related civilian research. By 1975, five out of eight federally funded research and development centers (FFRDCs) previously managed by universities for the Pentagon had been phased out or transferred to other sponsorship.*

In the long term, however, the protests had a more significant effect, for they helped trigger new demands for direct public accountability of the content of the basic research programs supported by military funds. This was a frontal challenge to the terms of the contract drawn up by Bush—and eventually endorsed by both the administration and Congress—after the Second World War. Such demands were occasionally made by student demonstrators—one suggested during a famous protest meeting at MIT on March 4, 1969, that efforts should be made "to prune out those items of the defense budget that are not directed specifically to military work."[46] But the students were not alone (nor, indeed, was it a major theme of their protests). President Johnson had already indicated his concern that the nation should see a return on its investment in basic science.[47] Indeed, skeptical voices were increasingly heard within the military itself; one influential study argued that the basic research sup-

---

* Although the process of separation is often seen as a victory for the protest movements, there was also often an internal logic, independent of student and faculty protest. Many of the contract research centers, spawned within the academic environment shortly after World War II, had since grown to mature adulthood, and separation often proved to be in the best interests of both parent and offspring. Although universities benefited from receiving substantial management and overhead fees from contract research, as well as from the research opportunities and specialized facilities made available to faculty members, such advantages "were often outweighed by the disadvantages of managing an organization whose objectives were increasingly divergent from the institution's principal missions of teaching and basic research," writes Walter S. Baer of the Rand Corporation.[45]

ported in the postwar years had contributed little to new weapons systems.[48]

The most influential skepticism, however, came from Congress, where it manifested itself in the so-called Mansfield Amendment to the 1970 Military Procurement Authorization Bill. When the bill came up for consideration by the Senate, an amendment was proposed. (It was actually introduced by Senator J. William Fulbright, though based on concerns explored in committee hearings held by Mike Mansfield.) The amendment stated that "none of the funds authorized to be appropriated by this act may be used to carry out any research project or study unless such a project or study has a direct and apparent relationship to a specific military function or operation."[49] In other words, the Pentagon could fund basic science only if it—and the scientific community—could show how it would contribute directly to specific military needs, and if Congress accepted their arguments.*

Perhaps overestimating the strength of the political lobby in favor of heavy government support of non-military-related research in universities, Mansfield and his supporters somewhat naively—and, it turned out, wrongly—predicted that much of the slack would be taken up by civilian agencies such as NSF.

The amendment was approved by both the Senate and the House of Representatives, and signed into law by President Nixon (Public Law 91-121, Section 203). Its formal effect was limited: when Pentagon officials went through 15,000 research projects to weed out those now disqualified from support, the research budget proposed for 1971 was reduced by only about $10 million out of a total of $1.3 billion. Far more significant in financial terms was the $64 million that Congress cut from DoD's planned research expenditure. Furthermore, the amendment itself was modified the next year, so that rather than research having to show a "direct and apparent" relationship to military needs, it was now merely necessary that there be, "in the opinion of the Secretary of Defense, a potential relationship."[52]

Nevertheless, the amendment encapsulated a growing feeling both inside and outside Congress that a lack of direct accountability meant that society was not getting the returns to which it was entitled from its two decades of investment in basic research, and that often federal agencies were being taken for a ride by the scientific community. It sought to reverse a formula to which both the military establishment and the scientific community had long paid lip service, namely that the promise of

---

* Eleven years later Mansfield was to say that he "never intended the amendment to affect the overall level of basic research supported by DoD," merely to ensure that research was linked to defined goals.[50] At the time, however, he made clear his concerns about "the undue dependency of American science on military appropriations," telling the House Science and Technology Committee that the role of DoD in sponsoring basic research should be "incidental rather than predominant."[51]

basic science to the military was sufficiently high to warrant virtually indiscriminate investment. Using this formula, scientists had enjoyed a high degree of autonomy in their choice of research topics; many freely admitted thinking up ways in which their pet research projects could claim some remote military connection in order to qualify for DoD funding.[53] Mansfield had ended this by demanding public accountability for the *substance* of research, not merely its conduct.

Just as the Rothschild Report in Great Britain two years later required many scientists to justify their research in terms of its value to a "customer" government department for which they were to operate as "contractors,"[54] so Congress now demanded a demonstration of relevance from those whose research was supported from the public purse. It was a requirement that explicitly permitted social judgments to be made on the content of individual research programs, precisely the form of democratic control that Bush and the scientific establishment had fought against so strongly—and successfully—twenty years before. And it was symptomatic of a broader disenchantment with Bush's philosophy. As one former Pentagon research administrator put it at the time: "The Mansfield Amendment is important, not because its direct effects have been great, but because it is the formal expression of deeper congressional concerns, the tip of an apparently large iceberg."[55]

Partly as a result of the Mansfield Amendment and demands for social accountability of basic research funded by the military, partly because of general pressure on the military budget resulting from the continued involvement in Vietnam (which pushed basic research to the bottom of the priority list), and partly because of the increased reluctance of university researchers to apply for DoD funding and thus be publicly identified as "bomb-makers"—even when they might still be qualified to receive it—military support for basic research in the universities dropped dramatically at the end of the 1960s. The decline had in fact started in 1965, well before the Mansfield Amendment was passed. After a heady period of growth, during which military support for basic research climbed to $263 million in 1965, there was a period of increasingly rapid decline. The budget had fallen 25 percent in real terms by 1971, and reached a nadir of just over half its 1965 level in 1975 real terms. Since this was a period in which the research budgets of other federal agencies were increasing, the Defense Department's share of total government basic research funding fell even more dramatically, from 20.1 percent in 1963 to 9.3 percent in 1975.[56]

The decline was felt in virtually all fields of science. Between 1971 and 1975, the DoD share of funding of university physics departments dropped from 32 to 19 percent, while the National Science Foundation's share increased over the same period from 19 to 35 percent. DoD support for engineering in universities dropped from 46 to 28 percent.[57]

This trend had not only financial but also political implications for science. For the budget decline helped reinforce the marginalization of scientists from positions of political influence, symbolized by Nixon's abolition of the Office of Science Policy and the President's Science Advisory Committee in 1973. Furthermore, the phenomenon was not confined to the United States; similar patterns emerged in other industrialized nations. The climate of the time was reflected in a report prepared for the Organization for Economic Cooperation and Development in Paris by a committee chaired by Harvey Brooks of Harvard University. The report predicted that research funding in OECD member countries would experience a continued "shift in emphasis away from defense, national prestige, and quantitative economic growth."[58]

Yet there were many prepared to fight against this trend, for the universities still had powerful friends in the Pentagon. John Foster, director of Pentagon research from 1965 to 1973 (and, like his predecessor Harold Brown, an ex-director of the Lawrence Livermore Laboratory), remained a firm supporter of the argument that basic research had a crucial role to play in meeting the military's needs for new technology, and that universities were the best place to do it. "National security requires nothing less than the best research talent offered," he wrote in an article in the *New York Times* in January 1970. Responding directly to critics who argued that military research had no place on university campuses, he contended that "the federal government must be free to enlist those talents wherever they are found—and they flourish particularly in the university community."[59]

The Pentagon soon found new justifications for the support of basic science. As it slowly disentangled itself from the morass of Vietnam, it turned its attention in a different direction, arguing that the Soviet Union had been modernizing its military forces to a point where the U.S. no longer enjoyed the technological supremacy it had been able to establish in the early 1960s. The threat of Soviet modernization was soon being used by DoD to protect research expenditure from those, even in its own ranks, who believed any extra money should be spent on buying more conventional weapons systems—and to justify rebuilding its links to the university scientific community, which was given deliberate priority over some of DoD's own research laboratories.[60]

Through such initially relatively small-scale initiatives, military funding for basic science increased slightly between 1975 and 1976, under President Ford, for the first time in a decade. However, it was under President Carter that the process sharply accelerated. Carter appointed Harold Brown, who had been Secretary of the Air Force under President Johnson, and then president of the California Institute of Technology, as Secretary of Defense.* To the delight of his former academic col-

---

* Brown's appointment prolonged a tradition by which critical policy decisions on military research have remained, since the last war, in the hands of a relatively small group of

leagues, Brown soon announced a commitment to increase the Pentagon's funding for basic science by 10 percent a year in real dollars for the following decade.[62]

The principal reason for the Pentagon's renewed interest in universities was, as already mentioned, the crucial contribution of basic science to military high technology. Originating during the McNamara period, pursued unsuccessfully as a "technical fix" to the Vietnam War, and resurrected as a response to Soviet military strength in the late 1970s, confidence in the military promise of high technology reached a new peak during the Carter administration. It was actively promoted by Defense Secretary Brown and his research chief, William Perry. It was also warmly endorsed by Carter himself—as well as by Wall Street—since it seemed to provide a way of reducing arms expenditure without sacrificing military strength.

Shortly after his arrival in Washington, Brown made it clear that the accelerated development of advanced military technology was going to be one of the key themes of his defense strategy, warning the Senate that the U.S. had barely kept up with the modernization and expansion of Soviet weaponry. "Given our disadvantage in numbers, our technology will save us," he told a reporter from *Newsweek* in 1980.[63] Perry frequently voiced his own confidence in Brown's "offset strategy," urging the U.S. to exploit what he claimed to be a five- to ten-year lead over the Soviet Union in areas such as microelectronics, computers, and jet engines.[64]

Perry was, in particular, the driving force behind a new military technology that epitomizes the use of basic science—the cruise missile. Early in 1977, as their principal answer to the Soviet's numerical superiority in conventional long-range missiles, Perry, Carter, and Brown agreed to push for rapid development and deployment of the cruise missile, which relies on sophisticated electronics to steer close enough to the ground for hundreds of miles to avoid enemy radar. Developments such as the cruise missile provided a direct boost to DoD basic research programs, since they generated new needs from materials science to microcomputers, frequently pushing at the frontiers of knowledge. For example, Perry established a major university-based research program in very high speed integrated circuits (VHSIC), which the cruise missile and other precision-guided munitions needed to process large amounts of infor-

individuals, each of whom, in the words of one member, Herbert York, "knew most of the others on a personal basis for a very long time."[61] Brown in turn is said to have recommended Frank Press for the position of presidential science adviser. The game of musical chairs continues. Foster, Brown's successor as Pentagon research director in the 1960s, had been his deputy at Livermore in the 1950s, and left government to join TRW, the company founded by Simon Ramo, to work on government missile contracts; the current holder of the position is Richard DeLauer, previously executive vice-president of TRW.

mation in short periods of time. Asked later what he considered to be his major achievement during his four years at the Pentagon, Perry replied that it had been his efforts "to reduce a twelve-year decline in DoD funding of basic technological research and to invest heavily in making smart weapons even smarter."[65] Perry's faith in technology was absolute —and at times he waxed lyrical. "You might say that we are following the Beethoven approach to weapons planning. Beethoven was famous for finding a good theme and hitting it over and over again. We think this is a good theme," he said of his efforts to apply computer technology to weapons development. "It lends itself very well to our industrial base, and we are pulling out the throttle very vigorously to exploit it to the full advantage."[66]

Explicit justification for increased DoD funding for basic science came in a report from a working group established in 1978 by the Office of Science and Technology Policy and its director, Frank Press. The panel was chaired by J. K. Galt of Sandia Laboratories (research laboratories in New Mexico run by Western Electric for the Department of Energy) and included four university scientists, three industrial representatives (from the Ford Motor Company, Ford Aerospace, and TRW Systems), and top officials from NASA and the Department of Energy. Quick to applaud the recent reversal in DoD support for basic science, the panel claimed that "it will make possible the quality and excellence essential to the research needed to maintain the strength of the United States."[67] The panel gave three reasons why the Pentagon should support basic science, which it claimed was "absolutely fundamental" to the Pentagon. The first two were relatively traditional. One was the need to help solve technological problems caused by gaps in knowledge; the second, to provide new concepts leading to major changes in technological and operational capability.

In addition to these reasons, however, the panel also stressed that basic science was "a source of insight for DoD policy-makers and others in evaluating and reacting to the possibilities inherent in technical proposals and in technological developments anywhere in the world." In other words, basic science was important to the military because of the same strategic value that private industry obtains by looking over the shoulder of university scientists to gather information about future markets, products, and processes. "The value of basic science lies in the perspective that new concepts afford in the review of technological initiatives available to the United States," the report said. "Identifying and using these less conventional results of research require great emphasis on appreciation of the significance of new knowledge to the national defense mission."[68]

Keen to minimize the impact of public accountability for the way research funds were distributed, the panel tackled the problem of "relevance" in military-sponsored research created by the Mansfield Amendment through a neat semantic sleight of hand. It recommended that "the criterion of relevance be applied primarily to broadly defined fields and subfields of science, rather than as a filter through which every individual project must pass"[69]—a distinction that, in practice, made the concept of relevance almost redundant (and thus social accountability irrelevant), since virtually every field of science can be described as relevant to some military need or another.

In line with the committee's recommendations, Defense Secretary Brown issued a directive in May 1979 requiring all service and defense agencies to ensure that their research programs were "relevant to broad science and engineering areas with potential relationship to a military function or operation." According to George Gamota, Brown's DDR&E, one of the prime functions of the memorandum was to take away some of the "misconceptions" the research community held about any lack of interest on the part of DoD in basic science, and to underline that it was no longer necessary "to scrutinize every research task and point your finger to a definite weapons system that will benefit from it."[70]

Brown's memorandum was a signal to the scientific community that DoD was prepared once again to support its activities enthusiastically, while respecting its demands for maximum freedom in the choice and conduct of research projects. DoD also followed the Galt panel's endorsement of efforts to reestablish an active relationship with the university research community, given in its claim that universities were "a logical place to expect the original and startling new ideas from research that result in scientific and engineering breakthroughs."[71]

The panel expressed support for other political objectives sought by the scientific community. For example, it stated that in selecting individual projects for funding, "judgment of the probable quality of the proposed research should be paramount"[72]—a return to the traditional peer review process by which the scientific community has passed its own judgment on the value of research without immediate concern for its ultimate utility.

With the Galt report in their hands, Brown and Press leaned heavily on the Office of Management and Budget and persuaded it to approve an extra $100 million in DoD funding for basic science in the administration's budget request to Congress for 1979. Congress added its own support to these initiatives, which were enthusiastically endorsed by the House Armed Services Committee in its authorization report for the fiscal year 1979 budget. The result was a 30 percent increase in DoD basic research between 1977 and 1980—and a 70 percent increase in DoD support for university research over the same time period.

The increases were accelerated by the Reagan administration when it came to power in 1981. The new administration's commitment to defense research was clear not only from its budget recommendations. White House officials signaled the general direction in which they anticipated the main thrusts of science policy to move by appointing George Keyworth as science adviser—a physicist who had spent virtually his whole professional life at the Los Alamos National Laboratory (the cradle of the atomic bomb) and whose own field of laser physics is an area of basic science in which the military has had a deep and sustained interest. Further evidence of the high priority given to the contribution of science to national defense came in the appointments to the new White House Science Council. Chaired by Solomon Buchsbaum of Bell Laboratories (who was a past member of the Defense Science Board), the council included other prominent members of the defense science establishment such as Edward Teller, the "father" of the hydrogen bomb, and Harold Agnew, previously Keyworth's boss as director of the Los Alamos National Laboratory.

The Reagan administration's commitment to military funding of basic science was formally acknowledged in a memorandum issued by the new defense secretary, Caspar Weinberger, in the summer of 1981, as budgets were being prepared for submission to OMB for the following fiscal year. Like his predecessor, Harold Brown, Weinberger stated that the national base of basic research was "inadequate" to meet future DoD needs, and he argued that substantial sustained growth in defense research was needed to restore this base. In the budget proposals submitted to Congress at the beginning of 1982, universities were told to expect a 16.5 percent increase in military-sponsored R&D funds—to a total of $736 million. Areas slated for special emphasis included free-electron lasers, submicron microelectronics, human tolerance to environmental stress, computer software, artificial intelligence and robots, physical oceanography, the development of new materials, and research on new propulsion systems for ships and guns.

Not surprisingly, this steady buildup of military-sponsored research has received enthusiastic endorsement from university leaders. Faced with declining support from civilian agencies, many looked increasingly toward the Pentagon to make up for the loss. For the first time in almost a decade, on April 3, 1981, three university presidents appeared before the research and development subcommittee of the House Armed Services Committee to express their support for the administration's moves. Presenting testimony endorsed by the American Council on Education, the National Association of State Universities and Land Grant Colleges, and the Association of American Universities, Edward Bloustein of Rutgers told the congressmen that "the university research base for defense preparedness is in some considerable disrepair," and that as a result "something vital to the nation's defense . . . is presently not taking place."[73]

Keen to encourage congressional support for the Pentagon's largesse, the university presidents played down the potential opposition on campuses; they told the congressmen that the mood had changed since the

1960s and that the Pentagon should have few qualms about seeking to reestablish close contacts. Robert Sproull, president of the University of Rochester and previously chairman of the Defense Science Board and director of DARPA, claimed that the protests on university campuses in the 1960s had been overplayed by the press, and that much defense-related university research had continued unimpeded. "We are in that same position today, and we are even more willing, and there is a completely different spirit among students and faculty on campus," Sproull informed the committee members.[74] George Gamota was equally reassuring, telling the *New York Times* that "the problems of the 1960s are largely gone."[75] Even some of those who had been among the Pentagon's critics in the 1960s seemed to have had a change of heart. Alex Rich, professor of biology at MIT and one of the signatories of a 1969 faculty statement deploring the misuses of science by the military, explained that although the Vietnam War had been a "moral abomination," the U.S. had since entered a new era. "The fact is we need a vigorous science program in our universities, and the Defense Department has a special responsibility," said Rich. "We used to get Naval support for biology at MIT; we'd like to get that again."[76] Several institutions, such as Rutgers University, revised rules passed eagerly by faculty members during the war so that they could once again accept classified research contracts.

There was direct support from the corporate sector, too. High technology companies in particular welcomed this new burst of DoD enthusiasm for basic research in universities, since many of them looked forward to profitable returns from the Pentagon's interest in advanced technology. Jacques Gansler has described how, with the government interested in performance as much as price, each of the modern "super-weapons" costs so much that large amounts of procurement money have become concentrated in a relatively few large companies, which are therefore able to make large profits on defense contracts.[77] TRW increased its operating profits on defense and electronics from $84 million to $168 million between 1978 and 1982, a period in which its profits on car and truck parts fell from $206 to $140 million.[78] But companies producing small specialized components also found themselves in a good position to benefit from the high technology emphasis. The president of Hughes Aircraft pointed out in 1982 that in that year, while the defense industry as a whole had been flat for the previous fifteen years, "in electronics we've seen 200 percent growth."[79]

With profits growing at this rate, many of the high technology companies soon attracted the interest of Wall Street investors. "Military Technology Is America's Gold," proclaimed an advertisement in the *New York Times* in April 1981, promoting a newsletter published by defense analyst W. Eliot Janeway, "the acknowledged authority on how to profit from an arms buildup." Janeway informed potential subscribers that the U.S. was entering the third major arms buildup since Pearl Harbor. As a result of new technologies and new political developments, however, the old-time defense stocks would not be the star performers. Instead, "sky-high premiums" would go to "space-cadet" military technologies. Janeway offered to show investors how to build their investment strategy around America's "greatest strategic asset," her advanced technology, adding that "the high technology defense play is the financial opportunity of the decade."[80]

It was not only the brokers who were enthusiastic about high technology for the military. The banking community also embraced the basic science–high technology defense strategy, since it promised to increase military strength without creating a major drain on the economy. In an editorial headed "Brains vs. Bucks," for example, the *Wall Street Journal* asked for a crash program on the cruise missile, at least doubling anticipated production rates. Missiles, it said, had become "our main technological lead" over the Soviets: "More missiles are the quickest and cheapest things that can be done for our strategic posture."[81]

An additional reason for corporate enthusiasm was the expectation that, just as it had done with the development of the first generation of computers during the war, and with many technologies since, the Pentagon would underwrite the basic R&D costs of what would later become profitable civilian technologies. Such were the hopes for DoD funding for a new generation of "supercomputers" to match those the Japanese were aiming to produce for the 1990s, computers that could carry out calculations 100 to 1,000 times faster than any already in existence and whose development costs would have been far too heavy for any one company to support.

If the corporate and university sectors have shared a common interest in the Pentagon's desire for new technology, they have also benefited from other elements in current defense strategy. One such element has been the desire of parts of the defense establishment to boost what it describes as the nation's defense industrial base (DIB)—the industrial infrastructure claimed necessary to ensure an adequate defense posture. The main impact on the research community has been to stress the contribution of universities toward maintaining the strength of the industrial base by producing the necessary scientists and technologists. Early warnings about the state of the DIB were made in a review panel of the Defense Science Board in 1976, subsequently updated by another DSB task force in the summer of 1980. Both panels suggested the need to build an industrial infrastructure that could guarantee its ability to meet defense needs over an extended period of time. And both stressed the role of universities as an essential component of this infrastructure.

Although the concept received little support from the Carter administration, under President Reagan planning for the renewal of the industrial base became a top priority at the Defense Department. It was strongly promoted by one of the sharpest critics of its claimed decline, Fred Iklé, and soon endorsed by Defense Secretary Caspar Weinberger. Weinberger told a meeting of the American Newspaper Publishers Association in May 1981 that the U.S. should be prepared "for waging a conventional war that may extend to many parts of the globe." This would require " a defense industry able to react quickly to wartime military needs."[82]

The universities were quick to capitalize on this new philosophy and the rhetoric that surrounded it. The nation's research laboratories, they argued, should be considered as part of the defense base—and hence share in any extra funding allocated for its reinforcement. The universities contended that they were needed both for their research, which would help this base raise its productivity, and to supply the scientific and technological manpower needed by the defense industry. Introducing a hearing of the House Armed Services Committee, chairman Melvin Price referred to the committee's previous hearings on the decline of the DIB and added, "I am afraid we have a similar situation in the academic community." With falling educational standards in schools and fewer engineers staying on in graduate school because of the attractions of the job market, "our engineering and scientific base is disappearing."[83] Bloustein of Rutgers told the committee that the general decline in support for research in the nation's universities during the 1970s created a situation that "bears a very important relationship to the industrial base," for it "leaves us wanting in *the university base for defense preparedness*"[84] (italics added).

The importance to universities of the DIB argument was that it presented the case for increased federal support not merely in terms of their short-term ability to contribute knowledge for specific military products —or even long-term technological strategies—but, just as important, in terms of their value as a base for future contributions. These, it was argued, could be maintained only through support for the educational and research infrastructure. Conventional forms of federal funding through research grants and contracts provided infrastructure support only to the extent that it could be justified as an "indirect cost." What the university community, as it has indicated in many reports, wants from the federal government is a source of *stable* funding.[85] The agencies that have traditionally supported the bulk of university research, such as the National Science Foundation, are finding this increasingly difficult to do. The DIB philosophy, however—like the National Defense Education Act, passed immediately after the Sputnik launch—combined with the new enthusiasm for basic research in the DoD as the apparent answer to the universities' needs.

This argument was used to meet university needs for research equipment. A report prepared by the Association of American Universities for the NSF in 1980 demonstrated a sharp decline in federal support for capital equipment since the 1960s.[86] The Carter administration responded with a budget proposal submitted to Congress in 1980 that the NSF create a new fund, totaling $75 million in the first year, to help universities upgrade their scientific equipment. The NSF proposal fell to other budget stringencies—first those imposed by Carter, later as one of the first "new initiatives" to be cut in the Reagan budget of March 1981. But the Defense Department soon picked up the ball, using the argument that the decline in the universities' research equipment created a threat to the national security. In its budget proposals for 1983 the Pentagon announced it was embarking on a five-year program to invest $150 million in university laboratory equipment. Each of the three services would contribute $10 million a year out of their annual allocation for basic research to meet this target.[87]

The Defense Department has also helped to fill a hole left by other agencies in graduate training. Increased federal support for postgraduates had also been identified in the late 1970s as one of the most pressing needs of the research community, yet again initiatives proposed for the NSF soon found themselves the target of the budget ax. Defense needs, however, provided a new rationale for federal support for graduate training. The Defense Department itself estimated that in 1981 it had 5,000 civilian and military openings in the hard sciences and engineering; many of the contract industries it relied on complained of the same problem. Partly at the AAU's recommendation, DoD announced early in 1982 that it was introducing a graduate fellowship program "as one means of increasing the supply of U.S. nationals trained in areas of science and engineering critical to the U.S."[88] It announced that it planned to award 125 graduate fellowships a year, at a stipend well above the conventional NSF level.

The Pentagon has thus shown its willingness to assist universities by providing increased research funds, support for research equipment, and subsidies for research training—all in the name of maintaining technological superiority over the Soviet Union on the one hand, and an industrial base capable of meeting the nation's long-term military needs on the other. In this way, it has offered universities the type of federal support that had become a scarce commodity from other federal agencies. And the Defense Department has been helping the universities in other ways. DoD funding has been used by several universities with active Pentagon support to increase their links with the private sector. In several cases, such as Stanford's Center for Integrated Systems (established with the aid of an $8 million grant from DARPA), DoD funding is being used as seed money to establish a major research facility expected to be heavily used by a wide range of private companies. Similarly, the University of Michigan, which recruited Gamota after he had left DoD, won a major contract from the U.S. Air Force to provide 75 percent of the funding for a new Center for Robotics and Integrated Manufacturing—a facility that many local companies, as well as Governor Robert Milliken, hope will turn Ann Arbor into a "world center of excellence in robotics research."[89]

Universities also received support from the Pentagon in their fight against social controls through government regulation. Many looked back with nostalgia to the immediate postwar era, when support through such institutions as the Office of Naval Research had provided maximum flexibility to university scientists with minimal accountability for the way in which research funds were used.* Like university scientists, many DoD officials considered that they could do their jobs best with the minimum of outside interference. The two communities shared a common distrust of democratic planning. Despite changes that had taken place in the intervening period, "DoD is regarded by universities as the most understanding and sensitive government manager of research," Sproull—a fierce critic of excessive government controls on research—told a congressional committee.[91] Indeed, DoD took little encouragement to help the universities argue against strictures laid out by the Office of Management and Budget in its Circular A-21. Pentagon officials repeated to OMB the universities' arguments that the result of the new rules, unless significantly relaxed, would be to decrease the effectiveness of the university research effort—and hence, implicitly, of the nation's security.[92]

The Pentagon's congressional allies put their own muscle behind the universities' case. With the active help of the House Armed Services Committee, a bill was hustled through Congress approving a shift from a procurement to a grants basis for defense research, a move that reduced the amount of form-filling required of university scientists receiving Pentagon funds—but a move that reduced as well the constraints under which they were required to work. In the floor debate, the change received heated opposition from both sides of the political spectrum. Armed Services Committee member William Dickinson defended the change by stating that it was "just another tool that DoD uses, just as any other agency presently uses." However, Jack Brooks, chairman of the Government Operations Committee, claimed that allowing the military to use grants rather than contracts for research projects could open the door to "millions of dollars of waste." Ron Dellums of California complained that "no one member of the Committee on Armed Services has given any particular reason why we ought to give the Pentagon this incredible freedom to spend extraordinary amounts of money," adding that "we should not in this incredible feeling of militarism feel we have

---

* Speaking on behalf of the Association of American Universities, David Saxon, vice-chancellor of the University of California, informed a Senate committee: "The program of the Office of Naval Research has often been cited as one of the most successful agency-university relations in our national experience. . . . Those days were labeled halcyon for good reason."[90]

to give the Pentagon every single thing that we think they want without any accountability." The complaints generated widespread support, but they were insufficient to counter the momentum of the military and university establishments, and an attempt to delete the new provision in the defense budget was narrowly defeated by four votes.[93]

On the surface, the change appeared relatively minor.[94] Yet it was symptomatic of the deeper trend, namely the way in which arguments about the importance of basic science to the nation's defense were being used to justify the weakening of social controls on the way that science is carried out and the way its results are put to use. At the same time, the extra money available for military research was being used to cement common political interests among the academic, the corporate, and the military research communities, forming a powerful coalition against demands for the direct democratic control of science.

If these three communities shared a common interest in promoting basic science in universities, they also shared an interest in rejecting some of the controls (such as a rigid interpretation of the Mansfield Amendment) that social pressure had led Congress to impose. But not all controls. When it was a question of those that, instead of placing science in the hands of the democratic process, tended rather to concentrate it in one of these three groups, then—as the robber barons had found with railroad regulation at the end of the nineteenth century—it was time for mutual compromise and accommodation if their combined political influence was going to be consolidated.

One area where a compromise between academic principles and military demands has been reached—to the exclusion of consistent demands for direct social accountability—is over the operation of the nation's two major nuclear weapons research laboratories: the Lawrence Livermore Laboratory in California and the Los Alamos National Laboratory in New Mexico, both managed for the Department of Energy by the University of California. Los Alamos was established in 1943 as part of the Manhattan Project to develop, construct, and test the atomic bomb; Livermore was created in 1953 to take over nuclear weapons research from the Lawrence Berkeley Laboratory. Both are operated by the university under a postwar agreement that weapons research should remain under civilian control; and both have been a continuous source of controversy among university faculty and students, many of whom have criticized the university link.[95]

The two laboratories have been responsible for most of the basic research behind every nuclear weapon in the U.S. arsenal. Administrators and scientists at the laboratories both argue in favor of maintaining links to the university. Not only does it permit laboratory staff to take on teaching commitments, but it also gives their work an aura of academic legitimacy that, laboratory administrators claim, has increased their ability to attract top-rate research workers. Equally important, being managed by the university means that the laboratory staff enjoys a much greater degree of freedom than would be the case if it were under government or industrial management.

The university's administrators, who benefit from a management fee of several million dollars a year, have also consistently defended the arrangement. Yet the appropriateness of an academic institution being responsible for laboratories whose main research is devoted to the creation of new weapons of mass destruction has long been a bone of contention among both staff and students on campus. Some critics argue that the university should sever its links with the laboratories altogether; in 1979, for example, over 800 faculty members signed statements calling for an end to the university's involvement with nuclear weapons R&D at the two labs as "inappropriate to a university's commitment to the free and open discovery and dissemination of knowledge."[96] Others, however, contend that if this were to happen, the laboratories would have little difficulty in finding another manager; already at the end of the 1970s, when the laboratory contract was coming up for its regular five-year renewal, a consortium of Midwestern universities submitted an alternative bid for the management contract. These latter critics have therefore focused debate on how university members could maintain responsibility for the laboratories and use this as a lever to direct their research toward more socially desirable goals.

One of the most persistent critics has been Charles Schwartz, professor of physics at the University of California's Berkeley campus. Schwartz argues that part of the reason the weapons laboratories remain heavily and successfully engaged in defense research is that the university "provides the laboratory management with a two-sided carte blanche; they are free of any supervision from within the university and yet the university name gives them independence from any other course of control."[97] To back his claim, he quotes the description by the Los Alamos laboratory's assistant director, Edward Hammel, of the role of the university as a "benevolent absentee landlord," since the "business" of the laboratories is primarily with Washington. "UC understands that and interferes in programs not at all," Hammel wrote in a memorandum in July 1977.[98]

Responding to faculty concerns, the university established a committee to look into its relationship with the laboratories when the contract came up for renewal in 1977. In its final report, the committee confirmed this lack of accountability to the university for the laboratories' research programs, stating that it was "particularly disturbed by the nominal leadership which the university provides. The laboratories enjoy a delightful autonomy within the protective shelter of the university, so delightful as to border on the licentious."[99] To correct this situation, it recommended that there should be greater involvement by faculty representatives in the administration of the two labs. However, this was rejected by the Board of Regents, and the contract was renewed virtually on the original terms.

It was the same when the contract came up for renewal in 1982. Under student and faculty pressure another report had been prepared, this time by a new university committee chaired by former UCLA vice-chancellor William Gerberding. It suggested that a board of overseers be established to review all aspects of the laboratories' programs "for the purpose of discharging the university's obligation to itself and to the public, as a public institution, to be completely informed about the work, classified and unclassified, undertaken by the laboratories." The report urged "significant faculty representation" on any such committee. Furthermore, membership on the committee was to be as open as possible, the prime requirement being not necessarily the technical knowledge, but "the experience, professional or other, conducive to the exercise of public responsibility in the broadest possible sense." [100] (This proposal generated enthusiastic support from former California governor Jerry Brown, who had first argued for complete separation, but then suggested implementation of the Gerberding committee's proposals for an overseeing board to review on a regular basis the major R&D programs of the laboratories.)

The idea of greater public participation in the running of the laboratory was, however, firmly resisted by the Department of Energy (DoE). In a letter to the university regents commenting on their decision to set up two overseeing committees to monitor scientific work and environmental health and safety at the labs, Duane Sewell, Assistant Secretary of Energy for Defense Programs, made the department's views on democracy clear. The university should accept its contractual management responsibilities "in order to execute them, not to subject them to the crucible of public debate," he stipulated, strongly hinting that DoE might seek another manager if democratic tendencies went too far. *[101]

DoE's opposition put the lid on efforts to open up the overseeing of the two laboratories. The Board of Regents rejected Jerry Brown's appeal to democratize the administration of the laboratories and voted by 15

---

* A report from DoE's Energy Research Advisory Board, which endorsed continuation of the existing relationship between the department, the university, and the laboratories, generated a certain amount of controversy over its peremptory treatment of public critics. Five members of the board issued a minority report complaining of a "degree of commonality" among the members of the study group that had looked at the weapons lab contract, most of whom were prominent members of the defense science establishment. The minority members complained that the review group had not looked at ways UC management of the labs influenced the interaction of their weapons-related and energy-related research. They also attacked the lack of democracy in the Energy Research Advisory Board's deliberations. "While the nature of some of the subject matter may have made the decision to hold closed meetings of the study group understandable, the time pressure that led the board to act on the draft report at a single meeting invites the conclusion that it viewed public input as a mere formality," they wrote. [102]

to 5 to negotiate a new management contract for five years from 1982. When the contract was eventually signed, it contained few changes from previous versions, accepting DoE's claim to control over research at the laboratory—subject to outside evaluation of its quality by other members of the scientific community—but rejecting demands that the research should also be scrutinized for relevance by the wider community. Protesters kept up the pressure. Several demonstrations were held in 1982 and 1983 outside the laboratories to protest their involvement in military research, frequently leading to arrests. And in May 1983 the California Assembly's Education Committee asked the Board of Regents of the university to study whether the laboratories could be converted to peacetime use—one of the protesters' chief demands—and passed a resolution stating that if the study showed this could be done, such a conversion should be carried out within three years.[103] But with no direct public leverage over the laboratories' work, there was little optimism that this would take place.

The debate over the public control of research at the two weapons laboratories had its origins in an earlier compromise, one that has recently taken on added significance as the precedent on which military and national security agencies are now extending their hold on a growing number of areas of science. This was the struggle that took place at the end of the Second World War between those who felt that all nuclear research should remain under military authorities and others who argued that it should be subject to civilian control. The result was the Atomic Energy Act of 1946 (revised in 1954), under which nuclear research carried out for both military and civilian purposes was to be run by the Atomic Energy Commission (AEC), responsible to the Joint Committee on Atomic Energy in Congress. Formally, the civilian commission represented a victory for those who had pushed for civilian control. Yet the military still kept its foot firmly in the door. The weapons laboratories, funded by DoE but producing research results subsequently developed by DoD weapons contractors, have all military aspects of their research placed under the control of a military officer installed within the AEC (now DoE) framework.*

Particularly significant for science was the fact that the AEC reserved the right to classify any scientific results in research related to atomic energy that it considered potentially dangerous in the hands of the enemy—whether or not the research that produced these results had been financed by the federal government. This soon became known as the "born classified" concept. The concept aroused controversy as soon as it was suggested. Many scientists felt there should be no secrecy attached to any type of scientific knowledge. Physicist Enrico Fermi, for

---

* In the early 1970s, the AEC was absorbed into the Energy Research and Development Agency (ERDA), which became the Department of Energy under President Carter.

example, claimed that "unless research is free and outside of control the United States will lose its superiority in scientific pursuit."[104] Reflecting such views, the original version of the atomic energy bill, proposed by Senator Brien McMahon, talked of the need for the "free dissemination of scientific information and for maximum liberality in dissemination of related technical information."[105]

During its deliberations on the bill, however, members of the Special Senate Committee on Atomic Energy adopted a more conservative position, justifying strict controls on information in the name of national security and abandoning a suggestion that free dissemination of knowledge should be the basic principle of information policy for nuclear energy.* Furthermore, the committee also dropped an effort to distinguish between "basic scientific" information, which would be free of any controls, and "related technical" information, on which controls would be imposed. Instead, it created the category of "restricted data," which left military authorities free to interpret what information could and could not be classified—even if scientists considered this basic science.[107]

Even some of those responsible for the legislation acknowledged the harshness of the restrictions. Two of the principal architects, James Newman and Byron Miller, wrote soon after the act was passed that even if it did not restrict the liberty of scientific thought, "it without question abridges the freedom of scientific communications." The controls on information were deliberately designed to regulate the interchange of scientific ideas; "even those data describing the phenomena and the laws of the visible universe are under interdict," they wrote.[108] In 1958 a congressional committee that had studied the Atomic Energy Act as a possible model for other legislation concluded that its provisions for the control of information were "a latent danger to the life of this democracy."[109]

But the AEC showed it had little concern for such political niceties and was prepared to use its powers to control scientific information to the full. In 1950, for example, it persuaded *Scientific American* not to publish an article by physicist Hans Bethe on thermonuclear weapons, even though it had already been set in type. National security officials personally supervised the destruction of the magazine's plates and removed all galley proofs of the article.[110] In the mid-1960s the act was used against a number of private research companies engaged in developing techniques for enriching uranium through gas centrifuge technology, on the basis that the dissemination of such technologies was a threat to national security since it could provide a cheap method for producing fuel for nuclear weapons.

* One British scientist has recently claimed that a major fire that broke out at the Windscale plutonium plant in Britain could have been avoided had this clause not been in effect, since it kept U.S. scientists from providing their British colleagues with information that would have prevented the fire.[106]

Some of these actions were based on justifiable fears. But it soon became clear that the borderline between legitimate national security concerns and the military's desire to control as much scientific and technical information as possible was a thin one—indeed, that claims of "national security" were frequently doing little more than masking efforts to extend this control as widely as possible. Particular conflicts arose in the late 1970s over the control of information about the explosion of atoms. Civilian researchers wanted to publish the results of experiments using laser beams to ignite small pellets of helium and deuterium gas, causing a miniature atomic explosion similar to that which takes place within the hydrogen bomb. These results offered a potential source of nuclear energy. Military authorities, however, insisted that the technology and the scientific knowledge on which it was based be kept entirely under wraps. Not only might it provide information about the mechanisms used in the design of nuclear weapons, but they also needed the laser for their own studies, since the pellet explosions can be used to simulate the effects of a nuclear blast and its impact on different types of material.[111]

For several years the military successfully used the "born secret" provisions of the Atomic Energy Act to block publication of information about experiments exploring civilian applications through a process known as "inertial confinement fusion" (ICF). Government officials defended their actions; Los Alamos director Donald Kerr asserted that the classification of the research had not affected its progress, on the grounds that "the well-known difficulties of the experiments are a much more profound impediment to progress than any administrative or statutory impediment that classification might provide."[112] Many scientists, however, disagreed. "The science of inertial confinement fusion would progress much faster if most of the physics was declassified," said a scientist at one of the small companies trying to exploit lasers as a civilian energy source, claiming that the classification of target design often prevented critical evaluation by university scientists.[113] The chairman of a committee established by the Department of Energy to study the classification of ICF said that he personally had "a lot more concern about the danger of inhibiting ICF energy applications by imposing security restrictions than about the danger of proliferation arising from a relaxation of those restrictions."[114]*

Another controversy over the use of the Atomic Energy Act to classify

---

* Further evidence of DoD's desire to use classification procedures to control the dissemination and use of data, as much as to prevent information from falling into hostile hands, was illustrated when the department told U.S. scientists not to discuss the results of thermonuclear "micro-explosions" caused by powerful electron beams described in a series of presentations by a Soviet physicist, L. I. Rudakov, during visits to U.S. laboratories in October 1976. As a reporter from *Science* put it, whatever the reasons for official silence, "it is hardly motivated by the urgency of keeping secrets from the Soviets."[115]

scientific data arose in March 1979 when the Department of Energy tried to prevent publication in the magazine *The Progressive* of an article by free-lance journalist Howard Morland giving details of how the hydrogen bomb works. Morland argued that he had collected all the information from public sources—including several documents discovered on the shelves of the Los Alamos public library. DoE replied that some of the details in the article were classified and that the magazine would therefore be in violation of the act if the article were published. Even though Morland had collected his information from "public sources," said DoE, some of this information had been released inadvertently, and although it was technically in the public domain, it remained classified.*[116]

The U.S. District Court for the Western District of Wisconsin upheld DoE's case against *The Progressive*, concluding that the information in the article could be considered as "restricted data" under the Atomic Energy Act. U.S. District Judge Robert Warren declared that even though the article did not contain enough information to enable a foreign power to build a hydrogen bomb, it could still assist such an effort by indicating which blind alleys should not be pursued.

The verdict was, perhaps, predictable, given the range of the government's power to control information about nuclear science under the terms of the Atomic Energy Act. In presenting his decision, however, Warren made a ruling with profound significance for the whole debate about the control of scientific knowledge in the name of national security. For in rejecting arguments about the unconstitutionality of efforts to control the freedom of publication, he suggested that this had to be interpreted in the context of the changing nature of war from a man-intensive to a machine- and technology-intensive activity. As a precedent for his decision, Warren cited the Supreme Court's judgment in 1931 that it was against the national security interest to publish the movements of troops in times of war. "Now war by foot soldiers has been replaced in large part by war machines and bombs," said Warren. Advance warning was no longer needed before a nuclear war could be commenced. "In the light of these factors, this court concludes that publication of the technical information on the hydrogen bomb contained in the article is analogous to publication of troop movements or locations in time of war and falls within the extremely narrow exception to the rule against prior constraint."[117]

Warren's words provided further confirmation of the *strategic* role that basic science has come to play in military planning. Despite the large

---

* DoE did not restrict its charges to Morland. Several scientists from various DoE laboratories wrote letters to Senator John Glenn and others giving reasons why they felt there was no longer a legitimate case to consider the information in the article as secret—some referred to an encyclopedia article by physicist Edward Teller several years previously in which much of the same information was presented. These scientists soon found that their own letters were declared classified as well.

amount of evidence presented by scientists to the contrary, who argued that most of the information was already well known, Warren decided that to publish the Morland article would create "direct, immediate, and irreparable harm" (a criterion established in a previous case when the *New York Times* successfully challenged a court injunction against publishing the Pentagon Papers). As a result, he established a legal precedent by which the publication of any scientific information could apparently be legitimately prevented if military authorities felt they had a good reason for doing so.

Warren's verdict set the stage for what was expected to become a classic legal battle up to the Supreme Court. The case, however, was abandoned by the government soon after a Madison, Wisconsin, paper published a letter from California computer scientist Charles Hansen containing the same basic information (the government had already successfully prevented the publication of Hansen's letter in a student newspaper at Berkeley). Nevertheless, the case remains a crucial watershed in the history of the extension of military controls over scientific information. Not only was it the first case in which prior restraint has been endorsed in the name of national security, but it was also the first time that the government had obtained full judicial endorsement of the extension of national security controls to scientific (or journalistic) activities.[118]

Until relatively recently the government's interest in controlling scientific information has been focused, as in the *Progressive* case, on the results of nuclear research. Yet as basic research in other fields of science has become increasingly pertinent to the interests and missions of defense and national security agencies—the principal reason, as we have already seen, for the growth in military funding of university research—so the pressure to broaden the range of such controls, even over the results of research funded by civilian agencies, has grown accordingly. One of the first areas to feel the effect was computer science, particularly that concerned with the study of computer-based codes as both a mathematical and a practical problem, a field known as cryptography.

Knowledge of how to make secret codes is often as valuable as how to break them; many of the code-making and code-breaking techniques developed during the Second World War remain classified, on the grounds that to release the details would give an enemy an indication of the type of information the U.S. is able to decipher. Furthermore, research into codes has, until recently, been a domain jealously guarded by the National Security Agency (NSA), responsible for ensuring the confidentiality of all government communications—as shown, for example, by its prosecution of *The Code Breakers*.[119] By the mid-1970s, however, two trends threatened the monopoly the NSA had until then been able to exercise over research into cryptography. The first was growing demand from the private sector for ways of protecting both commercial and personal information. This trend had escalated with the use of electronic data storage and transmission, which, unlike traditional methods, do not require physical access to information by someone who wants to intercept it.

The second trend was that cryptographic problems had become of growing interest to theoretical mathematicians studying what makes a mathematical problem easy or difficult to solve, drawing mathematicians into a field where much of their research overlapped with the problems being worked on by cryptologists. This was particularly true where the mathematics began to point toward sophisticated coding techniques based on mathematical problems considered virtually unsolvable, and where the decoding technique was therefore almost equally impossible to break.

Both trends contributed to growing pressure for what is known as public cryptography, the development of methods for coding and decoding data parallel to those developed by the security agencies. But they also resulted in a growing overlap between the interests of the intelligence communities and university research workers through narrowing the distinction between basic and applied research. As George Davida, associate professor of engineering and computer sciences at the University of Wisconsin, put it in testimony to a congressional committee: in computer sciences "there is very often little difference between theory and application." With the development of microprocessors, it had become "trivial" to take a procedure that someone developed theoretically and turn it into a machine that could encrypt, he explained. "It is difficult to draw the line between basic research and applications because there are many mathematical areas in computer science theory where there is a direct bearing on cryptography which would be difficult to restrict."[120]

This blurring of the distinction between applied and basic research posed a direct threat to the monopoly of the security agencies, which watched university scientists carry out and openly discuss research that they felt could seriously jeopardize their own work. Speaking at a meeting of the Armed Forces Communications and Electronics Association in January 1979, Admiral Bobby Inman, director of the National Security Agency, voiced growing concerns of many in the intelligence community. "There are serious dangers to our broad national interest associated with uncontrolled dissemination of cryptologic information within the United States," he said. "Unrestricted nongovernmental cryptologic activity poses a threat to the national security."[121]

Two events turned a smoldering conflict between the academic and intelligence communities into a full-scale public controversy. The first involved Davida, who had applied early in 1978 for a patent on a device to encipher and decipher computer information. Shortly after sending his application to the Patent and Trademark Office of the Department of

Commerce, Davida and a graduate student received notices stating that his patent application contained information "the disclosure of which might be detrimental to the national security." The notice warned Davida that he was forbidden to publish or disclose the invention, or any information related to it, to anyone not already aware of the details, subject to a fine of up to $10,000 and two years in prison.[122]

The letter produced a sharp outcry from the academic community, since Davida's work was sponsored by the National Science Foundation and was therefore unclassified; the chancellor of the University of Wisconsin, for example, told the NSF that the Patent Office's decision infringed upon the university's standard policy of research disclosure and, more fundamentally, established "a precedent which has a chilling effect on academic freedom."[123] After the matter had been taken up by the university with the Secretary of Commerce, Juanita Kreps, the restriction on the patent application was lifted—but not before it had raised broad concerns in the scientific community about the trends it represented.

These concerns were reinforced a few months later by an incident that involved a conference organized by the Information Group of the Institute of Electrical and Electronic Engineers (IEEE), which had planned a discussion on cryptography at its meeting in October 1977 in Ithaca, New York. Two months before the meeting, members of the group received a letter sent from a private address outside Washington, suggesting that the open discussion of crytography in a public forum where foreign participants might be present could violate the International Traffic in Arms Regulations (ITAR), part of the Arms Export Control Act passed by Congress in 1976 to control the export of technology and technical data with potential military applications. Again the action brought a strong reaction from university computer scientists, many of whom had previously looked on their work as basic research. One participant, Ronald Rivest of the Massachusetts Institute of Technology, had already described his scheme for an unbreakable code in that month's *Scientific American*, in an article purposefully written in such a way that the ideas could be used commercially. Concern increased when it was subsequently revealed that the letter's author, J. A. Meyer, was on the staff of the National Security Agency. An agency spokesman quickly dissociated the NSA from Meyer's actions, saying that it had "nothing to do with that letter" and that Meyer had been writing in a personal capacity. Yet suspicion remained strong that Meyer's views were widely held within the agency.* [124]

---

* The specific legal problem raised by the letter was whether a scientist's research results constitute "technical data," which, according to ITAR rules, are defined as "any classified information that can be used, or adapted to use, in the design, production, manufacture," or repair of "implements of war." The latter are defined by entry on the U.S. munitions list, which includes not only weapons and advanced computers, but also "cryptographic

The NSA tried to play down the two incidents. In the Davida case, Inman said later, the Commerce Department's decision had been a "bureaucratic error" caused by the misjudgment of a relatively low-level official, who had been unaware that the research was sponsored by the National Science Foundation. And the agency continued to insist that Meyer's actions were no reflection of NSA policy. Both incidents, insisted Inman, were the result "not of a faulty law, but of inadequate government attention to its applications."[126] Both, however, also contributed to growing tensions between the NSA and the scientific community over how research results in cryptography should be controlled—and by whom.

Already there had been controversy over the appropriate division of responsibility between the National Security Agency and the National Science Foundation, the civilian agency responsible for the research that the NSA was interested in. Early in 1977, two intelligence officers had visited the NSF's division of mathematical and computer sciences—the source of support for both Davida's and Rivest's research. They suggested that the foundation was operating outside a presidential directive that gave the NSA "control" over all cryptographic research. The NSF replied that it had not been able to find any such directive when the same question had been raised two years earlier. The intelligence officials then replied that in that case "they would have to get a law passed."[127]

Prolonged negotiations subsequently took place between the two agencies over how responsibility should be divided. NSF director Richard Atkinson wrote to Inman, suggesting that "a small unclassified research support program at universities ($2 to $3 million say) sponsored by the NSA would help prevent further problems."[128] Eventually a compromise was reached. The NSF agreed that all grant applications for cryptography research be shown to the NSA for comment prior to a funding decision. In return, the NSA would establish its own research fund, giving the agency direct control over those aspects of basic research that it was most interested in.

Even this, however, turned out to be controversial. Early in 1980 Martin Adleman, a computer scientist at the University of California and one of the original participants in the IEEE meeting, received a telephone call from the NSF saying that the agency was prepared to support only part of an application he had submitted to renew his research grant. The next day Inman telephoned Adleman to say that the NSA wanted to fund the rest of his research—the first that Adleman had been told of the NSA's interest in sponsoring his work. Initially Adleman was skeptical. "In the present climate I would not accept funds from the NSA," he

---

devices (encoding and decoding) and specifically designed components therefor, ancillary equipment, and especially devised protective apparatus."[125] Furthermore, responsibility for obeying the regulations rests with the person or company seeking publication, which may include the scientist at the laboratory bench.

told one reporter, who suggested that it was the first time the NSF had refused funds to a researcher for reasons independent of the scientific merit of the proposal.[129] "I'm shocked," said Rivest of MIT, claiming that the line between what is and what is not cryptography "is being pushed in a way that affects our ability to do basic computer science research."[130]

Further negotiations between the NSF, the NSA, and Adleman led to a compromise, and Adleman subsequently agreed to act as a guinea pig for a new system of funding university research by the NSA. But again the incident was widely discussed in the scientific community, for it raised concerns about the potential legal, constitutional, and political problems generated by the growing overlap of interests among the academic, commercial, and intelligence agencies on basic research in computer science—indeed, in science in general. After holding hearings on the controversy, the House Committee on Government Operations concluded, in a report published in December 1980, that efforts by the intelligence community to restrict public cryptography posed "enormous questions of constitutional rights."[131] Inman had already indicated that he would like Congress to give him the same authority as the federal government has under the Atomic Energy Act, allowing him to classify as "born secret" any work the intelligence agency thought might jeopardize the nation's cryptographic interests.[132]

The cryptography incidents also illustrate once again how growing ambiguity between basic and applied science—as well as between what is and what is not a security threat—has become intrinsically bound up with questions about the social control of scientific knowledge and the division of responsibility between civilian and military agencies. One NSF official, after meeting with the intelligence officials who claimed the foundation was trespassing on the NSA's territory, noted that the intelligence agency was partly motivated by a desire for power. "In the past the only communications with heavy security demands were military and diplomatic," he wrote. "Now, with the marriage of computer applications with telecommunications in electronic funds transfer, electronic mail, and other large distributed processing applications, the need for highly secure digital processing has hit the civilian sector. NSA is worried, of course, that public-domain security research will compromise some of their work. However, even further, they seem to want to maintain their control and corner a bureaucratic expertise in their field."[133]

The ITAR regulations, once considered by the scientific community as a relatively obscure set of government rules,* soon took on a much broader significance, for they became the basis on which the Department

---

* As the deputy director of the National Science Foundation wrote to the director of the State Department's Office of Munitions Control at the beginning of 1981: "The NSF, along with many individuals and institutions in the scientific community, has only recently become aware of the great potential impact on this country's science base of export laws and regulations."[134]

of Defense started to add restrictions to nonclassified university contracts. The first case in which this occurred was over research into very
high speed integrated circuits (VHSIC), a key component in cruise missiles and other new military technologies. When the Carter administration decided to develop the missile early in 1977, it began to lay plans for
a major research program into the scientific knowledge required for the
missile's key technology, its guidance computers. (These proposals were
eventually submitted to Congress at the beginning of 1979.) Keen to keep
overall control of the research under its own roof, the Pentagon argued
that its requirements were likely to be different from the research directions in which commercial computing was going, where the rapidly growing demand for consumer electronics was putting a high premium on
reduced price as much as improved performance.*

Citing the apparent reluctance of the U.S. commercial semiconductor
industry to adapt its output to defense needs, William Perry announced
"a new technology program intended to direct the next generation of
large-scale integrated circuits to those characteristics most significant to
defense applications." This program, he added, "will insure that the U.S.
maintains a commanding lead in semiconductor technology and that this
technology will achieve its full potential in our next generation of weapons systems."[136] The main purpose of the program, to be funded through
DARPA, was to investigate advanced computer and data-processing architecture and new approaches to computer aided design of complex-
function microcircuits. Also included, however, was research into the
materials and physical processes needed to achieve submicron geome-
tries—topics that are at the leading edge of basic research in materials
science. Perry suggested that a major DoD investment in these areas
could accelerate the development and application of VHSIC by about
five years.

The proposals generated an enthusiastic response from universities.
Soon Cornell, MIT, Stanford, and the University of California at Berkeley were "elbowing each other," in the words of the New York Times, to
get a piece of the $200 million that Congress approved for expenditure
on the VHSIC program over a period of five years.[137] However, while the
research wing of the Defense Department was eager to get on with the
work as quickly as possible, other Pentagon officials, supported by various members of the House Armed Services Committee, began to raise
concerns about the possibility that the results of the research could make
their way prematurely into the hands of military (or commercial) competitors. As a result, when the money for the VHSIC program was ap-

* In contrast to the 1950s and 1960s, civilian demand for computing had outstripped military needs, so that manufacturers were not automatically interested in new military markets. According to the Defense Science Board, only about 7 percent of the total
semiconductor market now goes for military applications, compared to 70 percent in the
late 1960s.[135]

proved, the House Armed Services Committee inserted language into its report on the authorizing legislation explicitly stating that the program was to be carried out within the ITAR framework. The implication was that government permission would be required for the export of any "technical data" developed in the course of the research, which could be interpreted to include the communication of basic research results to foreign scientists, even within the U.S.[138]

The potential impact of the ITAR regulations was severe, for, if scientific information was to be included in the category of "technical data," the rules directly challenged the tradition of open communication among scientists. A report commissioned from the Betac Corporation of Arlington, Virginia, jointly sponsored by Perry's office, DARPA, and the Office of International Security Affairs at DoE, pointed out that in the absence of strict formal restrictions, "control of the dissemination of data will require the voluntary cooperation of DARPA contractors"—in other words, universities accepting VHSIC research funding would be expected to police their scientists to make sure they complied with the rules. The Betac report also noted that "if voluntary efforts to limit dissemination are unsuccessful, stronger enforcement of existing export control regulations might have to be considered"[139]—a suggestion that led the House Government Operations Committee to comment that "researchers would be coaxed, cajoled, or bullied into withholding unclassified technical data they might generate in critical areas."[140]

Such, however, were the implications of the amendment insisted on by the House Armed Services Committee. In December 1980 the director of the VHSIC program in the Pentagon issued a memorandum to each of the three forces stating that export controls would, in line with the congressional language, be applied to the research under both ITAR, administered by the State Department, and the related Export Administration Regulations (EAR), administered by the Department of Commerce.* The principal targets were the prime contractors and their semiconductor suppliers. But given the difficulty in drawing the line between basic research and process technology—the same line that had proved difficult to establish in nuclear energy and in cryptography research—universities were not excluded from the amendment.

Thus, early in 1981, soon after the arrival of the Reagan administration in Washington, the Pentagon followed up its earlier memorandum with a second one to all universities involved in VHSIC research "suggesting" that in light of the need to comply with ITAR—as well as the uncertainty

---

* The Export Administration Act, which was revised in 1979, authorizes the imposition of export controls in the interests of national security, foreign policy, or the protection of the domestic economy from a drain on scarce materials. The act is implemented through the Export Administration Regulations, which require a license not only for technical equipment that might threaten these interests, but also for the export of "technical data"; export is taken to include transmission to a person who intends subsequently to leave the U.S.

about what precisely such compliance meant in practice—various procedures should voluntarily be adopted. Among these was the recommendation that no foreign nationals be employed as research assistants on DoD-sponsored VHSIC research, a suggestion that would have had a wide impact, since in some universities up to 50 percent of the research assistants in computer science came from abroad, filling a vacuum left by U.S. computer graduates who had departed for higher salaries in industry.[141]

Despite its delicate wording, the memorandum generated a strong reaction. The presidents of five major research universities—the four already described as "elbowing each other" for a share of the VHSIC research money, plus the California Institute of Technology, another major defense research contractor—wrote a joint letter to the Secretary of State, the Secretary of Commerce, and the Secretary of Defense. They complained vigorously about the controls the Defense Department was seeking to impose on basic, unclassified science. The letter pointed out that, although both ITAR and EAR had existed for several years, they had never previously been applied to basic science. "In broad scientific and technical areas defined in the regulations, faculty could not conduct classroom lectures when foreign students were present, engage in the exchange of information with foreign visitors, present papers or participate in discussions at symposia and conferences where foreign nationals were present, employ foreign nationals to work in their laboratories, or publish research findings in the open literature," the university presidents suggested.[142]

State Department officials, who have formal responsibility for administering ITAR, were conciliatory. James Buckley, Under Secretary of State for National Security, Science, and Technology Affairs, replied in a letter of July 3, 1981, that there had been "no change" in the Department of State's policy with respect to the application of export controls to the activities of universities.[143] Yet there were few signs of such a conciliatory attitude from the top of the Pentagon, or from the Department of Commerce, from which many of the strongest demands for stiff new controls on technology transfer had come. Indeed, even Buckley did not back away from the general thrust of the DoD memorandum, namely that academic scientists did not have any particular exemption from the requirements of the ITAR controls.

Furthermore, the Pentagon and the Commerce Department had already shown signs of wanting to extend the scope of ITAR controls over other parts of the academic domain. Even under the Carter administration, Pentagon research director George Gamota had admitted that the VHSIC controversy had been almost accidental, since computer research just happened to be the first area where the issue of applying export controls to basic scientific research had come up; it could have equally emerged in sponsorship of other areas, such as materials research.[144] The Pentagon already had its eye on other areas of research for potential restriction. By January 1980 the Critical Technology Implementation Interagency Task Group, charged by a presidential review memorandum to identify technologies that should be controlled under both ITAR and EAR, had produced a list of fifteen areas identified by the Defense Department, and ten by the Department of Energy, as "critical technologies"—each of which could be subject to the same restrictions as VHSIC research.[145] The list included computer networks, telecommunications, vehicular engines, underseas systems, and advanced seismic devices. In a later speech to the American Association for the Advancement of Science, Admiral Bobby Inman of the NSA indicated that the areas he was concerned about for national security reasons included "computer hardware and software, other electronic gear and techniques, lasers, crop projections, and manufacturing processes."[146] In some cases, even basic research in genetic engineering was considered an appropriate subject for export controls.[147]

Not only research projects are affected. The communication of scientific knowledge through public conferences, if these are attended by foreign nationals, can—as J. A. Meyer had pointed out in his letter to the IEEE Information Group—constitute an export of technical data under the terms of both ITAR and EAR. This was made clear to the officials of the American Vacuum Society when, in February 1980, they organized an international scientific conference in Santa Barbara on bubble memories—a technique for storing computer data which, ironically, was later largely abandoned by computer companies. Shortly before the meeting, the society was asked by the Central Intelligence Agency to provide a list of the topics that were going to be discussed. The conference organizers were subsequently told that under the terms of the Export Administration Act, permission from the Commerce Department was required, and that they should cancel invitations issued to scientists from the Soviet Union, Eastern Europe, and the People's Republic of China. All except the Chinese, already on their way to the conference, were contacted. When the Chinese arrived in California, the Commerce Department relented slightly, partly under pressure from the State Department, which did not want to antagonize relationships between the two countries. The organizers were told that the Chinese could be admitted provided that the conference discussed only technical data already in the public literature, or general trends in the research, and not the details of manufacturing processes. In addition, any foreign scientists were required to provide a signed guarantee that they would not pass on any of the information they learned at the conference to individuals from Eastern bloc nations.[148]

A similar incident took place some days later, this time when a Russian postgraduate student who had had a paper accepted for presentation at an international meeting on laser engineering and inertial confinement fusion was refused permission by the State Department to travel from the University of Texas, where he was studying, to present the paper.

Several Russian scientists were also refused visas to attend the meeting. Both incidents came at an embarrassing moment for the scientific community, since they coincided with a strong attack on the Soviet government's "interference" with the freedom of scientists, focusing in particular on the persecution of physicist Andrei Sakharov.[149]

Both these incidents took place under the Carter administration. When President Reagan arrived in Washington in 1981, enthusiasm increased for tightening up the application of ITAR and EAR regulations, particularly after the military crackdown in Poland at the end of 1981, when it was decided to use restrictions on access to U.S. science and technology as one form of direct reprisal against the Soviet Union. The most obvious manifestation of this was the administration's effort to block virtually all high technology sales to the USSR. But science was swept up as well, and controls were applied even more tightly.[150]

In December 1981, for example, a professor of engineering at Stanford University was informed by officials of the National Academy of Sciences that a proposed visit by Russian computer scientist Nikolai V. Umnov had been approved by the State Department only on certain conditions. Although one of the leading scientists in his field, Umnov was only to discuss the mechanical theory of robot locomotion—his area of research—and was not to be given access to control units or programming techniques for robots. No industrial visits were to be permitted. And except for documents approved for public release for unlimited distribution, Umnov was not to have any access to any other research funded by DoD, whether classified or unclassified.

Stanford vice-provost Gerald J. Liebermann wrote back to the academy saying that the university was not willing to accept responsibility for Umnov's actions, either on or off campus, during his stay. Subsequent negotiations between Stanford, the academy, and the State Department again resulted in compromise. The State Department backed away from some of its initial demands, and the conditions for Umnov's visit were relaxed slightly. Yet Stanford's letter staked a broader position on the steady encroachment of federal controls on basic research. Liebermann told the academy that the university felt that "federal export regulations should not apply to any of Stanford's activities on the grounds that our research programs represent basic and unclassified investigations, the results of which are generally available to the public through normal channels of scholarly publications, student theses, discourse among scholars, etc."[151] A press statement put out by the university explicitly linked Stanford's reaction to the earlier warning over the restrictions on VHSIC research, pointing out that "as predicted by the five universities' presidents nearly a year ago," the attempt to apply export controls to academic activities "has been spreading."[152]

Despite such protests, as well as the lack of any concrete evidence that universities were a significant source of leakage of sensitive scientific information,* many government officials continued to argue that the openness of the scientific community was seriously weakening the relative superiority of the U.S military forces and indeed was likely to become an increasingly popular Soviet target as the U.S. tightened up on the control of the export of technical hardware. The Pentagon, for example, published a brochure on Soviet military capability in 1981 that indicted official scientific exchanges, conferences, and symposia, and the entire "professional and open literature." All these, it claimed, enhanced Soviet military power by virtually giving away American science and technology. Complaints from Pentagon officials that the Soviets were stealing U.S. technological secrets frequently found a sympathetic ear and mouthpiece in conservative political circles in Congress. In a conference report on the authorization of funds to carry out the Export Administration Regulations, for example, the House Committee on Foreign Affairs said that its subcommittee on international economic policy and trade had reviewed "the means employed to circumvent U.S. export controls, such as illegal exports and re-exports, technology smuggling, industrial espionage, *exchange programs and conferences,* and foreign acquisition of U.S. high technology companies" (italics added).[154]

On April 2, 1982, President Reagan showed his sympathy with these arguments when, after several revisions, he signed Executive Order No. 12356, giving the national security agencies of the United States unprecedented authority to classify technical information as secret—including, if felt necessary, the results of basic scientific research. The executive order reversed a thirty-year trend toward declassification of scientific knowledge. On the surface, the new directive did acknowledge protests from the scientific community, with its specification that "basic scientific research information not clearly related to national security may not be classified."[155] Yet, as the American Association of University Professors pointed out, given the growing number of areas of science that could be claimed to fulfill such a requirement, combined with the discretionary powers placed in the hands of national security officials, the safeguard was very weak.† It concluded that the executive order "gives unprece-

---

* The academy's Corson Report, after examining both classified and unclassified files on the export of data, claimed the existence of a strong consensus "that universities and open scientific communication have been the source of very little of this technology transfer problem." The report added that "discussion with representatives of all U.S. intelligence agencies failed to reveal specific evidence of damage to U.S. national security caused by information obtained from U.S. academic sources."[153]

† In testimony to the House Armed Services Committee research subcommittee, NSF director Atkinson descibed how the increasingly sophisticated weapons systems being developed by DoD depend heavily on advances made possible by basic research. "The laser, high-speed integrated circuits, new materials, and the latest developments in computer science play an important role in our national defense and have all come about as a result of basic science," he said.[156] Significantly, as we have seen, each has also become the focus of controversy about the application of export controls to university research.

dented authority to government officials to intrude at will in controlling academic research that depends on federal support."[157]

But the administration was insistent. In reply to scientists who invoked the First Amendment to protect their right to communicate, the administration referred to the previous conviction of a company, Edler Industries, Inc., for exporting technical data relating to rocket and missile components.[158] In appealing its conviction, the company claimed that the First Amendment, which forbids laws that restrict freedom of speech, also guarantees the freedom to disseminate technical data. The Ninth Circuit court, however, rejected this argument on the grounds that since the technical data referred to in the export control legislation was significantly related to specific items whose export was regulated for national security reasons, the First Amendment was not a legitimate defense. During the Carter administration, the Department of Justice claimed that this decision left unresolved the broader question of the constitutionality of scientific knowledge in general, where this knowledge was not directly related to a particular technology on the munitions list.* However, the Reagan administration has subsequently used the Edler verdict to support its claim that restrictions on technical data—the basis on which controls on academic research are justified—do not infringe constitutional rights to free speech.

The Reagan administration made clear that it was going to place a rigorous interpretation on the power to control scientific information, which, it claimed, it had been given by the Export Administration and the Arms Export Control Acts. In August 1982, shortly before the opening of a meeting organized by the Society of Photo-Optical Instrumentation Engineers, the Defense Department, with the support of Defense Secretary Caspar Weinberger, informed many of the speakers due to present papers that their remarks would have to be cleared before delivery. Of the 626 unclassified papers due for presentation, 170 were eventually withdrawn, most not because they contained sensitive information, but because the Pentagon lacked the manpower to give the necessary clearance in time.

Keen to reduce tensions that such events were rapidly building in universities, leaders of the academic community soon began to negotiate a compromise with representatives of the military establishment. The National Academy of Sciences' Corson committee, supported by both several professional societies and the Pentagon, warned that excessive controls could themselves jeopardize the nation's long-term military, as

---

* Indeed, in an earlier memorandum to OSTP director Frank Press—kept under wraps until it was released into the hearing record of the House Government Operations Committee two years later—Justice officials gave their opinion that the application of ITAR controls to scientific knowledge was, in fact, unconstitutional "insofar as they establish a prior restraint on disclosure of cryptographic ideas and information developed by scientists and mathematicians in the private sector."[159]

well as economic, strength by obstructing the development of science. "To attempt to restrict access to basic research would require casting a net over wide areas of science that could be extremely damaging to overall scientific and economic advance as well as to military progress," the panel commented. The corporate high technology community agreed. All ten top research executives from major companies contacted by the Corson committee "either stated explicitly or implied that restrictions on scientific information would be deleterious to their companies' innovative and worldwide competitive posture."[160] As one panel member, the chairman of the executive committee of ITEK Corporation, later put it: "If we bind our hands and feet in basic science at universities, the nation is going to suffer, and ITEK's going to suffer."[161]

At the same time, however, the panel admitted the existence of "gray areas" where controls short of classification were warranted, and suggested a set of criteria. Indeed, it pointed out that a report produced by the Defense Science Board in 1976, under the chairmanship of Fred Bucy of Texas Instruments, had implicitly proposed that export controls be increasingly concentrated on these gray areas. Bucy had argued that to achieve maximum effectiveness, such controls should concentrate on "technological know-how" as much as finished products, since "design and manufacturing know-how are the principal elements of strategic technology control."[162] The Corson committee agreed that "it is at times as important to safeguard technical know-how in areas of rapid advance as it is to protect military systems themselves." It also suggested that research involving know-how was becoming more common in university laboratories for two reasons: first, manufacturing equipment and processes—for example, in microelectronics—were often only an extension of those developed to conduct basic research; and second, universities were being encouraged to move into areas closer to engineering design and product development than in the past.[163]

At the time, the Bucy report's recommendations, which were accepted almost verbatim by Defense Secretary Harold Brown in August 1977 and later incorporated into the revisions to the Export Administration Act, appeared essentially to be technical changes. But they soon took on a political character. Just as with the problems created by the growing links between the university-based scientific community and the corporate sector, the growing strategic importance of basic science (in particular, where it intersected with this area of "technical know-how") raised questions about how the appropriate institutional control mechanisms were to be developed, and how great an involvement was to be permitted to democratic institutions such as Congress and the courts. As the University of Wisconsin's vice-chancellor, Frank Cassell, had asked about the Commerce Department's attempts to suppress publication of the details of Davida's cipher device: "Should the executive branch of the government be able to prevent a citizen from speaking or publishing without some involvement by the courts? Should the executive branch of government be able to invoke the claims of 'national security' without demonstrating that our national security was genuinely threatened?"[164]

The goal of achieving national security is, of course, legitimate. As the Corson committee and most academics have now accepted, the important question is not *whether* national security considerations are going to be incorporated in decisions about the control of science, but *how* this should be done.[165] The difficulties of determining which actions are or are not in the national interest, and the fact that in the past such arguments were frequently made on explicitly political grounds, make it important that as much of the debate as possible be open to public scrutiny, even respecting the fact that certain types of information may have to be excluded for genuine security reasons. Most of the negotiation that has taken place, however, has involved relatively restricted access to decision-making. In the case of cryptography, the American Council for Education, which had recognized the severe problems raised by mandatory controls, agreed to set up an eight-member Public Cryptography Study Group (PCSG), largely at the prompting of Inman and the NSA. The group was directed to suggest ways of reconciling the conflicting goals of academic freedom and national security. The result was a proposal that all scientists working in the field should voluntarily submit their research papers for "comment" prior to publication to a review committee established jointly by the academic and intelligence communities.[166]

Buoyed by the apparent acceptance of his ideas by the ACE-sponsored study group, Inman launched an aggressive bid at the annual meeting of the American Association for the Advancement of Science in Washington in January 1982. He wanted to have the same process extended to other fields of research, such as computer hardware, lasers, and computer-based manufacturing processes, where, "publication of certain technical information could affect the national security in a harmful way." He suggested that, rather than a confrontation between national security and science, the two communities would be wiser to cooperate in achieving their respective goals: "A potential balance between national security and science may lie in an agreement to include in the peer review process . . . the question of potential harm to the nation." Inman concluded by telling his audience that they should move fast before the federal government was tempted to overreact, adding that "the tides are moving and they are moving pretty fast toward legislative solutions"[167]— a prediction that seemed borne out later in the year, when several bills were introduced into Congress demanding precisely such stiffer restrictions.[168]

Again the scientific community was quick to protest. William Carey of the AAAS described Inman's proposals for resolving conflicts through the peer review process as "nightmarish," since scientists did not want to be subject to "the whims of unknown people inside the walls of the military." NAS president Frank Press was more diplomatic, but still described the proposal as a "regressive step" and suggested that "the damage would be so great as not to warrant the little good it would do." And the Council of the AAAS, meeting the day after Inman's talk, passed a resolution stating that the association "opposed governmental restrictions on the dissemination, exchange, or availability of unclassified knowledge."[169]

Inman's comments, however, hit a sensitive spot. Many scientists virtually admitted that it was the *principle* of more government regulation —i.e., greater social control of their actions—rather than its specific form (or goals),that they were most concerned about. Already confronting the federal government over its attempts to regulate scientific research in other spheres, they winced when Inman asserted that "nowhere in the scientific ethos is there any requirement that restrictions cannot, or should not, when necessary, be placed on science." Society had recognized that certain kinds of scientific inquiry could be dangerous, he said, and had applied either directly, or through ethical constraints, restrictions on the research that could be done in those areas, as in the guidelines from the National Institutes of Health on recombinant DNA research. Why should national security dangers be treated differently? Indeed, Inman added, "the scientists' blanket claims of academic freedom are somewhat disingenuous in the light of the arrangements that academicians routinely make with private, corporate sources of funding."[170] Similar sentiments were later expressed by Assistant Secretary of Commerce Lawrence Brady, one of the administration's strongest supporters of tough export controls; he suggested that one weak spot was "the desire of academia to jealously preserve its prerogatives as a community of scholars unencumbered by government regulation."[171]

Donald Kennedy of Stanford was quick to respond for the liberals, claiming that to invent and then apply a new body of regulations to university research would cost more than it would gain. "If an entire technology is so critical in a military sense that it cannot be risked in an open environment, the government can classify it—thereby permitting the universities to decide, before the fact, whether they wish to accept the restrictions that come along with the work," he suggested.[172] It was a proposal that would let universities off the hook of more controls, but it would do little to prevent the research itself from being carried out—or from being carried out in secret.

Reflecting this general distrust of any form of social control on science was the fact that it was not only liberals who complained. The campaign against more federal controls received strong support from the conservative wing of the academic community as well. Robert Sproull, president of the University of Rochester—and an active campaigner for both more military research and less government regulation on university campuses—told a congressional subcommittee that as long as military secrets were not involved, scientific research should be carried out in the open.[173] The liberals even found themselves sharing an uncomfortable bed with arch-conservative Edward Teller, who had long argued that the more the Soviet Union was made aware of the strength of the U.S. military, the less likely it would be to try to challenge this power.[174]

If regulations *were* going to be introduced, however, the crucial question became who was going to decide on their content—and to oversee the way in which they were carried out. The report from the American Association of University Professors pointed out the dangers to democracy in the new powers to control scientific results granted under Reagan's Executive Order No. 12356. The report did accept the need for some form of classification system, provided that it stated which research should be treated in confidence according to national security needs that were "clear and compelling," thus enabling universities and their faculties to make "informed decisions" about their research. But it added: "Very different, and strongly objectionable, is a classification system that sweeps within it virtually anything that might conceivably be useful industrially, technically, or militarily to at least someone and that is administered by officials who feel compelled to classify as secret any information about which they have doubts."[175]

The most worrying aspect of Reagan's new order on the classification of technical knowledge is the degree of discretion it allows intelligence officials. Where they are uncertain, the executive order permits them to err on the side of caution, i.e., to impose controls even if these later prove unnecessary. The order also drops the condition that threats to national security need to be "identifiable," again making them more difficult to challenge (and giving security agencies a greater benefit of doubt in ambiguous instances). Both conditions reinforce the potential power of groups able to legitimize their actions by claiming that they are necessary to protect the nation from either external or internal threats with the minimum of public discussion.*

Even the scientific establishment's own suggestions, however, have frequently reflected a strong desire to keep control out of the sphere of full public debate. The conclusions of the ACE's Public Cryptography Study Group, for example, soon came under fire as an accommodation by members of a self-selected group (a number of professional societies

---

* The problem, as Mary Cheh, associate professor of law at the National Law Center, George Washington University, has pointed out, is a general one: "In court challenges, the government has claimed a national security justification for a wide range of actions including actions against Communists, aliens, politically motivated strikers, persons such as university professors whose loyalties were questioned, state governments involved in interstate conflicts, former CIA agents, newspapers publishing embarrassing information, and so on."[176]

had each been asked to nominate one member of the group), rather than the result of an open, democratic decision process. Davida claimed that voluntary prior restraint would have a chilling effect on cryptography research, that the NSA had a "seeming obsession with wanting to control cryptography."[177] Even the Corson committee suggested that the arrangement depended heavily on the judgments of technical experts in the agency—and that the integrity of such expertise could not be guaranteed in other circumstances.[178]

Indeed, reaction within the scientific community to the study group's proposals was far from unanimous. A scientist from the University of Rochester claimed in a letter to *Science* that the result of an NSA review of research proposals and the possible classification of research would be to reduce the amount of research carried out in the area. If the NSA wanted to exercise a policy of prior restraint, "it should either be forced to obtain a legislative mandate for such a policy or be made to test its current authority in the courts."[179] Various mathematical societies refused to endorse the study group's approach, claiming it was important to leave decisions over whether to comply with the group's procedures to individual scientists. Further criticism came from a panel assembled by the computer science advisory committee to the National Science Foundation, chaired by MIT computer scientist John Guttag. This panel also disagreed with the ACE's resolution of the issue, stipulating that prior restraint on publication was not the answer. "The study group says that this is the best deal we could have made, and that it would have been worse if we had gone to Congress for a bill. My position is that it is better to do this in public," Guttag said later.[180]

Despite such criticisms, however—as well as the reactions to Inman's proposals that the procedure be extended to all potentially sensitive fields —it was a variation on this approach that was endorsed by the National Academy of Sciences' Corson committee. On the basis that, if anyone was going to impose regulations, then the scientific community should retain maximum control over the way they were exercised, the committee recommended that in the "gray areas" in which restrictions were "undesirable yet warranted," a system similar to the voluntary prepublication review accepted by many cryptology research investigators be introduced. Scientific papers would be submitted to the contracting agency at the same time as they were submitted to scientific journals for publication. If scientists refused to accept modifications proposed by the agency, the government would have the ultimate right to classify the work, but the government would not have the power to "order" changes, and "the right and freedom to publish remain with the university."[181]

From one point of view, the Corson Report's conclusions represented an acceptable compromise between the academic community and the military authorities. Looked at from a different perspective, however, they can also be seen as a *political* bid to keep control of science in the hands of private decision-making, and thus remove it from the sphere of full public debate.* The strategy was successful in that the report's conclusions were subsequently used as the basis on which the Reagan administration attempted, under the guidance of the National Security Council and the Office of Science and Technology Policy, to develop a coherent policy for restricting militarily sensitive scientific data. Yet it is important that the report's apparently "liberal" message is not allowed to obscure the extent to which it justifed the further concentration of control over science in private hands.

The private sector shared the same concern for compromise with the security authorities as the universities, providing they were allowed where possible to maintain their own control over scientific knowledge. This was particularly true of companies involved in protecting computer data. At the working level, the relationship between such companies and the government was frequently close. NSA officials, for example, worked with IBM when the basic Data Encryption Standard was being developed in collaboration with the National Bureau of Standards, which had itself absorbed several NSA employees for the work.[183] (The links were strengthened when Lewis Branscomb, director of the National Bureau of Standards under President Ford, was appointed chief scientist of IBM in 1977.)

Given the close links established through joint research efforts, it was not difficult to find a mechanism by which the NSA and private companies were able to pursue their common interests relatively undisturbed by political constraints. In August 1981, the NSA announced that it was setting up a Security Technical Evaluation Center to encourage business to share its developments with the government. In return it guaranteed protection of proprietary rights. The center has provided an effective mechanism by which the two sides have been able to settle their differences out of the public eye—and thus reduce the amount of public criticism that some of the large computer manufacturers, such as IBM, might otherwise have made about controls on research data.[184]

Similar accommodation had been reached before. During the Second World War, when companies were prevented from seeking patents on discoveries the military wanted to keep secret, the Defense Department persuaded Congress to change the law so that a patent application could initially be made in a sealed envelope—with the patent coming into force only once the invention had been declassified and the envelope opened after the war's end. In practice the arrangement turned out to be highly profitable for the companies concerned, for it considerably extended the

---

* Indeed, the DoD-University Forum, set up by Kennedy of Stanford and co-chaired by him with DeLauer of the Pentagon, explicitly suggested setting up a committee of scientists from government, the universities, and industry which not only would determine those areas of science considered particularly sensitive, but would also review "the burden [of controls] on the vitality of research and engineering development."[182]

amount of time that a company was able to claim patent rights.[185] It was the same after the war, when companies were given rights to classified secrets that they needed to develop nuclear energy technology.

In return for such favored treatment, the private sector generally acquiesced in the general thrust of federal controls on scientific knowledge justified on national security arguments. Indeed, according to Harold Green of George Washington University Law School, the fact that American industry, which has had the largest economic stake in the exploitation of nuclear energy, has "consistently shrunk from contesting the imposition, however costly, of AEC, ERDA, and DoE information controls" is one of the main reasons that the "born classified" concept, with the threat to scientific communication that it presents, has survived for thirty-five years. "It reflects a realistic appraisal that industrial profit-oriented research might not prevail in constitutional litigation against what would be characterized as important national security considerations," Green told the AAAS meeting in January 1982.[186] Similarly, the desire of many high technology companies to profit from their participation in the VHSIC program is said to have contributed significantly to their acquiescence in the controls imposed by the government on the research carried out under this program.[187]

Since important issues of public policy are inevitably involved, many critics have demanded that discussions on appropriate controls should be channeled through democratically accountable institutions such as Congress and the courts. In the case of nuclear weapons research carried out under the auspices of the University of California—a public body, since it is a state institution—Charles Schwartz at Berkeley has argued strongly that more active overseeing is needed to meet the community's responsibilities for the research. "We need to build a constituency of people who understand that democracy dies when decisions are handed over to technical experts, or hidden beneath a veil of secrecy, or sold upon hysterical exaggerations of some external threat," contends Schwartz. "We need to work to bring the weaponeers under strict democratic control here at home before we can expect to make any serious progress in reducing the threat of nuclear arms by agreements between nations."[188]

The controversies over the *Progressive* trial and the NSA's campaign to develop a system of prior restraint on the publication of potentially sensitive research results—even if carried out voluntarily—have led others to demand that the conflicts be resolved through open democratic decision-making rather than being confined to those most closely involved. Mary Cheh suggests the need for new legislation to cover the ambiguities in the present situation, and to generate a democratic consensus on how decisions about the control of scientific information should be reached. "Given the unsatisfying conclusions of the *Progressive* litigation, it is imperative that Congress now confront the uncertainty it created when it first wrote a law with such sweeping and ambiguous information control provisions," she concludes in a major review of the legal implications of the court case.[189]

But the prospects for such legislative changes have been kept dim by the combined efforts of universities, the scientific establishment, private corporations, and intelligence and military agencies. Each has its reasons for limiting democratic participation in the application of controls to the conduct of scientific research and the transfer of scientific knowledge. None has shown any enthusiasm for subjecting such controls to what DoE Assistant Secretary Sewell referred to as the "crucible of public debate."[190] Proposals for legislative changes in the Atomic Energy Act, for example, put forward in a bill proposed by Representative Paul N. (Pete) McCloskey of California, found few sponsors in the scientific or corporate community, and soon became lost in the congressional agenda.[191]

Without open, democratic debate, however, the danger is that conflicts will be resolved with minimal consideration of broader public responsibilities—or of social goals that may not coincide with those of the main actors. The organization and conduct of research will again become essentially a technical operation, with consideration of ultimate ends dominated by discussion of means. The result is that scientists will continue to work on basic research for DoD while isolating themselves from debates about how their work is used, and that corporations, similarly, will remain happy as long as military technology contributes to their profits—and underwrites quantum leaps in new technology, such as the VHSIC program or fifth-generation computers. The military will remain free to contract the services of both, and to draw them into its escalating race of death.

Without full democratic participation, the debate over controls on military research is therefore likely to remain locked onto technical solutions to military challenges, and to deflect forces for genuine change. When Wiesner, as provost of MIT, turned down an invitation to endorse a one-day strike by the university faculty in 1969 to protest against the Vietnam War, he told the organizers: "I believe that a continuing study of the problems of the arms race, the needs of developing countries, and the problems at home would yield more results."[192] David Saxon, president of the University of California, told demonstrators that, rather than protesting against the MX missile or the university's responsibility for the weapons research of the two laboratories it manages for the government, they should consider the advantages and disadvantages of "a renewed effort by the United Nations to foster international cultural and intellectual exchanges."[193] Yet it was precisely the democratic opposition to continued U.S. involvement in Vietnam as much as the advice of scientists that helped persuade politicians of the need to withdraw. Similarly, campus demonstrations have played a significant part in raising national consciousness about the need for new controls on nuclear weapons. After nearly thirty years of the "technical fix" approach to arms control advocated by Wiesner and his colleagues, the world seems no farther from the dangers of a nuclear holocaust than when they started. It is now generally recognized that there are no technical solutions to the problems of arms control and limitation, only political ones.

After a period of relative quiet, voices of protest are beginning to be heard once more as opposition grows to the military control and uses of science. At the beginning of 1983, for example, the governing council of the American Physical Society passed a resolution condemning nuclear weapons, and suggesting various ways in which the government might act to reduce the threat of atomic holocaust. The move was strongly attacked by President Reagan's science adviser, George Keyworth, who argued that the society's action in mixing science and politics was "arrogant" and "extreme."[194] However a few months later, the physicists' act was implicitly endorsed by Pope John Paul II, who, in an address to the Pontifical Academy of Sciences in Rome, called on scientists to "desert the laboratories and factories of death"; he added that it was "the indubitable task of the scientific community to monitor scientific discoveries and see that they are not put to the service of war, tyranny, and terror."[195]

As we have already seen, it is not just the military which is opposed to direct forms of social intervention; equally strong resistance has come from universities and private corporations, the three groups forming a powerful coalition to protect military-related research from direct social controls. A clear example arose in the fall of 1983, when this coalition successfully defeated an attempt by citizens of Cambridge, Massachusetts to pass a local law forbidding work of any type—including research —on nuclear weapons within the city limits. Strong opposition came, predictably, from the Charles Stark Draper Laboratory, a contract research laboratory working primarily on inertial guidance systems for the Department of Defense which was separated from the Massachusetts Institute of Technology in 1972. But the move was also opposed by MIT itself, as well as Harvard University, on the grounds that a law banning nuclear research could set a "dangerous precedent" in giving local citizens the right to decide what type of research they were prepared to allow conducted in the city.[196] Resistance also came from local high-technology industries, many of which depend heavily on military contracts, others fearing more generally that the proposed law would make it more difficult to attract other similar companies to the area. The three groups mounted a vigorous television and press advertising campaign, run by a West Coast public relations expert and reportedly costing more than 20 times more than the efforts of supporters of what was to have been the Nuclear Free Cambridge Act. The success of the campaign, which resulted in the proposed law being rejected by 60 percent of local voters in contrast to 40 percent who voted in favor of it, was therefore as much a test of political muscle as of democratic will (earlier in the year, a non-binding referendum declaring Cambridge a nuclear free zone was passed by 74 percent of the vote).[197]

Of course "more research is needed," as Wiesner would argue, on arms control; of course the potential influence of international agencies should be reinforced to help maintain world peace. But as politicians know well, both slogans can be conveniently used to mask inaction. Bringing the arms race under control means fusing means and goals—making the individuals who contribute to it from the bottom realize the full significance of their combined efforts when seen from the top. And this applies to military research as much as, if not more than, any other area. In an environment where the actors are not neutral, and where they are frequently tempted to enter into pacts that mutually reinforce their respective political powers, trust is not enough. When a judge hearing the government's case against publication of the Pentagon Papers asked for details of the worst thing that could happen if the papers were published, the Defense Department sent over, under top security, a memorandum stating that if the Vietnamese knew certain codes had been broken, it would create a vast new array of problems. The case collapsed when a reporter present pointed out that the same information had already been widely publicized by DoD to demonstrate its success in breaking the code.[198] When Leo Szilard circulated a petition among fellow physicists during the Second World War pleading that the atom bomb not be dropped on civilian targets, he was restrained by Robert Oppenheimer on the grounds that military "experts" had informed him that the choice of such targets was essential. Only later did it emerge that the most "essential" reason was President Truman's desire to use the demonstrated effectiveness of the bomb as a bargaining chip with the Russians.[199] Such instances demonstrate the dangers of relying on technical experts and "national security" arguments, insulated from public scrutiny accompanied by the appropriate forms of democratic control.

4

SCIENCE AND FOREIGN POLICY: KNOWLEDGE AS IMPERIALISM

IN THE PREVIOUS CHAPTER WE SAW HOW THE INCREASING DIRECTNESS OF the contributions made by basic science to modern military technology has stimulated a growing desire by military authorities to place controls on the open communication of scientific knowledge. We also saw how, although in principle opposed to greater controls on science, both the academic and the corporate high technology communities have shown a willingness to accept them in a limited form; and that the compromise, established through negotiations between these two communities and those in the military establishment sympathetic to their arguments, was proposed in order to provide all three with protection against constraints they considered excessive, arbitrary, or unnecessary. So far we have concentrated on the way this compromise, although limiting the impact of constraints on the flow of scientific information, has at the same time reinforced a broader shift in control over access to science away from openly democratic institutions, helping to concentrate control in the hands of corporate or military decision-makers, subject to a minimal degree of social accountability. There is another perspective, however, from which we can view the increasing imposition of export controls on science. This is to look at the way they provide a significant extension of the use of science as a powerful instrument of foreign policy.

The principal target of recent controls placed on science to achieve foreign policy objectives has, of course, been the Soviet Union. Both the Carter and Reagan administrations, through actions ranging from the cancellation of bilateral scientific exchange agreements to the refusal to admit Soviet scientists to conferences in the U.S. or the imposition of strict constraints on those visiting U.S. laboratories, have provided numerous examples of the way science has been used as a channel for political leverage. If access to American science was dangled enticingly as a carrot for good behavior during the period of détente in the early 1970s, its withdrawal is now being brandished as a stick in the disenchantment that has followed.[1] The targets have been multiple, from the military crackdown in Poland to the treatment of Soviet physicist Andrei Sakharov. And in most cases the actions provoked as a response have been little more than gestures with limited impact. But this is far from the only domain in which control over access to U.S. science is being used increasingly for political ends.

In the case of the U.S.'s relations with other industrialized countries, for example, cooperation on scientific projects has long been used as a mechanism for building diplomatic bridges and helping to meet joint political goals. (The most explicit example of this has been the scientific activities organized within the framework of the North Atlantic Treaty Organization [NATO]). Emphasizing this point, the need for greater scientific collaboration was placed firmly on the agenda of the most recent economic summit meetings of the heads of the seven advanced industrialized nations, held in Versailles in 1982 and in Williamsburg, Virginia, in 1983.* The seven nations shared a common interest in cutting the costs of large research facilities; but the endorsement by the heads of state made it clear that the proposal for closer cooperation in science was also considered an integral part of harmonizing medium-term policies in both the economic and the political spheres. In the case of the less-developed countries, pragmatic arguments in favor of "scientific exchanges" are frequently even more transparent, given the vast gulf in scientific expertise between these countries and the U.S. Even the National Science Board, the policy council of the National Science Foundation, admitted in a statement issued in September 1982 that international scientific cooperation with such countries offered "eco-

---

* The countries attending were Canada, France, Italy, Japan, the United Kingdom, the United States, and West Germany; the meetings also included a representative of the European Economic Community. First suggested for discussion by French President François Mitterrand at Versailles in 1982, the commitment to closer collaboration in science was repeated at the 1983 meeting in Williamsburg, in the form of an endorsement of a working group that had identified eighteen areas in which such cooperation seemed both desirable and practical. It was subsequently cited in a self-congratulatory fashion by President Reagan in his covering letter to his administration's annual report to Congress on the role of science in international relations, required under Title V of the Foreign Relations Authorization Act of 1978.[2]

nomic, diplomatic, and other policy benefits going beyond the immediate needs of science per se."[3]

The new prominence of science in international relations is a direct reflection of the growing importance of science-based technology, ranging from microelectronics to biotechnology, not only domestically in the U.S. but also in the global economy. Modern technology has had several major implications for the structure of global trade. It has provided the transportation and communication infrastructures that have increased the interdependence of national economies. It has also made possible the rapid growth of multinational corporations, primarily (though increasingly less so) dominated by U.S. capital, by allowing the global decentralization of production under the control of a single organization. And it has placed technological innovation at the heart of economic decision-making of both developed and less-developed nations. The overall result has been to integrate the world increasingly into a single economic system, and to institute a single international division of labor.

The more the technological products and production processes that make this possible have come to depend on the fruits of basic science, the higher debates about the distribution and control of science have risen on the international agenda. Previously it was possible to identify three separate fields in which science intersected with foreign policy: the need to support science as an inherently international activity (for example, through arranging scientific exchanges with other countries), the need to provide a scientific or technical perspective on particular foreign policy topics (such as arms control or nuclear proliferation), and the need to address scientific problems that are global in nature (such as the buildup of carbon dioxide in the atmosphere).[4] Now the role of science in economic affairs has added a fourth dimension; and while the first three might be considered peripheral to the main thrusts of U.S. foreign policy, this fourth is central to its main concern, namely securing a global environment conducive to the steady expansion of the U.S. economy. "We have come to a transition," Lucy Wilson Benson, Under Secretary of State for Security Assistance, Science, and Technology under President Carter, told a congressional committee in 1978. "We are leaving an era in which science and technology were thought of as independent activities, throwing an occasional Roman candle into the foreign policy arena. We have entered an era in which the interactions between science and technology and foreign affairs are recognized increasingly as continuous and central to many of the important foreign policy problems with which we are dealing."[5]

In the process, however, science has also taken on a new political significance in international relations. A relative decline in the more overt forms of military and economic power of major industrial nations has led them increasingly to use their hegemony in science and technology to fight for positions of dominance in the international system. In a world where scientific knowledge has become what a report from the Organization for Economic Cooperation and Development describes as "intellectual capital,"[6] control of this knowledge, like the ownership of capital in its more conventional form, becomes the key to both economic and political power. Thomas Pickering, Assistant Secretary of State responsible for international scientific affairs under the Carter administration, has pointed out the political opportunities offered by the fact that the world wants access to U.S. science and technology: "The terms and conditions of that access can have a major impact on our political standing with affected countries."[7] Even more directly, Henry Nau, senior staff member for international economic affairs on President Reagan's National Security Council, has argued that increased global interdependence makes it possible for advanced countries to use the advantages of their superior scientific and technical expertise to impose "a more subtle and total form of imperialism than was possible in any previous period of history."[8]

At one level, the value of science to American capitalism in international trade remains primarily commercial, and can be measured in terms of the direct contribution it makes to company profits. Part of the recent rediscovery by multinational corporations that basic science is the key to competitive success in the global marketplace is the expectation that research should pay dividends from worldwide operations. Even more than virtually all other industrialized nations, the U.S. depends on high technology products as a substantial part of its most valuable exports. Between 1969 and 1979, for example, the U.S. trade surplus in R&D-intensive goods rose from $10.5 billion to $39.3 billion; during the same period its deficit in non-R&D-intensive goods went from $6.7 billion to $34.8 billion. A large proportion of the increase was due to sales of R&D-intensive goods to Third World countries—exports that rose from $4.5 to $23.3 billion over the same period. Fees and royalties paid by other industrialized nations for the use of American know-how increased over 350 percent (about 80 percent in real terms) between 1968 and 1978.[9] Overall, the economist Edwin Mansfield has calculated that more than 30 percent of an average multinational company's returns on R&D comes from foreign sales.[10]

The significance of the transfers of knowledge that take place through such transactions, however, is much broader than their commercial value. Included in the broad category of "R&D-intensive goods" is equipment that can be used to produce new goods that can subsequently compete with American products for the same markets. Such exports therefore carry a strategic significance, since they embody the capacity to compete, which, in the modern world, is itself a source of political power; those who own such technology are in a stronger position both economically and politically than those who do not. Evidence of this is underlined by the contrast between the enthusiasm that multinationals display in exporting new products, compared with their reluctance to export new production processes. One survey of twenty-three major companies by Mansfield showed that when new technology was developed as a product, in 72 percent of cases it was transferred abroad through a foreign subsidiary, 24 percent by unaffiliated licensing, and only 4 percent by direct exports. In contrast, when the technology took the form of a new process, foreign subsidiaries were used in only 17 percent of the cases; unaffiliated licensing was never used. In the remaining 83 percent of cases the innovation was transferred through the export of resulting products, i.e., with the process itself remaining protected at home.[11]

This has direct implications for our arguments about the control of science. As we have seen in earlier chapters, it is precisely in its contribution to new process technologies that basic science has taken on its new economic significance. Advanced processing techniques require an increasingly sophisticated knowledge of the nature and behavior of basic materials and substances, often the same information that scientists, for ostensibly different reasons, are pursuing in the basic research laboratory and may need to build into their own laboratory production equipment. Conversely, the desire to restrict the dissemination of new processing technologies is particularly strong in science-based industries such as electronic machinery and chemicals, where companies need access to the latest innovations in the use of computers, semiconductors, integrated circuits, and advanced techniques in chemical production.[12] Indeed, the Organization for Economic Cooperation and Development has recently agreed to define a particular subset of high technology products as a "technological control" category—i.e., products providing technological control—and it characterizes these as embracing "*activities linked to research and development,* computers, telecommunications, machine tools" (italics added).[13]

Furthermore, it is precisely because of the key nature of these "control technologies" that the science on which they frequently depend has increasingly become a target for export controls. Shifting the emphasis of such controls from technological products to design and manufacturing know-how was, as we have already seen, the main recommendation of the 1976 report produced by a subcommittee of the Defense Science Board chaired by Fred Bucy, president of Texas Instruments, and subsequently included by Congress in the revisions to the Export Administration Act made in 1979.[14] The explicit intention of the change was to make controls on access to technology with potential military uses more efficient and more effective. But the change had several clear commercial advantages for high technology corporations. It left them relatively free to offer their products for sale on the world market, and it also legitimated arguments that they be permitted to tighten their control over the dissemination of process technologies, and thus by implication over the scientific results on which their development depended.

Take, for example, advanced university research into semiconductors and microelectronics. Even though much of this can be counted as basic research—and has indeed been supported by the Department of Defense —as much effort has been put into protecting the results of the research from flowing prematurely to commercial competitors as into keeping the results from countries that might be a military threat. It has been the same situation with biotechnology. The key nature of scientific developments in the field—many of which have taken place in U.S. universities, and have been financed by public funds—has made access to science highly desirable. In both cases, as we have seen, control over the results of scientific research tends to be concentrated increasingly in the hands of private decision-makers. And access to these results is determined by what meets these private interests.[15]

The power provided by this control over access to strategically important areas of basic science has been used in different ways. In the case of the Soviet Union, leverage over the country's internal policies—for example, its treatment of dissidents—has been attempted by directly cutting off the flow of scientific information in such critical areas. With industrial allies, the goals have been more complex. The current enthusiasm for high technology, and the basic science that supports it, is part of a global restructuring being undertaken to escape the economic recession of the late 1970s and early 1980s. On the one hand, each country is attempting to maximize its own strength in key areas of advanced technology, determined to stake as large and as influential a claim as possible to the new international division of labor that this process of restructuring is bringing about. On the other, the countries share a collective interest in regulating—or "rationalizing"—overall competition to make sure that no one nation is able excessively to exploit its advantages in a way that makes the system as a whole vulnerable either to internal collapse or to external threat. Furthermore, individual countries may be tempted to use their scientific strengths to impose economic or political goals that may not be shared by others.

It must be remembered that, despite much recent hand-wringing,[16] the U.S. is still the most powerful producer of science in the world. And it has already shown how this position can be used, deliberately or unconsciously, to weaken the effectiveness of the scientific efforts of other nations, even those considered its political allies. One way has been through gaining cheap access to scientific expertise, for example in biotechnology, where U.S. companies have drained off much of Europe's best scientific talent,[17] or in computer software.* Another is by offering

---

* One international merchant banker describes how, as part of what he describes as the "massive and highly profitable U.S. penetration of Europe," companies such as IBM, Hewlett-Packard, and Digital Equipment Corporation have quickly realized that "very effective European software talent can be harnessed for projects such as development of systems products with worldwide applicability at a cost far below that of their counterparts in the United States." The result, he suggests, is that "U.S. companies are having their cake and eating it too, as far as Europe is concerned."[18]

a more favorable climate for venture capital investments; many European venture capital companies set up to invest in new, high technology companies have placed most of their funds in the U.S.[19] A third way this hegemony is exercised is through the power it gives the U.S. to withdraw from international scientific agreements without fear of diplomatic reprisals, as was the case when the National Aeronautics and Space Administration backed out of a joint mission to the sun planned in cooperation with European space scientists.[20] Finally, it allows the U.S. to exact political favors in return for access to the fruits of American science; early in 1983, for example, the Department of Commerce agreed to let an American company ship microchip fabrication equipment to an Austrian company only after Austria had reluctantly signed an agreement to tighten the flow to the Soviet Union of high technology exports originating in the U.S.[21] Similar arrangements were said to have already been made with Sweden, Finland, India, and Hong Kong.

Each of these is an example of ways in which U.S. hegemony in important areas of science has—whether intentionally or not—undermined the ability of other developed nations to compete on equal terms, either by draining key scientific or financial resources, or by limiting the opportunity for independent maneuver.[22] Perhaps the heaviest impact, however, has been on the less-developed countries (LDCs) of the Third World. These countries are faced with a dilemma. They provide some of the largest markets for the products of the new technologies, either in microelectronics (such as those applied to mass education or long-distance communication), or for health and agricultural products developed by the latest techniques in biotechnology (such as vaccines or new food crops). At the same time they are even more vulnerable than the industrialized nations to the social distortions that can result from the fact that control of the science underlying these technologies lies increasingly in the private rather than the public domain, and that the applications of this science are therefore primarily determined by private profit rather than social need.

The foreign companies chasing such markets in the less-developed countries have two principal goals: the first is to maximize their profit; the second is to minimize competition. Many Third World countries complain that the combination of these two factors has several undesirable implications. One is that the technology sold to them is inappropriately matched to local needs and resources; another is that it can be excessively priced since, in the absence of effective competition (or with the allure of well-known brand names) markup rates are often high. A third complaint is that it makes them excessively dependent on foreign supply sources, and that this dependence can sap local initiative and undermine efforts to pursue indigenous patterns of development that may be better suited to local conditions.

Their dependence is reflected in R&D statistics. These show that virtually all the world's research and development is carried out in the industrialized nations; the less-developed countries of Africa, Asia, and Latin America between them spend less than one-twentieth of the global R&D budget, even though they contain three-quarters of its population. To put it another way, the U.S. currently devotes over $200 a year on research for each of its inhabitants, whereas in most Latin American countries the equivalent figure is less than $5, and in many of the poorer countries of Africa and Asia it is less than $1. Colin Norman has calculated that whereas the U.S. spends $175 a year on agricultural research for each of its farmers, for the world as a whole that figure is 30 cents.[23]

Statistics alone tell only part of the story. When one begins to ask more detailed questions, an even more skewed picture emerges. Many scientists in the Third World work for international corporations on projects selected by foreign executives and intended primarily to benefit stockholders in the industrialized nations. Some work in the luxury goods sectors in which many high technology products fall, unrelated to the most pressing social needs and priorities of the countries to which they belong. Others work in fields of pure science, where the agenda is set by the scientific communities of the industrialized nations, with no significant links to local productive actvties. The overall amount of research in LDCs directed toward solving their own problems has been calculated to be as low as 1 percent of the global R&D budget, with the rest aimed at improving the quality or quantity of exports or adapting foreign products to local markets.[24]

This imbalance even within the research carried out in LDCs raises crucial questions about who controls the overall research effort in these countries, what the implications of this pattern of control are for the forms of knowledge that emerge, and the extent to which new technology incorporating this knowledge meets the real needs of the communities into which it is introduced. For the forms of social control that operate through science are not merely the results of external dependency. Many of the newly industrialized countries have been at the forefront of those demanding increased domestic control over science and technology. Yet in practice the thrust of this strategy, as seen from a domestic perspective, is often identical to that already described as taking place in the U.S. The private sector, evoking the claims of economic efficiency and the logic of market demand, uses its control of science and technology to reinforce its own domestic political power.

The less-developed countries need access to modern science in order to develop both socially and economically. To do this effectively, however, requires the indigenous ability to *control* this science, and thus to determine its content, in order to be able to generate the ability to respond to domestically defined needs. Increasingly, however, the results of scientific research required by such countries are also being acknowledged as valuable private assets by the world's multinational corporations and are being concentrated in the public and private laboratories of the industrialized nations. According to one estimate, only 1 percent of the R&D sponsored by multinational companies is carried out in the LDCs.[25] The multinationals are prepared to let the LDCs have their access to their research results—but at a double price. On the one hand, the science embedded in new technological products becomes a commodity bought and sold according to the conventional rules of the marketplace, often at a price the LDCs cannot easily afford. On the other, the acceptance of science in commodity (i.e., private property) form implies the acceptance of the social relations that create and are expressed through this form. These social relations are frequently in direct conflict both with the institutional arrangements needed to ensure that scientists work on the areas of greatest indigenous importance and with efforts to apply that science to the most pressing areas of social need.

The general picture that emerges from this overview of the use of science in foreign policy is that the increasing concentration of control over science in the hands of the corporate community and its isolation from democratic decision-making, described domestically in earlier chapters, is reproduced at the international level. Indeed, in many ways it is merely a component part of this broader international movement. The U.S. is seeking to preserve its position at the top of a hierarchical system in which each country's position is increasingly determined by the size of its handle on the new "control technologies" and on the science that promotes them. George Keyworth, President Reagan's science adviser, describes U.S. leadership in science and technology as an "economic imperative" and speaks of the need, as the newly industrialized countries move toward taking a bigger share of manufactured goods, that "we, along with the other advanced nations, will increasingly have to shift to ever higher technologies and services."[26]

Yet this hierarchical structure to the world economy, which both encourages and is in turn sustained by the centralized control of access to scientific knowledge,[27] has important political implications that directly mirror the anti-democratic tendencies we have already outlined on the domestic front. Restricting the access of those lower down on the hierarchy to modern science only reinforces their lack of political power, increasing their vulnerability to the pressures and demands placed on them from above. In some cases, countries relatively near the top may be able to resist such pressures; in one recent new initiative, for example, several countries in Western Europe have agreed to pool their resources in advanced computer research in an attempt to avoid eventual domination by the U.S. or Japan.* Those at the base of the pyramid are in a

---

* The European program, known as ESPRIT (European Strategic Research Program on Information Technology), was originated in 1983 with an initial target budget of $1.3 billion over a five-year period.[28]

much weaker position. The increasing control over science being exercised by the countries that form the core of the global economy—and by the private institutions that exercise such control within these core countries through their privileged access to science—merely accentuates the powerlessness of those on the periphery, condemning them even more forcefully to a life of deprivation, while at the same time reducing their ability to explore alternative development strategies that may be more appropriate to their real needs and resources.

The use of science in helping to achieve foreign policy objectives has evolved steadily in the period since the Second World War. It was stimulated initially by America's successful development (and subsequent use) of atomic weapons; indeed, in many ways, as we have seen in the previous chapter, the controls developed at the time for nuclear science have since provided a paradigm for broader efforts to use science and technology as a diplomatic lever in the contemporary world. In a stroke, the atom bomb moved science and technology to the center of the world's diplomatic stage, both as a foundation for military power and as a tool for diplomatic influence. The U.S.'s clear leadership over all other nations in the fields of nuclear science and technology gave it new sources of leverage, an opportunity that it was quick to exploit.

The influence, however, could be effective only if the U.S. itself retained control of nuclear technology and the science on which it was based, and this goal was not shared by all. In the years after the war, some members of the scientific community tried to place firm reins on the genie they had let out of the bottle.[29] The atom bomb had made them painfully aware of the destructive potential of a science that had, since the Scientific Revolution, been almost uniquely associated with material progress. They lobbied hard for the creation of a body which would place the future development of nuclear energy for both civilian and military purposes under international control. A group chaired by David Lilienthal, chairman of the Tennessee Valley Authority, and including prominent scientists such as Vannevar Bush and J. Robert Oppenheimer, proposed the plan in a report prepared for Assistant Secretary of State Dean Acheson, based on consideration of the basic technological factors affecting the development of an international control system for all aspects of atomic energy.[30]

Negotiations with the international community, however, were entrusted to a delegation headed by the Wall Street financier Bernard Baruch and three other leading members of the banking establishment. Firmly instructed by Congress not to compromise America's military power by divulging too many atomic secrets, Baruch presented his own watered-down version of the plan to the United Nations Atomic Energy Commission, on terms that rapidly proved unacceptable to the Soviet Union. After four years of negotiations, the proposals failed to gather the necessary support within the United Nations and the initiative collapsed, helping to open the door to the proliferation of nuclear weapons and the escalating arms race that has since occurred between the two major nuclear powers.

High on the list of reasons for the collapse of the negotiations was Soviet distrust of U.S. motives (admittedly complemented by U.S. distrust of Soviet motives). The U.S. repeatedly asserted its intention to relinquish atomic weapons, yet it never reached the point of defining the conditions and timing of what it would consider to be acceptable controls on its own nuclear technology. This reluctance only emphasized suspicion that the Americans wanted to retain essential control of nuclear technology while giving the appearance of vesting this control in an international body.[31] Furthermore, reflecting broader political feelings in Washington, the American delegation was unwilling to negotiate on issues, such as the limitation of national sovereignty, that were clearly unacceptable to the Soviet Union. Again the implication was that international control of nuclear science and technology, which meant voluntarily relinquishing U.S. hegemony in this field, was unacceptable to Congress—and to Wall Street.

A second initiative was more productive, at least from the U.S. point of view. This was the government-backed campaign known as Atoms for Peace, aimed at promoting the worldwide sale of nuclear energy for civilian purposes. First outlined in a speech by President Eisenhower before the United Nations General Assembly on December 8, 1953, and followed up with a United Nations conference two years later, Atoms for Peace had the explicit goal of averting the military buildup of nuclear weapons by diverting nuclear materials to peaceful purposes. It was also designed as a propaganda response to Soviet proposals for a worldwide ban on all atomic weapons and efforts to take the lead in developing the civilian uses of atomic energy.

The initiative helped establish patterns for the international control of atomic energy, most significantly through the creation in 1956 of the International Atomic Energy Agency (IAEA), and the Non-Proliferation Treaty of 1968, which established a system of international safeguards over nuclear fuels and materials. Yet in practice the effectiveness of the control system was once again undermined by U.S. reluctance to cede either military or commercial control over its own nuclear technology. IAEA itself was limited in its effectiveness by a dual responsibility for both the promotion and the regulation of nuclear power. The safeguard system was also limited by U.S. reservations, with the result that direct encouragement was given to the transfer of nuclear technology before reliable international safeguards had been established—a basic flaw that still exists in the IAEA system.[32]

The desire to promote civilian applications of nuclear energy was also tempered by caution about encouraging the U.S.'s commercial competitors. Both the Nuclear Energy Agency (NEA) and EURATOM were established to foster commercial interest in Europe in U.S. nuclear technology. However, concern that the United Kingdom, which already had a strong government-backed program in nuclear research and development, could capture most of the world's nuclear energy market meant that U.S. support for NEA was initially lukewarm. EURATOM's role was confined to safeguards and promotion; again one of the aims of the agency was to provide a means by which the U.S. could control and keep a watch on potential competitors. As noted earlier, it has even been suggested that U.S. unwillingness to share basic scientific knowledge about nuclear reactions was a major contributing factor to the fire that occurred in a graphite pile at the British nuclear facility at Windscale in 1957.[33]

From the U.S. point of view, the Atoms for Peace initiative was successful. It created an institutional framework within which the U.S. was able to reap a maximum economic and political advantage from its position of world leaderhip in nuclear science and technology, by establishing the conditions under which the U.S. could profit from the foreign sales of nuclear technology, while essentially retaining control of that technology in economic, political, and military terms. Atoms for Peace also laid the basis for subsequent efforts by U.S. diplomats to contribute to the domestic development of nuclear power by opening up markets for the infant U.S. nuclear industry, while providing opportunities for the industry to demonstrate nuclear power abroad before introducing it at home. (As Warren Donnelly, of the Congressional Research Service, has pointed out: "Underlying the publicized, idealistic purposes of sharing U.S. nuclear science and technology were pragmatic, practical considerations of advantages to the United States."[34])

In the initial postwar decades there was little motivation to use other areas of science in the same way. Science was recognized as a valuable mechanism for encouraging greater cultural cooperation between nations and for greasing the wheels for political, economic, and military cooperation—but not necessarily seen as an integral part of such cooperation. This, for example, was the basic message of a report produced for the Department of State in 1950 by Lloyd V. Berkner.[35] Strongly reflecting the then-dominant Cold War ideology, the report emphasized the importance of science and the interchange of scientific information as an effective tool of counterpropaganda. It laid down the guidelines that for more than a decade prescribed the department's philosophical approach to science and technology; it also suggested the creation within the State Department of a new post of science adviser and special assistant to the Secretay of State. The main emphasis was on science as an international, cultural activity. Apart from an almost ritual endorsement of international scientific activities, science took a low place on the diplomatic agenda for most of the 1950s. For example, the Office of the

Science Adviser in the Department of State, established in 1951, became moribund four years later, while the number of overseas science attachés administered by the office fell from a peak of eleven in 1952 to zero at the end of 1955.[36]

Not that there was a lack of enthusiasm on the part of the scientific community. Scientists were keen to place themselves at the disposition of the state and to help meet its foreign policy objectives, often as expressed through foreign aid programs. James R. Killian, President Eisenhower's science adviser, proposed a strengthened science program in the State Department in an article in *Science* in January 1961.[37] President Kennedy's Science Advisory Committee suggested in a report to Secretary of State Dean Rusk that the post of science adviser in the department be raised in status, a proposal that was translated in the summer of 1962 into the decision to establish an Office of International Scientific Affairs. Efforts to boost the research activities of the Agency for International Development, initially resisted by many of the agency's staff, were supported in particular by AID's second administrator, David Bell. (Recruited by Kennedy from the faculty of Harvard University, Bell later became executive vice-president of the Ford Foundation and a key figure behind the ill-fated plans to establish an Institute for Scientific and Technical Cooperation under President Carter.[38])

Apart from the Kennedy staff in the White House, however, such proposals received little support in political circles. The post of science adviser in the State Department continued to languish in relative obscurity and financial poverty for most of the 1960s. The same was true of the proposals for an enlarged research office within AID. The President's Science Advisory Committee suggested a research budget of $100 million a year, but Congress—like many senior aid administrators—was skeptical of the whole venture; it placed an initial ceiling of $6 million on the project. After a slight expansion, the initiative fizzled, and the research office was eventually absorbed into the agency's "war on hunger" program in 1968. Even a report from the National Academy of Sciences published in 1965, which advocated greater attention to the role of science and technology in development, did not prove any more successful in attracting and keeping the attention of policy-makers.[39]

The lack of direct political interest in science at anything significantly more than a propaganda level was reflected in the first United Nations Conference on Science and Technology for the Benefit of Less-Developed Areas, held in Geneva in 1963. The conference itself provided an opportunity for the scientists of the developed nations to draw up an agenda of what they considered to be the major scientific and technical needs of the Third World. The report of the conference, ambitiously entitled *World of Opportunities*, is full of flamboyant promises about how science and technology will "bridge the gap between the haves and the have-nots" and quell the "revolution of rising expectations."[40] Two thousand papers were presented to the conference, most of them arguing that the solution to world development lay in the massive transfer of science and technology from the industrialized North to the underdeveloped South. In practice, however, the conference achieved little, and its general impact on political thinking was low. The fruits of the science-technology cornucopia failed to trickle down as predicted in the years that followed, and the general historical verdict on the conference was that it had virtually no political or scientific consequences.[41]

In the late 1960s and early 1970s, however, a new factor arrived on the scene that was to transform the whole debate. This was the rise to economic power and political influence of giant multinational corporations such as Exxon in oil, IBM in computers, General Motors in automobiles, General Electric in electrical goods, and Goodyear in rubber and tires. Technological developments, particularly in communications and transportation, created the conditions under which capital could break the geographical constraints binding production to its financial or management base. Multinationals were able to exploit their new ability to move capital, materials, credit, managerial expertise, and even trained labor from one country to another according to a strategy designed solely to maximize overall profitability. Two important components that could also now be moved around freely were technical skills and intellectual property—in other words, scientific knowledge in its material and commodity forms. Both became central elements in the creation of the new international division of labor by which U.S. capital was able to organize its productive operations on a global basis while maintaining centralized control.

The expansion of U.S. capital through the actions of multinational companies soon met with strong opposition. In Europe governments rapidly began pumping more money into their research and development budgets in order to meet what French politician Jean-Jacques Servan-Schreiber labeled "the American challenge."[42] Reaction was even stronger among the LDCs. Many of the latter had only just emerged from the shadows of colonialism. Yet they began to feel that the economic dependence imposed by the actions of the multinational corporations was not significantly different from the political dependence to which they had previously been subject. Multinational companies were identified by the newly independent nations of Africa, Asia, and Latin America as the principal mechanisms through which new forms of dependency were being created.

The control by these companies of the main channels of technology transfer was soon recognized as particularly crucial. Operating largely outside the control of individual sovereign states, multinational corporations were able to make decisions about the transfer of technology and science independent of local decision-making processes—and often in defiance of them. Buoyed by the apparent success of the oil-producing nations in achieving a significant increase in the price of oil sold to the industrialized nations by organizing themselves into a cartel, the LDCs began to flex their own political muscles. Calls for international controls on technology transfer soon became a staple component of the strategy through which they sought to expand their emancipation from economic domination by the industrialized nations.

The broad strategy was described as the desire to create a new international economic order, whose goals were to improve the terms of trade between developed and less-developed nations, as well as access to the developed nations' capital and technology. Countries belonging to the so-called Group of 77 quickly characterized scientific and technological dominance as an expression of the new form of economic imperialism. The potential effectiveness of this strategy, given the degree to which the countries that supported it also offered a lucrative new outlet for sales of Western technology, was not lost on the multinational corporations. "The Group of 77 is probably more unitedly organized today in an assault on the citadels of technology than on any other single effort," warned Elliot Richardson, a past Secretary of Commerce and a leading spokesman for the liberal wing of American international capital, at a meeting organized by the American Association for the Advancement of Science in 1979.[43]

Richardson's warning reflected a deep-seated concern in the corporate community. Many senior executives had been shaken by the successful negotiating strategy of the Organization of Petroleum Exporting Countries (OPEC). Multinational corporations soon recognized the need for a political response to this challenge to their hegemony over the international system. On the one hand, it meant strengthening the links between the industrialized countries themselves and limiting the possible damage caused by intra-capitalist competition. On the other, it meant providing a common bargaining front to the Third World, one that would secure access to new markets without accepting the terms such countries were demanding for that access.

One outcome was the creation of the Trilateral Commission in 1973, largely due to the efforts of David Rockefeller, chairman of the Chase Manhattan Bank. This is an informal assocation of leading members of the commercial, banking, and political establishments in the three principal regions of the industrialized capitalist world—Japan, the U.S., and Europe—hence the description "trilateral." Its purpose has been to promote the economic policies of these countries insofar as they affect the operations of multinational capital, and to encourage the coordination of their responses to the political demands of the less-developed countries.[44]

The strategy of the private sector soon found active support in government circles. The State Department was encouraged to pay close attention to both the needs and the potential diplomatic value of multinational corporations in achieving its foreign policy objectives. A report prepared by the Commission on the Organization of the Government for the Conduct of Foreign Policy under the chairmanship of Robert D. Murphy, and presented to President Ford and to Congress on June 27, 1975, spoke of the need for "coherence" in foreign policy in a "rapidly changing, interdependent world." Such coherence was to be explicitly achieved through the exercise of U.S. political power in the attempt at "shaping an international order" and "managing interdependence."[45] Science and technology were quickly drafted to help achieve these objectives.

The State Department was already being urged to make more use of science and technology in diplomatic affairs by Congress (with the backing of the scientific community). Legislation passed in 1973 led to the creation of an expanded Bureau of Oceans and International Environmental and Scientific Affairs (usually known by the abbreviation OES) after President Nixon had abolished the White House Office of Science Policy. A report from the Congressional Research Service, produced at the request of a congressional subcommittee, urged the U.S. to make active use of its scientific and technology strength to achieve foreign policy objectives: "The U.S., as the principal national exponent in technological achievement, ought therefore to be recognized as diplomatically preeminent, but also ought to accept the responsibility for leading the way in the application of technology to the achievement of goals shared with the other nations of the world," the report stated.[46] Congress itself passed new legislation specifically mandating the State Department to increase its scientific and technological activities, agreeing with the Congressional Research Services criticism that "only meager resources have been spared to search for ways to turn technology to the achievement of diplomatic goals."[47] (The same criticism had long been made, with apparently little effect, in the scientific community.)

Given the new importance of these issues for multinational corporations, which in the aftermath of the 1973–74 recession began looking increasingly toward the LDCs as a source of new markets and as financial borrowers, the State Department, in contrast to the two previous decades, now needed little persuasion to move science and technology to the center of the diplomatic stage. A key figure in this strategy was Henry Kissinger. A close student of debates over the control of nuclear energy in the 1950s,[48] when the U.S. seemed to have successfully used controls on science and technology to achieve commercial, political, and military goals simultaneously, Kissinger was keen to extend the same negotiating techniques across the complete range of science and technologies that other industrialized nations and the Third World wanted, exploiting the desires of both for the fruits of U.S. research.

Kissinger's confidence was strengthened by the successful use of scientific exchange agreements as a public manifestation of the détente negotiated with the Soviet Union by President Nixon, itself promoted by visions of the Soviet Union as a long-term market for American capital and technology. Science and technology had the advantage of offering a worthy and apparently neutral mechanism for U.S. diplomacy, which encouraged both commercial trade and a form of dependency that, it was hoped, could be manipulated to minimize political aggression. As a headline in *Science* expressed it: "U.S.-Soviet Summit: Make Science, Not War."[49] This approach was particularly attractive in the politically conscious post-Vietnam period, when the Pentagon Papers trial and exposés about the activities of the Central Intelligence Agency were creating deep skepticism about the morality of some of the techniques that had been used to achieve foreign policy objectives in the past. It also exploited the fact that the Soviet Union and the nations of Eastern Europe were beginning to turn to Western technology as a solution to their own economic problems. So great were their demands in this area that their cumulative balance of payment deficit and debts with the West rose from $8 billion in 1972 to $80 billion in 1981.

Kissinger's strategy toward the less developed nations was outlined in a series of speeches to the United Nations. In April 1974 he laid the groundwork in an address to the U.N. General Assembly in which he claimed that "no human activity is less national in character than the field of science . . . no development efforts offer more hope than joint scientific and technical cooperation."[50] One year later, in another major speech to the U.N. (delivered in Kissinger's absence by U.N. ambassador Daniel Moynihan), the proposals had become more concrete. Developed and less-developed countries, he said, shared a common interest in the orderly development of a "single global system of trade and monetary relations," which meant that while the advanced nations had an interest in the growth of markets and production in the developing world, "the developing countries have a stake in the markets, technological innovation, and capital investment of the industrial countries."[51] Kissinger outlined nineteen separate initiatives that would, he believed, improve the access of developing nations to U.S. science and technology, while helping to restore rationality and order to the global system. Further proposals along the same lines were added in a speech to the United Nations Conference on Trade and Development (UNCTAD), held in Nairobi in 1976.

To those close to Kissinger, his strategy was clear. According to one of his speech writers, Kissinger "thinks that America's ability to contribute money and run the world in the old-fashioned way of the 1950s and 1960s is now over. What we can contribute—and what the world wants—is our technological capabilities."[52] Dixy Lee Ray, a former chairman of the Atomic Energy Commission who had been appointed the first head of OES early in 1975, was less flattering in her description. Ray claimed that the leadership of the State Department had a difficult time thinking of science and technology "as anything other than convenient hand-maidens." Kissinger, she said later, considered scientific capability and management as "bargaining chips" in a political game. "It means that you're saying to another country, 'If you do what I want in some sort of political situation, or alignment, or whatever, then you'll get access to our science and technology.' "[53]

Not surprisingly, Kissinger's initiatives did not receive wholehearted support from the scientific community, even from those members who welcomed the greater prominence given to science and technology in foreign affairs. To many scientists, the short-term political motivations were too blatant. Ray herself resigned in a well-publicized huff in the middle of 1975, complaining in a letter to President Ford that the bureau she had headed for less than six months, which was supposed to offer advice on scientific questions related to diplomatic initiatives, had no independent voice and "can do little but acquiesce in the policies set by others."[54] She cited as an example a large-scale energy research agreement with Japan, which she was told about only after it had been signed.

But the private sector, too, had its reservations about Kissinger's strategy. It agreed with the goal of persuading both developed and developing nations to accept the fruits of American science and technology in return for political favors—including an agreement not to challenge the political conditions on which it was offered. The main reservation of corporations, however, was that the strategy involved a degree of sometimes unpredictable government intervention into their own efforts to control access to the scientific and technical knowledge on which their global power was increasingly based. (Many were upset that they had not been consulted by Kissinger prior to his U.N. speeches, and complained that it was often difficult to relate Kissinger's broad promises to the practical actions of the State Department.[55]) Kissinger's attempts to exploit U.S. science and technology to gain diplomatic advantages had coincided with the growing realization that for domestic corporations too, privileged access to science and technology was the root of economic success in the world marketplace. These ideas were also gaining a foothold in the State Department. William Casey, then Under Secretary of State for Economic Affairs (later director of the Central Intelligence Agency under Reagan), told the Industrial Research Institute in October 1973 that, although productivity, prices, exchange rates, and trade barriers were all important sources of the economic strength of U.S. companies, "today we consider none of these more important than supporting science to nourish technology, and enlisting technology to pay our way in the world."[56]

This was the period at which it was becoming clear that external trade was a vital component of the U.S. economy—and that the comparative advantage of U.S. capital in international trade rested primarily on science-based industries such as electronics and computers, new energy technology, the technologies needed to exploit the resources of the ocean bed, and, most recently, biotechnology and genetic engineering. The more U.S. corporations realized that their commercial success in international markets depended on their ability to exploit the strategic advantages offered by American science, the more insistent they became that access to this science was not a gift to be given away to either developed or developing nations—even in exchange for political favors. Instead, it should be carefully regulated so that its political use did not threaten their own power.

Furthermore, it had previously been possible to maintain a distinction between science and technology, and to argue that even if technology transfers needed to be regulated to avoid giving away excessive power (for example, through the proliferation of nuclear weapons), scientific knowledge could be freely offered as a "public good." Increasingly, however, science had become part of the same universe—at least that strategic science which, through its close and direct links to advanced production technology, both developed and less-developed nations feel is the most relevant to their social and economic needs, and are therefore most interested in obtaining from the U.S.

The reservations expressed by the private sector were rapidly absorbed into State Department thinking. Following Dixy Lee Ray's resignation, a report on the position of science and technology within the department was commissioned by Casey's successor as Under Secretary of State for Economic Affairs, Charles W. Robinson.* The report was prepared by the former head of the National Aeronautics and Space Administration, T. Keith Glennan, who went out of his way to sound out and include the opinions of the corporate community. In June 1976 a meeting was held in New York at which Glennan met with executives from several multinational corporations. The meeting was organized by Herbert Fusfeld, director of research for Kennecott Copper and a past president of the Industrial Research Institute. Companies represented at the meeting included American Cyanamid, AMAX, RCA, Sperry Rand, American Can, and General Electric—all multinationals that carried out substantial trade with the Third World and were therefore concerned at the extent to which the Kissinger strategy might be challenging their power in the marketplace. The participants agreed that the relationship between private-sector technology and foreign policy "poses serious difficulties for both foreign policy and business opportunities if not resolved." They demanded a coherent government position that was "both reasonable and effective," suggesting that industry should be given the oppor-

* Robinson was subsequently appointed Deputy Secretary of State by Kissinger and, after leaving the Ford administration at the end of 1977, was immediately appointed with Kissinger to the executive board of the trilateral commission.

tunity to consult in advance with government officials over major proposals in the field of international technology transfer.[57]

Glennan's report faithfully reflected the comments he received from such executives. One of its main recommendations was that close liaison be established between industry and the State Department to ensure "maximum benefit on matters of common interest." In particular, he suggested that the Bureau of Oceans and International Environmental and Scientific Affairs should "assist industry . . . to deal with the problems involved in the export of its technology." Glennan had already proposed to the multinational corporation representatives at the New York meeting that the bureau, the main focus for scientific affairs in the State Department, also become the focus for "establishing rapport with industry on technological issues."[58]

Thus, by the time President Carter arrived in Washington at the beginning of 1977, top officials in the State Department were already "preparing to act on the problem of science and technology,"[59] and the groundwork had been thoroughly laid for a broad-based attempt to integrate science and technology into foreign policy in a way that suited the needs of U.S. private corporations. Carter himself quickly came under pressure from the scientific community to increase the role of science in foreign affairs. Soon after his election, he received a letter from five past presidents of the American Association for the Advancement of Science, suggesting the need for greater efforts in this direction.[60] Far more important in determining Carter's strategy, however, were his links to the East Coast banking and corporate communities—the world of international capital. These links were established primarily through his recruitment to and participation in the activities of the Trilateral Commission, the members of which had been largely responsible for promoting Carter's candidacy as the Democratic nominee for President in 1976.[61]

Among the Trilateral Commission members appointed to senior positions in the new administration was Zbigniew Brzezinski, professor of public law and government at Columbia University in New York, who became Carter's National Security Adviser. Brzezinski had helped David Rockefeller to conceive and establish the Trilateral Commission in 1973, and he served as its executive director until joining the Carter administration at the end of 1976. Like Kissinger, he was firmly convinced of the value of science and technology as tools of foreign policy. In his book *Between Two Ages: America's Role in the Technetronic Era*, published in 1970, Brzezinski set out his version of the Trilateralist credo, describing his belief that the industrialized nations were entering an age in which technology—and especially electronics, hence the neologism "technetronic"—was increasingly becoming the principal determinant of social change. Cooperation in science, he suggested, could help cement the political alliance between industrialized nations claimed necessary to ward off nationalistic pressures in the interests of free trade and capitalist solidarity. Indeed, Brzezinski portrayed international collaboration in science and technology as central to efforts to create a new global alliance of the advanced capitalist nations, proposing, for example, the creation of a "permanent information linkage . . . between the universities of New York, Moscow, Tokyo, Mexico City, and Milan" to provide a "cross-national pooling of academic resources." Such a development would form part of a "more rational division of labor in research and development," which would, of course, considerably facilitate the coordinated control of access to this information.[62]*

As we have seen, Harold Brown, another active Trilateralist (whom Carter is said to have first met through their joint membership on the commission), established the framework by which the Carter administration absorbed basic science into its military strategy. Similarly, Brzezinski's ideas—broadly shared by other members of the commission—helped create the framework by which science was integrated into the domain of foreign policy. The main thrust of this approach, as Brzezinski saw it, was to use U.S. hegemony in science and technology to rationalize competition between advanced capitalist nations (for example, by sharing the costs of major research facilities), while at the same time reinforcing the hierarchical structure of the global economy by ensuring that control of the strategically important areas of science and technology remained concentrated in institutions at the top of the pyramid.

This was the broad brief given to the various prominent members of the Trilateral Commission who were put in charge of crucial negotiations on international science and technology issues. Elliot Richardson was made ambassador to the Law of the Sea Conference; his task was to negotiate an international treaty that would prevent an anarchistic free-for-all for the riches of the seabed, without providing other countries with excessive access to the advanced techniques of seabed mining that Third World countries were demanding as a prerequisite for fair competition. Gerard Smith, previously North American chairman of the commission, was given responsibility for finding a way of using the U.S. hegemony in nuclear technology to impose conditions on the use of this technology by other countries (for example, by the ultimately unsuccessful efforts to discourage the spread of nuclear reprocessing, which, it was claimed, would increase the availability of weapons-grade plutonium). And Trilateralist Lucy Wilson Benson, previously chairman of the National League of Women Voters, was appointed to the new position of Under Secretary of State for Security Assistance, Science, and Technology, a position in which she was responsible for the preparations for the

---

* Significantly, from the point of view of our later discussion in Chapter Six of the use of arguments about science and technology to provide a depoliticizing veneer of neutrality to economic debates, Brzezinski acknowledged that he was suggesting "an approach to international economic relations that is increasingly depoliticized *in form*, even if the ultimate underlying purpose remains political" (italics added).[63]

United Nations Conference on Science and Technology for Development—preparations which, as we shall see below, were carried out with comparable objectives.

The Office of Science and Technology Policy was included in Carter's strategy. It was made clear to Frank Press, soon after his appointment as director of the office and as Carter's science adviser, that helping to mold diplomatic relations with other countries was expected to be one of the main functions of the new office. Press shared many of Carter's—and Brzezinski's—views about the value of science in international affairs. Indeed, Press's own international contacts—through, for example, his involvement in planning for the International Geophysical Year in 1957 and his chairmanship of the National Academy of Sciences' committee for scholarly communication with the People's Republic of China—seem to have been among the reasons that he was selected for the job. And he later expressed a conviction that "scientific and technical assistance is a key linkage between the U.S. and the LDCs, *one that has been underutilized in the past*" (italics added).[64]

In a message to Congress in March 1979, Carter staked out the parameters for increased government involvement with science and technology in international affairs. He argued that although much international cooperation in science and technology takes place through private academic or commercial channels, there was a growing role for governmental participation as other nations made new commitments to scientific and technological growth. He listed four themes that were shaping his administration's policies: pursuing international initiatives to advance U.S. R&D; strengthening scientific exchanges; formulating programs and institutions to help the LDCs use science and technology; and cooperating with other nations to manage technologies with global impact. Carter was frank about his motivations: "If used wisely, these future opportunities for scientific and technological cooperation can further our foreign policy objectives."[65]

Perhaps the most explicit use of science as a diplomatic tool was its role in opening up political and economic relationships with the People's Republic of China. Brzezinski had long argued that it was in the long-term interests of the U.S. to create a new relationship with China, both to establish a political counterforce to the Soviet Union and to develop China as a market for U.S. products. A visit by Brzezinski to Peking revealed that China was interested in buying advanced technology from the U.S. and that there was a possibility of skirting stalled diplomatic talks by encouraging contacts through science and technology.[66] His visit was therefore followed by a number of visits by leading members of the U.S. science policy establishment, culminating in a science and technology agreement signed by Chinese Vice-Premier Deng Xiaoping in Washington on January 31, 1979. This agreement covered such programs as the development of a satellite communications system, expanded academic exchanges, the exchange of plant materials for genetics research on crops, and cooperation in high energy physics.

The tactic was successful in helping to create new political bonds between the leaderships of the two nations and in enhancing the opportunities for U.S. industry to participate in China's ambitious modernization efforts.[67] The number of scientific exchange agreements increased steadily—by 1983 there were more than twenty—and paved the way for a substantial quantity of high technology exports. Already, however, there were signs that other parts of the administration were less than happy about those agreements, which appeared to threaten strategic interests. In particular, the Defense Department objected strongly to the promise to sell to the Chinese an advanced version of NASA's earth-mapping satellite LANDSAT. Eventually a compromise was reached, but it was made clear that trade in high technology with even those "friendly" countries unlikely to pass it to the Soviet Union was not going to remain free of controls.

Even greater difficulties were experienced with Carter's attempts to provide scientific assistance to the less-developed countries through a proposed Institute for Scientific and Technical Collaboration (ISTC), intended to be a major new federal agency which would channel both public and private scientific and technical assistance to Third World countries. Packaged in a form acceptable to the corporate community, ISTC was promoted in glowing terms;* one memorandum, for example, promised that it would be "the jewel of U.S. development aid," since it was going to make available on a stable and reliable basis "one of the best and most desirable commodities—American know-how."[68] However, after three years of lobbying by the administration, ISTC failed to generate the necessary congressional support, and what had started life as a proposal for a politically autonomous agency equivalent in size and stature to the National Science Foundation ended up as no more than a new bureau within the Agency for International Development, with extra funding amounting to little more than $12 million a year.

The history of ISTC helps throws some important light on the federal government's approach to the use of science in foreign affairs—and the reaction of the scientific community and the private sector to these efforts. For in many ways it symbolized the failure of the Kissinger strategy, namely the idea that the government should play the dominant role in providing advanced scientific knowledge to the LDCs. The concern was that this could threaten the private channels through which this same knowledge could be transferred while ensuring that access to industrially important know-how and the conditions under which it was used re-

* Indeed, the institute was often described as a government-backed substitute for the efforts of the Rockefeller and Ford Foundations in this direction.

mained firmly under the control of the corporations to which this know-how "belonged."

The idea of separating science and technology from other aspects of foreign aid had been on the political agenda since proposals of the President's Science Advisory Committee in the early 1960s.[69] A decade later, an International Development Institute was endorsed by President Nixon and submitted to Congress, but failed to win the necessary backing, largely because it was seen as a way of assisting potential competitors to U.S. corporations in the Third World by giving them unregulated access to U.S. technology. Kissinger's list of proposals to the U.N. in September 1975 had included the setting up of a similarly named International Industrialization Institute, but this idea too remained grounded, primarily for the same reasons.

Virtually all proposals to create a new focus for research related to Third World needs had been enthusiastically supported by the scientific community. Many scientists were dissatisfied with what they considered to be the inadequately exploited potential of American science to help the LDCs and the generally low priority given to research by official aid agencies. Moreover, a new government-funded research institute was a potential source of funding for their own research. Indeed, the National Academy of Sciences had been one of the main sources for Kissinger's proposed International Industrialization Institute. Writing in *Science* in 1975, George S. Hammond, foreign secretary of the National Academy of Sciences, and Murray Todd, executive director of the National Research Council's Commission on International Relations, suggested the creation of "an institutional capability for the purpose of facilitating the access of developing countries to 'overdeveloped' world scientific and technological activities in universities, research institutes, government laboratories, and the private sector."[70]

More significant, in light of the experience with Kissinger, the idea of creating an institutional channel for technical assistance to Third World countries, particularly one able to deal with such countries on a bilateral rather than a multilateral basis, was—at least initially—appealing to the private sector. Companies that had expressed concern about technology being used by the White House and the State Department as a lever to achieve short-term political goals welcomed the suggestion that a new institute be created that would oversee technology and knowledge transfer arrangements at one step removed from immediate foreign policy pressures, i.e., without posing a direct threat to their interests. Furthermore, these companies saw the possibility of a government-sponsored institute as legitimating and defending their own claims to proprietary rights over transferred knowledge. The Chamber of Commerce, for example, suggested that the U.S. government "should consider establishing an office that could serve as the central focus where business firms— and transferee nations—can take problems that arise in connection with arrangements to transfer technology, and that can help the process of monitoring, negotiating, and resolving disputes."[71]

The stage had therefore been set by the time Carter and his advisers put together their foreign policy strategy. Brzezinski himself, like Kissinger, had already endorsed the idea of a Technical Assistance and Research Institute, put forward by President Nixon's National Planning Association in 1969, explicitly arguing that developed countries should create new institutional channels for technical aid to the countries of the Third World that were "not subject to political pressures" from these countries.[72] To help develop this strategy, he recruited as adviser to the National Security Council Henry D. Owen, a co-founder of the Trilateral Commission and director of foreign policy studies at the Brookings Institution in Washington, D.C.

Owen soon arranged for the State Department to sponsor a report on development assistance strategies from Brookings. The report was prepared under the close guidance of an advisory committee chaired by David E. Bell of the Ford Foundation (and AID administrator under Kennedy). In addition to several university scientists and administrators, this committee included executives from Exxon and Citibank. It proposed the creation of a separate development research institute that would, among other roles, function as "a catalyst and coordinator of U.S. scientific, technical, and educational activities related to development problems."[73]

In developing the strategy for setting up such an institute, Owen established a close working relationship with Frank Press and the Office of Science and Technology Policy. (Significantly, when Press was criticized in the *New York Times* for his failure to establish public advisory committees, it was Owen who leapt into print in his defense, claiming that the advisory function on important technical issues had been well served by nonpublic means.[74]) Press in turn recruited Eugene Skolnikoff to organize OSTP staff work on plans for the institute. (Skolnikoff had worked in the science adviser's office under Presidents Kennedy and Johnson and was now professor of political science at the Massachusetts Institute of Technology; he was later appointed chairman of the German Marshall Fund.)

By the end of 1977 Owen had prepared a paper suggesting, in line with the Brookings report, the creation of an autonomous International Development Foundation reporting directly to the President. This was to have a headquarters staff of 200, with ten to twelve regional offices and an annual budget of between $500 and $700 million. The Office of Management and Budget, however, soon indicated that it would oppose any major expenditure on an agency that was free of direct control over the way the money was spent. Reflecting OMB's position, Frank Press wrote in a memo to Owen that OSTP's "preferred option" was the creation not of a separate institute, but of a "semiautonomous" science, technology, and development foundation, which would generate most of its initial funding and staff from the scientists and technical staff then working for the Agency for International Development.[75]

The OMB-OSTP view prevailed. In a speech delivered in Caracas in March 1978, Carter announced the creation of a new, semiautonomous Agency for Technological Cooperation—eventually known as the Institute for Scientific and Technical Cooperation. A planning office was esablished under the wing of OSTP and AID. As described in August 1978, the goals of the institute were "to expand knowledge and increase availability of technology and skills needed to meet critical problems of people in developing countries."[76] Typical areas for short-term research projects included new agriculture technologies, satellite technology, information systems, forestry and energy, tropical diseases, and contraceptive technology. And an advisory board was set up, chaired by Bell, who had been influential in shaping the original Brookings study and apparently hoped the institute would take over responsibility for some of the foundation's activities in the Third World. At the beginning of 1979, the Carter administration asked Congress to approve the creation of the institute and allocate $25 million in new funds for the fiscal year 1980, together with the transfer of $66 million of research being carried out by AID.

If the scientific and humanitarian goals of the institute were unimpeachable, the way in which they were to be pursued—given the political interests on which they inevitably impinged—was more controversial. The scientific community was lukewarm in its enthusiasm for the administration's plans. Even a semiautonomous institute, in the community's eyes, ran the risk of being too closely tied to the broader demands of foreign policy. They preferred something more independent, less immediately amenable to government control. Many of the critics organized themselves into a group known as the Council on Science and Technology for Development (chaired by ex-NAS president Frederick Seitz) and put their weight behind a counterproposal, being developed in Congress by the staffs of Senator Adlai Stevenson, Jr., and Representative George Brown, for a more independent institute. Taking as a model the freedom from direct government intervention that Vannevar Bush had established for the National Science Board after the Second World War, they argued that the institute should be run by an independent board with executive policy responsibility, to whom the director of the institute was responsible, rather than a purely advisory council, with the director answering to government agencies. In other words, control of the institute and the science and technology that passed through it would be firmly placed in the hands of private rather than public decision-makers.

Despite their criticisms, the scientists and politicians who proposed this alternative arrangement eventually came around to endorsing the administration's proposal as the only one that was likely to succeed in Congress. They persuaded the administration to add the word "science" to the institute's title, turning it into the Institute for Scientific and Technical Cooperation (ISTC).[77] But their support was never whole-hearted—one of several factors that contributed to the eventual failure of the whole initiative.

From the administration's point of view, the idea of ISTC, while legitimating its actions by appealing to the apparent neutrality of science and technology, was clearly recognized to have an important political role. The message was more subtle—and more long-term—than Kissinger's, but not much different in substance. The U.S. was prepared to offer the best of its science and technology to developing nations through ISTC, but on condition that these countries adopted what the U.S. considered to be appropriate development strategies, in both economic and political terms, and respected the terms—such as the proprietary rights of multinational corporations—on which it was offered. Frank Press had pointed out in his memo to Henry Owen that ISTC had both a scientific and a political function. Opportunities for collaboration and trade with the U.S. would be "adversely affected" if other countries responded to the technical needs of the Third World, he said; "thus more effective use of science and technology will serve expanding foreign policy requirements, as well as direct development objectives." He criticized the idea of an autonomous agency on the grounds that "the opportunities for the foundation to contribute to the other aspects of our bilateral assistance effort would be fewer."[78] The administration's interest in using science and technology to mold development strategies is also shown in one ISTC planning document that claims "a consensus that scientific and technological advances, when employed within an appropriate policy and management framework, can be important factors in *determining the rate and direction* of economic and social development" (italics added).*[79]

However much the scientific community distrusted the degree of government involvement planned for ISTC, the institute still received substantial support from parts of the private sector. Many companies were particularly interested in the administration's intention to use the ISTC

---

* Further evidence of the administration's goals appeared in a speech to UNCTAD V in Manila on May 11, 1979, given by Carter's ambassador to the United Nations, Andrew Young—another Trilateral Commission member. Young announced the U.S.'s continued opposition to a "second window" demanded by less-developed countries on the fund that had been set up to stabilize commodity prices; but he suggested that ISTC "will be prepared to join with the second window in organizing, manning, and financing specific research and development projects related to commodities."[80] Young's remarks brought the comment from the Center of Concern, a Washington-based religious group involved in Third World issues, that "the only relationship the U.S. government is interested in with the Third World is one in which the U.S. does the organizing, manning, and financing—in other words, where it is in control."[81]

to both open up and secure channels for transferring their scientific knowledge and technical know-how to the so-called "middle-tier" countries in relative security. These countries made up a growing market for U.S. know-how—yet they had also proved to be one of the chief sources of demands through multilateral bodies such as the United Nations for radical reforms of the conditions of technology and knowledge transfer. ISTC was a convenient way of exploiting the market for technology and scientific know-how while warding off political demands by Third World countries for greater control of both.

From the beginning, there was indeed a strong private-sector involvement in the planning for ISTC. Scientists joined the administration in arguing that ISTC would bring the private sector more effectively into the development process and "encourage mechanisms for U.S. companies to help in building self-reliant capabilities in the developing world."[82] The executive director of the Council of the Americas, an organization representing almost 75 percent of American companies doing business in Latin America, told a congressional committee that ISTC, by bringing government and industry together "to create the kind of know-how and knowledge that are needed for productive purposes overseas," was "an important vehicle for bringing greater private participation into the policy process regarding science and technology cooperation between the U.S. and developing countries." In particular, he said, it would help create a "demand pull for technology from this country."[83]

Yet even the strength of private-sector support turned out, in practice, to be mixed. Although some companies saw ISTC as a useful tool, others argued that there was a need for less—not more—government involvement in technology and knowledge transfer. In other words, they believed that the private sector was strong enough to determine on its own the conditions under which the developing world would be permitted access to their science and technology.

The administration remained committed to its goal. By the summer of 1979—two years after the initial proposal had been made by Owen—both the House and the Senate had passed legislation authorizing the creation of a new institute. This was sufficient for Father Theodore Hesburgh, leader of the U.S. delegation to the United Nations Conference on Science and Technology, to announce Congress's approval and the imminent formation of the institute as a sign of U.S. good faith toward the Third World.[84] Yet the announcement proved to be premature. The Senate refused to pass the legislation needed to provide the new agency with a budget. In doing this, it was responding directly to the criticisms of a small group, led by Senator Dennis DeConcini of Arizona, who argued that the work of the proposed institute would unnecessarily duplicate that already being carried out by AID, and that therefore there was no reason why anything more than a reorganization of AID was needed. Negotiations failed to break the deadlock, and without the necessary funding, the whole project was stillborn.

The reasons for ISTC's failure to cross its final legislative hurdle were complex. DeConcini certainly waged a tenacious campaign against the institute, partly motivated, it was claimed, by his failure to obtain an administration position for one of his supporters. Whatever the personal motivations, however, DeConcini's opposition to ISTC struck a responsive chord in the hearts of senators with other concerns. Some criticized the proliferation of government agencies and the apparent duplication of the existing responsibilities of AID, and they were reluctant to grant further increases to the foreign aid budget. Others, however, resented the fact that the ISTC proposals represented a deliberate effort to place research on Third World needs more directly under the control of private corporations and universities, removing it from its traditional home in AID—where, whatever the uses to which it had been put, it remained responsive to direct control by Congress.

This was certainly the fear within AID itself. Not only did the agency's scientific and technical staff resent the implication that they were doing a poor job, but agency administrators were also concerned that they would lose an important part of their power base. Their fears were justified, for the general feeling in both the scientific community and the private sector, based on past experience, was that continued AID control of these programs was "totally inconsistent" with what the institute was supposed to achieve, since the agency seemed preoccupied with managing day-to-day assistance programs.[85] Hence the proposal to transfer AID research programs to ISTC. AID officials were, unsurprisingly, against this proposal. They had already expressed their objections to the Brookings report, which had used AID's previous lack of attention to research to support the case for a new International Development Foundation (IDF) from which ISTC later developed. Under the subtitle "An Idea Whose Time Has Come? or Old Wine in New Bottles?" the AID reply claimed there was "a very real danger" that the proposed institute might become the captive of U.S. university and private voluntary organization personnel. It advised that "for both substance and tactical reasons, AID might be better off supporting the IDF proposal," but it made clear staff feeling that any new organization should be created within and under the control of AID, not outside it.[86]

Such fears were backed up by evidence that it was precisely from such private institutions that the ISTC planners were seeking political support. An investigation of the ISTC planning office, carried out at DeConcini's request by staff of the Senate Appropriations Committee, revealed a pattern of lobbying that the institute's opponents were quick to exploit—not least because the use of public funds for such purposes is technically illegal. The investigators, for example, found a list of 200 individuals, many in the corporate world, who appeared to have been contacted with the request that they ask their congressmen to support the ISTC legislation. They also found a draft letter to various university presidents explicitly suggesting the types of arguments they might put to their congressmen—and in at least one case, a reply indicating that universities anticipated receiving future research funds from the institute they were lobbying for.[87]

On the basis of such evidence, the report concluded censoriously that there had been "a planned and concerted effort by federal officials to contact a broad spectrum of private industry and university officials and other outside parties to seek their support for the authorization and funding of ISTC."[88] In substance it revealed little unusual in the way Washington works; as Daniel Greenberg commented, it "had the ring of Rip van Winkle telling the cops that there's gambling in Atlantic City."[89] Nevertheless, the use of appropriated funds to lobby for congressional support of new legislation is technically illegal, and the report's conclusion therefore provided ample fuel for DeConcini's attack on the institute. It also demonstrated clearly who the ISTC proposal had been aimed to please, namely those institutions already engaged, as we have seen in previous chapters, in tightening their control over science and laying down the conditions under which other groups—including other countries—would be permitted access.

The problem with ISTC in the form eventually proposed by the Carter administration was that, despite its efforts to meet the wishes of the academic and corporate communities, it lacked sufficient support from any particular constituency to see it through the legislative process. At the same time it generated sufficient opposition to make sure that, without such support, it was unlikely to succeed in obtaining congressional approval. DeConcini's hatchet work was made easier by the reservations of those who might otherwise have been ISTC's most enthusiastic supporters. The scientific community, pointing to their experiences with the National Science Foundation, never fully accepted the argument that the institute should not be allowed the autonomy that a properly "scientific" organization might have expected—i.e., control by scientists and their corporate peers. A meeting organized by the Aspen Institute program in science, technology, and humanism in the summer of 1978 recommended "as much independence as possible from U.S. foreign policy."[90]

On the other side of the political spectrum, several organizations directly concerned with the Third World had their own reservations. In particular, they criticized ISTC planners for the relatively low level of involvement by Third World representatives in the development of plans for the institute (a shortcoming the planning office itself admitted). They also expressed concern that ISTC would promote forms of science and technology that would encourage greater dependency on the industrialized nations while not necessarily addressing the most immediate needs of the Third World. "Central to our reservations is the question of the development philosophy underlying ISTC," the Center of Concern commented. "Evidence so far indicates a development model which gives insufficient attention to self-reliance and breaking the ties of dependency."[91]

As for the private sector, its own enthusiasm for ISTC waned as it realized that Third World unity behind demands for easier access to Western science and technology was losing some of its initial strength—and that multinational companies were more likely to be able to arrange such transfers on their own terms, either independently or working directly through AID, than they were with any new government-financed body. Eventually a code of conduct for the operation of multinationals was signed, but it was a voluntary code, with no government-backed sanctions. Moreover, it included the provision that Third World governments receiving transferred knowledge and technology should guarantee reasonable safeguards of confidentiality—in other words, that they agreed to respect the commodity form of scientific knowledge and patterns of control expressed by its dissemination through private rather than public channels.[92]

The collapse of the ISTC initiative, therefore, ultimately reflected a rejection of the Kissinger-Brzezinski strategy by the very forces it had originally been designed to protect and promote. Congressional actions did lead to the creation of a new Bureau of Science and Technology within AID, with an initial budget of an extra $12 million—an initiative which, as we shall see below, took on further significance under the Reagan administration as a channel for applying the private technology and technical know-how of U.S. companies to the LDCs. But it was a pale reflection of what Carter and fellow Trilateralists Kissinger, Brzezinski, and Owen had previously considered desirable.

If the ISTC initiative represents the failure of a *positive* strategy devised by the Carter administration to plug the private sector into the scientific and technological needs of the Third World, we now pass to what might be described as the success of a *negative* strategy in the same field. This was U.S. participation in the United Nations Conference on Science and Technology for Development (UNCSTD), held in Vienna in the summer of 1979, whose origins lie in demands made by the LDCs at the beginning of the 1970s for more equitable access to the world's science and technology. Such demands potentially posed a double threat to U.S. interests. On the one hand, they were likely to reduce the financial gains that private companies stood to make through the "sale" of this science and technology by requiring that it be made available to Third World countries on nonmarket terms. On the other, they presented a direct challenge to the hierarchical patterns of control that the industrialized nations, as a bloc, were able to exercise over the emerging international division of labor through their control of advanced science and technology. Both were causes for defensive action.

UNCSTD was proposed by the U.N. General Assembly in December

1976 to update—and, it was hoped, provide a more politically realistic approach than—the conclusions of the first U.N. conference on science and technology for development, held in 1963. This, like the earlier Atoms for Peace conference, on which its planning had been based, had turned largely into a science fair, where the rich nations competed against each other to sell their technological wares to the poor. The proposal for a new conference was picked up eagerly by Kissinger, who saw UNCSTD as an opportunity to negotiate a settlement to the growing tensions between North and South over technology and knowledge transfer. Indeed, Kissinger offered to host the meeting in Washington, and it was only after lengthy negotiations that it was finally agreed to hold it on relatively neutral ground in Vienna.[93]

Kissinger had few doubts about where the major constituency, at least in the United States, was for such a conference. The initial planning for the U.S. strategy was carried out almost entirely through contacts with the private sector, and it concentrated on the terms and conditions of the transfer of scientific and technical knowledge to the LDCs. Kissinger's own involvement reached a climax on November 17, 1976—after the presidential election in which Ford had been voted out of office—with a day-long meeting in Washington organized by the Department of State and largely dominated by representatives from the private sector. Reflecting a desire by private corporations to reap the maximum financial advantages from such transfers, while minimizing the political control they might be required to give away, the first point made by the panelists, according to a summary prepared by the State Department, was that "privately owned U.S. technology should be made available in an orderly way that takes into account the legitimate concern of U.S. enterprises to avoid excessive risks and restrictions."[94]

Members of the scientific community soon realized that, as far as Kissinger was concerned, their involvement was to be limited to those areas that were directly related to potentially commercial technology, and that Kissinger's main interest—as it had previously been with nuclear energy—was the political implications of the terms and conditions of access to this science and technology, rather than their substance. In November 1976, shortly after Carter had won the presidential election, five past presidents of the AAAS complained to Cyrus Vance, the Secretary of State–designate, that the U.S. preparations were placing a disproportionate emphasis on the problem of the transfer of proprietary technology rather than on the "substance" of science and development.[95] In a similar vein, Frederick Seitz, president of Rockefeller University in New York, and Rodney Nichols, the university's executive vice-president, wrote to Carter on behalf of a number of scientists, engineers, and physicians who had formed themselves into a group called the Council for Science and Technology in Development; they put forward a list of areas in need of scientific attention in the LDCs.[96] Their letter became the basis of a study by the National Research Council of the National Academy of Sciences (of which Seitz was a past president), commissioned by the State Department. The result was a list of what were considered to be the priority needs of Third World countries, divided into five areas: industrialization; health and nutrition; food and climate; energy and natural resources; and urbanization, transportation, and communications.[97]

To Seitz and his fellow scientists, concentrating on the terms of LDC access to Western science and technology was an unnecessary politicization of the issues. In a letter to OSTP director Press that reflected support for a development research institute, Seitz suggested that "if certain countries push the conference's agenda toward contentious political issues, the position of the United States should remain sufficiently flexible that we could pursue our objectives outside the framework of the conference."[98] In making such a suggestion, Seitz was repeating a familiar theme often heard from scientists, namely that the problems of development could be simply cured if left to scientists and engineers, with politicians removed from the picture.*

Yet there was a recognition in official circles from an early stage that the substance of the U.N. conference was by definition political. Both the LDCs and Kissinger had in their separate ways acknowledged that neither science nor technology was neutral in the context of international diplomacy—indeed, that conflicts over access to science and technology were becoming *the* central conflicts over economic growth and development strategy. William Carey, executive officer of the AAAS, predicted (accurately) in 1977 that the conference would be "a face-off between advanced and deprived countries, in a charged atmosphere, with science and technology as hard currencies in the new diplomacy."[100]

The same awareness was not lost on members of the Carter administration. Frank Press made this clear in an address to the Council on Foreign Relations in New York in February 1978. He cautioned that UNCSTD should not be too ambitious in scope by trying to address all development-related issues, and should focus on those related to science and technology. "Yet we must be careful not to adopt an overly technocratic view of the conference," he told his audience. "We must realize that discussions with the developing world about science and technology are really about the core issues of economic wealth, expertise, and

---

* In the early 1960s Walter Schilling intimated that "the scientist's profession inclines him to look at problems in terms of searching for a solution to them. When this perspective is turned to the problems of international politics, however, the scientist's approach often appears open to the characterization of 'naive utopianism or naive belligerency.' His approach to international relations appears simplistic and mechanistic. It is almost as if he conceived of policy being made primarily by forward-looking, solution-oriented, rational-thinking types like himself."[99]

power."[101] Jean Wilkowski, appointed by Carter to head the State Department's preparations for the conference, was equally explicit. UNCSTD "is a political conference," she told a congressional hearing, since the principal issues were LDC concerns about inequality and dependence. "Those are really the catalytic forces that gave cause to this conference. It's the desire of the developing countries to overcome this technological dependence and overcome this inequality."[102]

Identifying and agreeing on the areas of scientific and technological need in Third World countries were perhaps the easiest task facing the organizers of UNCSTD. Indeed, it was one that many considered inappropriate. Conference secretary-general Frank João da Costa frequently reminded audiences that "science and technology are not the subject matter of this conference," and it was only under pressure from U.S. scientists and others that he reluctantly added the topic "science, technology, and the future" to the Vienna agenda.[103] Much more difficult— and the source of the tension between North and South that already became openly expressed during preparatory negotiations—was disagreement about the *way* these needs should be addressed, both in technical and in political terms.

The LDCs, negotiating through the Group of 77, started from the position that global inequity in the distribution of science and technology was a reflection of broader economic and political inequities. Hence, they argued, eliminating the former could only be achieved by addressing the latter. One of the clearest statements of this position was made in the report of a symposium held for African scientists and science policy-makers in Arusha, Tanzania, in January 1978. The report stated that African countries in particular found themselves on the periphery of the global economy, dependent on the center for scientific and technological knowledge and thus faced with no option but to accept both on the terms set by this center. Those attending the Tanzanian conference demanded "a new International Science and Technological Order" which would ensure "an optimal application of science and technology to development in its broadest and most forward-looking sense." The international community, they said, should acknowledge that there was an urgent need to liberalize the conditions relating to the international flow of knowledge. In one of its most controversial passages, the so-called Arusha Declaration stated: "It must be accepted universally, for a start, that technological knowledge is the common heritage of mankind."[104]

To U.S. corporations, this demand encapsulated their worst fears and suspicions. Treating such knowledge as a public good, rather than a private commodity, struck at the heart of the operation of multinational corporations and the power relations on which their activities were based. The prospect of science and technology being treated as the "common heritage of mankind," an idea initially used to refer to the potential exploitation of outer space or the ocean floor, implied a resource that should be made freely available to all. And this in turn, if endorsed by the United Nations, would imply that all technology-related knowledge—including the results of scientific research on which private companies in the industrialized countries depended increasingly as the key to power in the world economic system—should be made freely available to anyone who wanted it.

The business community remained adamant about the terms of its cooperation with the LDCs. Nat C. Robertson, chairman of the international subcommittee of the federal science and technology committee of the Industrial Research Institute (whose 258 member companies perform 85 percent of the privately funded research in the U.S.) warned that demands from LDCs for free access to Western science and technology "would dilute the proprietary rights of private-sector firms." He expressed enthusiastic approval for a passage in the U.S. national paper to UNCSTD that argued that technology transfer should be an effort "in which private industries or organizations enjoy due protection, and due return on their investment." [105]

At the international level, the same concerns were expressed in a report prepared by a group of twenty-six U.S. and European executives from major multinational corporations. [106] This group stressed the need for "flexibility" in negotiations between developed and less-developed countries. In practice, however, this meant that if less-developed countries wanted access to the science and technology being offered by the developed countries, they must accept the terms on which it was being offered. The group's chairman, James D. Grant of CPC International, emphasized that "both parties must be satisfied with the arrangement if a successful investment is to be made." On the one hand, this meant that a company should attempt to accommodate a host country's social and economic objectives. At the same time, however, "transnationals must receive a return for their investment and proprietary knowledge." [107]

Inevitably, it was the terms and conditions on which the LDCs would be given access to the scientific knowledge of the developed countries, rather than the precise nature of the science relevant to their needs, that became the focus of UNCSTD. These debates about technology transfer set the framework for debates about science. The Third World nations came to Vienna with a set of sweeping demands, focusing in particular on three critical issues that had not been resolved during preparations for the conference in New York. Each of these issues directly challenged the hierarchical patterns of control over access to scientific knowledge that the developed nations were attempting to reinforce.

The first proposal made by the LDCs was that the United Nations engineer a major shift in the global allocation of research and development resources by creating a new research fund with a target budget of $4 billion by 1990, perhaps raised through a system of international taxation on international trade in manufactured goods. Although it sounded a massive sum, the result would have been to raise from 5 to 7 percent the Third World's share of the global R&D budget. The second demand was for Third World control of U.N. programs concerned with applying science to development, in particular by the creation of a new focus within the U.N. system that was under its control. The third major stumbling block was over demands for major changes in the terms of technology and knowledge transfer; this was illustrated by the proposal that the conference should endorse a "program of action" that included demands for preferential low-cost access to patented technical information on the grounds that the LDCs should be given "full access" to the science and technology of the industrialized world.

None of these three demands was acceptable to the developed countries, even though they were prepared to agree that, in principle, scientific and technological self-reliance in the Third World was to be encouraged. Almost unanimously they pleaded poverty on the first request, an "unnecessary duplication of institutional structures" on the second, and the inappropriateness of trying to resolve the third at Vienna, since it was already being addressed by other negotiations within the U.N.[108]

The U.S. delegation was among the firmest in resisting the Third World's demands. On the surface, its approach appeared conciliatory. As noted earlier, the delegation head was Father Theodore Hesburgh (chairman of the Rockefeller Foundation, a director of both the Council of Foreign Relations and the Chase Manhattan Bank, and president-elect of the American Council on Education's Business–Higher Education Forum). He read out a statement from President Carter affirming that the U.S. was willing to support "all practical endeavors that can help us overcome endemic problems such as food scarcity and the energy crisis." Hesburgh himself spoke of the "anomaly" that 95 percent of world R&D is conducted by the developed nations, argued strongly for "cooperation not confrontation," and agreed that "transferred technology is often inappropriate to local needs as well as wasteful and insensitive to environmental impact." The U.S., he said, was prepared to join "reasonable ventures that strengthen worldwide scientific and technological cooperation."[109]

The catch lay in whose definition of "practical" and "reasonable" was to be used. The U.S. delegation was operating within the framework of Presidential Review Memorandum 33, prepared in the spring of 1978, which had laid out U.S. policies responsive to the North-South dialogue and other policy requirements in order to develop a U.S. position for science, technology, and development. The basic thrust of its instructions was to maintain the appearance of negotiation without giving the Third World any increased control over U.S. scientific and technical resources. U.S. negotiators stuck closely to the lines prepared for them, aided by the presence of a number of senior corporate executives as "advisers" to the Vienna delegation (e.g., Lewis Branscomb, chief scientist of IBM; William May, chairman of American Can Company;

Fletcher Byrom, chairman of the board of Koppers Company; and Frank M. Gimsley, vice-president of the Caterpillar Tractor Company). In a corporate sermon that directly reflected the corporate community's input into the State Department's preparations, Hesburgh asked for "a more equitable relationship between the developing countries and international private enterprise, so that in the global transfer of technology the interest of both is enhanced."[110]

The demands of the private sector had, from the earliest stages, been at the forefront of U.S. planning for UNCSTD. Hesburgh had made it clear to Congress that "the conference can be an effective mechanism to acquire new trade and investment opportunities for American industry."[111] At the preparatory meetings in New York, the American delegation had complained that an early draft of the plan of action produced by the U.N. secretariat "does not give balanced attention to the constructive role and contributions of the total private sector throughout the world."[112] And the delegation in Vienna received congressional support in its attempts to retain private rights over the allocation of knowledge. Representative Don Fuqua, chairman of the House Science and Technology Committee, "repeatedly expressed concern lest the UNCSTD 'program of action' violated the patent clause of the U.S. Constitution" through its demands for free access to the fruits of American research.[113]

The final outcome of the conference was a series of compromises that reflected the corporate world's support for a greater scientific capability in Third World nations, but its opposition to demands for any significant shift in control over their scientific or technological resources. The conference turned down the LDC proposal for a major new fund, although it did agree to a more limited initiative, namely a two-year interim fund under the auspices of the United Nations Development Program (UNDP), with a target of $250 million of voluntary contributions. The LDCs were prepared, reluctantly, to accept this as the only source of extra research funds likely to emerge from the conference. Their hopes were high for significant contributions from developed nations. The U.S. delegation had already been told by the State Department that it could endorse this proposal and that "the U.S. would contribute its fair share"[114]—which, on the basis of its contribution in other fields, the LDCs expected to be about $50 to $60 million.

The second compromise was over institutional changes within the United Nations system. Here the U.S. eventually agreed to accept the creation of a new Center for Science and Technology in New York. It also agreed to the enlargement of the Economic and Social Council's Committee on Science and Technology for Development to become a "committee of the whole"—i.e., one on which all members of the United Nations would be represented. The enlargement of this committee was one of the key Third World demands, since they hoped it would be a vehicle for controlling the allocation of research funds. Yet the committee's power was immediately emasculated when it came to discussion of the relationship between the new committee and the interim fund. The LDCs wanted the committee, on which they would have a majority, to decide on the projects selected for funding. The developed countries, however, opposed this. Ultimately a compromise was adopted under which, although the new committee was responsible for the principal "directions" that the fund should move in, it would not have any direct control over the funds. Thus the interim fund provided the Third World with a new source of support for their scientific activities, but little power over it, since the allocation of funds remained essentially under the control of the donor countries. The U.N. rearrangements, in contrast, provided the Third World with new power, but no resources through which to express it. Neither arrangement was likely to challenge the overall distribution of control over science and technology that UNCSTD had set out to achieve.

The impact of the conference was reduced even further when Congress refused to endorse even the relatively small $15 million contribution to the new fund that the administration eventually asked for in its budget request for 1981. In fact, there was little positive enthusiasm for the new fund in the White House, where many saw it as competing for congressional approval with their own pet project, ISTC. Indeed, despite Carter's warm message of support to the Vienna meeting, the general attitude of the executive branch to UNCSTD seems to have been dismissive. Early OMB skepticism about the conference is said to have led to the decision (later reversed by Congress) not to identify the planning office as a line item in the 1979 budget appropriations.[115] Frank Press, the principal link between OMB and the State Department during the conference preparations, made no reference to the conference at all in a subsequent review of the international activities of his office during his period as Carter's science adviser.[116]

Given this lack of administration enthusiasm, the interim fund soon became an easy target of OMB budget cutters, and the proposed U.S. contribution was eliminated entirely from the administration's budget requests two years later. The failure of the U.S. contribution to materialize, together with skepticism in several other major aid-granting countries—in particular Canada, Japan, and the United Kingdom—meant that the UNDP had great difficulties in getting the new fund off the ground. After two years, it had raised less than $40 million toward the originally promised target of six times this figure. Although it received 900 requests for assistance from over 100 countries, it had been able to act on only one in ten of these by the beginning of 1983.*

* The U.N. General Assembly, in Resolution 37/244 of December 20, 1982, approved the creation of a permanent U.N. Financing System for Science and Technology for Development, based initially on the operations of the interim fund. Although its aim was a budget for 1983–85 of $300 million, its prospects of raising this were even dimmer than those of the original fund.

From the perspective of the Third World countries, UNCSTD therefore turned out to be a major disappointment. An editorialist for a Mexican science magazine pointed out that the sum the UNDP's interim fund had been able to raise represented the cost of a small warplane or the budget of a little ministry in a small developed country. "The lesson of all this is that the developing nations must make their own decisions and assume greater responsibility if they wish seriously to increase their R&D capabilities," the magazine wrote.[117] Ward Morehouse of the Council for International and Public Affairs commented in the *New York Times* that "the results of the conference were nil"; he went on to suggest "a moratorium on large and indifferently prepared global problem-solving conferences while we continue to search for more effective ways to link international dialogue to the meaningful and concrete ways to fulfill unmet needs."[118]

From the U.S. point of view, however, the conference was a success, for it had contained the Third World's challenge to the dominant patterns of control over Western science and its applications to modern technology. A reporter described one U.S. delegate as returning from Vienna "elated" by the conference outcome.[119] During the conference itself, the initial resistance of almost all the industrialized nations, even to proposals that they knew they were eventually prepared to accept, paid off, for they had to make only comparatively slight concessions over the organization of scientific activities within the United Nations system. The U.S. had not been forced into giving away anything that it had not wanted to, and conversely had managed to retain for its private corporations full control over their science and technology. At the same time it had successfully avoided any breakdown in negotiations that could have triggered a more critical response from the Third World and created further barriers to the international dissemination of U.S. science and technology through channels more amenable to centralized corporate control.

Indeed, as far as private corporations were concerned, the conference was a success precisely because it did little to disrupt, and in many ways reinforced, the status quo. Harvey Wallender of the Council of the Americas said later that he felt most multinational corporations would tend to disregard completely what had happened at the conference, preferring to pay attention to what government policy-makers said in private, not in public U.N. meetings.[120] Similarly, the World Bank said it did not foresee any major impact on its R&D or technology transfer policies as a result of the conference.

What unites the histories of ISTC and UNCSTD are the growing efforts by the private sector to defend their privileged access to scientific knowledge, in particular that knowledge which has become the key to their technological competitiveness. In both cases, government action—whether exercised domestically through federal agencies or internationally, in collaboration with other advanced nations, through the United Nations—was supported only to the extent that it helped corporations exploit this knowledge without giving away any control over it. The net result was to strengthen the patterns of control over science in the hands of private-sector institutions in the industrialized nations, providing other countries access to it only if they were prepared to accept the rules of the economic and political game that ensured the continued dominance of the core over the periphery in the global economy.

Such a policy was endorsed even more strongly by the Reagan administration when it came to Washington in 1980 than it had been by the Carter administration. The Kissinger-Brzezinski strategy had already come under heavy fire from the conservative wing of the Republican party, which argued that *any* government-based attempt to regulate the flow of private science and technology was an interference with free trade. This was claimed true regardless of whether the regulation was proposed by Trilateralists (in the interests of "managing global interdependence") or the Group of 77 (in the name of global equity). At the same time, however, the Reagan administration accepted the basic premise on which the strategy had been constructed, namely that U.S. science and technology could be dangled as a reward for political good behavior, and thus used as a tool by which this "good behavior" could be manipulated.

Continuity with the past was soon revealed by Secretary of State Alexander Haig, Jr. In an address given on August 11, 1981, on "A Strategic Approach to American Foreign Policy" that directly echoed the ideas of his previous mentor, Kissinger, Haig claimed that developed and less-developed nations share a "mutual interest in modernization," and that "Western capital, trade, and technology are essential to this process."[121] He also made it clear that he was prepared to offer U.S. technology to the Soviet Union if it restrained its intervention in world trouble spots. In a speech to the World Affairs Council of Philadelphia in October 1981 (shortly before a meeting of the heads of the world's developed and developing nations in Cancún, Mexico), Reagan himself offered research and technical assistance in areas such as energy and agriculture as an alternative to financial aid—cheaper and more effective in both a technical and a political sense.[122] In this spirit, new scientific cooperation agreements were reached with several "middle-tier" developing countries, including Brazil and India.

At the same time, however, Reagan and his advisers made even clearer than the Carter administration the political terms under which scientific and technical assistance was being offered to other nations. Haig, in his speech, said Reagan recognized that "the essence of development is the creation of additional wealth rather than the selective redistribution of existing wealth from one part of the world to another"—an explicit formula for the support of Third World capitalism, and a rejection of the political strategies for redistribution being pursued by the LDCs through the United Nations system. He even argued that security assistance was being provided to right-wing regimes in Latin America and elsewhere "in recognition of the crucial link between modernization and stability." * [123]

The premises of the Kissinger-Brzezinski-Carter strategy—that diplomacy had an important role to play in protecting the terms and conditions on which U.S. science was made available to the Third World—therefore remained valid. So too did the tactic of using scientific agreements with Third World countries to pursue other political goals. When Indian Prime Minister Indira Gandhi visited Washington in the summer of 1982, for example, a high-level task force was appointed under the guidance of Reagan's science adviser, George Keyworth, to draw up a list of projects on which scientists from the two countries could collaborate. One of the goals of the White House was to help mend political bridges that had been seriously weakened by Congress's refusal to let India continue to receive U.S. fuel for its nuclear reactor at Tarapur, since India had not agreed (as required under the Nuclear Non-Proliferation Act of 1978) to open all its nuclear installations to international inspection. [125] At the same time India agreed with Washington that it would tighten up the export to the Soviet Union of high technology originating in the U.S.—the price it was prepared to pay for increased access to U.S. science.

The Reagan administration also continued its predecessor's policy of using scientific exchange agreements with the People's Republic of China to smooth the way for increased sales of high technology goods. A series of new agreements covering nuclear physics, transportation, aeronautics, and biomedical science were signed in May 1983 with China's Commission on Science and Technology—despite the cancellation of most cultural and sports exchange agreements after the U.S. had granted political asylum to a Chinese tennis player. The agreements were signed a few days before the first meeting of a Joint Commission on Chinese-American Commerce, during which the U.S. Secretary of Commerce, Malcolm Baldridge, Jr., had announced a significant increase both qualitatively and quantitatively in the transfer and sale of U.S. technology to China—an arrangement described by the Chinese authorities as "a total success."

Further continuity was maintained by the Reagan administration in shifting the emphasis of foreign aid from economic to scientific and

---

* Richard Allen, at the time Reagan's National Security Adviser, went even further in a television interview broadcast just before the Cancún meeting. He said that although reducing the foreign aid budget was justified on the grounds that "the problems of the less-developed countries are not going to be solved simply by the massive infusion of money," the Reagan administration believed that "emphasis on technical assistance, particularly in a free democratic and capitalist system, will yield positive results." [124]

technical assistance, a trend actively encouraged by the new administrator of the Agency for International Development, M. Peter McPherson.
The legislation originally intended to establish ISTC was used to support
a new Program for Scientific and Technological Cooperation within
AID, while the agency itself created a new Bureau for Science and Technology. Despite its more modest size—funding for both 1982 and 1983
was held at $10 million—the new program carried out many of the tasks
that had previously been destined for ISTC; half of the money went to
support research proposals from scientists in both the U.S. and the
LDCs, while the other half supported a project administered by the
National Academy of Sciences to support networks of LDC institutions
in exploring unexploited technologies of potential economic value to
those countries. Placed in charge of AID's Bureau for Science and Development was Nyle Brady, who had already been tapped by the Carter
administration as the first director of ISTC, and who had returned to
Washington in anticipation of taking up the latter position, having previously been director of the International Rice Research Institute in the
Philippines.

Brady soon made it clear that he saw one of his principal responsibilities as improving the access of developing nations to U.S. science and
technology in both the public and the private sectors—but particularly
in the latter. His position was squarely in line with the administration's
general approach to foreign aid. One dimension of this strategy was to
emphasize bilateral rather than multilateral links, since these can be
more easily tied to politically acceptable objectives. Another was to encourage—as recommended, for example, in the Glennan report of 1975
—greater direct private-sector involvement in developing aid strategies,
stressing the role of the market rather than public institutions in the
creation, adaptation, and dissemination of new technologies.

The Bureau for Science and Technology, again in line with previous
proposals for the ISTC, became one of the principal channels in the
State Department through which this private-sector linkage was firmly
established. The attractions of such a relatively low-key approach to
development assistance have been described by Columbia University
economist Nathaniel Leff. In an article in the review Orbis, he pointed
out that the desire of the LDCs to exercise control over transferred
knowledge inevitably implied conflict with multinational companies,
which were concerned to maintain the confidentiality of their know-how
and to avoid "leakages" and thus potential losses in other markets. He
suggested that, as a result, AID should request bids from American companies to provide know-how to the LDCs, engaging the private sector in
the contracting-out programs that AID had long carried on through
university research departments. Leff emphasized that "this would has-
ten the transformation of American firms from sellers of goods to sellers
of know-how in less-developed countries." [126]

Here again we come to the crux of the matter. Selling "technology" abroad is something that can be done in a relatively straightforward commodity relationship. Selling "know-how," as Leff pointed out, is something different, since one is selling something much more valuable: the capacity to produce. The competitive advantage enjoyed by U.S. companies in the global economy lies as much in their science-based know-how as in their technology, hence the push to move this to the center of international trade. Yet the control of the application of this know-how remains important. If it is sold as a commodity on the open market (or even given away, with no strings attached, as part of a foreign aid package), such control is abrogated; if it is included as part of a bilateral agreement between governments, the handles on its application remain accessible. The more scientific knowledge becomes an essential component of this know-how, the greater the desire to put science under these same controls.

For private corporations, therefore, it is less attractive to arrange for the transfer of know-how under contract to the developing country than to a U.S. agency that can be depended on to protect their interests. Companies reap a double advantage. On the one hand, as Leff put it, "by increasing the attractiveness, both to firms and to LDC governments, of an alternative to direct foreign investment, the policy would reduce the intrusive presence of MNCs [multinational corporations] in the less-developed countries."[127] Similarly, protection for private property and the social relationships that it embodies would be increased. Under the new arrangement, the multinational corporations provide the know-how and reap the financial and political benefits, with AID and the State Department using the conventional forms of diplomatic leverage to make sure that MNC control of this know-how is maintained. The advantage of this arrangement, as the head of a U.S. company working in Mexico put it in evidence to a congressional committee, is that "when you sell . . . technology in terms of technical assistance, you control that technology."[128]

One of the clearest examples of this shift from the Carter administration's Trilateralist approach to knowledge transfer to the more naked free-market strategy of the Reagan administration lies in their different handling of negotiations leading up to the signing of the United Nations Law of the Sea in December 1982. The facts can be put quite baldly. Discussions about a Law of the Sea, designed to regulate a wide range of activities associated with what had previously been treated as the "high seas," began in the late 1960s. One section dealt with the terms of access to the minerals on the seabed, and the distribution of the advanced technology needed to exploit them. Despite broad differences in approach between developed and less-developed nations, both the Ford and the Carter administrations made substantial efforts to reach a mutually acceptable accommodation with the less-developed countries, and had almost succeeded by the time Carter left office at the end of 1980. The Reagan administration, however, made it clear soon after coming to power that it disagreed with its predecessors' position. It demanded further major changes to the draft treaty—at that time virtually completed after numerous rounds of negotiations—and these were unacceptable to the majority of participants. The gap proved to be unbridgeable; when the treaty was finally signed in December 1982, the U.S. was not among the signatories.

On the surface the reasons for the U.S. change of heart appeared relatively straightforward. The Ford and Carter administrations had both argued that although the treaty extracted a high price from U.S. corporations that wished to engage in exploitation of the seabed, it was worth the return, namely an internationally agreed-upon legal framework defining the rights of all parties to access to the world's oceans for civilian and military purposes. The Reagan administration disagreed. It claimed that the price was too high, that U.S. mining companies were being asked to give away too much of their proprietary know-how in mining technology. It argued that adequate protection could be achieved by other means, including a mini-agreement signed late in 1982 with West Germany, France, and the United Kingdom—and if necessary by military force.

Beneath the surface arguments lay deeper ideological motivations. For Third World nations, the Law of the Sea Treaty was seen as a way of engineering a redistribution of scientific and technical know-how and expertise from the developed to the developing nations—and thus, like UNCSTD, directly challenging the dominant global patterns of control over advanced technology and the related scientific and technical knowledge. The treaty requires, in particular, that mining companies who wish to exploit the seabed for valuable metallic nodules can do so only if they make the technology and know-how they have developed to do this available to an international organization known as the Enterprise. This organization would then be able to carry out the same activities, parallel to the mining consortia into which the corporations had organized themselves, with the profits going directly to benefit the less-developed nations.

In the mid-1970s, U.S. negotiators, shaken by the effectiveness of the Arab oil embargo and acting largely under Kissinger's instructions, were prepared to go some way toward meeting Third World demands in order to guarantee future access to an important source of minerals needed by U.S. industrial producers. Ironically, many of the legal concepts in the draft treaty agreed to in principle at the end of 1980 originated in the U.S. President Johnson, for example, had spoken in 1966 of the need to ensure that "the deep seas and ocean bottoms are and remain the legacy of all human beings."[129] Furthermore, the suggestion that mining companies be given licenses in return for fees, taxes, and making their mining technology available to an International Seabed Authority had been put forward by Kissinger in 1976 as a suggested compromise between the demands of the industrial and the developing nations. Failure to agree on a treaty, he warned at the time, would result in "unrestrained military and commercial rivalry and mounting political turmoil."[130]

Pressure to achieve an acceptable treaty was maintained under the Carter administration, which appointed Trilateralist and ex–Commerce Secretary Elliot Richardson as chief negotiator. Richardson made considerable negotiating progress, and by the end of 1980 a draft treaty seemed all but ready for signature by virtually all the world's nations, including the U.S. Yet already the treaty had become the target of a virulent attack from the more conservative wing of U.S. capital. Two particular objections were voiced. The first was directed against the specific attempts to develop an international regime to take mining techniques and know-how from the developed countries and give it to the LDCs. The second challenge took the form of a wholesale rejection of international institutions such as the United Nations as a framework for regulation of either economic or technological activities, and in particular of the idea of engineering a global redistribution of wealth through the "New International Economic Order."

Generously supported by benefactors of conservative causes, in particular the Sarah Scaife Foundation of Pittsburgh, critics of the treaty mounted a full-scale attack.[131] One group, chaired by Fletcher Byrom, chairman of the board of Koppers Company and a member of the U.S. delegation to UNCSTD, complained in a report for the World Affairs Council of Pittsburgh (financed by the Scaife Foundation) that "U.S. policies toward the Third World have all too often been motivated by human rights and essentially 'political' considerations, to the exclusion of economic and closely related national security considerations" (the last comment referred to the fact that agreeing to an international treaty was seen as mortgaging future U.S. supplies of "critical minerals" such as magnesium to the whim of the developing nations).[132] Similarly, Daniel James, a consultant to the conservative National Strategy Information Center on the Law of the Sea negotiations, wrote to the *Washington Post* on April 27, 1981, in support of the Reagan administration's decision to review the U.S. position. "The central objection to the treaty is that it would establish an International Seabed Development Authority, which would exercise virtual supranational dominion over the ocean's depths in a manner as Orwellian as its name, abridging our national sovereignty and *ruling the destinies of U.S. private companies,*" he stated[133] (emphasis added).

It became clear from such comments that critics were objecting not merely to details in the draft treaty, but to the whole principal of international regulation of technology and knowledge transfer, which would, they claimed, reduce U.S. hegemony in critical areas of new technology. When the Reagan administration arrived in Washington early in 1981, the critics had powerful allies in influential positions. As president of United Technologies Corporation, for example, Secretary of State Haig had previously attacked the "common heritage international regime" envisaged in the draft Law of the Sea treaty as "inimical to private-enterprise market principles and the interests of the Western industrialized nations." He had gone on to say that the U.S. would in particular be injured since "it would be required to relinquish many of the advantages of its current technological leadership." [134]

In January 1982, after a detailed review by the State Department, the Department of Defense, and the National Security Council, President Reagan held a press conference in which he listed the areas in which the draft treaty required changes if it was to be acceptable to the U.S. One of the most important was the demand for the elimination of provisions for the mandatory transfer of private technology. [135] Four weeks later, just before the final negotiating session in New York at which it became clear that the U.S. demands were not acceptable to the majority of other participants, the head of the U.S. delegation to the treaty talks, James L. Malone, explained the administration's thinking to a congressional committee. "There is a deeply held view in our Congress that one of America's greatest assets is its capacity for innovation and its ability to produce advanced technology," Malone said. "It is understandable, therefore, that a treaty would be unacceptable to many Americans if it required the U.S. or, more particularly, private companies to transfer that asset in a forced sale." [136] (Elliot Richardson, who as Carter's negotiator had already reached what he felt was a reasonable compromise on this point, disagreed with this characterization. He claimed that, rather than destroying the idea of private property, "the treaty is indispensable to creating property rights in seabed minerals and a legal framework without which investment will not occur." [137])

At one level, the debate over whether or not the U.S. should endorse the treaty separated the liberal from the more conservative wing of U.S. capital, broadly corresponding to the split between Democrats and Republicans. Richardson, complained in an article in the *Washington Star* that "this is an issue which appears to be drawn between the internationalists and the free marketeers." [138] He and other representatives of the internationalist wing of American capital strongly criticized the Reagan administration's decision on the grounds that it would provoke further anarchy in international trade relations.

Yet the Reagan administration's actions in rejecting the treaty must also be seen in a broader historical context. Kissinger's approval of the international regulation of deep-sea mining and the transfer of related scientific and technical knowledge had been a direct and calculated response to the militancy of the Third World's opposition to multinational corporations at the beginning of the 1970s. By the early 1980s, much of this militancy had evaporated, while the multinational corporations' desire to keep a hold on this knowledge had increased. Split by internal differences that seriously weakened their bargaining capacity, the Third World no longer presented the same threat to the expansion of U.S. capital. Indeed, countries such as India, Mexico, and Brazil were themselves becoming net exporters of technology and know-how and had little desire to become subject to the same controls they had previously insisted be imposed on others. There was no need for broad international agreements when the same goals could, it was argued, be achieved by other means (ranging from bilateral negotiations through "security assistance" to the destabilization of hostile regimes). Sea-mining technology was itself used as a potential instrument of persuasion. The counsel for the National Oceans Industries Association warned that U.S. companies would not do business with companies belonging to countries that had signed the treaty.[139]

Seen in this light, the Reagan administration's refusal to accept the Law of the Sea Treaty, signed by 119 other countries in Jamaica on December 10, 1982, was an expression of confidence among U.S. multinationals in their ability to control more directly the demands of less-developed countries on Western science and technology. As such, it is linked directly to the strategy adopted by AID to exploit the economic and political potential of U.S. science and technology. Both represent a shift away from the Carter strategy of requiring active government participation. The shift was, in fact, already occurring while negotiations over ISTC and UNCSTD were taking place, and contributed significantly to the failure of negotiations in each case. In both cases government direction, sanctioned by public debate, has taken a back seat as the principal determinant of the strategy for applying American science to Third World needs. The driver's seat is increasingly occupied by U.S. capital, keen to exploit its private technical and scientific knowledge while maintaining as much control over it as possible.

Subsequent moves by the Reagan administration to promote a "mini-treaty" among those few industrialized countries that already possessed or held an interest in the technology needed for deep-sea mining reveal the other side of the coin, namely the desire to regulate competition *among* the advanced nations to ensure that their mutual hegemony is maintained. The U.S. persuaded Britain, France, and West Germany to sign an interim agreement in November 1982, and the four countries agreed to support a private arbitration agreement signed by the five main deep-sea mining consortia. The idea was to encourage orderly competition among the companies, but to provide complete protection for the technology and know-how they had developed for lifting the metallic nodules from the seabed. The strategy was to attempt to use the technological lead of the U.S. companies, protected in this way by the terms of the mini-treaty, to undermine the effectiveness of the main U.N. treaty. As one lobbyist for the mining consortia put it: "Without the technology supplied by American companies, it's unlikely that anyone will mine the seabed."[140]

The significance of the Reagan administration's actions regarding the Law of the Sea lies in how they encapsulated its approach to the global distribution of control over advanced technology, as well as the science on which it depends. Just as the administration had complained that attempts to achieve a redistribution of technical know-how through the U.N. system that challenged the dominant position of its mining companies would set a precedent for negotiations in other spheres, so its own strategy offered a precedent for an alternative approach, namely that all such issues should be resolved through the mechanism of the market. Rejecting Third World claims that their lack of technology made fair competition impossible, the administration continued to insist, as Malone put it in his statement to Congress, that U.S. interests "will best be served by developing the resources of the seabed as market conditions warrant."[141]

In the case of seabed mining, the research whose results the mining companies wanted to stop being forcibly transferred to Third World nations was still relatively "applied" science. Yet, as we have seen previously, the distinction between applied and basic research, particularly when it has a direct relationship to advanced industrial processing techniques, is rapidly disappearing. And the results of such areas of basic science are, with the Reagan administration's blessing, being increasingly approached in the same way, namely according to the philosophy that distribution should be determined by the demands and incentives of the market, rather than based on any social judgment of need or equity.

This is becoming the case with biotechnology. The impact of technological developments based on recent scientific findings in the fields of cell biology, molecular genetics, and recombinant DNA is likely to be as great, if not greater, on the developing as on the developed nations. Potential applications cover areas such as disease prevention and treatment, animal breeding, food production, plant care, and new sources of energy. Furthermore, they are sufficiently close to realization to make the commercial prospects attractive. As a report from a committee of the National Academy of Sciences put it: "Compared with many traditional development programs, the anticipated results from biotechnology appear to be cost-effective and within the time frame and general manpower requirements of most developing countries."[142]

The range of such applications has led many biotechnology companies to put a special emphasis on products such as vaccines against hepatitis-B and foot-and-mouth disease; indeed, it appears that the prospects of global sales have led some biomedical research laboratories to increase their emphasis on parasitic diseases and other ailments that primarily affect developing countries. The agricultural research also has wide potential LDC application—for instance, the research into increasing plants' ability to fix nitrogen or to tolerate unfavorable growing conditions—and this, too, has attracted considerable commercial interest. The result, as one of the U.S.'s leading molecular biologists, Nobel laureate David Baltimore, has remarked, is that "at the moment, this work is being driven more by profit motive than by anything else." At the same time, Baltimore points out, "almost all of the biotechnology is found in the developed world." (Baltimore, director of the Whitehead Institute at MIT, went on to warn: "It is not prudent to maintain a continual dependence on the developed world, where much of the current work is profit-oriented—not a solid base on which to build solutions to local problems"[143]—a statement later underlined when one biotechnology company, International Plant Research Institute in California, announced that a failure to find sufficiently profitable markets for its disease-resistant cassava had led the company to redirect its research efforts toward the needs of U.S. food processors such as low-fiber wheat, tomatoes high in solids, and vanilla-flavored cereal crops.)

Aware of the danger that the combination of these two factors could create new chains of external dependency, Third World countries have established plans for an International Center for Genetic Engineering and Biotechnology under the auspices of the United Nations Industrial Development Organization (UNIDO). Approved in principle at the beginning of 1983, the center will carry out research on industrial processes using genetic engineering techniques and train scientists and technicians from developing countries in ways of using them, in line with a previous statement by the agency's director that biotechnology "could galvanize and broad-base the industrial structure of developing countries and impart new directions to industry, agriculture, and energy."[144] The need for such an initiative was strongly endorsed by a team of six leading molecular biologists—four from the United States—who visited universities and government institutions in thirty-four cities throughout sixteen countries. Despite this, the U.S. State Department decided not to support planning for the new center, citing among its reasons "unanswered questions on patent rights and cross-licensing"[145]—in other words, fearing that the center could undercut the market interests of American corporations (many of which own exclusive rights to basic biotechnological processes through their links with university molecular biology departments).

Such conflicts between public and private demands on research relevant to Third World needs have already begun to emerge. Early in 1983, scientists from the West Coast biotechnology company Genentech agreed to cooperate with research workers from the New York University Medical School on efforts to develop a malaria vaccine, potentially one of the most significant contributions of biotechnology to Third World health problems. Genentech promised to clone cells producing the antigen needed for the vaccine; in return, however, the company demanded exclusive rights to market the resulting vaccine. The New York University researchers refused, pointing out that their work was partly supported by the World Health Organization, which expected in return access to any new products resulting from the research. And WHO was not prepared to grant any one company the rights to the vaccine— particularly in the light of growing demands from Third World countries that they be given the resources to establish their own vaccine production facilities. Genentech, not without a certain public rancor, withdrew from the project.[146]

The experiences with biotechnology illustrate the new rules of the game that are coming into play over the international dissemination of science. Previously it had been possible to make a relatively clear distinction between science and technology, and to argue that even if technology should be transferred primarily through the private marketplace (a position itself frequently challenged by the LDCs), the results of science should be made freely available. Yet the more the distinction between applied science and basic science becomes blurred, the more arguments are heard for treating scientific results in the same way as technical know-how. In earlier chapters we saw some of the domestic implications of this switch, with increasing interest by both the corporate and the military communities in university basic research being accompanied by pressures from both for increased control over this research. What we find is the same process now taking place in the international arena, where the traditional idea that the results of scientific research should be made freely available to anyone interested is now being increasingly displaced by the idea that they should be bought, sold, and bartered as private property.

The change has important implications for the role of science in foreign policy. Where science has in the past been used as a tool of international diplomacy, it was largely considered a *neutral* tool, in the sense that scientific (as opposed to technological) issues, although important in themselves, tended to be peripheral to the main concerns of international relations. In contrast, through the significant contribution of research-intensive products to the balance of payments of the industrialized nations, as well as a direct contribution to new processing techniques in key sectors of industry, science is rapidly becoming an integral element of international economic policy. The political implications of this structural change, rather than any lack of desire to help the nations of the Third World on the part of individual negotiators, explains the lack of success of ISTC, UNCSTD, and the Law of the Sea negotiations.

To understand the new international politics of science, it is therefore necessary to see them as a reflection of the new international division of labor—that is, as part of a global system of production, largely controlled by international banks as multinational corporations, and within which the ability to determine the terms and conditions of access to Western science increasingly constitutes one of the mechanisms by which this control is exercised. It is not only the less-developed countries that complain. A moderate Labour member of the British House of Commons writes that given "the realities of the power and autonomy of the multinationals . . . any science policy with the remotest chance of being effective must include guidelines on how to force or induce multinational corporations to conform to that policy."[147]

At top diplomatic levels, however, the issue is seen differently. For the most advanced industrialized nations it is a question, as Brzezinski once put it, of broadening "the scope of educational-scientific and economic-technological cooperation" as a way of strengthening their political and economic links.[148] (Somewhat similarly, a recent report on international trade from the National Academy of Sciences states: "Nowhere is our national welfare more interwoven with that of our allies than in the fields of science cooperation and high technology trade."[149]) The significance of scientific collaboration in rationalizing the costs of research between these countries, while at the same time reinforcing their dominance over the global economy,* was reflected by its inclusion for the first time on the agenda of the economic summits held in 1982 and 1983. The second of these, held at Williamsburg, endorsed a report prepared over the previous year by senior science advisers of the seven heads of state, listing eighteen areas where cooperation was beginning, ranging from research on fusion energy to biotechnology. Cooperative science projects had in the past "sometimes been less than effective because they failed to take sufficient account of the growing interface between technical activity and the socio-politico-economic environment," said the report. "A new thrust and fresh political will are needed from the highest level of government" to ensure better cooperation and to keep interdependence in the diffusion and use of science from becoming "a cause of conflict" or a source of "weakness in the future."[150] The final communiqué from the Williamsburg summit "noted with approval" the report and encouraged further work on the eighteen collaborative projects it listed.[151]

The less-developed countries are not excluded from this scenario. "As developing countries create infrastructures in science and technology, our own countries should recognize the constructive role which they are able to play," advised the report.[152] Yet, as has been repeatedly made clear to them, their participation is supported only to the extent that they are prepared to recognize the new rules of the game. For a start, this means recognizing the increasing primacy of the market as the principal

---

* Five countries alone—the U.S., Japan, West Germany, France, and the United Kingdom —account for 70 percent of the industrialized world's exports to the LDCs.

channel for the transfer of scientific knowledge and respecting the control over this knowledge that multinationalf corporations are able to exercise—for example, by concentrating research activities in the industrialized nations and limiting the dissemination of scientific knowledge through the use of protected patents. (Five out of every six patents in the LDCs are owned by foreign companies, and many are never exploited but are merely used to ward off potential competitors.[153])

The problem is that political implications can often undercut the development of what Peruvian economist Francisco Sagasti has called the need for an "endogenous scientific capability,"[154] namely a capacity for independent decision-making on science and technology priorities when powerful external groups already have a keen interest in the outcome of these decisions The situation these countries face already limits their ability to maneuver, and proposals for the future threaten to limit it even more. A U.S. businessman suggests that "from a rational point of view, we need a restructuring of the world economy, with the United States, Western Europe, and Japan competing in the high technology capital goods area, and the LDCs with low technology, labor-intensive products."[155] A panel of U.S. academics and business leaders—coordinated by the economist Henry R. Nau (then professor of political science at George Washington University and later appointed a senior staff member of President Reagan's National Security Council)—proposes that these countries restrict their import of high technology production processes and thus the export of high technology products, in order to avoid excessive competition with the industrialized world.[156] In making recommendations to President Reagan on steps to increase U.S. competitiveness, the Business–Higher Education Forum, established by the American Council of Education, insists that one requirement is for "better protection of the intellectual property of U.S. firms conducting business in less-developed countries."[157] Each of these demands, while perfectly "rational" for the industrialized nations to make, is arguing for a division of labor in which the economic interests of the "core" nations remain dominant over the aspirations of the periphery. And this in turn means a greater concentration of control over the science essential to new production processes within both sets of countries.

The same problems exist with international information systems. Many less-developed countries have suggested that comprehensive systems giving information on the science and technology available from the industrialized nations would be a useful tool for their own development strategies. The proposal is supported by those multinationals who see it as a useful way of increasing foreign sales of their technical know-how. Some, however, point out that such systems will always suffer from the fact that no company will insert the data most crucial to its economic strength. Thus the chairman of Texas Instruments points out that "it is not likely that sensitive information (possibly the most useful in the eyes of the developing countries) would be made available to such a 'public' information system."[158]

In such circumstances, efforts to establish an effective, autonomous research capability in the less-developed countries face substantial obstacles. The goal has been widely endorsed; a declaration from the Pugwash Council on guidelines for international scientific cooperation for development, for example, states that "countries of the South must build up an autonomous capability for problem-solving, decision-making, and implementation in all matters relating science and technology to development."[159] Yet there are strong pressures in the opposite direction. For example, Anil Agarwal, director of the Center for Science and Environment in India, has described how solar energy reseach workers in India mounted a sharp protest campaign against one state's intention to order solar pumps from a company set up by a former World Bank economist and a scientist from the Massachusets Institute of Technology. The Indian scientists, from the state-owned electronics company, argued that if the government wanted to exploit the results of domestic research, it should not allow the import of foreign technology when a domestic equivalent was likely to become available, even if this might prove to be more expensive. "Importing technology could speed up industrial development, but it could also undermine local R&D efforts, thus promoting technological dependence and the economic and political dependence that follows," writes Agarwal.[160]

A similar situation also exists in Brazil. A study of the Brazilian electronics industry showed that "lack of technology research" and the fact that the industry was controlled by decisions from foreign centers appeared to be the cause of its technological dependence and the almost total predominance of foreign enterprises in that sector. As the president of one Brazilian company complained: "It is incontestable that the activities of subsidiaries of multinational firms, in most cases, must follow the global policies of the parents. In general the 'know-how' utilized is also important, having been developed in the research centers of the parents. This practice assures control of the technology furnished to subsidiaries, remaining dependent on the parent for innovation."[161]

The structural constraints imposed on the LDCs by the place allotted to them—both technically and politically—at the bottom of the international division of labor has led to suggestions for some radical remedies. One is for a partial "de-linking" from the global economy, under which a country would deliberately sever links in certain fields of science and technology wih the industrialized nations in order to promote conditions for more autonomous development.[162] A variation of this, suggested by Ward Morehouse of the Council for International and Public Affairs, would be for international agreement to be reached on a limited number of "technologies for humanity," where the research would be carried out and the technologies developed and disseminated entirely in the public domain. Two candidates suggested by Morehouse for such treatment are malaria vaccine and nitrogen fixation.[163]

Yet already—as we have seen in the case of the dispute between Genentech and WHO over the rights to the production of malaria vaccine —private corporations are tightening their control over the scientific knowledge that offers the most effective way of producing such technologies. And the power that they have to do this underlines the fact that science and technology are only a part of the problem. Although both are clearly necessary components of development strategies, the deepest roots of the problems facing the poor in Third World countries are cultural, social, and political. In other words, they are located in the global distribution of power that both permits and is in turn reinforced by private control over the fruits of modern science. The historical record shows that without changes in the distribution of this power, the massive transfer of Western science—on whatever terms—is unlikely to achieve its full development objectives. "The transfer of technology from rich to poor countries, especially through the private market channels of transnational corporations, has not helped in the relief from poverty and hunger in the Third World," writes Surendra Patel, chief of the Technology Transfer Division of UNCTAD. Although industrial output has grown impressively, the transfer of Western science, technology, and capital has not led to significant improvement (in either relative or absolute terms) in the living conditions of the people. "Most of the Third World remains ill-fed, ill-clad, ill-housed, and illiterate," says Patel. "The economic and social changes witnessed in the recent past can best be described as dependent development."[164]

Meeting the full potential of autonomous development means breaking the cycle of dependency. And this in turn means that the LDCs need to generate the poltitical ability to challenge not merely the terms under which they are currently allowed access to Western science and technology but, more fundamentally, the power relationships that let the developed countries set these terms—power relationships increasingly expressed through the internal dynamics of global trade and the dominant position within it of multinational banks and corporations. Such a challenge, however, strikes at the heart of the pattern of international relationships that the U.S., no less than the other advanced industrial nations, is currently seeking to establish through the integration of science into foreign policy—a pattern in which the centralized control of access to science in the hands of private institutions has become more, not less, important. The stakes have been raised on both sides.

=== 5 ===

SCIENCE
AND SOCIETY:
PUBLIC PARTICIPATION
VS.
DEMOCRATIC CONTROL

WHEN WILLIAM D. MCELROY, DIRECTOR OF THE NATIONAL SCIENCE Foundation, appointed a special assistant in June 1972 to promote the agency's research into the ethical implications of modern science, his action carried an ironic symbolism. Selected for the post was an attorney who, among various previous posts in the State Department, had been head of the counterinsurgency task force for Southeast Asia under both the Kennedy and the Johnson administrations.[1] The irony lay in the fact that his post at the NSF held certain similarities to his previous responsibilities. For the function of the new program, as many agency officials saw it, was not merely to stimulate a new field of research, but also to fulfill a more political role by refurbishing an image of science that was becoming increasingly tarnished by public criticism. And one of the goals of this exercise—like that of any counterinsurgency strategy—was to defuse the destabilizing influence of this criticism and prevent it from evolving into a movement that could seriously challenge the traditional patterns of control over science exercised by the scientific and corporate communities.

Criticism of science had grown rapidly in the preceding few years. Prior to the end of the 1960s, although isolated parts of science and its social applications through technology had attracted public attention—in particular over the development of nuclear weapons—there had been no overall questioning of its role in contemporary society; science in the period since the Second World War had been almost unanimously identified as a force for social progress. This was followed, as we have seen in previous chapters, by a period of growing skepticism. Questions increased about the desirability of unregulated technological growth, based partly on an awareness of the environmental damage inflicted by many science-based industrial processes, as well as the health and safety problems that these processes often created for both industrial workers and the outside community. Doubts raised by other by-products of technological progress, from cancer-causing chemicals in food through supersonic transport planes to fragmentation bombs in Vietnam, led to a fundamental questioning of the idea that the social applications of science were almost invariably beneficial. And this in turn prompted many to suggest that society's ability to produce new scientific knowledge was rapidly outstripping its ability to keep such knowledge under proper control.[2]

Much of the criticism, focused through groups ranging from Citizens' League Against the Sonic Boom to Friends of the Earth, was aimed at the failure of traditional political institutions to prevent the new problems associated with science and technology from emerging and to deal with their results. In particular it was argued that these institutions had failed to inject social values into decision-making on scientific and technological issues, other than those that promoted maximum economic growth or military strength. In response, political leaders sought to develop mechanisms that would make up for the deficiency. The legislative and the executive branches of government competed with each other for public favor by passing new legislation and establishing new institutions that would integrate a wide range of environmental and social parameters into decisions about the development and deployment of new technologies.* And reacting to charges that many of these decisions had been made in the past with excessive secrecy, the new laws and the institutions they created were designed to accommodate greater public participation in the decision-making—for example, by providing opportunities through legislation such as the Federal Advisory Committee Act of 1972 for public comment on proposed regulatory decisions or open attendance at the meetings of agency advisory committees.

Yet pressure from critics often extended beyond a mere demand for the consideration of new parameters and opportunities for public expression in the traditional decision-making process. Their criticism of the way decisions had been made in the past included a political dimension,

---

* The most important of these were the National Environmental Protection Act of 1969 and the decision to establish the Environmental Protection Agency; the Occupational Safety and Health Act of 1970, setting up the Occupational Safety and Health Administration within the Department of Labor; the Clean Air Act of 1972; the Water Pollution Control Act of 1972; and the Toxic Substances Control Act of 1976.

in that they claimed that the fault lay partly in the patterns of control behind the decisions about science and its applications. Remedying this, it was suggested, also required the redistribution of power, both in the narrow sense of greater public access to and control over science and technology, and in broader terms that addressed the fundamental social and political structures of U.S. society, ranging from its universities to its private corporations. Such demands frequently became expressed in terms of a desire for greater public participation in decision-making. But a more general distrust of the individuals and institutions that had led the U.S. into the morass of the Vietnam War on the one hand, and the environmental crisis at home on the other, provoked a revitalized grass-roots democracy that sought a firm grasp on the principal handles of political power.

The two approaches to the problems raised by the social impact of science, although frequently overlapping, nevertheless reveal a basic conflict between two styles (or tendencies) of political strategy. The first, favored by those who seek a "rational" approach to the problems by the imposition of solutions reached through a consensus of experts, can be characterized as the *technocratic approach*. Even when encouraging participation in the process of reaching consensus, this approach leaves unquestioned the basic political structures through which the solutions, usually expressed in technical terms, are to be put into effect. In contrast, the second approach stresses the importance of procedures as much as goals, arguing that the rationality of solutions offered by experts is often illusory, and that the best protection against this is to exploit to the full the opportunities for wide participation in making decisions, not merely talking about which decisions should be made. This approach acknowledges greater confidence in the opportunities for participation offered by federal and state legislative bodies, by the courts, and by broader political movements such as public interest groups and labor unions, and bases its strategies on the assumption that the solutions to the problems caused by the applications of science require a redistribution of political power as much as the insight of technical expertise. It can be characterized as the *democratic approach* to technological decision-making.

It will immediately be seen that the democratic approach directly challenges the technocratic approach. On the one hand, it questions the assumptions on which suggested solutions to social problems are left largely to scientific and technical experts; on the other, it threatens the political basis on which these suggestions are put into practice. It was the democratic approach that rose to prominence in the late 1960s and early 1970s, buoyed by widespread public criticism of science and technology. Indeed, what has previously been characterized as the second phase in post–Second World War science policy, when research budgets went into decline and demands for the "social relevance" of research programs dominated the more traditional criteria by which funding for basic science had been justified, was largely an acknowledgment that science and technology should be managed by increasing the direct impact of democratic choice. In contrast, I suggest, the third phase of science policy, which we are now entering, is characterized by the reverse process, namely a reascendancy of the technocratic approach over the democratic approach as the dominant form of political strategy. As such, it forms a crucial component of the new politics of science.

In previous chapters we explored some of the principal trends that have taken place in terms of the management of science during this new era, emphasizing the way control over access to the fruits of scientific research is increasingly being concentrated in the hands of corporate and military elites, assisted by those in government and universities who support the primacy of private over public decision-making on questions involving production and the social applications of science. In this chapter we shall look in greater detail at the way the new corporate and government confidence in basic science has been complemented by a resurgence in the use of ideas about science to justify the technocratic approach as the dominant style of political management. Before doing so, however, we need to examine how, even during a period in which the democratic approach to decision-making appeared to be gaining acceptance and impact, the political challenge it represented was successfully contained, to such an extent that the technocratic approach—and the process of decision-making by elites that lies behind it—was never seriously threatened.

Various techniques have been used to limit the impact of demands for a redistribution of power over science and its social applications, despite an apparent opening-up of decision-making. One has been the ability to control the structure of the decision-making agenda—for example, by deciding which forms of public participation will be permitted at which stage, and what their final impact is going to be. A second has been the power to lay down the boundary conditions for participation, determining which types of argument will be considered by decision-makers, and thus defining the limits of legitimacy in both technical and political terms. By the use of such techniques, as we shall see, a gap has been successfully maintained between public participation in decisions about science and technology and the placing of such decisions under direct democratic control. Understanding how this has been achieved is an important part of any attempt at devising a long-term strategy by which the conflicts between science and democracy can be resolved.

The debate over political strategy has covered not only the applications but also the very practice of science. For the two decades after the Second World War, exploiting the formula established by Vannevar Bush, the scientific community was left largely to itself to decide how to distribute the research funds that it had been allocated from the public

purse. Even when it became fashionable to demand relevance in research, it was usually left to scientists to determine how they should
reach their set objectives. As public criticism of some of the uses of
science began to grow, however, so pressures for greater participation in
decisions about the conduct and direction of scientific research generated a strong political appeal. Many argued that the public had a fundamental right to take part in deciding both where and how research funds
should be spent, since it supported the research through its tax dollars,
shared many of the risks that the research created, and benefited from
the application of the research results.[3]

The demands for greater participation, as in the Mansfield Amendment (see Chapter Three), posed a fundamental challenge to the social
contract that had been drafted between the scientific community and
the federal government by Bush and his colleagues in the immediate
postwar period. Scientists had previously argued successfully that they
could operate with the greatest effectiveness if they were insulated from
direct political pressures; in broad terms this was interpreted as a mandate under which the public had agreed to grant scientists the right to
determine the directions of basic research and the appropriateness (if not
always the scale) of research methods. In return, scientists offered vague
promises that they would come up with discoveries that would ultimately
prove of substantial social value.

The principles were often ferociously defended by scientists whenever
they came under fire. During fierce debates over the regulation of research using recombinant DNA techniques, for example, comparisons
were frequently drawn to the persecution of historical figures such as
Galileo, or to the distortions that political pressure could impose on
science, illustrated by the case of the Russian geneticist Lysenko. Both
were used to reinforce the claim that science should resist efforts to make
it conform to socially accepted norms. Hugh DeWitt Stetten, the first
chairman of the National Institutes of Health's Recombinant DNA Advisory Committee, at one point talked of freedom of scientific inquiry as
virtually a constitutional right, suggesting that it should be treated in the
same way that "we have learned to treat freedom of speech."[4] Molecular
biologist and Nobel laureate David Baltimore, referring to efforts by
fellow biologists to oppose a commission being suggested by Senator
Edward Kennedy to regulate such research, warned that "our success or
failure will determine whether America continues to have a tradition of
free inquiry into matters of science or falls under the fist of orthodoxy."[5]

Often, however, such claims were little more than thinly veiled efforts
to deny the fact that by its size, scope, and rapidly broadening impact,
science had inevitably become a social endeavor to which it appeared
increasingly legitimate, both to politicians and to the public, to apply
standard norms of social behavior. The claim that freedom of research
should be recognized as a constitutional right could lead to precisely that

indifference to the social impact of science that had been responsible for many of the problems it had helped to create. What scientists such as Baltimore characterized as the "fist of orthodoxy" was seen by groups who favored strict environmental controls on such research, such as Friends of the Earth and the Natural Resources Defense Council, as a legitimate effort to make scientists more directly accountable for their actions to the society that supported them. By appealing to academic freedom as a defense against such demands, scientists appeared to be demanding a license to follow their curiosity wherever it led, almost in defiance of public calls for caution.

There was, admittedly, nothing particularly new in political controversy being generated by the social impact of new scientific knowledge— nor in efforts to regulate technology through government intervention. Actions taken in the nineteenth century ranged from legislation to prohibit the manufacture of fraudulent vaccines to a federally sponsored research project aimed at discovering the cause of boiler explosions on river paddleboats, which ended with the scientists proposing not only technical remedies but also a possible set of regulations by which they could not be imposed. During the early years of the twentieth century, complaints ranged from the effect on consumers' health of food additives, such as caffeine and sodium benzoate, to the occupational hazards of new production techniques, for example in the chemical and food-processing industries. In the early 1950s, even though overall public confidence in science and technology was at its peak, there were still several areas of concern. The most obvious was the spread of nuclear weapons that followed the development of the atomic and hydrogen bombs during and immediately after the Second World War. But it was also during this period that fears of the carcinogenic properties of artificial food additives led Senator James J. Delaney to introduce one of the strictest rules controlling the applications of science ever passed by Congress, an amendment to the Food and Drug Act requiring that the government set a zero tolerance for any chemical found to cause cancer in laboratory animals.

Until the mid-1960s, however, the debate about the steps needed to mitigate the less desirable social effects of modern science remained primarily confined to professional circles. Indeed, health or environmental hazards identified with new technologies were generally sold to the public—and accepted—as an unfortunate but inevitable price for technological progress, heavily outweighed by the many material benefits that such progress was expected to bring. Confidence remained high that even where science had created problems, more science would successfully resolve them. By the end of the decade, however, the reaction was very different. Many had begun to argue that the price of unrestricted scientific and technological progress was too high. Major changes were demanded in the way science was applied to new technology, and the way this technology was regulated, to make both more compatible with broader social and environmental goals than those of technical and economic efficiency. And the criticism was extended to include the way the scientific community conducted its own affairs.

Many separate events were responsible for this change in attitude toward science, but few had a greater impact than the publication in 1962 of Rachel Carson's *Silent Spring*, a damning indictment of the idea that science and progress were necessarily synonymous.[6] Carson was not the first to point out the hazards to wildlife presented by new chemical pesticides, in particular DDT. In the late 1950s, biologists had already become alarmed about the unexplained deaths of robins and other birds exposed to the chemical when it was being used to control the vectors that carried Dutch elm disease, and the list of victims had grown rapidly.[7] Nor, perhaps, were her criticisms the most rigorous; much of Carson's data about the potential carcinogenicity of DDT, later to prove crucial in debates about its threat to human health, was somewhat speculative. What Carson did, however, was to bring together in a popular form the evidence against DDT from a number of separate scientific disciplines, building these into a generalized critique of the narrow focus of contemporary science and technology, of their apparent blindness to broad social and environmental effects, and ultimately of the gulf between the values of the laboratory and those of the surrounding society.

Scientists complained vociferously that Carson had taken various scientific facts "out of context" to build a critique that was far from objective, and that her views were misinformed and distorted. One review in *Chemical and Engineering News* was headlined "Silence Miss Carson," while another in *Science* dismissed her concerns over public health hazards with the claim that "most scientists who are familiar with the field . . . feel that the danger of damage is slight."[8] Significantly, both reviewers were prominent members of committees established by the National Academy of Sciences to look at the health and environmental effects of chemical pesticides. But *Silent Spring* was not written as a mere summary of the scientific data—nor did its author claim to be objective. The book was a polemic, designed to raise alarm signals and to stimulate a public response. In this it succeeded impressively. The public was already concerned by disagreements among "experts" about vaguely defined threats from modern science that ranged from fallout from nuclear tests to fluoride in drinking water; it was thus more than receptive to Carson's arguments. A general feeling was spreading that not all the results of modern science were necessarily beneficial to society, and furthermore that scientists were often unable to predict or control the impact their discoveries would have. Through Carson's work—complemented later by others such as Barry Commoner, Paul Ehrlich, and Ralph Nader—the debate about the impact of DDT on the environment in particular, and about the growing price of scientific and technological progress in general, turned from a professional debate among chemists, industrialists, and health professionals into a full-scale public, political issue.[9]

The impact of this shift was not limited to the public. Many scientists began to recognize the legitimacy of some of Carson's arguments, in particular the picture she painted of a countryside devoid of wildlife if the use of chemical pesticides continued to escalate with minimum regulation. These scientists raised their own questions about the new social impact of science and technology, and thus added considerable legitimacy—if not political weight—to public concerns. The President's Science Advisory Committee, under the direction of its chairman, Jerome Wiesner, prepared a report in 1962 on the use of pesticides. Although not going as far as Carson, the report was still highly critical of some of the practices it found, and was warmly endorsed by President Kennedy. It recommended both an orderly reduction in the use of nondegradable pesticides and the eventual elimination of persistent toxic chemicals. The committee did not stick to technical issues; one of its more controversial recommendations was that responsibility for the regulation of new pesticides should be transferred from the U.S. Department of Agriculture to the Department of Health, Education, and Welfare, a move that directly challenged the close relationship between the agricultural industry and its supporters both in Congress and in the Department of Agriculture.[10]

Toward the end of the decade, other issues stimulated further concern both inside and outside the scientific community. These raised questions not only about the desirability of some of the new technologies being introduced or proposed but also about the way decisions about them were made. One source of concern was the supersonic transport aircraft (SST), launched by the Kennedy administration and promoted by the aerospace industry as the next logical step in intercontinental air travel. As the costs of the project escalated, the companies contracted to carry out the design encountered more difficulties than predicted, and public awareness of the noise and environmental damage it was likely to cause increased, so opposition to the project began to mount steadily. The SST soon became the target of a coalition of scientists, economists, and environmentalists, who warned that it would produce intolerable noise at airports, prove totally uneconomical to operate, and severely damage the earth's ozone layer, resulting in unpredictable climatic changes[11] The scientists' concern was later heightened when it became apparent that President Nixon was misrepresenting advice he had been given by his scientific advisers, implying that they were in support of the SST program when in fact many had grave reservations about it. One member of PSAC, Richard Garwin, who had chaired a committee that had produced a confidential report highly critical of the SST, told a congressional committee in personal testimony in May 1970 that "there has been less than adequate, and in many cases distorted, information available for this decision process."[12] Eventually the SST program was canceled by Congress in March 1971—representing one of the environmentalist movement's most dramatic victories in its fight against the inevitability of technological progress, since it indicated for the first time that environmental risk could be considered sufficiently important to head off the introduction of a sophisticated technology. It also confirmed the need for greater surveillance of the way scientific advice could be distorted for political ends.[13]

Another target of the scientific community's criticisms of political distortions of its advice was the proposal in 1967 by President Johnson's Defense Secretary, Robert McNamara, to deploy a limited number of anti-ballistic missiles (ABMs) at selected sites around the U.S. as protection against Soviet attack. The proposal itself was widely criticized in the scientific community, this time on the technical grounds that the system was not likely to produce the type of protection that McNamara was claiming. Scientists such as Garwin and Hans Bethe, for example, argued that the ease with which the proposed ABMs could be deceived by decoys would inevitably limit their effectiveness. Again there was resentment at the fact that McNamara and his director of research, John Foster, were misrepresenting advice from scientists that they had been given in confidence, emphasizing to Congress advice that supported ABM deployment and keeping quiet about many of the criticisms. Foster informed a congressional committee that a scientific advisory committee had told the Secretary of Defense that the Safeguard ABM "will do the job that the Department of Defense wants it to do." But one member of the advisory committee—a prominent high energy physicist—later told the same congressional committee that "Dr. Foster's remarks indicate that we made recommendations that in fact we did not make."[14] It was a situation that left many scientists disenchanted with the role they were being placed in as advisers to the executive branch.

Disenchantment was not restricted to the government's science advisers. In addition to specific criticisms of DDT, supersonic aircraft, and the anti-ballistic missile proposals, a large sector of the scientific community was increasingly critical of the U.S.'s military involvement in the war in Vietnam and its use of the products of the nation's research laboratories—criticism which, again, rapidly flowed over into the public arena. Indeed, one of the significant aspects of the anti-war movement was that university scientists played a significantly larger role in leading opposition to the administration's policies than their colleagues in the arts and social sciences. A survey of the disciplinary affiliations of those who had signed public advertisements in support of university teach-ins during the late 1960s and early 1970s revealed that the proportion of scientists was consistently higher than that from other disciplines.[15] Many of the scientists expressed their opposition to the war through criticism of the military use of modern science, for example in chemical defoliants or electronic anti-personnel devices. Such subjects became a hot topic of controversy at meetings of the American Association for the Advancement of Science, where leading members of the scientific establishment were frequently accused of collaborating with the administration's policies on Vietnam through providing technical advice to the Department of Defense and carrying out classified military research on university campuses. The protests were also significant in that they triggered the creation of militant grass-roots organizations such as Science for the People, which grew out of Scientists and Engineers for Social and Political Action (SESPA), and which became the principal focus of a new critique of science. By emphasizing demonstrations and confrontation, rather than petitions and discreet top-level pressure groups, the new groups broke sharply in both substance and strategy from their predecessors in the immediate postwar period, which, while strongly criticizing the immoral uses to which science had been put (in particular, to the development of nuclear weapons), nevertheless maintained that science as such remained "neutral" and was free of any direct guilt.[16]

The political response to charges of environmental and social indifference in applying science to technical and economic goals took place at two levels. The first was largely pragmatic. It concentrated on finding ways of "picking roses without getting cut by the thorns," as Alex Capron, professor of law at the University of Washington, has described it.[17] Attempts were made to find ways of assuring that science would be applied to socially responsible goals by developing methods for integrating social values—suitably laundered of subversive political content—into scientific and technological decision-making, in particular by introducing strict new environmental, health, and safety regulations covering scientific experiments and the introduction of new technologies. These, it was hoped, would be sufficient to lead to better technological choices. It was a strategy supported by the corporate community, since it appeared to allow social goals to be met without interfering excessively with the marketplace. An editorial in *Fortune* in 1971 claimed the need for a "discriminating political judgment that will permit and support certain new technologies . . . and will discourage or suppress other technologies,"[18] while banker David Rockefeller suggested that "there may have to be new laws to force consideration of the quality of life dimension so that more socially responsive firms will not suffer a competitive disadvantage."[19]

There was, however, a second dimension in the response of both the scientific and the corporate communities. This was a reaction to the *political* challenge that the social critique of science and technology represented. If doubts were being expressed about the directions in which science was leading, this inevitably raised questions about the way control over science and its applications was exercised—and who should be permitted to exercise it. Criticism concentrated on the essentially private channels through which this control had been exercised in the past, with decisions about science left primarily to the scientific community, and about its applications to the corporate and military communities. Pressure grew for a more direct and explicit role for social institutions, ranging from community groups to congressional committees, in applying a social direction to technology and, ultimately, to science.

While the scientific community was prepared to meet the challenge of encouraging applications of their work that did not have unacceptable social side effects, it was equally concerned that in the process it should not give up the relative autonomy and freedom from direct social controls it had previously been able to negotiate with its political paymasters. Where these were threatened, it fought hard to defend them. Many scientists espoused the claim made by the philosopher of science Michael Polanyi in 1962 that "the soil of academic science must be ex-territorial in order to secure its control by scientific opinion."[20] If the public was clamoring at the gates, their demands should be listened to and—where they were considered legitimate—acted upon. But that was as far as outsiders should be allowed to get; the boundaries to democratic intervention in science itself were to be clearly marked.

This defensiveness toward demands for greater social accountability on the part of the scientific community is illustrated by various initiatives either adopted by or impressed on the National Science Foundation. These tended to exhibit a constantly shifting balance between, on the one hand, an apparently genuine desire to respond to pressures to make science "socially responsible," and, on the other, a concern that these pressures should not significantly challenge the control either of the practice of science by the scientific community or of its applications by private corporations. Thus, while the NSF was prepared to expand its research agenda to include investigation of the social impact of science, it made strenuous efforts—frequently supported by its allies in Congress—to ensure that the boundaries of this new activity were sufficiently restricted to prevent it from becoming the base of a major challenge to the dominant patterns of control over science.

One example of such boundary setting is to be found in the early history of the NSF's program of study in the Ethics and Values in Science and Technology (EVIST). The goal of this program has been to support research into the "ethical rules and social standards that govern the conduct of scientific and technological activities, including the selection of research priorities and the applications of research results." Although it grew out of more general concerns both inside and outside the scientific community, the specific impetus for the program was a symposium on human rights sponsored by the Joseph P. Kennedy Foundation in Washington in 1971. The participants at the symposium produced a statement calling for more research into "the social and ethical consequences of scientific decisions," and urging that "wisdom—and not just knowledge—become a determining factor in the direction of technological advances affecting human life."[21] NSF director William McElroy soon recognized how important it was for the scientific community itself to keep a handle on any such studies. Responding to the symposium, Hermann Lewis of the NSF prepared a paper on how a research program addressing the topics could be initiated by the foundation. The result was the proposal for a new program of research, funded jointly with the National Endowment for the Humanities, known as Ethics and Values in Science and Technology.

The initial reasoning behind EVIST operated at two levels. Several top NSF officials were prepared to accept the pragmatic arguments in favor of more research into the ethics of scientists. Since its creation, EVIST has supported research into topics that range from the social impact of computer and telecommunications technologies to the value and ethical conflicts that arise out of the corporate and social roles played by science in a modern industrial society. Projects being funded in 1981 ranged from "ethical issues in the use of biological monitoring for occupational health" to "value presuppositions in scientific textbooks."[22]

Behind the pragmatic response, however, was a political reaction aimed directly at raising the public's opinion of the inherent value of science and thus heading off demands for greater social control. A memorandum from McElroy to members of the National Science Board written in December 1971, only two months after the Kennedy symposium, points out that apart from the actual knowledge that might be gained and distributed through the program's activities, the public image was to be important, since the EVIST program could provide benefits for the supporters of science by generating favorable publicity. "A number of projects more or less related to this area have already been supported by various organizational units of the foundation," McElroy indicated. "It is now proposed to approach this matter in a more overt, visible, and active manner."[23]

From the beginning there was also a conscious effort to make sure the program did not provide the platform for a broad political critique of science and technology and the way its social applications were largely determined by private interests. Harvey Brooks, a member of the National Science Board, wrote a letter to McElroy in January 1972 outlining some of his concerns about how the EVIST program would fit into existing controversies over the applications of science and showing how he felt the research agenda should be deliberately structured. "I think it is quite important to be alert to the preservation of some kind of balance in such a program," Brooks stressed. "There is some danger that an anti-technology or anti-industry bias may be disproportionately represented in the unsolicited proposals received. This may make it necessary to carry out some beating of the bushes for proposals of a more pro-technology or pro–private enterprise character in order to secure a more balanced program."[24] EVIST's first coordinator, Louis Levin, was reassuring. "You may be sure that we will tread carefully in this whole area, at least as long as I am involved in it," he replied to Brooks. "I agree with you that it is a most important area, but also one that could get us into trouble."[25]

In another example of boundary-setting, NSF officials seem to have been successful in their efforts to avoid getting directly involved in mainstream public controversies over science. At least in the early years, more EVIST grants were awarded to explore the effects of changing social and ethical standards on the conduct of scientific work (issues that could be dealt with inside the conventional political framework of the scientific community) than to explore the effects on people outside this community of specific scientific developments that could have provoked demands for more controls on science (controls that might have directly threatened certain lines of research).[26] The balance changed in later years as the program gained in legitimacy and became viewed as more of a safety valve than a threat by the scientific community. But mainstream support never seems to have been much more than lukewarm, and when the Reagan administration came to Washington, EVIST had to fight hard both inside and outside the NSF for its survival.

The dilemmas confronted by the scientific community in responding to demands for social accountability were reflected in Congress. Supporters of science (such as the more dominant members of the House Science and Technology Committee) and its critics locked horns in debates over whether or not it was desirable to place social controls on science and on the development of new technologies, and if so, how this should be done. Such tensions rapidly surfaced over a proposal by Senator Edward Kennedy to complement EVIST with a new "Science for Citizens" program within the NSF. Kennedy's idea was based directly on the concept of "public interest science" developed by scientists such as Frank von Hippel and Joel Primack, justified by the examples of Rachel Carson and others who had provided warnings of the unanticipated side effects of science and technology, and enthusiastically supported by consumer advocate Ralph Nader. It stemmed from successful campaigns over the previous decade for greater community participation in decisions previously left to professional groups in other areas of social policy, ranging from university curricula to environmental planning.

Von Hippel and Primack first discussed the concept of what they called "public interest science" in an article in the journal *Science* in 1972. They used recent technological controversies, such as those over DDT and the SST, to argue for a full opening-up of technological decision-making, with the government subsidizing public interest groups that lacked the competence or expertise to mount complex technical arguments or challenge such arguments when made by others. "The way in which technical experts make their services available to society can significantly affect the distribution of political power," Primack and von Hippel later wrote. "If scientists make available to the citizen the information and analysis he needs for the defense of his health and welfare, they can help bring about more open and democratic controls on the uses of technology."[27] In a similar vein, Nader complained at a meeting of public interest groups in 1973 that in areas such as nuclear safety, radiation hazards, arms control, job safety, and safe drinking water, it had been "difficult to get scientists and technical experts to testify about the potential hazards that may be involved [as] most tend to push the establishment line."[28] Senator Kennedy's staff referred to the potential dangers of offshore oil drilling and recombinant DNA research as examples of issues where the public, aided by suitably qualified scientists, should play a greater role in scientific decision-making.[29]

Yet there was by no means a consensus, even within Congress, that this was a desirable objective. Kennedy introduced his proposal for a Science for Citizens program into the National Science Foundation's authorization bill when it came up for discussion in May 1976. The initial purpose of this proposal was to provide citizens groups engaged in challenging technological decisions with sufficient funds to give them access to a source of the relevant technical information. The Senate soon agreed, largely at Kennedy's prompting, to earmark $3 million for the NSF to improve the public understanding of policy issues involving science and technology and to "facilitate the participation of students, engineers, graduate and undergraduate students in public activities aimed at the resolution of public policy issues having significant scientific and technical aspects."[30] The program was to include public service internships; the organization of forums, workshops, and conferences to bring scientists and nonscientists together; and the setting up of "Public Service Science Centers" to make scientific information available for local needs. Kennedy's proposals built on plans initially prepared by the NSF itself at the request of Congress, and submitted to Congress in February 1976, but adopted a more activist approach.[31] Even so, the bill did not go as far as some of its supporters had hoped. Von Hippel, for example, had argued for fellowship programs to allow scientists to work with public interest groups, as well as a new journal of "public interest science," but neither was included in the Senate bill.

In any case, the congressional debate over the Science for Citizens Program was heated. Several members of the House Science and Technology Committee, reflecting comments widely expressed by the scientific community, objected to its activist tone. A leading critic was Mike McCormack, an outspoken supporter of the nuclear industry, who claimed that the funds would be used to support nationwide efforts to prevent the spread of nuclear power stations, along the lines of the state referendum that had been held in California.[32] Nor was there much enthusiasm for the proposal within the NSF. The foundation had already taken various steps to enlarge what it considered to be public participation in its decisions, but these attempts had largely focused on involving more members of the scientific community. In its report to Congress on the Science for Citizens Program, it talked of expanding membership of its advisory committees, but only from groups that already comprised the nation's "science base," not the general public.[33]

The different perspectives emerged even more sharply when the program came up for funding the next year. McCormack complained of federal subsidies going to "self-styled groups of private citizens who have a particular perspective that they want to impose upon the public and . . . want to use federal bucks to do it."[34] In support of the program, Representative Tom Harkin accused that to try to limit efforts to provide scientific and technical data to citizens involved in "debates that are going to drastically effect our lives is, I think, to take a very nondemocratic attitude toward our whole society."[35]

Largely as a result of McCormack's opposition, which was reinforced by other members of the House Science and Technology Committee, Kennedy's ambitious plans were cut back. In 1977 the program was provided with a budget of $1.2 million, instead of the figure of $3 million that Kennedy had proposed. Even more significant, Congress insisted that strict limitations be placed on who could receive funds from the program, thus clearly defining what were considered to be the legitimate limits of federally sponsored public participation in scientific and technological decision-making. Original plans had intended to encourage scientists, engineers, and students to participate actively in public policy debates on scientific and technical issues. Excluded from the final bill, however, were political lobbyists and intervenors, as well as groups that the Internal Revenue Service had identified as being substantially involved in propaganda or attempts to influence legislation. The NSF itself had justified such restrictions on the grounds that they might run into legal problems if they found themselves funding citizens groups that subsequently turned around and sued another branch of the government. But the overall result was to defeat much of Kennedy's original objective, since the constraints placed on the program by Congress meant that the NSF was not permitted to subsidize technical assistance to citizens' groups that in practice were likely to be the most in need of it and at the same time the least able to afford it.[36]

The pragmatic and the political responses to public criticism of science and its social applications coincided even more effectively in the rise of the technology assessment movement. At the end of the 1960s, demands for more sophisticated technology assessment became a principal focus of the scientific community's response to outside criticism. As a method for bringing social and environmental values into an integrated system of decision-making, it seemed to epitomize the "rational" approach to social problem-solving that appealed to scientific minds. (Michael Baram, for example, has described this systems view of technology assessment as aiming "to demonstrate that citizens, corporations, and public institutions are all interrelated in specific patterns and thereby share responsibility for rational planning and decision-making."[37]) Furthermore, it brought about this integration without excessively upsetting the basic political mechanisms by which control over science and technology was exercised. In other words, technology assessment was a way of deflecting demands for a redistribution of power by expressing its strategy in terms of ultimate goals—namely a harmonious correlation between technological development and social needs—rather than the political desirability of the procedures used to achieve these goals. Indeed, technology assessment was often deliberately pursued as a means of reducing political conflicts to technical terms, immediately favoring technocratic over democratic styles of political decision-making. For all these reasons, it was not surprising that many leading members of the scientific community played a leading role in Congress's decision to establish an Office of Technology Assessment in 1972.

The scientists' interest in the systems approach to social problems embodied in technology assessment was not a spontaneous reaction to a new set of problems, but had a long history. In the 1930s leading members of the scientific community, particularly in Europe, had frequently made demands for the rational allocation of social resources part of a broader plea for the application of the scientific method to social planning (one that led several toward Soviet-style Marxism).*[38] During the Second World War many of these scientists successfully applied their ideas about rational management to problems such as supply routes and bombing strategies, developing techniques that eventually became the basis for the postwar growth of systems analysis and operations research. In the late 1950s and early 1960s the target of this approach shifted to social problems such as arms control and developing countries; indeed, at one point Jerome Wiesner wrote that underdevelopment was essentially a question of systems analysis.[40] By the end of the decade the social impact of new technologies appeared a ripe field for applying the same approach. A report from the National Academy of Engineering pointed out that in the early 1960s the use of systems analysis had done much to rationalize decision-making involving policies and practices in the area of national security and defense; it went on to suggest that in a similar

---

* Elsewhere I have suggested that the relationship between science as a mode of explanation of the natural world and proposals for the "scientific" organization of social life can be traced back to the Renaissance, if not beyond.[39] The broader contemporary implications of this relationship are discussed in Chapter Seven.

way "we believe that in the 1970s the practice of technology assessment could provide a more productive basis for decisions about the appropriate utilization of technology for social purposes."[41]

Although the Office of Technology Assessment (OTA) was formally a creation of the U.S. Congress, the scientific establishment played a crucial role in both its conception and birth. Prominent scientists provided many of the initial ideas on which Congress based its legislation. Their endorsement helped to ensure an apparently objective legitimation for this approach to policy-making about science and its social applications, and for the claim that technology assessment could be seen as a politically neutral, value-free technique. In the process, however, they also reinforced efforts to establish strict limits on the extent to which direct public pressure should be allowed to influence science and technology policy.

Some of these limits were already revealed in a report on *Applied Science and Technological Progress*, prepared in 1967 by a blue-ribbon panel established by the National Academy of Sciences. The report reflected the willingness of the scientific community, faced with growing demands that research should be made more directly relevant to social needs, to introduce social parameters into the determination of research priorities. But it also warned of what it saw as the dangers of excessive democracy. The panel was chaired by Harvey Brooks, dean of engineering and applied physics at Harvard University and chairman of the National Academy's Committee on Science and Public Policy. Commissioned by the Science and Technology Committee of the House of Representatives, it argued that the scientific community should be more responsive to socially determined priorities in deciding how research resources were to be distributed. But it also suggested that "the public is often tempted to dump large amounts of money into the solution of problems that are perceived to be of social importance, without adequate consideration of feasibility or economic efficiency." The committee therefore warned against attempts to apply what it considered excessive democratization to science, in other words, a process that challenged the scientists' own priorities. "Real dangers are involved," it said, "when the nonscientist attempts to impose his own value system on what should be largely scientific decisions."[42]

In 1969 the academy published a second report commissioned by the same congressional committee. Under the title *Technology: Processes of Assessment and Choice*, this report established the basic framework within which later congressional discussions about technology assessment in general—and the creation of the Office of Technology Assessment in particular—were carried out. The committee that prepared the report was again chaired by Brooks. Its members represented a broad cross-section of the corporate and university research establishment, as well as several prominent historians and sociologists of science and technology.* Its report to Congress spoke at length about the need for a broader perspective on technology and its application to social needs, as well as the value of a new political focus for technology policy. "Advances in science and technology have brought advances in our ability to anticipate the secondary and tertiary consequences of contemplated technological development and to select those paths best suited to the achievement of broad combinations and objectives," the report said. "The challenge is to discipline technological progress in order to make the most of this vast new opportunity." To help do this, it supported the establishment of a new mechanism for technology assessment that would "introduce a greater degree of objectivity into the process and inject a body of criteria and assumptions that reflect a wider set of interests and values than do the specialized organizations currently engaged in fragmented assessment activities."[43]

If this call for more rational policy-making was the pragmatic side of the case for technology assessment made by the academy committee, the political element was not far behind. The report warned that, frightened by the untoward side effects of technological change and frustrated by their inability to humanize its direction, "people with much power and little wisdom will lash out against scientific and technological activity in general, attempting to destroy what they find themselves unable to control." Public participation was to be encouraged, on the basis that "decisions affecting the course of history require the broadest possible public participation and should not, even if they could, be delegated to narrow elites, whether scientific or political." But such participation was to be restricted to "well-defined channels," while "mechanisms should also be provided to filter out for summary treatment truly frivolous or irresponsible claims"[44]—a suggestion that left open the political question of who was to determine the criteria for frivolity or irresponsibility.

Furthermore, criticism of the private sector was to be deliberately muted. It was, insisted the report, "crucial that any new mechanism we propose foster a climate that elicits the cooperation of business with its activities. Such a climate cannot be maintained if the relationship of the assessment entity to the business firm is that of policeman to suspect. The needed climate requires that private industry be encouraged to find

* Committee members included Hendrik V. Bode, previously a vice-president of the Bell Telephone Laboratories, who had become professor of systems engineering at Harvard University; Raymond Bowers, professor of physics at Cornell University and previously a staff member of the Office of Science and Technology; Edward C. Creutz, vice-president for research and development with Gulf General Atomic Ltd. and a member of the Manhattan Project team at Los Alamos; A. Hunter Dupree, one of the leading historians of American science; Milton Katz, Henry L. Stimson Professor of Law at Harvard Law School and one of the principal architects of the Marshall Plan for reconstructing Europe, which he headed between 1950 and 1951; and Morris Tanenbaum, general manager of the engineering division at Western Electric.

its own technical solutions—not compelled to follow solutions formulated from above."[45] It was therefore clear from the beginning that technology assessment was being proposed as a means of ultimately reinforcing, rather than challenging, the basic patterns of control over science and technology, and that as such, it was conceived in a political framework that sought to minimize the imposition of publicly determined needs on unwilling private decision-makers.

The academy report established the conceptual framework for the subsequent legislative history of the Office of Technology Assessment. Emilio Q. Daddario—chairman of the science, research, and development subcommittee of the House Science and Technology Committee, and the original architect of the OTA legislation (whose conception is said to have taken place during a lunch with Wiesner, then provost of MIT)—often referred to the report's conclusions during congressional negotiations to legitimate his proposals. Brooks testified frequently on Capitol Hill in favor of the OTA, and he acted as a consultant to the Daddario subcommittee; in particular, he is widely credited with having written the section of the initial legislation that details the organization of the OTA.[46] As on other occasions, the scientific establishment's need for political support in achieving particular goals—both offensive and defensive—coincided with the committee's need for legitimation from the scientific establishment to achieve its own objectives within the congressional arena, namely an expansion in both the scope and the importance of its role at a time when neither was to be easily gained by arguing for more money for basic science.

If the academy report captured the twin functions that technology assessment was expected to have for the scientific community—the pragmatic response to social pressures combined with the political rebuttal of demands for greater direct social control of science and technology—these factors were also largely to blame for the checkered legislative history of the OTA. There was no lack of support in Congress for the pragmatic aspects of technology assessment. As early as 1966 a report from the science, research, and development subcommittee had warned of the "dangerous side effects which applied technology is creating, or is likely to create, for all humanity."[47] Daddario subsequently claimed that "Congress is becoming aware of the difficulties and dangers which applied science may carry in its genes."[48] The floor debate on the proposal to establish the OTA provided ample opportunities for legislators to demonstrate their concern about the impact of science and technology on society. Speaking in the Senate in May 1971, for example, Senator Warren Magnusson, chairman of the science subcommittee of the Senate Commerce Committee, suggested that "this measure would provide for steering and managing this potent force for change so as to be sure that our technologies do not create unexpected, unwanted consequences or develop a mindless, self-renewing momentum that might threaten the treasured human and humane qualities of our society."[49] Nor was the political value of the OTA in meeting the challenges of the so-called anti-science movement ignored by Congress. In the same debate, Magnusson added that he was introducing the OTA legislation at a time when "sounds of protest are mounting to 'turn technology off.' This motto can only promote a senseless confrontation between technology and society, to our peril."[50]

Equally significant, the OTA was acknowledged by many members of Congress as providing them with a way of challenging the technical basis of decisions coming from the White House. Disagreements over the ABM plans of McNamara and the environmental hazards of SSTs had convinced legislators that they needed to strengthen their hand with respect to the executive branch on political decisions involving science and technology. Many had been made acutely aware of their lack of access to scientific information when new data about the impact of supersonic transport on the ozone layer were released only hours before a major vote in the Senate on the administration's plans for the SST; their unease was only heightened when evidence emerged that the executive summary of a technical report on the environmental impact of SSTs had been slanted to give a more favorable conclusion than the body of the report itself—for example, by describing the climatic effects of thirty Concordes as "smaller than minimally detectable."[51] As Charles Mosher, the senior Republican on Daddario's subcommittee and a co-architect of the OTA legislation, put it in one floor debate: "We in the Congress are constantly outmanned and outgunned by the expertise of the executive agencies. We desperately need a stronger source of professional advice and information more immediately available and entirely responsible to us and responsive to the needs of our own committees."[52]

The desire to develop an alternative source of technical advice was nurtured by scientists themselves after Nixon, deeply suspicious of the role that many leading members of the scientific community had played in the anti-war movement, and angry that various members of his Science Advisory Committee had publicly stated their opposition to his policies on ABMs and SSTs, decided in 1973 to abolish both PSAC and the position of the President's science adviser. Spurned by the White House that had previously given them political status, if not direct access to power, many scientists turned to Congress. Indeed, their enthusiasm for the OTA initiative, and the prominent role that, at least in its originally intended form, it gave to scientists as advisers on major policy issues, prompted *Wall Street Journal* columnist Jude Wanniski to criticize the whole venture as "Teddy Kennedy's Shadow Government." In a column that clearly reflected the inside thinking of the Nixon administration, Wanniski—later a prominent adviser to presidential candidate Ronald Reagan—stated that the White House was concerned about the OTA because it has just finished "a general housecleaning of administration 'science experts' " who were really nothing more than "political operatives for the Nixon opposition." * The White House, said Wanniski, felt that "the OTA will provide an operating base for those scientists who have been opposing Nixon's defense policies across the board." The charge was supported by a quote from Kennedy aide Ellis Mottur, one of the principal strategists on pushing the OTA legislation through Congress, that as long as the White House had an advisory apparatus, it had been the focal point in the country for science policy: "If it's not now in existence, an operation like [the OTA] will become the central science policy institution in the country."[54]

If the political impact of the OTA had been restricted to the way in which it strengthened the effectiveness of the legislative branch in formulating new laws and making decisions on complex technical issues, it would probably have been created with little fuss (apart from those occasions when it trespassed on territory jealously guarded by a particular congressional committee). Already two such institutions were in place and functioning effectively, namely the General Accounting Office, which investigates the use of federal funds authorized and appropriated by Congress, and the Library of Congress, which, together with its Congressional Research Service, provides a basic reference service. Supporters of the OTA argued convincingly that, given the increased importance of science and technology to a wide range of political issues, the new office was needed to complement (rather than duplicate) efforts of the existing two (a conclusion that was later confirmed in a study carried out for the House Science and Technology Committee[55]).

Both inside and outside Congress, however, it was soon recognized that the concept of technology assessment also contained a more subversive component, namely that it could become the kernel of a new form of social planning by offering a powerful handle on technological policy. The report from the National Academy of Engineering appeared to hit at the heart of the free enterprise system in arguing the need for greater responsiveness to social goals. "Competition rarely rewards and often penalizes behavior that is socially desirable in the larger context," it stated.[56] The subsequent report from the National Academy of Sciences hinted at the need to increase centralized control over technological decisions when it stipulated that "the challenge is to discipline technological progress in order to make the most of this vast new opportunity."[57] Senator Magnusson, in proposing the OTA to the Senate, quoted Ed Wenk of the Congressional Research Service as suggesting the need to

---

* There was some irony in the fact that the Nixon administration's plans for the SST had been strongly defended by then presidential science adviser Edward David—now a prominent member of the Republican science policy establishment. David had at one point issued a statement, co-signed by thirty-four other prominent scientists and engineers, claiming that the Senate's opposition to the aircraft, later vindicated by the commercial failure of the Anglo-French Concorde, was "the wrong approach to dealing with new technology."[53]

"find a standard by which we can steer [technology] to meet our collective social goals."[58]

The political potential of technology assessment as opening a path to
a national technology policy held both a promise and a threat to the
scientific and corporate communities. The promise lay in the opportunity that, if kept under control, it presented those who believed that
social problems could be solved through a consensus of scientific experts
with a mechanism for injecting their solutions into the public policy field;
the threat lay in the danger, as these two communities saw it, that the
same mechanism could also be used for imposing socially determined
objectives on their activities, i.e., for public control of what many considered should be private decision-making. The scientific community,
through the reports produced for Congress, had recognized in the public
questioning of science a threat to its own political autonomy unless this
questioning was deflected; in the same way, private corporations saw in
technology assessment, unless equally carefully handled, the threat of
social control over their investment and development strategies.

The reaction of the private sector to this threat of greater centralized
control ranged from hostility to resignation, depending on their views
about the desirability of a national technology policy. Some companies
expressed open skepticism, suggesting that the OTA was going to concern itself with "technology harassment and technology arrestment"
rather than technology assessment. The aerospace industry, having seen
its plans for a supersonic aircraft shot down by analysis of its economic
and environmental impact, and wary that increased public involvement
in decision-making could lead to further setbacks, claimed that it was
"spooked" by the OTA bill.[59] Business Week reported that many businessmen "are questioning whether technology assessment is a threat to
their operations."[60] Other corporate leaders, however, were prepared to
accept the OTA as the price of meeting public demand for greater social
responsibility, anticipating—correctly—that its more threatening aspects could be adequately kept in check through congressional and scientific allies. Carl H. Madden of the U.S. Chamber of Commerce
reflected in 1973 that "we're simply entering a new era of policy analysis.
The era of technological laissez-faire is coming to an end."[61]

The history of the OTA became a tortured reflection of the political
tensions under which it was born. Despite intense lobbying, the more
conservative wing of the private sector was not able to prevent the bill
from becoming law, although the corporate community as a whole did
succeed in having the concept of "early warning" removed from the
legislation on the grounds that it invoked the destructive potential of
intercontinental ballistic missiles as a metaphor that should be applied to
all technology; the wording was changed to talk about "early indications."[62] But from the beginning it was clear that the OTA was not going
to be able to operate with the independence from conventional political

pressures that many of its original promoters, particularly those in the scientific community, had argued for.

In the final legislative debate, for example, original plans to have the OTA run by a panel of outside scientists, engineers, and public interest representatives were amended, after opposition from Representative Jack Brooks, the powerful chairman of the House Government Operations Committee. Instead, a central role was given to members of Congress. Harvey Brooks had proposed a thirteen-member OTA governing board in which the seven public members—expected to include several eminent scientists[63]—would have a majority over the remaining members, who would comprise two senators, two representatives, and the directors of the General Accounting Office and the Congressional Research Service. But under the terms of an amendment suggested by Jack Brooks and inserted in the legislation that was eventually passed in 1972, the OTA is run by a bipartisan board with six members from the Senate and six from the House of Representatives, with an equal number of Democrats and Republicans, plus the OTA director. The scientists, together with other "public interest representatives," were moved sideways to become a "Technology Assessment Advisory Council," whose powers were substantially more limited.[64] It was also made clear that the OTA was meant to complement, not substitute for, the work of existing congressional committees—for example, by the fact that it could initiate inquiries only at the request of a committee chairman.

Daddario, having resigned from Congress to make an unsuccessful bid for the governorship of Connecticut, was appointed the first director of the OTA in 1973. The appointment was not a success. Although well-acquainted with the issues, Daddario was cautious about taking a strong stand on controversial issues; he insisted, for example, that all hints of policy recommendations be omitted from OTA reports. Daddario managed to avoid alienating those members of Congress on which the OTA's survival depended. But the price was the frustration of those who had expected bolder initiatives; instead, they received a series of expensive but unremarkable reports from outside contractors, which often shed neither heat nor light on important congressional controversies.

The scientists on the advisory council lost no opportunity of blaming Daddario's failures on excessive politicking.* On stepping down as the first chairman of the OTA's advisory board in 1976, Harold Brown commented that "few of us on the council, I believe, would say that we are satisfied with what has been accomplished, compared with what we

---

* Several of the scientists on the council—such as its first chairman, Harold Brown; his vice-chairman, Edward Wenk; and his successor, Jerome Wiesner—had been associated with President Kennedy's Science Advisory Committee. Brown had previously been director of the Lawrence Livermore Laboratory, Pentagon research chief, and Secretary of the Air Force under both Presidents Johnson and Nixon, then president of the California Institute of Technology, and was later Secretary of Defense under President Carter.

hoped for and still believe possible."[65] The solution, Brown and others argued, lay in granting the OTA greater independence, with a larger, more qualified staff of technology assessment "experts," moving it a step closer to a system of rational policy-making on technological issues with minimum interference from openly democratic politics. In 1975, for example, advisory council members had recommended to the board that OTA staff themselves be permitted to suggest topics for analysis that had not been proposed by any particular committee, and that the office be given extra funds for funding outside groups to study "early-warning type issues."[66]

But if Daddario had upset the scientific community by refusing to shake himself clear of allegiances to his former congressional colleagues, he also failed to develop a reputation for the OTA that could have deflected such criticism. Daddario resigned in 1977 amid continuing complaints that the OTA had failed to live up to its initial promise. A report from the House Commission on Information and Facilities in 1976 said that the OTA "remains substantially short of reaching levels of performance reasonably expected of an information resource of its size and cost and access to expertise"[67]—picking up Brown's suggestion that the office should turn down requests from Congress that were technical feasibility or economic studies, rather than genuine assessments.*

Daddario's departure led to a bitter fight over his successor in which new tensions emerged, this time not between Congress and its outside advisers, but between rival political factions within the legislative body itself. Both Senator Kennedy, who had become chairman of the OTA board, and his aide Ellis Mottur, who had been given a staff appointment at the OTA, were accused of seeking to secure the post for Mottur. The personality clashes over succession attracted most of the media attention; behind this, however, there was a political basis to the dispute. Kennedy had spoken out strongly in favor of increased public participation in OTA activities, in particular in the detailed assessments of new technologies that it carried out. More conservative Democrats, in particular Olin Teague, the powerful chairman of the House Science and Technology Committee and also a member of the OTA board, took strong exception to Kennedy's populism. "Kennedy is using the board for personal political purposes," complained Teague in 1977.[69] Mottur lobbied hard for the

---

* Physicist Barry Casper described the first years of the OTA's existence in terms of the "dog that did not bark," a reference to the Sherlock Holmes story whose denouement lay in Holmes's conclusion that the guard dog didn't bark because the culprit was its master. "The most striking feature of OTA's record so far is the systematic exclusion from its agenda of controversial new programs," Casper wrote early in 1978, citing topics before Congress such as the B-1 bomber and the liquid metal fast breeder reactor which the OTA had all but ignored. "One way to avoid charges of bias is to be superficial and eschew controversial issues; that has been the OTA approach," continued Casper. "With a few notable exceptions, OTA reports have been bland and superficial."[68]

position of director, but this too backfired by provoking further angry reaction from Kennedy's opponents, such as Teague and Republican congresswoman Marjorie Holt.

Partly as a result of the opposition to Kennedy's populism and Mottur's ambitions, the OTA looked in a different direction for its new director. After a highly publicized search headed by Jerome Wiesner, then chairman of the advisory council, it came up with Russell Peterson. A former governor of Delaware, and before that director of research for the Delaware-based du Pont chemical company, Peterson took a very different tack from Daddario, one that was much closer to that being recommended by the scientists on the advisory council. He frequently expressed his determination to bring a "holistic" approach to technology assessment, which he defined as placing the analysis of new technological trends in the fullest possible social and environmental context. In a speech to the American Association for the Advancement of Science in early 1978, Peterson expressed his conviction that "while we pride ourselves on our perceptions of truth in our areas of specialty, we must widen them to include a holistic perspective. Otherwise what is really important is not always obvious."[70]

Peterson's attempts to turn the OTA into an independent think-tank, minimizing its involvement in conventional politics, met with the approval of the scientists on the advisory council. So too did his approach to technology assessment, which closely paralleled the scientists' problem-solving, systems view of political conflict over technical choices and priorities. Under Peterson's guidance, for example, the OTA staff undertook a systematic effort to produce a priority list of topics in need of attention, worthy of the best scientific traditions of Francis Bacon. (This was the scientific method suggested by Bacon in his *Novum Organum*, which conceived of the scientific community as a vast army of knowledge collectors.[71]) Soliciting nominations from 4,500 individuals and organizations, supplementing these with their own suggestions, the staff came up with 4,293 possible topics for study. These were synthesized into 286 proposed topics, which were then narrowed to 32—the top 5 being alternative national energy futures; alternative global food futures; national water supply and demand; health promotion and disease prevention; and the productivity of U.S. croplands, forests, and wetlands.[72]

Such an approach was in line with the recommendations for the function of a technology assessment office that had been sketched out both in the NAS report and in the original congressional legislation drafted by Harvey Brooks and others. But if the new autonomy satisfied the scientists, since it removed disputes over technology from political arguments that many found excessively messy,* this time it was at the expense of

---

* A common view of politics held by scientists is summed up by Leo Szilard in a short story in which a dolphin comments on a defunct human society, saying "political issues were

congressional support. Several members of the board felt that the contents of the priorities list strayed too far from what Congress considered to be the most important legislative concerns. Some members of the OTA board argued that the OTA should concentrate on specific technical issues rather than attempting a global analysis of social priorities. One complained that Peterson was trying to create "a sort of Brookings Institution in the Congress." In a press release, Senator Orrin Hatch accused the OTA of "a disturbing pattern of ignoring congressional oversight and service."[74]

Peterson resigned in 1979, after only one year in the post, to become the president of the National Audubon Society. This time it took the board relatively little time to find a successor—John (Jack) Gibbons, previously director of the University of Tennessee's Energy, Environment, and Resources Center. Gibbons quickly adopted a low-key approach to his job, keen to buy peace with both sides. He has eschewed the broader vision of his predecessor, emphasizing the need for the OTA to "earn its keep" by responding to the specific contributions it is able to make to current congressional concerns. At the same time, he has concentrated on producing competent technical reports that meet many of the criteria laid down by his scientific advisers, talking, for example, of "cutting issues into bite-size pieces" that can be assimilated into the congressional decision process without presenting any fundamental challenge to this process.[75]

Gibbons's approach has proved to be an effective survival strategy for the OTA, which managed to survive virtually intact after the arrival of the Reagan administration, despite being a favorite target of conservative attacks. Yet the price of survival has been not only a narrowing of horizons, but also a retreat from technology assessment to technology analysis. Individual technologies are studied within closely defined technical and economic parameters, frequently avoiding some of their more conventional implications. Efforts to scan the horizon for emerging problems have been heavily cut back. Gibbons has referred to the dangers of "wrestling with a many-headed hydra that you cannot get your arms around successfully"[76] in attempting to assess all the social implications of a new technology, in particular trying to draw up a balance sheet of its costs and benefits. It is an approach that ruffles few feathers, but the result has been to create an institution that is much more limited than what many of its original supporters had hoped for.

One example of this compromise is the OTA's report on applied genetics.[77] As a subject of intense public and congressional controversy in

---

often complex, but they were rarely anywhere as deep as the scientific problems that had been solved . . . with amazing rapidity because they had been exposed to discussion among scientists, and thus it appeared reasonable to expect that the solution of political problems could be greatly speeded up also if they were subject to the same type of discussion."[73]

the mid-1970s, genetic engineering became an obvious topic for the OTA to tackle. The OTA staff proposed a broad-ranging study of the full social impact of the new techniques at the height of this controversy in the fall of 1976, but was dissuaded by members of the advisory council. A more limited report, prepared after several drafts, quickly became a best-seller when it was published in 1981. It presents a careful evaluation of the technical and commercial potential of the application of the recombinant DNA techniques to industrial production processes, with a listing of areas, such as pharmaceuticals and agriculture, in which the new technology is anticipated to make its greatest impact. Yet there are many areas of the social impact of genetic engineering—in particular, its application to humans—that are ignored.

OTA director Gibbons described the omission as the result of a lack of time. However, it also seems to have been an attempt to circumscribe the limits of "assessment" and define what was a legitimate impact for study primarily in terms of conventional technical and economic criteria. The effect of this and similar reports has been—as Harvey Brooks and other members of the scientific community had wished—to leave the distribution of power over science and technology undisturbed. They neutralize any efforts to use technology assessment to shift decision-making from the private to the public arena, or even to draw up a balance sheet of the benefits and costs of the new technology (initially proposed as one of the OTA's principal functions). One of the most vocal critics of the OTA's approach, who had argued vociferously for a broader approach to a social assessment of the impact of genetic engineering, embracing a range of ethical and political questions, found himself described as "stubborn" for trying to influence the direction of the assessment after the end of a planning workshop and screened out of the review process for drafts of the project report.[78] Perhaps it was a signal of the clear limits being placed on the concept of public participation in technological decisions, at least as far as institutional approaches to technology assessment were concerned. And in such ways the OTA has tended to reinforce the technocratic over the democratic style of decision-making—as many of its scientific proposers always intended it should.

Perhaps no other topic demonstrated the extent to which scientists successfully headed off demands for greater social control of their own activities than the debate over the safety of recombinant DNA research. What started as a relatively straightforward—if unprecedented—concern over the potential dangers of a new research technique rapidly escalated into a full-scale confrontation between the scientific community and its critics, which brought to the surface many of the tensions over public participation in scientific decision-making that had been festering for the previous decade. Extravagant charges were liberally exchanged by both sides. The more extreme critics warned of monsters and uncontrollable diseases escaping from university laboratories and accused scientists of "trying to play God" by altering the genetic makeup of living organisms. Scientists in turn accused the public of wanting to destroy freedom of inquiry and claimed that strict safety regulations would prejudice the many commercial applications that genetic engineering promised.

The confrontation came to a head in the late 1970s over attempts by various congressional committees to establish a legal framework for the regulation of DNA research. Few scientists were enthusiastic about the principle that the regulation of the research should become enshrined in law, although most were at the time prepared to accept some legal solution as an inevitable outcome. Two aspects of proposed legislation, however, sent shock waves through the scientific community. One was the proposal that local or state legislatures, responding to grass-roots pressure, be permitted to impose tighter restrictions on the research than those developed in Washington. The second, a suggestion of Senator Edward Kennedy, was that a national commission be set up to oversee all aspects of the regulation of recombinant DNA research, including the licensing of laboratories. The commission would be made up of individuals appointed by the President—and scientists would not necessarily be in a majority. Both proposals presented a direct challenge to the decision-making prerogatives of the scientific community, generating fears that they would set a precedent for bringing other areas of biological research under government regulation.[79] An intense lobbying campaign was initiated, orchestrated largely by the American Society of Microbiologists, and it managed to take the wind out of the sails of a powerful movement in Congress in favor of legislation. Within a short period of time, virtually all legislative proposals were dropped.

The scientists' lobbying of Congress was one of the more visible manifestations of the political role played by the leaders of the scientific community in structuring public involvement in the regulation of recombinant DNA research in order to minimize its impact. From an early stage in the DNA controversy, however, many had realized that by publishing a famous letter to Science and Nature in 1974, suggesting a moratorium on all recombinant DNA experiments until methods had been established guaranteeing that they would be carried out in adequate safety, scientists had for the first time turned the regulation of basic science into a public issue.[80] As Nobel laureate James Watson was later to complain: "The minute the moratorium was announced, in effect we had invited the public to join in the decision-making process."[81]

The authors of the letter to Science were members of a group established by the National Academy of Sciences and chaired by Paul Berg of Stanford University. The letter itself, which followed concerns expressed at the Gordon Conference on Nucleic Acids the previous year, suggested the moratorium as a precautionary step, prior to holding an international conference to discuss how the potential hazards associated with the research might be contained. As a voluntary constraint by scientists, who agreed not to carry out certain types of experiments, it was unprecedented in the history of science—a fact that largely explains the intense public interest that such an apparently small act immediately aroused.[82]

The conference suggested in what rapidly became known as the "Berg letter" was held at the Asilomar conference center on the California coast in February 1975. Already there were warnings from some of those present that the public was not likely to stay out of the decision process for long, and that scientists should take the political initiative if they wanted to remain free of social controls. Roger Dworkin of the University of Indiana warned that the responsibilities of self-regulation were not to be taken lightly: "Any appearance of self-serving will sacrifice the reservoir of respect that scientists have and will bring disaster upon them."[83] Facing the apparent reluctance of many participants to even discuss what safety guidelines were appropriate for which type of experiments, given the many uncertainties involved, Sidney Brenner of Cambridge University in England cautioned that "if the collected wisdom of this group doesn't result in recommendations, the recommendations may come from other groups which are less qualified." Brenner went even further to propose that the meeting should recommend harsher guidelines than it felt necessary, in order to avoid external controls on their work. "The issue that I believe is central is a political issue," Brenner explained. "We live at a time where I think there is a great anti-science attitude developing in society, well developed in some societies, and developing in government, and this is something we have to take into account."[84]

The warnings of Dworkin and Brenner were soon brought home by public reaction to the scientists' decisions at Asilomar, to which both the domestic and the international mass media gave substantial coverage. The scientists present at the meeting recommended that experiments using recombinant DNA be classified into three categories of risk. Reflecting Brenner's advice, the final document was more stringent than the proposals of the three working parties that had contributed separate sections. Yet even this was insufficient to deflect subsequent criticism. Indeed, even though they accepted the need for guidelines as self-defense, the participants at Asilomar seemed to have largely failed to anticipate the general pressure their discussions helped to generate—rather than head off—for greater public involvement in science policy at all levels.

Four months later, some of this pressure surfaced at a hearing in Washington at which several of the participants of the Asilomar meeting were closely questioned by Senator Kennedy and members of his health subcommittee, which was responsible for overseeing the biomedical research of the National Institutes of Health (NIH). Donald Brown of the

Carnegie Institution of Washington gave the conventional argument in favor of the autonomy of the laboratory. He told the subcommittee that although the public was entitled to participate in decisions about how scientific advances should be applied, only scientists were qualified to direct the research itself and determine how it should be carried out. "Scientists have the special knowledge to recognize potential hazards of their research and to devise constructive solutions," he claimed.[85]

Other witnesses at the hearing, however, disagreed. "Actions taken by scientists alone are not sufficient," said Halsted Holman of the Stanford University Medical School. "When knowledge is treated as a private possession . . . the public remains ignorant and may become apathetic or hostile."[86] Picking up and expanding on Holman's theme, Kennedy asserted that the actions taken by the scientists during and after the Asilomar meeting were inadequate because "scientists alone decided to impose the moratorium and scientists alone decided to lift it." The factors under consideration, however, extended far beyond their technical competence, said Kennedy. "In fact they were making public policy. And they were making it in private."[87]

The political warning was not lost on Donald Fredrickson, NIH director, and as such responsible for administering the guidelines under which recombinant DNA research was to be carried out. Fredrickson soon realized that such pressure would only be provoked by stonewalling, but that its impact could be reduced by careful handling. "We were aware that we were embarking upon a rare opportunity for innovation in the public governance of science. A fumble could mean loss for all concerned," Fredrickson later stated.[88] The stakes were indeed high, for the Berg letter had opened a crack in the whole edifice of autonomy for science by publicly acknowledging a role for social and ethical considerations in which scientists admitted they had no particular claims to expertise or experience.

Fredrickson was soon persuaded that if actions taken by the scientific community were to be effective in heading off demands for outside controls, it was essential that they be carried out in a manner that was immune from legal challenge. Thus, soon after NIH prepared its first set of guidelines, a public meeting was held at which they were openly discussed. The meeting was carefully structured to give more time to the critics of the research than to the supporters, since its purpose was not to develop a consensus—or even to discover what the critics had to say —but merely to be able to demonstrate, if later challenged, that in reaching its eventual conclusions on the guidelines, opposing points of view had been adequately listened to. Similar arguments were used to convince Fredrickson that he should publish full documentation of the public aspects of the debates over controls on research. Few were expected to pore in detail over the lengthy volumes that emerged; but failure to keep a full and continuous record of the unfolding debate, Fredrickson was warned, would probably allow control of the situation to pass completely from the hands of the scientific community.

The first version of the guidelines covering recombinant DNA research was published in the summer of 1976. It laid out physical and biological containment provisions under which certain types of experiments could be carried out, and listed others that were forbidden without the express permission of the director of NIH. But even though political considerations were dressed in the apparent neutrality of technical language about safety levels, they were never far below the surface.[89] At the time, many scientists argued that the guidelines were stricter than necessary; indeed, the subcommittee responsible for drawing up the guidelines had been persuaded to tighten up a first draft after public criticism that it did not reflect the consensus reached at Asilomar.[90] Later, however, several of those who had been engaged in the early discussion admitted that the additional margin of safety had been an effective way of stalling external pressure for social controls.[91]

In the years that followed, the guidelines were reduced in strictness by a series of steps. Each step, as it was taken, was justified by NIH by referring to some new knowledge that had come to light. Frequent reference was made, for example, to the outcome of preliminary risk assessment experiments showing that the dangers of the use of recombinant DNA techniques in the laboratory were less than originally feared, or to the discovery that genetic material from different organisms combined spontaneously in nature, leading to the argument that there was nothing particularly artificial about achieving the same in the laboratory.

At the same time, however, the rate of deregulation was carefully controlled by NIH to ensure that it did not provoke political demands for external regulation of the scientific community by moving too fast. With the warnings of Dworkin and Brenner still ringing in his ears, as well as similar advice from attorneys from federal agencies such as the Food and Drug Administration, Fredrickson took care to move at a speed that allowed safety precautions to be relaxed, but without allowing congressional legislators or others to argue that the scientific community was being irresponsible in deregulating itself. Several members of the Recombinant DNA Advisory Committee (RAC), set up under the 1976 guidelines to advise the NIH director on how the guidelines should be interpreted and changed, acknowledged the political role they were playing. In a letter to *Science*, written in 1977, Wallace Rowe of NIH put the situation explicitly: "The decision to specify containment levels for particular experiments was primarily one of policy, being based on value judgments as to how to respond to a problem for which there was an inadequate data base, and not based on a rational estimate of the probability of risk."[92]

Most scientists, of course, were eager to reduce the impact of safety controls as quickly a possible in order to continue with experiments that few considered particularly dangerous. This itself brought complaints, and not only from outside critics. In 1979, Professor Roy Curtiss of the University of Alabama, whose successful development of a disabled—and hence biologically safer—bacterium capable of expressing foreign DNA had been influential in persuading Congress to forgo federal legislation, cautioned against overestimating the margin of safety and proceeding too rapidly with loosening the containment requirements. Curtiss told Fredrickson that adherence to the guidelines "has not hindered our work," and that a recommendation from the RAC that all experiments using the disabled vector be exempt from the guidelines was premature. Such a proposal, he continued, was not based on objective review of available scientific evidence, but was "based more on the politics of science than on the data of science."[93]

Fredrickson, however, was playing a delicate political game himself, convinced that the long-term political interests of the scientific community required balancing the pressure from scientists for less regulation against the threats of external action if he moved too fast. Such threats came from two directions, local communities and Congress. Many local legislatures had already decided to take action into their own hands. The most dramatic instance was in Cambridge, Massachusetts, where the mayor, Alfredo Vellucci (long an antagonist of local academic institutions such as Harvard and MIT) held a series of dramatic hearings. Vellucci suggested that all research using recombinant DNA techniques should be banned. Aftr eight months of deliberation, a special task force recommended a more moderate approach, which allowed the experiments to continue under the supervision of a city biosafety committee. But Vellucci's actions had set a precedent. Other local authorities soon followed Cambridge's example in requiring all research within their jurisdiction—not just that supported by federal funds—to be carried out under the NIH guidelines. These included Amherst, Massachusetts; Princeton, New Jersey; and Berkeley, California. The states of New York, Maryland, and California each deliberated about introducing legislation.[94]

These local initiatives provided a backdrop for a series of debates that took place in front of congressional committees in 1977. Building on a growing groundswell of public sentiment in favor of strict controls, and stimulated by critics of the research both inside and outside the scientific community, twelve separate legislators had introduced bills into Congress addressing the regulation of DNA research. What worried scientists most about these initiatives was the possibility that local community groups would be given powers to determine the conditions under which recombinant DNA research could be carried out in university laboratories. Both NIH and many scientists argued strongly that if legislation was to be introduced, the federal government should be able to preempt state laws. "I felt very strongly that [local regulations] would be unjustified by the known facts and create intolerable confusion in so universal and mobile an activity as this kind of basic laboratory research," Fredrickson said later. "Had Congress come to a vote on statutory control, the most important issue it could have debated would have been that of preemption of all other standards by federal ones."[95]

Several legislators, however, continued to insist that the norms of democracy should allow local authorities to determine their own safety rules. Senator Kennedy argued strongly that the public ought to be involved at the ground level in decisions about how research should be conducted, in other words, "in the scientific development as well as the application."[96] He introduced into the Senate a bill, initially drafted by the administration, extending the NIH guidelines to cover all recombinant DNA research. But Kennedy's version omitted all reference to federal preemption, which NIH, reflecting the dominant views of the scientific community, had proposed in its own initial draft.

Kennedy's refusal to support federal preemption of efforts to place science under the control of local communities was a key factor in provoking the scientific community to action. Harlyn Halvorson, who had asked to testify at the hearings held by the Kennedy subcommittee but had had his offer refused, seized the offensive. After consulting experienced lobbying groups such as the American Civil Liberties Union, Halvorson persuaded the council of the American Society for Microbiology (ASM) to approve a recommendation that "all responsibility for regulating actions relative to the production or use of rDNA molecules should be vested in HEW" and to go on record as favoring "uniform national standards."[97] Scientists attending the 1977 Gordon Conference on Nucleic Acids signed a statement expressing their concern that the benefits of rDNA research would be denied to society "because legislation and regulations will stifle free inquiry." Even the board of Americans for Democratic Action, prompted by one of its members, condemned the Kennedy proposals by pointing out that strict control of science in the past had preceded excesses such as Lysenkoism and "some of the inhuman practices in Nazi Germany."[98] Philip Abelson of *Science* summed up the general attitude of the scientific community: "Public fears may yet overcome scientific judgment, and what many scientists believe to be bad legislation may be enacted."[99] Molecular biologist David Baltimore described the situation that he and his colleagues found themselves facing in challenging Kennedy's proposals for a national commission: "The new biology has become the new politics in a very concrete manner: biologists are spending their time in the halls of Congress trying to prevent the establishment of the first commission to control basic research."[100]

The ASM-inspired lobbying was successful. Kennedy announced in the fall of 1977 that he was withdrawing his bill, asking merely for a one-year moratorium on changes to the guidelines and for continued, though unspecified, lay involvement in the process of "evaluation, development, and implementation of our national policy toward science and medical research."[101] He subsequently appeared to lose interest in federal regulation of recombinant DNA research, perhaps partly due to the fact that his chief legislative assistant, Larry Horowitz, spent a year working in the California laboratory of Stanley Cohen, one of the harshest critics of the guidelines. At Horowitz's prompting, Kennedy was able to use an escape clause that Halvorson, taking a leaf out of the professional lobbyists' book, had suggested for legislators required to explain their shift in position—namely that the bulk of the evidence collected during the past two years suggested the research was not as risky as was once perceived."[102]

If scientists won the battle with Kennedy, however, they had not yet won the war against community control. Early in 1978, Representative Paul Rogers introduced a new bill into Congress. This time university administrators joined their scientific colleagues in the fight for federal preemption. A group known as "Friends of DNA" worked closely with Rogers's superior, Harley Staggers, to draft an alternative bill that would minimize the potential for local control of recombinant DNA research. The administrators claimed that legislation that endorsed the right of local communities to determine what should and what should not be done within university laboratories could set a dangerous precedent for demands for increased control over other university activities.[103]

Industry representatives, who had stayed out of the earlier debates on the safety question, now added their voices to those of university scientists and administrators. Many were worried that either community or congressional involvement in decisions about the conduct of research would be used as a precedent to support other claims to community control of their own research efforts, and that this might prejudice the commercial exploitation of the research. Arthur Whale, general patent counsel for Eli Lilly Corporation, commented at a hearing on the Rogers bill that its passage would be unique in providing for legislative intervention in private research efforts, since the bill would extend the NIH guidelines to cover research in the private sector. "It would subject basic research activities to unprecedented federal controls, and it would do so in this case at the critical initial phase of recombinant DNA research."[104]

Indeed, even after the main push for legislation had run out of steam, the American Society of Microbiologists continued to push for federal preemption and to express its opposition to "a patchwork of local controls," which, it claimed, would result in scientists traveling aound the country to find communities where regulations were least restrictive. In testimony to the Senate science subcommittee chaired by Senator Adlai Stevenson, Jr., in November 1977, Halvorson repeated the ASM's basic arguments: "The steady proliferation of local community activity to limit, impede, or halt DNA research impresses on us, no matter how reluctantly, the need for minimal interim federal legislation . . . [that] should provide for federal preemption over local laws."[105] In other words, regulation was acceptable if it was technocratically controlled from the center, but unacceptable if it was likely to be democratically controlled from the grass roots.

At the same time, scientists continued to argue that knowledge generated since Asilomar reduced the overall need for strict regulation. Many expressed this view at a hearing held by the science, research and technology subcommittee of the House Science and Technology Committee, chaired by Roy Thornton of Arkansas. The subcommittee was sympathetic, and helped stall any progress on the Rogers bill.* Public interest and environmentalist groups such as Friends of the Earth and the Environmental Defense Fund, along with their supporters in the scientific community, argued that the scientific uncertainties still surrounding the research demanded a conservative approach to safety and environmental precautions. Yet faced with the opposition, they found themselves with dwindling political support in Congress. Eventually this support evaporated completely, and all proposals for congressional action—whether requiring federal preemption or not—were dropped from the legislative agenda.

If the scientific community, with the support of its congressional and corporate allies, was successful in fending off legislation at either the state or the federal level, it also managed to neutralize pressure for greater public control of the Recombinant DNA Advisory Committee. This pressure was partly fueled by NIH's own behavior. NIH administrators had been widely criticized for suggesting revisions to the guidelines in 1978 on the basis of the conclusions of a closed scientific meeting in June 1977, at which the results of early risk assessment experiments were discussed, even before the results of the experiments had been published in the open literature. A statement summarizing the meeting's conclusions was aggressively publicized to boost public confidence in the safety of recombinant DNA research, claiming that the results showed that disabled laboratory bacteria "cannot be converted into the epidemic pathogen by laboratory manipulation with DNA inserts."[107] Over 100 scientists signed a letter objecting to the publicity being given to this conclusion before the data on which it was based had become available. Others questioned the significance being attached to the results. The Department of Public Advocate of the State of New Jersey, in a typical comment, claimed that the conclusion was a "borderline red herring." Scientists concerned with the hazards of using the strain, *E. coli* K-12, had never maintained that the strain was the central hazard, but had argued that it was so fertile that hybrid plasmids might be transferred to

---

* Three years later, having left Congress and been appointed chairman of the Recombinant DNA Advisory Committee, Thornton expressed his "great personal satisfaction" that the subcommittee had "slowed the rush toward federal regulation."[106]

wild strains. "To leave out this factor is equivalent to ignoring and leaving unsaid the possibility of a core meltdown in a nuclear reactor and merely stating that a nuclear reactor is safe because there is no danger of a nuclear explosion," a report from the department stated.[108]

Criticism of the absence of public discussion of the research before it was used as the basis of policy recommendations triggered demands for greater public participation in the activities of the RAC. Indeed, Fredrickson later admitted that it had been a "mistake" to move before the conference conclusions had been published in the open scientific literature.[109] Despite opposition from scientists, Joseph Califano, Secretary of Health, Education, and Welfare, announced that he was expanding the number of public interest representatives on the RAC from two out of twelve to six out of twenty. At the same time, he increased the required public participation in the Institutional Biosafety Committees (IBCs), established at individual universities and research institutions to oversee observance of the NIH guidelines.

Yet expanding public representation on the committees responsible for implementing the guidelines turned out in practice to be little more than a public relations move. The inclusion of critics on the RAC helped legitimate its decisions by giving the impression of greater pluralism, and the presence of such critics frequently resulted in a greater discussion of controversial decisions than might otherwise have taken place. However, the appointments did little to alter the political dynamics of the committee, on which scientists—often those who were directly involved in carrying out the research they were regulating—remained in the dominant position. Scientists at NIH were even able to exercise considerable influence over the choice of public interest representatives, vetoing those they felt would be too troublesome—in other words, those who might transcend what were considered to be the legitimate boundaries of the public debate, and cast regulatory issues in explicitly political rather than technical terms.

In practice, therefore, the presence of public interest representatives on the RAC, many of whom were openly critical of the dominant role of scientists on the committee, did not slow the pace at which the guidelines were dismantled. Objections that adequate risk assessment experiments —one of the main recommendations of the Asilomar conference—had not yet been completed were frequently answered with the claim that such experiments were no longer necessary. When caution was exercised in deregulating, it was usually based on the fear that moving too fast would provoke a backlash from either Congress or local communities, rather than any conviction that the caution was necessary on scientific grounds.

One of the clearest examples of this process came in the fall of 1981 when the RAC debated a proposal from committee members David Baltimore and Allan Campbell that the guidelines be turned into a voluntary code of practice. The two scientists argued that there was no longer a case for applying stricter constraints to rDNA research than to conventional research projects. The referred to what they claimed was a growing consensus among scientists that research using recombinant DNA techniques to transfer genes between organisms was no more dangerous than conventional research with the same organisms. The majority of the members of the RAC were prepared to accept this position, endorsing the publication in the *Federal Register* of a proposal that the guidelines be transformed into a voluntary code of conduct, that the makeup of the Institutional Biosafety Committees be left to individual research institutions, and that containment requirements for most experiments be yet again significantly reduced.

The RAC's proposals were based primarily on an assessment of the scientific arguments that had been put to it about the apparent lack of significant danger associated with most recombinant DNA experiments, providing these were carried out according to what was accepted as "good laboratory practice." When the proposal was made public, it was greeted enthusiastically by individual scientists, many of whom had long objected to the guidelines as unnecessarily burdensome. (In a typical reaction, Paul Berg of Stanford University commented that the guidelines were now dispensable, since "based on the substantial amount of experience and experimentation with the recombinant DNA methodology during the last six years, there is widespread agreement that the risks that were once thought to be so plausible are actually remote or possibly nonexistent."[110]) The political response from institutions rather than individual scientists, however, was very different. The prospect that the guidelines might become no more than a voluntary code of practice— i.e., that the federal government was now backing away from its efforts to regulate recombinant DNA research—was already beginning to restimulate debates about the need for local control at the state and community levels to make sure that good laboratory practices were, in fact, followed. In California, for example, the Health Committee of the State Assembly held two hearings on the effectiveness of the NIH guidelines. After the hearings, committee chairman Arthur Torres announced that he was considering introducing new legislation requiring all scientists in the state to observe the recommended containment procedures. Staff aides made it clear that the decision on whether to proceed with new legislation would depend largely on the outcome of further discussions by the RAC on the proposal to make the guidelines voluntary.*

The renewed intensity of local debates, many inspired by the plans of emerging biotechnology companies to build new laboratories or produc-

---

* The California bill, although passed by both the State Assembly and Senate, was later vetoed by Governor Edmund G. Brown, Jr., on the grounds that it could discourage the growth of biotechnology industry in the state.

tion plants, rekindled fears in both universities and companies of new attempts to impose local controls over their research, in the absence of central guidelines administered by NIH. Genentech, for example, repeating the arguments put forward previously by the American Society for Microbiology, wrote to NIH that "the alternative to the attentiveness of NIH could well be a patchwork of local and state regulations which might impede our national progress and do nothing to assure additional safety."[111] The Industrial Biotechnology Association, representing a number of other small biotechnology companies, expanded on the corporate motive for opposing local controls. It claimed that "one significant reason for adherence to a uniform system of federal guidance and overseeing is our belief that such an approach *is more compatible with commercial development* and the benefits it brings to society than would be a system of local requirements" (italics added).[112] University IBCs issued similar warnings about local controls. Writing on behalf of the committee on the regulation of hazardous biological agents for the Harvard Medical School, committee chairman Thomas O'Brien stated: "It is our concern that the relaxation of the NIH guidelines would lead some local communities to regulate this activity with different standards. The impact of such an occurrence could be devastating to the scientific community."[113]

The warnings did not go unheeded. The threat that California and other states might introduce new legislation dominated the discussion when the RAC met to consider the public comments on its proposal to abandon the guidelines as a regulatory requirement. Given the unexpectedly strong opposition from both university and corporate IBCs, the RAC members were quick to back off from their previous proposal; they adopted a compromise resolution that, while suggesting a relaxation of containment requirements, still maintained the mandatory regulatory structure established five years previously. It was explicitly accepted that the decisions had been made for political rather than scientific reasons. Yet there was little consideration of the fact that local controls might reflect legitimate local concerns. One member warned that if the federal government made the guidelines voluntary, it would become a "political football" at the state and local levels. "The guidelines are a protection against politicians . . . whipping up a public frenzy behind them,"[114] he admonished.

Chairman Ray Thornton justified the continued existence of the regulatory apparatus as "a means of affording good communications between the scientific community and public policy-makers."[115] Yet the political pressure was, as ever, present. Thornton had previously received a letter from his former colleagues and the scientific community's chief allies in Congress, the members of the House Science and Technology Committee, suggesting that it would be "prudent" for the RAC to continue in existence as a way of keeping public criticism at bay.[116]

It was the first time in almost six years that the committee had reversed itself on a major policy decision. In the process, it demonstrated an awareness that keeping the public out of laboratory decision-making could be most effectively achieved not by dismissing criticism out of hand, but by a carefully tuned response that, to modify Alex Capron's metaphor, allowed it to continue picking scientific roses without being hurt by the political thorns. The decision to retain a system that dramatically reduced the substance of controls while keeping their application firmly in the hands of the scientific community was a decision clearly made on political, not scientific, grounds. It maintained a process by which the scientific community, while responding to the public's concerns about the potential health hazards of recombinant DNA research, had successfully contained the political challenge to its autonomy by retaining firm control of the overall shape of the decision-making process, whether by establishing its agenda, by defining the boundaries of dissent, or by keeping local protest groups out of the picture wherever possible. The new politics of science had come of age.

The histories of the Office of Technology Assessment and the recombinant DNA debate have several factors in common. Each originated in public concerns that society's ability to produce new scientific knowledge seemed to be greater than its ability to provide adequate protection against the less desirable implications or applications of such knowledge. In the case of the recombinant DNA debate, the arguments focused on the desirability of social controls on the practice of science and the activities of scientists; with the OTA, the concerns focused on the other end of the spectrum, namely the way science was put into practice through technology. And each generated an institutional response that has revealed substantial pragmatic value. Despite a shaky start, the OTA has settled down to producing a series of technically competent statements analyzing the possible patterns of development of a range of new and existing technologies, generating sufficient bipartisan support in Congress to ensure its continued survival. Similarly, the National Institutes of Health, through the development of the rDNA guidelines and the activities of its Recombinant DNA Advisory Committee, have—so far at least—managed to ensure that research using recombinant DNA techniques has been carried out without creating any of the damage to humans or the natural environment that had initially been feared.

Politically, however, each has tended to reinforce the dominant patterns of control over science and technology by heading off what the scientific and corporate establishments considered excessive demands for greater democracy. This has been achieved despite the fact that public participation has been high. The OTA is able to point to the large number of participants on its advisory panels who come from private industry, labor unions, environmental and consumer groups, professional societies, and university departments to demonstrate the efforts that it puts into trying to establish a broad consensus on each of the reports it produces. Furthermore, the new office has, as intended, increased the ability of Congress to discuss complex technical issues with the executive branch of the government. But the OTA has not provided the broad mechanism for steering technology toward more socially desirable ends, for weighing the social costs against the social benefits of new technologies, or even for scanning the horizon of scientific and technological possibilities—which were among the tasks envisaged by many early supporters.

It has been the same with the regulation of recombinant DNA research. Again the level of public participation in the recombinant DNA debate was substantial; indeed, former NIH director Fredrickson has referred to the RAC, with its several public members, as "one of the most useful 'cultural' innovations to come out of the rDNA controversy."[117] Yet the significant decisions remained largely within the hands of the scientific community, and public interest representatives consistently found that they were unable to exercise any significant leverage over the committee's decisions. After attending and analyzing committee meetings over a period of several years, one persistent critic of the RAC's procedures commented, that "while NIH officials have claimed that 'the public has been consulted no less than the scientific community' . . . what was called 'public participation' in hearings . . . was largely an illusion: the critical views developed in those forums had little or no real impact on NIH policy."[118]*

The pattern that emerges from these and other developments has important implications for the future of science and technology policy within a democracy. Increased awareness of the broad social impact of science and technology has, as described at the beginning of this chapter, mobilized the public around issues such as chemical pesticides, carcinogens and the workplace, toxic wastes, and nuclear power. Pressure has subsequently grown for greater participation in decisions about such technologies and the science on which they are based.[120] New institutions such as the OTA and the RAC have, in principle, provided a forum within which negotiations over the potential hazards of new areas of

---

* A similar analysis could be made about public participation in federal energy decisions through membership of the Energy Research Advisory Board, or indeed virtually any other body with the same function. (See, for example, the comments in Chapter Three on the ERAB discussion about weapons research at the Lawrence Livermore Laboratory.) Nancy Abrams and Joel Primack have criticized the treatment of public participation in hearings organized by the Department of Energy and public workshops run by the Environmental Protection Agency and the Nuclear Regulatory Commission over the disposal of radioactive waste in comparable terms. They argue that "the agencies permit public participation either too early, when plans are extremely vague, or too late, when the public is presented with a *fait accompli*. Public participation is not integrated into the decision-making process and is thus generally viewed as a sham."[119]

science and their social applications can take place, one step removed from the conventional political process. In addition, the desire for participation has been legitimated in a large number of new regulatory laws passed in the early 1970s, each of which required substantial public involvement in decisions such as setting acceptable levels of chemical residues, or even deciding which experiments could be carried out on human subjects.[121]

However, if such developments reflected the first steps toward direct democratic control of science and technology, they did not go unchallenged. The response of the leaders of the scientific and corporate communities, as we have seen with the OTA and the rDNA dispute, was not to deny the political nature of these debates, but to redefine the field of discourse in such a way that their political impact was tightly circumscribed. The NAS report made clear its intention of doing this when it argued that its intention was "to raise the level of political discourse, not to eliminate it." One purpose of this extended discourse was to allow "citizens' groups, private associations, or surrogate representatives to make their views known,"[122] but decisions were still to be left to conventional power groups. The practical outcome is that public participation has been used to legitimize decisions still made largely by private decision-makers, rather than to shift the political basis on which they are made. Dissent has been successfully contained and neutralized. Even advisory functions tend to have been carried out within the same closed universe of discourse. The input of public representatives is accepted if it reflects the values that exist within the accepted range of consensus, but is rapidly dismissed as irrelevant or disruptive if it tries to question the boundaries of this consensus.

By confining attention to relatively limited areas, the result has frequently been to exclude broader issues about the social impact of new technologies. In the case of the Recombinant DNA Committee, for example, it was decided by NIH officials at a relatively early stage that the committee would confine itself to the safety aspects of the research and would not concern itself with other social impacts, such as the potential moral or ethical questions raised by the widespread use of the techniques.[123] Thus, when a suggestion was made that the committee pass a resolution condemning the use of genetic engineering techniques for military purposes, it was decided that this was not a topic on which the committee was entitled to express an opinion. Similarly, when at the end of 1982 the committee approved a proposed experiment to insert the diphtheria toxin gene into a bacterium for cloning, its main concern was whether the experiment would be carried out safely. Virtually no attention was given to why anyone should want to carry out the experiment. Indeed, there was virtually no concern for whether it was in compliance with the Biological Weapons Convention of 1972, in which the U.S. agreed not to produce biological weapons—even though it was an experiment that could have potential application to the development of such weapons, and despite several scientists' insistence that the data it was designed to produce could be equally well obtained by other means.[124]

Similar limitations emerged in the work of the OTA. In its several reports on genetic engineering techniques, the social effects assessed were primarily technical and economic. No attention was given to the moral and ethical questions raised by the potential application of these techniques to the manipulation of human genetic material. Furthermore, neither the RAC nor the OTA addressed political questions about the way in which the new techniques altered the balance of control over biological processes (both human and nonhuman)—an issue consistently raised by public interest groups.

The result is that when new issues arrive on the political agenda, they tend to be dealt with in the same *ad hoc* fashion as they were even before the concept of technology assessment was invented. In the summer of 1983, for example, author Jeremy Rifkin persuaded fifty-five prominent religious leaders and six scientists to sign a resolution demanding a ban on the genetic engineering of human reproductive cells on the grounds that such intervention could lead to altering the human species. When criticized over the all-or-nothing tone of the resolution, several signatories admitted to reservations but defended their initiative on the grounds that no one appeared to be addressing the potential problems that seemed to be emerging, and that it was necessary to stimulate a broad public debate. "There has to be a discussion of this, and I don't see it coming from the scientific community," insisted the Roman Catholic bishop of Richmond, Virginia.[125]

The irony, therefore, is that greater public participation and scrutiny may in fact be reducing the degree of democratic control over technology policy by encouraging a form of populism that disguises the way existing power structures are being reproduced. In the early 1970s, for example, Congress made much play of the fact that it had responded to the concerns of the environmentalists by requiring environmental impact statements for new federally sponsored projects. Many millions of dollars and thousands of hours of computer time have subsequently been spent on producing the fat documents required to meet the new legal conditions. Whether they have improved the quality of decision-making —or whether the same effects could have been achieved at much lower cost through alternative, more direct means of public participation— remains an open question.

Certainly the technical quality of the reports has frequently been low, reflecting the fact that the main purpose of the studies has been procedural rather than scientific, often intended to justify decisions rather than to enlighten them. According to one critic, writing in *Science* in 1976: "Many politicians have been quick to grasp that the quickest way to silence critical 'ecofreaks' is to allocate a small proportion of funds for any engineering projects for ecological studies. . . . Impact statements seldom receive the hard scrutiny that follows the publication of scientific findings in a reputable scientific journal."[126] Others claim that by turning the attention of the environmental movement to the courts and away from forms of more direct action, the effect of impact statements has been to divert the political energies of the movement in a direction where, in the long run, they are likely to have less overall impact.

Indeed, one critic, Sally Fairfax of the Resource Policy and Management Program at the University of Michigan's School of Natural Resources, has gone so far as to describe the National Environmental Policy Act as a "disaster" for the environmental movement and for the quest for environmental policy. Fairfax suggests that litigation under NEPA, and preoccupation with the NEPA process, cut off potentially significant developments in the direction of governmental agencies' responsibility for environmental protection, and in the involvement of citizens in the deliberative processes of the agencies: "It turned environmentalists' efforts away from questioning and redefining agencies' powers and responsibilities and focused them instead on analyzing documents." Among the criticisms made by Fairfax is that it has distorted the direction of scientific inquiry by putting tremendous amounts of money and efforts into applied rather than pure research. The "science" of the impact statements, she argues, is neither disciplined nor cumulative. "Proper scientific inquiry must proceed gradually, under the full scrutiny of a skeptical and disciplined profession. It cannot be rushed or obliged to take positions on current issues if it is to be credible or valid. It seems reasonable to suggest that one of the long-term effects of NEPA will be the distortions it has caused in the science it relies on."[127]

Fairfax's argument, in brief, is that by trying to make environmental impact analysis a scientific rather than a political procedure, both the science and the policy aspects are distorted—and that its effect, contrary to widely made claims, has in fact been to stifle public involvement in decisions about important environmental issues as much as to open it up. The same statement might be made of technology assessment in general. The promise of technology assessment was that it would ensure a better balance of the costs and benefits of scientific and technological progress by allowing for more democratic participation in the selection of technical choices. Genuinely opening up the channels for such participation, however, would have required a substantial shift in control over decision-making away from private and into public channels. This, as we have seen, was a step that neither the scientific, the corporate, nor the political establishment was willing to take.

Other countries are already pursuing different strategies for involving members of the community in the technology assessment process.[128] Frequently the approach is more overtly political, such as providing labor unions with an explicit opportunity to exercise substantial control over new technologies that are introduced into the workplace. In Scandinavia, for example, various experiments in technology assessment are being introduced that would permit unions direct control—or at least veto power—over new technologies both within and outside the workplace if it is felt that their social costs outweigh their economic advantages. Similarly, in Britain labor unions have the right to nominate four members to the Genetic Engineering Manipulation Committee, who serve on the committee not in their personal capacity—as is the case with the members of the RAC—but as representatives of the members of their unions. It can be argued that this difference has resulted in a more genuinely democratic process for regulating recombinant DNA research, even though more of the British committee's meetings have been held in closed session than has been the case with the RAC.[129]

The approaches adopted elsewhere are not necessarily the most appropriate for the U.S. Nevertheless, they frequently reflect a more overt recognition of the need to address problems raised by the social impact of science in an explicitly political framework. It is not a question of making science as an intellectual practice more democratic; no one is pretending that the layperson's judgment on complex scientific issues should be given the same weight as that of scientific specialists in the field, or even that each specialist's opinion is of the same value. The danger, however, occurs when the scientist's distrust of democracy in his or her field of research is extrapolated into a domain where this distrust is no longer justified, that is, when the decisions involved are social and political rather than purely scientific or technical. In such circumstances a denial of democratic procedures is, *de facto*, a reinforcement of the opposite, namely rule by powerful elites.

In the next chapter we shall discuss various cases in which such extrapolations have served a political function while, conversely, political judgments have been cloaked in an aura of scientific neutrality. What the present chapter has shown is that as control over access to science has become increasingly important to the corporate community, not only has the scientific community helped in the tightening of this control, but it has also helped to head off efforts at moving control in the opposite direction, namely toward greater direct democracy. If democratic control of science and technology is to be achieved, the lesson of the recent past is that it must be founded on a more substantial strategy than merely the rhetoric of public participation in decision-making.

= 6 =

REGULATING TECHNOLOGY: SCIENCE AS LEGITIMATION

SHORTLY AFTER TAKING OVER AS THE NEW ADMINISTRATOR OF THE ENVIronmental Protection Agency (EPA) in March 1983, William Ruckelshaus addressed a meeting of the National Academy of Sciences in Washington. Ruckelshaus succeeded Anne Gorsuch (now Anne Burford), who had resigned after escalating public and congressional criticism of her management of the agency made her a political liability to the Reagan administration. The first task therefore facing Ruckelshaus was to raise the internal morale and, even more important, the external credibility of the agency. Both, he suggested to the scientists gathered at the NAS, could be achieved by giving greater weight to the importance of science in regulatory decisions. Ruckelshaus told the scientists that the EPA was not going to emerge from the disorganized situation in which it had been left by Burford without a significantly higher level of public confidence in its activities. "The polls show us that scientists have more credibility than lawyers or businessmen or politicians, and I'm all three of these," he quipped. "I need your help."[1]

Several months earlier, in a separate incident, James C. Miller, chairman of the Federal Trade Commission (FTC), had reacted angrily to the accusation that he wanted the commission to ignore some of the data it used to support charges against companies of deceptive advertising. Miller had proposed introducing stricter criteria by which the claims of advertisers were to be judged misleading. When it was suggested that this would make it more difficult to bring charges against a company, since it would require more rigorous proof of deception, Miller defended the proposal on the grounds that it was part of an attempt to institute "more scientific standards" for regulation at the FTC. "Surely readers would not deny the need to base regulatory action upon good, scientific evidence," he wrote in reply to an article in *Science* questioning his proposal. "I do not object to the statutory ban [on 'deceptive acts or practices'] but I would like the word 'deception' more clearly defined."[2]

These are but two examples of a tendency that has been increasing significantly in recent years to justify regulatory activities affecting new technologies by claiming that they are "scientific." In the case of the EPA, the concept was used to raise the agency's public credibility during a period in which the Reagan administration remained committed to reducing the burden of environmental controls on private industry, and after the demonstration that the more explicitly political approach adopted by Gorsuch generated strong public opposition. With the FTC, it was used to justify a suggested move that would have reduced the weight of regulation on advertisers, for example, by shifting the burden of proof of honesty versus deception from industry to the FTC's Bureau of Consumer Protection, and requiring less evidence to substantiate claims in advertisements.[3] In both cases, the intention was to use the apparent objectivity of science to suggest that the regulatory policies being followed or proposed were the result of a technical rather than a political choice. Each, it was claimed, was merely challenging the efficiency of *means* rather than the desirability of *goals*.

The tendency has been pervasive, particularly as regulatory decisions have become more controversial and both their economic impact on and opposition from industry have grown. Those either opposing new regulations or seeking to have existing ones weakened have done so by challenging their scientific rationality. Demands from industry are made for "proof" and "certainty" of environmental or health damage before regulations are introduced for new technologies. A detailed description of the relationship between "cause" and "effect" is said to be necessary before any action is taken against the former in order to prevent the latter. Corporate lobbyists contend that scientific questions should be answered before any regulatory action is taken; if only partial answers are available, then regulations should be based on scientific judgments.*

---

* In a memorandum to the EPA, for example, written soon after the Reagan administration came to power, a consultant and former director of Dow Chemical suggested that "at the very beginning of her term the administrator could declare that regulatory rules, standards, and decisions will be formulated on the basis of high-quality scientific evidence, and if evidence is lacking decisions will be based on the best scientific evidence available."[4] Gorsuch seems to have accepted such advice; in describing the principles on which the Clean Air Act was to be revised, for example, she announced that new standards would be based on "sound scientific data demonstrating where air quality represents real health risks."[5]

In a growing number of ways, an appeal to "scientific" rather than "political" judgment has become the touchstone separating "good" from "bad" regulation. A drastic reduction in methods for evaluating toxic wastes, for example, was proposed by one top EPA administrator as part of "our plans for application of 'good science.'"[6] Describing the overall strategy, George Keyworth, President Reagan's science adviser, told a congressional committee early in 1983 that the administration wanted to "reduce the excessive burden of federal regulations by improving the rational basis on which those regulations are made."[7]

On the surface, such pleas for scientific rationality in regulation appear highly desirable. If science could tell us which new technologies cause identifiable social problems, the precise nature of these problems, and the exact relationship to their cause, then regulation would be a simple matter of social priorities and technical means. Unfortunately this is not the case, since, as scientific problems, each of these remains surrounded by uncertainty. A lack of detailed knowledge about the transport of chemicals in the atmosphere means that no one can "prove" in a rigorous way that smokestack emissions from one U.S. state cause a specified increase in deposition of acid rain in a particular Canadian province. No one can state with certainty what amount of depletion of the ozone layer will cause a specified increase in temperature on the earth's surface, or why exposure to one chemical will cause cancer while exposure to a closely related one will not. Nor can anyone demonstrate that an Army veteran exposed to nuclear fallout during bomb tests in the 1950s who subsequently dies from leukemia contracted the disease because of his exposure. Some technologies—such as DDT, thalidomide, or Kepone—cause such acute health or environmental damage that they can be readily identified as dangerous and controlled (usually by banning). But chronic threats, often caused by low-level exposure to large populations over a long period of time, present a much more difficult challenge to both science and regulation.[8]

Given the degree of uncertainty involved, the assumed cause-effect relationship on which regulations are based must inevitably involve a considerable amount of personal judgment. Some of this will be technical judgment, such as the degree of statistical fit between the scattered points on a graph and the smooth curve that they are claimed to approximate. But other elements will be more subjective, not only in the explicitly social sense (such as determining levels of "acceptable risk") but even within the domain of science itself (for example, the choice between rival models of causality or the significance of animal data for conclusions about humans). Given the many uncertainties and judgments involved, clear and uncontestable demonstrations of scientific "proof" or "certainty" are impossible in almost all such cases. Thus, demands for such proof and certainty before actions are taken are often little more than attempts to prevent the action from taking place or to restrict its effect to a minimum. But decisions proposed or made for a mixture of scientific and political reasons are defended on the grounds that they are dictated by the science alone; the statement from Keyworth quoted above, for example, *assumes* that more rational regulation will be less burdensome on the private sector. It is by surrounding such decisions and judgments in what the phenomenologist Edmund Husserl described as a "cocoon of objectivity" that science is used as legitimation.[9]

This presentation of political arguments in apparently neutral "scientific" language is, I suggest, another key feature in the new politics of science. We have already seen how the broad social regulation of new science-based technologies introduced at the end of the 1960s and the beginning of the 1970s contained two components: a set of apparently pragmatic restrictions setting limits on the degree to which either individuals or the natural environment would be exposed to technologies with potentially hazardous consequences, and a more explicitly political component increasing public participation in the procedures by which these restrictions were established. In the previous chapter we concentrated on the second of these, demonstrating how the degree of democratic control expressed through public participation had been carefully controlled, often with the direct help of the leaders of the scientific community. We now turn back to the first area to see how arguments about scientific rationality are used to limit the substantive content and impact of regulation itself—or, more accurately, to defend restrictions on regulations against external criticism.

In public discussion, defenders of scientific rationality in regulation often claim that the choice is between emotion and irrationality, on the one hand, and science and rationality, on the other. The implication is that the latter are, almost by definition, preferable to the former. To characterize the conflict in this form, however, is fundamentally misleading (just as it is misleading to describe the more militant critics of contemporary science and technology as "anti-science" when, in fact, what they are criticizing are the social and political values on which this science is supported, and which subsequently become expressed through it). A more useful characterization is to place the conflict in explicitly political terms, suggesting—in line with the model used in the previous chapter—that it is the result of a conflict in the political forms of regulation. The choice, again, is essentially between two approaches to the regulation of technology: the *democratic*, embracing values that supporters describe as humane and socially just, and critics deride as emotional and irrational; and the *technocratic*, defended by the same critics as scientific and rational, criticized by others as unfeeling and anti-democratic.

Characterized in this way, we can see how the demand for a "scientific" approach to regulation fits in neatly with the other trends toward the reassertion of the "technocratic" over the "democratic" described in earlier chapters. It helps reinstate the social prestige of science—since scientists are now projected as those who will solve the problem of producing effective regulation, rather than those who created the need for regulation in the first place. It reasserts the value of technical expertise as a legitimate source of social judgments. It reduces complex social problems caused by the impact of science and technology to a form that can be handled within the dominant norms of technical and economic rationality, in other words requiring that solutions display both technical efficiency and economic profitability. It ties in neatly with the idea that politics is a pragmatic, not an ideological, activity—an idea that tends to dominate the political discourse in Washington, both in Congress and in the federal agencies.* Finally, it manages to achieve all this without upsetting the existing distribution of political power; indeed, often by encouraging a greater concentration of decision-making in private hands.

For all these reasons, we can place industry's dedication to "the proposition that 'good science' should be the foundation for good regulation" (to quote Julius Johnson of Dow Chemical[11]) in the same category as the claims made by the engineer Frederick Taylor at the turn of the century to use a "scientific" approach to factory work as the basis of "good management."[12] In both cases, the stated goal was to improve the efficiency of procedures, and indeed in each case, provided sufficiently narrow criteria were used, this goal was achieved. In the process, however, both provided a mechanism by which the control of these procedures—rapidly becoming more complex—could be securely placed in the hands of a managerial class. Scientific regulation, no less than the "scientific management" invented by Taylor, has an important political component, one that cannot in either case be disguised merely by the linguistic terminology in which its elements are described.

Again we can break recent experience into three postwar periods. In the first, covering the two postwar decades, few questioned the scientists' possession of technical expertise, nor that this expertise should, where considered appropriate, be used as a legitimate basis for policy decisions. The power and prestige of scientists were such that one physicist-turned-author, Ralph Lapp, described them as the "new priesthood."[13] The priesthood reached the zenith of its power during the Kennedy administration, a period when, according to historian Arthur Schlesinger, Jr., "the governing attitude in the White House was that public policy is no

---

* An example of this belief is the statement of one professor of political science, criticizing the reduction in EPA research funds proposed by the Reagan administration early in 1982: "Policy-making in this country, more than in any other country I know of, relies heavily on scientific-technical information. . . . The Congress has consistently preferred approaches to policy that work to those that are ideologically consistent or clean. It is the rejection of ideology and the preference for pragmatism that explains the Congress's consistent support for research and development."[10]

longer a matter of ideology but of technocratic management."[14] Even in the Johnson administration, when basic science came under close questioning for the first time since the end of the Second World War, the status of scientists as technical experts on social issues remained relatively high; it was merely that they were being asked to direct their expertise away from the laboratory.

Public disenchantment, however, was rapidly setting in. Faced with a growing gap between public concerns about the environmental and health threats caused by pesticides, radioactive fallout, or occupational carcinogens, and statements by eminent scientists—subsequently disproved by events—that such concerns were unjustified, the credibility of scientific experts began to pall. In several cases the process was accelerated by the use of scientific advisers to defend positions adopted for overtly political reasons. As was indicated in the last chapter, at one point the head of the White House's SST office announced that it was "the considered opinion of the scientific authorities who have counseled the government on these matters over the past five years" that the operation of the aircraft would not cause significant damage to the atmosphere or the environment; when the technical reports were later published, after strong congressional pressure, it was clear that what the scientists had actually said was very different.*[15] It was the same with the proposed construction of the Safeguard Anti-Ballistic Missile System. Here again the administration paid little attention to the substance of the advice it was given by its scientific advisory boards about the technical weaknesses of the proposed system; nevertheless, it frequently referred to the fact that it had consulted these boards to justify its proposals.

Another controversy surrounded the potential dangers of cyclamates, artificial sweeteners with strong commercial attraction since they were ten times cheaper than sugar and could be sold in soft drinks as "nonfattening," yet which were discovered at the end of the 1960s to cause bladder cancer in laboratory animals, as well as being associated with birth defects and genetic damage. When public criticism, this time supported by a National Academy of Sciences committee, questioned the escalating use of cyclamates, the Secretary of Health, Education, and Welfare, Robert Finch, set up a technical committee that told him what he—and the food industry—wanted to hear, namely that despite the potential danger, cyclamates could contine to be sold provided they were

* One scientist involved in a study undertaken by the National Research Council of the National Academy of Sciences for the Nixon administration on the environmental impact of the supersonic transport claimed later that "it did not appear to me that the academy's advice was being sought on what damage was likely to be produced by the booms from a supersonic transport, or whether such a transport should be built—that decision was apparently a *fait accompli*—rather, the academy was being asked to do a 'whitewash job' on a publicly unpalatable undertaking. All information on this subject which came to me subsequently is consistent with that original judgment."[16]

labeled a nonprescription drug. A year later, under mounting public, congressional, and scientific pressure, the same committee reversed its decision and supported a ban on all over-the-counter sales; in doing so, it cited "new" scientific evidence which, a congressional inquiry revealed, had already been considered, but given less weight, in its earlier findings.[17]

The cyclamate story was perhaps the most blatant case in which the tailored advice of a committee of scientific and medical "experts" was used to give scientific legitimacy to decisions reached largely on nonscientific grounds—initially apparently in order to give cyclamate manufacturers time to sell their existing stock, later to avoid the appearance of accepting congressional criticism. Coinciding with the broader criticism of the economic, military, and social contributions of basic science described in previous chapters, such cases fueled the general pressure to open up the decision-making process to allow full public scrutiny of the use of science in policy decisions. The "demystification" of the expert became a frequent demand. Few challenged the right of the expert to make technical decisions and judgments; it was when a cloak of expertise was used to shroud the nontechnical ways that decisions had been reached that the most vigorous criticism was provoked.* As scientists suffered financially from the reduction in funds and political power, they also lost out on social status. No longer could the government justify a decision to do something just because—it claimed—its scientists had advised it to do so.

By the end of the 1970s, however, demands that scientists should remain on tap, not on top, had also begun to falter. Their return to political favor was, as we have seen in earlier chapters, part of a broader swing from public back to private decision-making on technological issues claimed essential for restructuring the nation's industrial base. The widespread involvement of the federal government in the active promotion of new technologies had helped to create both heavy pressures on public spending and a shift from the private to the public control of social resources, which U.S. capitalism was no longer prepared to support as its economic problems worsened. Efforts to steer technology in directions that would not be chosen if left to the marketplace alone, however socially desirable, were claimed to be reducing the effectiveness of investment strategies based solely on a desire to maximize the rate of

---

* Joel Primack and Frank von Hippel, citing cases such as the SST, the ABM, cyclamates, and the pesticide 2,4,5-T, claimed in 1974 that keeping the activities and reports of scientific advisory committees confidential had "made it possible for government spokesmen to create the public image that federal policies for technology follow directly from the facts and analyses provided by technical experts, even when these policies have been in reality politically motivated and technically misguided. It is intolerable that the government advising system has been so easily subverted and turned into a propaganda device for tranquilizing instead of informing public opinion."[18]

private profit. If the nation's industrial base was to be made more efficient, in particular by concentrating on factors that encouraged the growth of science-based industries, so too did its forms of social and political management need to be streamlined. And one way of doing this was to "reform" the basis of regulation so that it became compatible with, and not a restriction on, continued technological change and economic growth. It was a goal to which scientists stood ready to contribute.

Conscious of the previous decline in their political power and social prestige, which they associated with excessive intervention in their affairs, members of the research community—in both the academic and the corporate sectors—frequently became some of the most articulate proponents of more efficient management of technology through a reduced government role and a more "scientific" approach. As far as research was concerned, they argued for the need to shift government policy on science away from a "demand pull" approach, implying tight political controls on research programs, and toward an approach providing greater freedom to the private sector to set priorities. In doing so, however, the research community helped set the framework for what was rapidly to become an intense national debate over the extent to which the nation's economic problems could be blamed on a decline in the rate of technological innovation, in turn the result of excessive regulation based on nonmarket criteria.

An alternative approach—that regulation could be made more efficient by making it more scientific—had indeed been offered by leading members of the scientific community at the beginning of the 1970s as part of the technology assessment movement. But, apart from its integration into the planning of the Office of Technology Assessment, it had been largely ignored as being out of tune with the growing populism of the time. A significant example can be found in a report prepared for the Organization for Economic Cooperation and Development by a group of science policy experts chaired by physicist Harvey Brooks of Harvard University, the chief architect of the OTA. Entitled *Science, Growth, and Society*, the report, like the NAS reports on technology assessment for which Brooks had also been largely responsible, warned against allowing excessive participatory democracy in decisions about technology. It also suggested that science offered "a wider intellectual base for the control and orientation of technology—a more subtle and more complicated role" than merely providing a source of new technology.[19] Thus the OECD report was already suggesting scientific regulation as an alternative to the more explicitly democratic forms then coming into favor, particularly in the U.S.*

---

* In suggesting science as an "intellectual base" for illuminating "the implications for various social values of alternative technological choices," Brooks and his fellow committee members explicitly invoked a concept of science as "systematic knowledge and inquiry,"

As the economic problems of the U.S grew worse toward the middle of the decade, the political environment became more sympathetic toward such an approach. In particular, this approach offered a mechanism for making environmental, health, and safety regulations more compatible with the values of the market, since in principle it promised to reduce complex social problems to neatly quantified form. Furthermore, scientists promoted their arguments as a way of encouraging greater technological innovation. Typical views were expressed at a workshop organized by the National Academy of Engineering (NAE) and the National Research Council's Academy of Engineering at Woods Hole, Massachusetts, in August 1976. The workshop was attended by several leading members of the corporate research community such as Lewis M. Branscomb, chief scientist of IBM, and J. Fred Bucy, president of Texas Instruments, as well as prominent academics and government officials. A report presented to the workshop and prepared under the supervision of N. Bruce Hannay (foreign secretary of the NAE and vice-president for research and patents at Bell Laboratories) spoke of "increasing concern" about the "gap between the potential technical and entrepreneurial vitality of the U.S. and its actual performance." It claimed that excessive social controls through regulation were a primary cause of a reduction in U.S. technological leadership in the world. The workshop participants endorsed the report's conclusion that a general inquiry should be organized into ways and means of fostering technological innovation in the United States. Setting the tone for the debates to follow, the report suggested that the inquiry should not look at ways of encouraging greater direct federal involvement in promoting innovation, but rather "should range broadly over tax policy and incentives, regulatory policy, anti-trust practices, and other federal laws and policies affecting innovation."[21]

Complaints about the impact of regulation on technical innovation had found little sympathy at the beginning of the 1970s, when the main body of regulatory legislation was eagerly passed by a rebellious and populist Congress; indeed, this was generally considered to be the legitimate goal of the regulation. Nor were its full implications realized. For example, the National Environmental Protetion Act of 1970, which required that environmental impact statements be prepared for all major federally financed development projects, was initially seen as relatively limited in its effect. Yet despite the weaknesses described in the previous chapter, the new law still turned out—as environmentalist groups were soon able to demonstrate in a series of court challenges—to offer a lever for citizens' groups to influence corporate investment plans

---

which seemed to have more to do with their general systems view of the world, discussed in the previous chapter as an attempt to deny the political nature of technological decisions, than with the models accepted by philosophers of science.[20]

and thus a channel for public input, however limited, into technology policy.

Many of the environmental regulations contained a "technology-forcing" component, based on the idea that if a corporation was obliged to meet certain environmental or health standards, it would carry out research to develop new technology to meet these standards that it might not have done if technological choices had been left to the criteria of market demand and profitability alone. A typical example is the catalytic converter for car exhausts, strongly opposed by Detroit when first proposed as being beyond the scope of existing technology at a reasonable cost, later adopted with little difficulty when the auto industry found more efficient ways to meet government air pollution standards.

If the environmental legislation increased community involvement in corporate decision-making about new consumer technologies, a corresponding voice was given to the labor unions through the Occupational Safety and Health Act, signed by President Nixon in 1970. This act emerged from a series of labor struggles, in particular those of coal miners, steelworkers, and auto workers, for cleaner working conditions. Not only did the act establishing the Occupational Safety and Health Administration (OSHA) within the Department of Labor provide a legal framework for tightening up the safety conditions in industry, but in principle it also provided workers with rights to participate in decisions about the conditions in which they were prepared to work—and thus ultimately in the technological design of their jobs. To many of its supporters, the act was an attempt to establish a degree of democratic control over the impact of technology by helping to shift power from employers to workers. Sheldon Samuels of the Industrial Union Department of the AFL-CIO has claimed that "what businesses are really complaining about is the basic thrust of the [Occupational Safety and Health Act], which gives workers rights that enable them to participate in the determination of their own level of risk." [22]

Even if the shift in power turned out to be largely imaginary, the Occupational Safety and Health Act nevertheless helped to sustain a new militancy at the rank-and-file level of the labor unions, where members saw it as a chance to challenge not only the control of the workplace by management, but also frequently the control of the traditional labor agenda by the union hierarchy. In both senses, health and safety issues were directly linked to questions of control over working conditions—and ultimately to decisions about the introduction of new production technologies. Local action groups argued that unless workers began to fight for the right to control their own working conditions, they would never be able to make their workplaces healthy and safe. [23]

Opposition to the new social regulation and the potential leverage that it provided community groups and labor organizations over technological decisions soon began to coalesce in the corporate community. The

Business Roundtable, for example, was formed in 1972 by companies such as du Pont, Alcoa, and General Electric as a lobby group to fight against new regulations whenever possible. During the 1970s steady resistance came from corporations to each new regulation proposed by Congress or OSHA. Congressman Paul Rogers told a meeting of the American Association for the Advancement of Science in 1978 that U.S. industry had "fought every inch of the way against every environmental health requirement; every dollar invested to reduce deadly coke oven emissions, to control arsenic and lead from copper smelters, to block unnecessary radiation exposures, to curb toxic sulfates and nitrate particles from coal combustion has come only after protracted political and legal struggles."[24]

By the mid-1970s the corporate community had begun to realize that, taken individually, the new regulations resulted primarily in additional costs; taken in aggregate, they formed a major political challenge, even on top of the new channels they provided for public participation. For they threatened to significantly shift the balance of power over technological decision-making into the hands of the state. Gerald R. Laubach, president of the Pfizer Corporation, complained that a "state-mandated" scientific orthodoxy was developing, using actions to regulate drugs taken by the Food and Drug Administration as evidence of "an issue of state control."[25] One prominent public relations consultant for the chemical industry, the author of a book entitled *Will the Corporation Survive?*, talked openly of what he described as "galloping socialism," warning that U.S. private enterprise was about to collapse under government controls.[26] A survey in 1975 by the American Management Association revealed a growing feeling that the hegemony of capital over technical change was in danger. One president complained: "Our country will become a socialized welfare state by the year 2000." Another voiced fears about an excess of democracy: "Social responsibility can be integrated into existing structures, but if the tail wags the dog it is unlikely that most businesses can survive."[27]

To community, environmentalist, and labor groups, the strong regulations passed by Congress were an expression of democratic will and a deliberate choice to place the objectives of a clean evironment and a healthy citizenry above that of maximizing private profit. But, to the corporate community, the regulations became seen as a direct challenge to their "right to manage." Expressing the views of many industrial executives, Murray Weidenbaum (writing as professor of economics at Washington University in St. Louis, later chairman of the Council of Economic Advisers under the Reagan administration) claimed that as a result of "outside bodies" becoming involved in political decisions through social regulation of technology, companies were—wrongly in his opinion—being required to respond to social responsibilities rather than concentrate on profit-making. The most fundamental aspect of regulation, he complained, was the "weakening of the entrepreneurial character of U.S. industry" caused by "decision-making . . . being moved to the public arena.[28]

The industrial backlash turned into a full-scale attack on regulations during the Carter administration. The administration, however, had depended heavily on the environmental and labor constituencies during the presidential election campaign of 1976. It soon found political difficulties in more overt strategies that were stiffly opposed by these social groups. For example, when Carter's first anti-inflation chief, Robert Strauss, suggested that social regulations should be one of the first targets of a coordinated anti-inflation drive, he quickly generated the animosity of the then powerful environmental movement. Strauss was forced to back down by the public outcry.

The Carter administration found a safer route in delegating the task of devising anti-regulation measures to its economic and scientific experts. White House economists such as Charles Shultze, chairman of the President's Council of Economic Advisers, and Barry Bosworth of the Council on Wage and Price Stability (COWPS) started to demand—with the concurrence of both the corporate community and the science policy office—a strict demonstration that new regulations were both economically and technically achievable without excessively disrupting the vitality of U.S. capitalism.

There were obvious political contradictions between the two approaches to regulation, broadly representative of the opposing wings of the Democratic coalition, with environmentalist and labor groups on one side and the liberal corporate establishment on the other. These contradictions broke into the open over efforts to reduce the exposure of textile workers to cotton dust. The dust had been identified as the cause of byssinosis, or brown-lung disease, said to affect almost 85,000 of the 560,000 workers annually exposed to it in the textile industry. OSHA announced early in 1978, after more than three years of deliberation, that it was introducing new regulations reducing permissible exposure to cotton dust from 1,000 to 200 micrograms per cubic meter of air for yarn manufacturing.

Following protests from textile manufacturers about the costs of implementing the new regulations, the White House submitted the regulations to the new Regulatory Analysis and Review Group for evaluation. (The Regulatory Analysis and Review Group had been set up by the Council on Wage and Price Stability with the active support of the Office of Science and Technology Policy to review regulations introduced by the various government regulatory agencies.) COWPS, with the backing of the textile industry and the science policy office, claimed that these regulations were unacceptable since they would result in excessive costs, estimating for example that they would require the industry to make an initial investment in new machines of $625 million, plus considerable additional annual expenditures. OSHA replied that it was not responsible for considering the costs of preventive actions if these did not cripple the industry involved, since its principal responsibility was to find the most effective way of protecting the health of workers. Carter himself initially supported his economic advisers, but he backed down under pressure from senior union leaders, as well as Secretary of Labor Ray Marshall and OSHA administrator Eula Bingham. The OSHA standards were implemented with only relatively minor modifications.

The problems encountered by the Carter administration in seeking to reduce the burden of regulation on the private sctor by explicitly political means increased the need for an alternative strategy. This new strategy took the form of attempting to secure a national consensus on the need to "reindustrialize America"—and then arguing that a reduction in regulation was necessary to reach this goal. Industry had for some time been suggesting that federal regulations affecting technological innovation should be formulated in a fashion that reinforced, rather than challenged, the basic dynamics of the marketplace. The Industrial Research Institute, the principal association representing research managers in the private sector (and dominated by large companies such as du Pont and Exxon), produced a report on technological innovation which suggested that "the most useful way to diminish the barriers and disincentives to innovation omnipresent in the present regulatory climate in the U.S. would be the maximum use of market-adjusting economic incentives, as opposed to legal restrictions and penalties, in attempting to meet regulatory goals."[29] The Committee for Economic Development (CED), another business lobby group, produced a report on innovation from its subcommittee on technology policy, chaired by Thomas A. Vanderslice, senior vice-president of General Electric; it similarly called on the government to reduce social constraints on technological innovation, arguing for the need to "consider the impact of regulatory policies on technological innovation as a means of achieving the nation's economic objectives."[30] Government should be aware of business's need for "the proper balance of constraints and incentives to enable us to achieve our economic and social goals," Vanderslice later explained.[31] The CED report warned against too much direct government involvement in attempting to stimulate innovation; instead, it should concentrate on supporting basic research, on increasing the incentives for innovation— such as more liberal tax and patent policies—and removing disincentives by relaxing regulation. The direct promotion of research toward socially determined objectives was not the answer.

The corporate community, much of which had actively supported Carter as a presidential candidate in 1976, was not slow to bring its suggestions to the White House once he took over the presidency. They persuaded the administration to look for ways of making regulatory decisions "more compatible with a desire to innovate," as Carter's Assistant Secretary of Commerce for Science and Technology, Jordan Baruch, later described it.[32] In turn the administration quickly recruited its new science adviser, Frank Press, to help in this task by emphasizing the need to integrate a more scientific perspective into regulation policy. Soon after taking up his new post, Press was visited by top research managers such as N. Bruce Hannay and Arthur Bueche, vice-president for research and development at General Electric (and a prominent science adviser to both Ford and, later, Reagan). Presumably they advanced the claims of the earlier Woods Hole report, for which Hannay had been largely responsible, blaming excessive regulation (among other factors) for a slowdown in technological innovation.[33] Press also sought out a number of business leaders from technology-intensive companies to listen personally to their complaints and demands. As Press later put it: "There were remarkably similar points and themes which came out of these meetings about what the government should stop doing—that is, government policies that impeded industrial innovation—and what the government should start doing to foster such innovation."[34]

Apparently convinced by many of industry's arguments, Press accepted that the decline in innovation was "clearly a question of national importance," and he immediately placed it high on the science policy agenda.[35] Following these early contacts, Press and his staff established an unprecedently close working relationship with the corporate research community. As Jules Blake of the Industrial Research Institute—which openly described itself as a "free-enterprise, free-marketing group"—was later to write in a letter to Science: "During the last four years there has been some important interaction established by the OSTP with the industrial research community." Furthermore, Blake emphasized, this interaction had been carried out without the adversarial relationship that often existed in the interaction between industry and some federal agencies: "We in the industrial R&D community feel that our voice has been heard.[36]

Industry therefore had little difficulty in impressing its message about the need for reform in the federal government's approach to regulation. Carter himself—with his background in nuclear engineering on the one hand, and his close ties to the Eastern banking establishment and multinational capital through membership on the Trilateral Commission on the other—showed himself, like Press, to be sympathetic to the business viewpoint. According to Press, Carter had originally thought that the problem of regulation was merely one of excessive paperwork, but he was soon made to realize by leaders of the corporate and industrial community "that the issue was much wider."[37] The voice of the private sector was clear and insistent in its demands on the administration, arguing that federal regulation was hampering innovation and should therefore be reduced. At times Press appeared cautious about his own conclusions.

At one point, in a speech at MIT in May 1978, he suggested that "it remains to be seen . . . whether in our regulatory actions we have leaned too much one way or another." Industry, he argued, might be giving a distorted picture of the impact of federal regulations. Describing his talks with industry executives, he commented: "I rarely heard recognition of the other sides to these arguments. . . . Prior to the new rules, many products were not adequately tested and evaluated in terms of environmental and consumer safety before marketing, hence the public demanded much of that regulation."[38] At other times, however, he showed little doubt that, as industry claimed, the burden of federal regulation was excessive.

Largely in response to the private sector's and the scientific community's suggestions, Press agreed to recommend to the President a broad-ranging review of industrial innovation along the lines recommended by the National Academy of Engineering workshop two years previously. The White House responded enthusiastically to Press's suggestion, one official claiming that a broad study of innovation "fits nicely with a whole set of themes that are developing for the President: inflation, productivity, unemployment, and balance of trade."[39] It agreed to establish the Domestic Policy Review, the first such high-level and broad-ranging review of government innovation policy for twenty years. The review itself was made the responsibility of the Department of Commerce rather than OSTP itself, and placed under the wing of Baruch. The goals of the policy options to be presented to the President, according to domestic policy adviser Stuart Eizenstat, were to "ameliorate any negative impacts existing federal policies have upon private-sector R&D and innovation in a way consistent with other national goals."[40]

Much was made by members of the Carter administration of the breadth of opinion the review was supposed to incorporate. But both the structure of the review itself and the way in which it was carried out made it clear that the exercise was largely directed at building consensus within political circles over what the corporate sector considered wrong with government policy and what should be done about it, rather than looking objectively—in a technical, an intellectual, or a political sense—at the process of innovation. Over 100 senior industry executives were involved in various aspects of the review, and prominent industrialists were appointed to head the key advisory committees. William M. Agee, president and chief executive officer of the Bendix Corporation, headed the advisory committee on economic and trade policy; Thomas O. Paine, chief executive officer of Northrop, and Jack Goldman, group vice-president and chief scientist at Xerox Corporation, co-chaired the advisory committee on federal policy in industrial innovation; another committee was chaired by Thomas Vanderslice of GE and the Committee for Economic Development.

There were, admittedly, representatives of other groups besides the industrial community. In particular, two of the advisory committees, one concerned with labor and the other a public interest advisory committee, had members who represented a very different viewpoint. But their presence turned out in practice to be little more than a token gesture, since few recommendations from either committee received any significant endorsement from the White House. Members of these two committees were not surprised, given the initial structure of the review. "Witness, for example, the absurd inequality of the situation in which we find ourselves," said the public interest advisory committee in its report, pointing out that in contrast to the many top industrialists on advisory committees dealing with specialized topics within the subject of industrial innovation, there were only fifteen representatives of diverse public interest gathered in one advisory committee, which was supposed to cover all facets of the subject.[41]

Sponsorship of the innovation review by the science adviser's office might have implied a totally objective study. In fact, as the structure of the review and the process by which the final recommendations were selected made it clear, the study was largely a political maneuver from the beginning. The industry representatives who had come to see Press early in the Carter administration's term of office were not looking for lengthy scientific analysis; rather, they were seeking legislation for their claim that American capitalism was being shackled by social controls on both new and existing technologies. The measures they wanted the science policy office to endorse were essentially political measures, designed to promote the economic efficiency of the private sector by reasserting the right of capital to control the application of scientific knowledge to market-determined needs. And part of this was a redefinition—accompanied by a relegitimation—of the basis on which regulatory decisions were made.

The conclusions of the innovation study largely reflected its corporate origins. The study itself resulted in over 200 recommendations being passed to the Department of Commerce. These were reduced to a short list presented to the White House. On October 31, 1979, flanked by Commerce Secretary Juanita Kreps, Press, and Baruch, Carter announced the results. After a familiar résumé of the reasons technological innovation was important to any advanced industrialized economy, he listed various measures that the administration was intending to pursue as a result of the policy review. These included increasing the efficiency of government technical information services, "clarifying" clauses in the patent law, and boosting efforts to reduce the weight of regulation.[42] As important as the specific recommendations, however, were the political assumptions on which their selection was based. These implied—as the corporate sector had been insisting—that the nation's economic difficulties were largely caused by the fact that technological innovation was being held back by excessive government intervention, and that innovation could be restimulated only by passing principal responsibility for technological decisions back to decision-makers in the private sector.

The political nature of the conclusions was emphasized by the fact that the question of how the government should behave to enhance innovation lacked the intellectual consensus that Carter's announcements of the review's conclusions implied. Indeed, the National Science Foundation consistently insisted that the innovation problem was not as serious as some were suggesting (a pronouncement somewhat embarrassing to the Commerce Department, since, if anyone, the NSF might be expected to provide an objective assessment of technological change). The NSF said there was little hard evidence that the rate of technological innovation was in a serious decline—or that government regulation was significantly to blame.[43] A report from the the Congressional Research Service stated succinctly: "It is possible to paint a uniformly negative (or positive) picture of U.S. industrial innovation only through a selective use of indicators."[44] Even economist Edwin Mansfield, in a later speech to the American Economics Association in New York in December 1982, claimed that data pointing to a slackening in the overall rate of innovation in the U.S. were "so crude and incomplete that it would be foolish to put much weight on them." Jean-Jacques Salomon, head of the science policy directorate at the Organization for Economic Cooperation and Development in Paris, writes that "it would be wrong to conclude that there has been any 'decline' in science and technology in the United States . . . [,which] remains the greatest world power as far as research and innovation are concerned."[45]

For the purposes of the innovation review, however, as well as the public relations campaign that industry carried out to back up its claims, such doubts were seldom admitted. Given the nature of the exercise and the political conditions under which it was carried out—Baruch admitted that the Commerce Department had concentrated on producing recommendations for the President that were "politically do-able" and "would secure the necessary political support"[46]—the outcome was not indeed to reflect the pluralistic thinking that existed within the academic community about the social and economic roots of technological innovation. Indeed, even if one concedes a slowdown in the rate of technological progress, other explanations existed outside the industrial community, but they received little attention from policy-makers, since their political implications did not point in the desired direction.

Some blamed any apparent slowdown on the monopolistic practices of large corporations, which tended to discourage innovation in their smaller competitors. (Herbert Holloman, for example, who had been the first Assistant Secretary of Commerce for Science and Technology under President Kennedy in the early 1960s, and was later director of the MIT Center for Policy Alternatives, claimed that the monopolistic position enjoyed by large firms led them to oppose dramatic changes in the production process. Effective innovation, in his opinion, required "an economy not dominated by giant monopolies which cannot be entered by other firms who threaten the monopoly."[47]) Another target of criticism was the shortcomings of U.S. management. These were highlighted in studies carried out by Robert Hays and William Abernathy of the Harvard Business School, who pointed out that other countries experiencing the same pressure as the U.S.—including stringent social regulation— had still been able to raise their levels of productivity. Where competitors had concentrated on producing superior technological products, however, American managers had increasingly directed their attention to an exaggerated emphasis on quantitative rather than qualitative analysis, to a preference for servicing existing markets rather than creating new ones, and to a "devotion to short-term returns and 'management by numbers.' "[48]

A third line of argument also received little support from policy-makers, even though it was often promoted by individual companies to their shareholders. This was the argument that regulation frequently *stimulates* technological innovation, and can indeed provide a spur to greater market competitiveness—either directly, by providing new markets for companies that produce technologies that make production processes cleaner and safer; or indirectly, by requiring companies to invest in new equipment that is not only cleaner and healthier but also more efficient. Union Carbide told its shareholders that the increasing application of mandatory government standards had "significantly increased air pollution control markets" over the previous five years; American Cyanamid was similarly optimistic, indicating that despite short-term costs of regulation, "the longer-term prospects hold many opportunities for socially responsive and profitable management."[49] Similarly, the U.S. textile industry was given a major boost by tough government regulations on exposure to cotton dust, which caused it to get rid of much of its old, inefficient machinery and invest in the latest production equipment capable of producing better-quality fabrics at higher speed.[50]

None of these alternative explanations, however, contained the message that American capitalism wanted to hear. Nor, indeed, did it wish their thrust to be the principal message conveyed to the American public or to politicians. Rather, a vigorous campaign was conducted to persuade the public that a slowdown in innovation existed that was the direct result of excessive federal regulation of the production process—not of capital's own failures. Many companies took out full-page advertisements in the national press claiming that overregulation was strangling invention and discouraging the R&D necessary to produce new technologies.* Robert

* An observer pointed out that one company that did this, Gould Electric, was spreading the message shortly after it had been fined $283,050 for polluting inland waterways, the largest such fine ever levied on a private company.[51]

F. Dee, chairman and chief executive officer of Smith Kline Corporation, stated defiantly: "Our present technology lag has been engineered
in large part by government."[52]

The media campaign had a number of objectives. The most obvious
was to cast social regulations, designed to protect workers, consumers,
or the environment, as obstacles to the complete spectrum of science,
technological innovation, productivity, economic growth, and ultimately
social progress. Dire warnings were issued about what would happen if
nothing were done to reduce public control of the private sector. Regin-
ald Jones, chairman of General Electric, and one of the fiercest critics of
government controls, warned of a "new mood" in America that could
"bring the grand enterprise of science and technology to an ignominious
halt."[53] The National Agricultural Chemicals Association, a lobby group
formed to fight the government's efforts to increase controls on new
chemicals and fertilizers, put out a press release provocatively entitled
"Excessive Regulation Threatens Food Supply."[54]

Behind this was a less explicit agenda, namely an attempt to establish
a semantic framework that would help legitimize the anti-regulation
campaign by expressing its objectives in the apparently neutral languages
of science and common sense. In order to do so, the media campaign
also set out to reestablish a positive image of science and science-based
progress in the public's mind to neutralize the criticism that had been
directed at both over the previous decade. Linguistic terminology played
an important part in this process. A reductionist language was used to
distinguish "unnecessary" regulations, often claimed to be the results of
applying "bad science," from those admitted to be necessary, but only if
they could be shown to be based, in contrast, on "good science."[55] Research aimed at social objectives, such as protecting the environment or
the health of workers and consumers, was labeled "defensive," allowing
companies to argue that they were being forced by government (and thus
implicitly against their will) to undertake such an activity. Similarly,
research and development was divided into that which contributed directly to company profits, and that carried out for broader social reasons.
Reflecting such distinctions, the vice-president for research and development at Lever Brothers complained about the increasing number of
toxicologists employed in the research laboratories of the chemical industry, commenting that this represented a major drain on the industry's
scientific resources, since "toxicologists don't innovate."[56] The clear implication was that industry's definition of a "productive" scientist was one
who helped to produce new technologies and technological processes,
not one who tried to protect the public from their side effects.

The media were quick to pick up and amplify both the content and
the form of the messages being fed to them by the public relations campaign. In an article headed "Vanishing Innovation," the *Business Week*
reported that "the future health of the nation's economy, many experts

believe, requires a much more benign environment for industrial R&D than has existed over the past decade." Welcoming the Carter Domestic Policy Review, the magazine stated that "far too many R&D dollars are being spent by companies to meet federal safety, health, and environmental regulations, rather than to develop new products and processes."[57] The *New York Times*, in an editorial on "America's Technology Lag," suggested that opportunities should be sought "to eliminate regulations that impede innovation."[58] *Time* spoke of "The Innovation Recession," referring with little hint of contention to a "shocking decline of American ingenuity, otherwise known as R&D," quoting Arthur Bueche of GE on an apparent collapse in American values, and referring to "another fear expressed by many scientists: [that] a growing share of government-sponsored R&D is not true research at all but only the quest for instant remedies to satisfy the rising number of regulations flowing from Washington."[59] In such ways the mass media helped frame the issues in a language consistent with the political goals of the corporate sector.

The publicity campaign was aimed at legitimizing efforts to reduce social obstacles to the increased profitability of the nation's industrial base, and thus to the expansion of American capitalism. If there was a price to be paid in terms of fewer anti-pollution measures or more dangerous workplaces, the American public was told that the long-term gains would justify the sacrifice. "We must choose which effort—quality of life or reindustrialization—will be given first priority over the next ten to fifteen years," claimed sociologist and White House consultant Amitai Etzioni. His neutral-sounding term "reindustrialization" was enthusiastically taken up by both the Carter administration and the mass media to support the argument that there was, as far as they saw it, no such choice. According to Etzioni: "Government policy will have to be consciously directed toward encouraging investment at the expense of public and private consumption. This is what reindustrialization is all about."[60] An advertisement by U.S. Steel, picking up on Etzioni's characterization, quoted the company's president, William R. Roesch, as describing reindustrialization as a vital necessity.[61]

The American people, however, were being asked to do more than sacrifice a clean and safe environment. Also being rescinded were political rights that had been won over the previous decade for participation in major decisions about the shape and direction of technological change. Stringent regulations expressed a strong desire that technology should respond directly to social priorities and needs. The movement toward regulatory reform—or regulatory relief, as it later became less euphemistically known—aimed at reducing the need to observe social priorities in corporate planning by circumscribing the political challenge to decision-making that regulations represented. The frequently heard claim that regulation increased unemployment, for example, was partly intended to weaken those constituencies that put public need above private, corporate priorities.[62]

The political goal was to reduce the legitimacy of demands made by the critics of corporate America, from environmentalist groups to labor unions, for a prominent role in setting national social and economic priorities. Science policy—and indeed the very structure of scientific debates about the need for regulation—helped accomplish this disenfranchisement by legitimizing corporate demands. As one activist engaged in building links between the environmental movement and the labor movement has written, the struggle against the "scientization of innovation and regulation policies" is also "a fight over power, control, prerogative, and participation. It is a battle over the boundaries of our democracy. Not surprisingly, it is always a hotly contested fight, for a great deal is at stake."[63]

Yet the political contradictions that had surfaced in the dispute over the cotton dust standards took their toll. The White House was unable to resolve fundamental conflicts between its obligations to different wings of the uneasy political alliance spanned by the Democratic party. Attempting to placate both wings placed limits on the results of the OSTP-initiated policy review of industrial innovation. During the review itself, industry had pushed hard for major concessions in two areas: increased tax relief for research and development, and a substantial decrease in the burden of regulation. On both they were to be disappointed. The Carter administration claimed it was putting off any changes in tax policy until a later package of tax changes, and that regulation was already being adequately tackled in other areas. Conversely, those traditional Democrats who had persuaded the Commerce Department to propose a strongly interventionist industrial policy—later dismissed by Press as a "kind of corporate statism tinge"[64]—failed to win much support in the White House. The Domestic Policy Review, widely hailed when announced as timely and necessary by both sides of the Democratic coalition, including an industrial community expecting a more sympathetic response, fizzled like a damp fuse. Indeed, such was the equivocal nature of the principal recommendations that they failed to win much support from either side. Industrialists jumped on the lack of any major changes in tax policy, regulatory policy, or patent policy. Labor and environmentalist groups pointed out that they had gained even less; they complained that "the old whipping boys are being dragged out," as one labor official described the references to excessive regulation and other social controls as impediments to innovation.[65]

Behind the scenes, however, the currents were already running in industry's favor, and against the labor unions and environmentalists. Although—as the Strauss and cotton dust incidents had already indicated—the political support from these latter groups made it difficult for the Carter administration to make a direct attack on regulation, its economists, aided by its scientific advisers, continued to develop strategies for cutting back the impact of regulation by less overt means. One of these was to try to bring the regulatory agencies under the more direct control of the White House and the Office of Management and Budget, since this would make it easier to mold regulations to the specific demands of economic and industrial policies favoring increased innovation and reduced social controls on private enterprise.

Historically, executive branch agencies such as the EPA and OSHA, and the "independent" bodies such as the Consumer Product Safety Commission and the Nuclear Regulatory Commission, originated in separate congressional actions determined by the need to respond to specific social demands. This has allowed agency heads both diversity in approach and a degree of independence from other areas of administration policy in interpreting their mandates. One reason is that the agencies enjoyed enthusiastic support from the congressional committees and public pressure groups that had helped set them up, as well as considerable autonomy in establishing new regulations. Under the Carter administration, these agencies, frequently staffed by those who had previously been active in the public interest movement, took aggressive positions on a wide range of environmental, health, and safety issues—i.e., on the need to apply tough controls to the social applications of science. They argued that, although Congress had demanded firm action when the agencies had been created at the beginning of the 1970s, successive Republican administrations had been reluctant to apply the full rigor of the law, while public participation in decision-making had, as we saw in the previous chapter, made little substantive impact.

Diversity and political independence allowed the agencies to follow a strategy that was not tied to the coattails of the economic arguments being used elsewhere in the Carter administration. Unsurprisingly it was not a popular strategy with the administration's economists—or its science policy advisers—both of whom felt the agencies should be reined in. At a meeting organized by the American Association for the Advancement of Science, presidential science adviser Frank Press complained: "We now have a regulatory structure that is highly segmented, wide-ranging in its impact, economically important, highly politicized, very aggressive, relatively independent, and almost totally uncoordinated."[66] In an attempt to bring the regulators into closer line, various linking mechanisms were established. The regulatory agencies themselves established an Interagency Regulatory Liaison Group (IRLG) to coordinate their activities and actions on individual hazards. Against this, White House economists, with the active participation of Frank Press and other OSTP officials, set up a Regulatory Analysis Review Group (RARG), headed by the chairman of the Council of Economic Advisers; the intent was to seek to minimize the economic impact of new regulations. A

Regulatory Council was also established to publish a Regulatory Calendar of future regulations.

In describing these new arrangements, the official line was that they were based on the need for more rational management of regulatory decision-making. The Regulatory Council, Press told the AAAS, had been established "to bring some coordination and consistency into the regulatory system." Press emphasized the need for "greater scientific rigor" in regulatory programs and went on to pick up an argument made earlier by Charles Shultze of the Council of Economic Advisers that the development of the federal regulatory process was at about the same state in its evolution as the federal budget process had been before the creation of the Bureau of the Budget in 1921.[67]

Yet there was also a political motivation in the reorganization. Press admitted the need to balance social goals "without denying ourselves the benefit of new technology."[68] Bowman Cutter, executive associate director of OMB (and a close ally of Press in efforts to increase federal support for basic science), told the same AAAS meeting that the main reason for greater coordination over regulation was to make it easier to make trade-offs between different social and political objectives, such as protecting the environment on the one hand and stimulating economic growth on the other. (OMB had previously been unsuccessful in trying to get seven agencies voluntarily to agree on a common approach to the control of toxic substances.) Presidential inflation fighter Alfred Kahn, speaking before a sympathetic audience at the American Enterprise Institute, had few doubts that the incentive for streamlining the regulatory agencies was to bring them under tighter control by the economists and the economic logic of the administration. He described the Regulatory Council, for example, as an attempt to introduce "both economic and scientific rationality" into the regulatory process. This meant not only setting common priorities, but also "knocking heads together to see that the regulatory agencies, pressed by the council on the one hand, and by RARG on the other, follow the lead of the President."[69]

The Office of Science and Technology Policy itself took the lead in trying to integrate the regulatory agencies into a single bureaucratic system by getting them to agree on a common scientific basis for their actions. In February 1979, for example, scientists at OSTP suggested a single scientific organization which would be responsible for identifying and characterizing potential carcinogens across a range of government agencies, based on an expansion of the National Toxicology Program established the previous year by the Department of Health, Education, and Welfare.[70] Such efforts had both a scientific and a political dimension. The first was to ensure intellectual consistency among the rules introduced by the different agencies; the second was to undercut those agencies that the White House felt were being too aggressive in pursuing their legislative mandates.

Central to the overall strategy were moves, supported by OSTP, to bring the individual programs of the regulatory agencies under the tighter control of the Office of Management and Budget and the Council of Economic Advisers. During the Carter administration, OMB played an increasingly important role in determining which regulations were to be developed, applying an economic logic to regulatory decision-making that often cut directly across the social priorities that had been set for the agencies by Congress. Environmental health professor Nicholas Ashford of MIT speculated in public whether OSHA decided to accept the advice of the Council on Wage and Price Stability to soften new restrictions on exposure to acrylonitrile because it accepted the economists' arguments or because "they were responding to the potential threat that RARG would take the issue to the President, as it had done with the cotton dust standard." Ashford went on to suggest that the assessment of an agency's economic impact by groups such as the Council of Economic Advisers—or, for that matter, OMB—might well be seen as "strategies to reorient various legislative mandates to their own point of view."[71]

The efforts by Carter's science advisers to place regulation on a more "scientific" basis were part of a broader effort to subordinate the social control of technology through environmental, health, and safety regulation to the rules and values of the marketplace. A similar goal lay behind a complementary strategy, often promoted enthusiastically by industry and its supporters in Congress and the White House, and legitimated by those who claimed that regulation should be based on a more scientific approach. Under this strategy, decisions about the control of technology were to be made on the basis of a cost-benefit assessment (CBA).

Initially, much of the regulatory legislation passed by Congress in the late 1960s and early 1970s had paid little explicit attention to economic considerations, on the grounds that once society had decided what it wanted to be protected from by a conventional process of democratic choice, it was up to the private sector to follow such decisions in the most economical way it could discover. The Occupational Safety and Health Act of 1970, for example, makes virtually no reference to economic factors that might influence regulatory decisions, but merely states that measures must be taken to protect the health and safety of workers from significant harm. As Eula Bingham, head of OSHA under President Carter, put it: "Worker health and safety . . . are to be heavily favored over the economic burdens of compliance."[72]

Despite intense opposition from industry, this interpretation has been upheld by the Supreme Court. In 1978 the textile industry brought a court challenge against the new restrictions introduced by OSHA to protect workers from brown-lung disease as a result of exposure to cotton dust. The industry claimed, as the administration's economists had claimed in trying (unsuccessfully) to have the restrictions significantly weakend by the White House, that the new regulations were excessively restrictive. They complained in particular that OSHA had not taken sufficient notice of the costs required to meet the new standards in deciding the level at which they had been set. After a series of court decisions, the industry's challenge was finally overruled by the Supreme Court in 1981. The Supreme Court ruled that Congress, in passing the original legislation, had not intended that safety measures be applied only to the extent that they imposed acceptable costs to the industry involved.[73]

Expressing worker safety purely as a social goal, however, was a direct challenge to forms of decision-making based primarily on economic criteria, the principal calculus of private corporations. The deliberate exclusion of economic considerations became an increasingly frequent target of industry's attack on regulations, and in 1979 Carter signed an executive order requiring the publication of a "regulatory analysis," showing the expected costs and benefits of a regulation before it was introduced. Many of industry's criticisms were shared by Carter's science adviser, Frank Press, who told the AAAS meeting in his 1979 speech that one of the problems with regulatory agencies is that they tend to concentrate on single-priority objectives, with less consideration to other effects, "especially cost." He went on to suggest that scientists should, as a result of their intellectual training, be in favor of more cost-benefit and risk-benefit analysis. "Science is essentially rational, and as scientists, we generally support more analysis and fact-gathering to bring reason to bear on our regulatory decision," he contended.[74] (Congressional supporters of reduced regulation often voiced similar arguments. Republican Congressman Donald Ritter, an engineer from Philadelphia, introduced a bill into Congress in the fall of 1981 that would extend the cost-benefit approach to full-blown risk analysis. According to Ritter, the purpose of his bill was "to bring a higher level of scientific input to decisions by regulators."[75])

Many criticisms can be made of cost-benefit analysis. One is the moral argument that it is ethically wrong to apply narrow quantitative criteria to human health and human life, since this reduces to a crude economic assesment the criterion of value that must inevitably be used. Environmentalist David Doniger, for example, of the Natural Resources Defense Council, told a congressional subcommittee that "there is simply no morally and socially acceptable way to trade human life and such things as the survival of other species to conventional economic products."[76] A second argument is that the results of such analysis are frequently wrong —and hence can be seriously (and sometimes deliberately) misleading. The most widely cited example of this is the calculation made by the chemical industry in the early 1970s that the proposed, stringent restrictions on workers' exposure to polyvinyl chloride (PVC) would impose such a heavy burden on the plastics industry that many firms would be forced into bankruptcy. One study predicted costs of between $65 and $90 *billion*. In practice, the industry soon showed itself ingenious at developing ways of meeting the new standards. Combined with the stimulus to invest in new plants and equipment, the regulations helped the PVC industry to substantially increase its profit levels at a total cost of less than $1 billion. In 1978, Secretary of Energy James Schlesinger told Congress that complying with new beryllium standards would cost $150 million; the real cost turned out later to be about $4 million.[77]

Perhaps the most fundamental criticism of cost-benefit analysis, however, is that it distorts often complex and politically charged decisions by reducing them to a form that fits neatly into the technocratic ways of making regulatory decisions. The political assumptions on which the calculations are based, and which they therefore effectively reproduce, are masked by what physicist John Holdren has labeled the "tyranny of illusory perception."[78] Cost-benefit analysis is seldom used, even in private business, as a way of *making* decisions, since decision-makers are usually well aware of its methodological deficiencies; more frequently it is a device for defending or justifying decisions made for a complex set of technical, economic, and political reasons—or for attacking such decisions made by others (as, for example, the commonly cited estimate by conservative economist Murray Weidenbaum that social regulation costs the U.S. economy $100 billion a year—a figure frequently wielded by those who claim regulations to be excessively restrictive, but attacked by others, such as economist William K. Tabb, as a gross overestimate of the cost that completely ignores many of the benefits).[79]

The "scientific" techniques of cost-benefit analysis frequently obscure political questions of equity, justice, power, and social welfare behind a technocratic haze of numbers, tending to substitute the calculations of few for the judgments of many. Testifying before a congressional committee, an attorney for the Natural Resources Defense Council in Washington, Richard Ayres, complained that "cost-benefit analysis allows costs to flow to small groups and benefits to large groups, and vice versa. It is concerned with efficiency but not with equity. It is deceptively precise and ignores ethical and moral choices."[80] Yet because of this very fact, the technique has many attractions, not merely for government officials drawn to the solid defense that an argument based on numbers —rather than subjective opinion—appears to give, but also for the business community. On the one hand, it allows them to exclude from decision-making those factors that cannot be adequately quantified (such as equality of opportunity); on the other, it offers a technique by which decisions can be justified by producing a list of benefits, however chosen, longer than a list of costs.

Efforts by the Office of Science and Technology Policy to put regulation on a more scientific and economic footing, both directly by reinforcing the power over regulations exercised by White House economists and indirectly by encouraging the wider use of cost-benefit analysis, were widely applauded in the liberal community. William Carey, the executive director of the American Association for the Advancement of Science, claimed that "the role of the science adviser in helping to rationalize regulatory hysteria in the interests of productivity and reduction of uncertainty has been striking."[81] Yet if the intellectual case was appealing, the political implications were frequently overlooked. For attempts to legitimize looser regulation by appealing to the need to accelerate technological innovation, to bring the agencies responsible for implementing regulation under the greater control of economic policy-makers, and to justify the economic tools of cost-benefit and risk-benefit analysis as a "scientific" answer to social problems were each part of the broader strategy already described in earlier chapters, namely to shift the control of science and its applications through technology from a *democratic* to a *technocratic* approach.*

If there is a clear difference in the two approaches with regard to public participation in scientific and technological decisions, the same difference is reflected in their assumptions about the problem of regulation. Indeed, using a term loosely borrowed from the philosophy of science, we might describe them as offering competing regulatory paradigms. In general, the democratic paradigm sees the real (and potential) problems created by science and technology from the point of view of the individuals or social groups that directly experience its effects, rather than those who seek to profit financially from its exploitation. In principle, it optimizes technological decisions for caution rather than recklessness, safety rather than risk, and public need rather than private profit. It is also based on the fundamental premise that responsibility for managing technology, both for promoting it and for dealing with its unwanted side effects, should rest with those directly affected by its applications.

The technocratic paradigm sees the management of technological innovation and regulation very differently. The purpose of innovation is characterized as the need to maximize the use of available resources (including human labor power, if this is needed, but excluding labor power as a resource if this is considered unnecessary, regardless of the human consequences). It optimizes for private profit and tries to make a "best estimate" of risk, using this to fine-tune the regulatory apparatus so that it presents the minimal economic burden to the private sector. It accepts that those who promote technology bear a responsibility to protect individuals and groups from risk, but places such concerns within the broader calculus of economic profitability. It will err if necessary on

---

* Ashford of MIT, in opposing Ritter's legislative proposals, claimed that "the location of a centralized entity for performing comparative risk assessments within OSTP undermines the basic consideration that risk management decisions are social policy decisions which are based only partly on hard sciences." Attempts to separate the scientific basis for these decisions from other considerations relevant to social policy design were "misguided."[82]

the side of caution; but it will be equally cautious of overestimating risks and adding extra costs to the costs of production, as well as engendering the political risks posed by stringent regulatory institutions. Above all, the technocratic paradigm seeks to locate responsibility for promoting technology and controlling the risks associated with it in the hands of the corporate decision-maker, ignoring the unbalanced distribution of economic power that exists in the market, and arguing that, in the long run, market forces and the "hidden hand" that is supposed to keep them in check will ultimately prove to be the most efficient basis for regulation.

Where the Carter administration was caught between environmentalist and labor groups on the one hand and economists expressing the views of the private sector on the other, the Reagan administration faced a different dilemma. For while the more liberal wing of the Republican party, symbolized in particular by Vice-President (and ex–Trilateral Commission member) George Bush, was prepared to accept the need for a moderate degree of regulation—provided it could be made compatible with the decision-making procedures of private capital—the conservatives were demanding an all-out political offensive against any public regulation of the private sector. In this context, demands for more "scientific" regulation became part of a strategy to rein in the more extreme wing of the anti-regulation movement, since many in the private sector feared that this itself could provoke a backlash that might challenge their long-term interest.

The need for less regulation was one of the key planks in Reagan's platform as presidential candidate in 1980. It served a double purpose. For conservative industrialists, the traditional backbone of the Republican party, Reagan offered a more realistic chance than Carter of reducing the burden of government controls. (Significantly, Reagan's "business advisory committee" included some of the strongest critics of government regulation, such as John Hanley, chairman and chief executive officer of Monsanto; Fletcher L. Byrom, chairman and chief executive officer of Koppers Company and a member of the policy committee of the Business Roundtable; and Richard S. Schubert, vice-chairman of Bethlehem Steel.) To blue-collar workers, the appeal was broader, for regulation could be presented as the epitome of the evils of Washington "interference" in local issues, and even as a major source of unemployment.[83] Addressing a meeting of the Economic Club in Detroit in May 1980, Reagan appealed simultaneously to both constituencies by claiming that "the auto industry is virtually being regulated to death."[84]

Several of the Reagan administration's first acts in power reinforced and accelerated the initiatives that had already been pursued by the economic and scientific advisers to the Carter administration. One of his most significant moves was to sign Executive Order No. 12291, requiring all executive branch agencies to conduct regulatory impact analyses

(RIAs) before either publishing proposed rules or issuing them in their final form, and requiring such rules to be submitted to the Office of Management and Budget for review and "suggestions" before they were implemented. The prologue to the order set out two requirements that all new rules were expected to fulfill: that their anticipated benefits should outweigh the costs, and that they should represent the "least burdensome" way of achieving regulatory goals. In one step the executive order established two of the top priorities of the "regulatory reformers" of the Carter administration: the requirement for full cost-benefit analysis and, through this, a tightening of the White House's control over the regulatory agencies. The result, in the words of OMB officials, was "to transform what had been a useful economic tool into an imperative of federal decision-making." * [85]

Just as under President Carter, these efforts were eagerly supported—and endorsed—by the science adviser's office. Whenever he presented a summary of the Reagan administration's approach to science policy, the President's science adviser, George A. Keyworth, included a reference to the need to apply science to regulatory reform. Addressing the AAAS soon after arriving in Washington, Keyworth claimed that OMB's new review process of federal rule-making was "an essential adjustment to a period when we overreacted and created a climate of uncertainty and an excessively adversarial relationship between government and industry." [87] He used identical words the following February in a speech to British members of Parliament. [88] The previous month, speaking before executives of the Monsanto Company in St. Louis, he argued that reducing the burden of government regulations meant that "corporations will not find it necessary to conduct broad 'defensive R&D'—aimed at regulatory compliance—and will be able to use these funds for more productive channels of research." [89]

In making such statements, Keyworth was doing little more than repeating the lines delivered to him by the administration's economists, such as Murray Weidenbaum, chairman of the Council of Economic Advisers. They were not scientific statements, but coming from the mouth of the science adviser, they gained greater credibility. Nor was Keyworth's support merely rhetorical. The Regulatory Reform Task Force established under Vice-President Bush decided to abolish the

---

* Christopher DeMuth, administrator of information and regulatory affairs at OMB and executive director of the Regulatory Reform Task Force set up under Bush, confirmed the political function of the cost-benefit requirement. He argued not only that it strengthened judicial oversight by requiring agencies to place on record the economic consequences of their decisions, but that it was "even more powerful as an instrument of executive oversight," since the presidency was the office of government "most suited to advancing a consistent program against narrow political pressures" and was "far more likely than Congress or the courts to take a broad view of the economic interest of the society, and far more able to impress this view on the federal bureaucracy." [86]

Interagency Regulatory Liaison Group, which under the Carter administration had been a forum in which regulatory agencies could join in a common front against the administration's economists (for example, in proposing a cancer policy based on broader definition of a potential carcinogen than industry's scientists and economists were prepared to accept). But recognizing the potential value of central scientific review —to complement and help legitimize the economic review carried out by OMB—the task force re-created the IRLG as a new Interagency Science-Health Coordinating Group. Keyworth was appointed to chair the new group, a position previously held by one of the regulatory agency heads.

Parallel with these developments, however, were the actions of the new appointees to the agencies, who appeared little concerned with problems of public credibility and legitimacy, and more with vigorously prosecuting what they saw as a broad mandate to significantly reduce the impact of their respective agencies on the private sector. Often they, too, defended their actions by claiming they were based on "scientific" arguments. When, for example, Anne Gorsuch, administrator of the Environmental Protection Agency, was challenged over how she could reconcile the agency's needs for more scientific research with major reductions in its research budget, she replied that the quality of research did not necessarily depend on an ever-expanding budget. "Our emphasis is on quality, not the amount of money we can spend," she contended.[90] Previously, she had announced that amendments to the Clean Air Act would be based on "sound scientific data." Secretary of the Interior James Watt, challenged over his submission of names for potential members of the science advisory board to the Republican National Committee for approval, pointed out that he had checked the names with the National Academy of Sciences.[91] And OSHA officials, justifying the decision to dismiss a scientist who had criticized the agency's failure to act firmly against formaldehyde after it had been shown to cause cancer in laboratory animals, claimed that OSHA "lacked confidence in the data" on which the conclusions of carcinogenicity were based.[92]

It soon became obvious, however, that such quasi-scientific arguments were only skin deep. Few were convinced that the EPA was committed to building a better base of scientific knowledge about environmental problems when it acquiesced in a cut of almost 40 percent in its research budget between 1981 and 1983.[93] Those scientists who were not reappointed to advisory committees after having black marks laid against their names by the Republican National Committee were not convinced that selection had been made purely on scientific merit, particularly when all those approved by the committee were appointed. OSHA's stand on formaldehyde was undercut by a panel of scientists (none of whom had been consulted before firing the internal dissenter, Peter Infante); the panel countered that there was a "sound scientific basis" for regarding formaldehyde as a human carcinogen.[94] Similarly, evidence began to trickle out of the agency of other cases—for example, the chemical ethylene oxide—where recommendations from scientific advisers for strict regulation had apparently been overruled by the agency's head, Thorne Auchter.

Such distrust fanned broader criticisms about the actions of the regulatory agencies under their new bosses. When Gorsuch resigned under pressure from the White House in March 1983, it was largely as a result of the growing weight of political charges that were building up against the agency, in particular that it had been collaborating excessively with private industry in drawing up its new regulatory programs. But behind the more public debates, resentment against the agency's actions was building rapidly in the scientific community, which was increasingly appalled at the way suspect interpretations of scientific data were being used to justify the agency's actions (such as its refusal to take any action against those industries that many scientists felt were the clear source of the acid rain falling on Canadian provinces close to the U.S. border). Even more significant, disenchantment with the heavy-handed efforts to torpedo the effectiveness of the regulatory agencies was growing in industry, which feared that the agencies were themselves becoming an obstacle to "rational" decision-making.

As early as October 1981, the journal *Automotive News*, no great fan of strict automobile regulations, wrote of the turmoil in the EPA: "What was once a robust, dynamic entity has shriveled to a gray shadow of its former self racked by internal dissension, [and] run by people with little expertise in environmental issues."[95] Industry made its position clear. Beneath the ideological rhetoric, it was more interested in forms of regulation that fitted comfortably with its own decision-making procedures than in less regulation for the sake of it. A survey of 316 firms carried out by the College of Business Administration at the University of Oregon confirmed that industry wanted regulatory reform, not regulatory elimination. It found widespread support for the introduction at the state and local levels of "the rational, efficient administrative procedures generally found in the management of business and government," according to the study's director.[96]

Congress too was getting restive. Bipartisan support began to grow for a new round of regulatory reform—this time addressed not to the zeal of the regulatory agencies under the Carter regime, but to their lack of action under Reagan. Republicans grew increasingly concerned that this could turn into a major political liability during the 1984 presidential and congressional elections. Conversely, Democrats spotted the opportunity for making quick political gains. And agency heads such as OSHA's Auchter, having seen the writing on the wall with Gorsuch's departure, discovered a new enthusiasm for tough regulations. The regulatory reform bandwagon, having apparently overstepped the mark, was put smartly into reverse.[97]

This move back to the center was symbolized by the appointment of

William Ruckelshaus, EPA's first administrator under President Nixon, as the successor to Gorsuch. Ruckelshaus quickly moved to reassure an increasingly skeptical Congress that he intended to restore the agency's image, accepting the immediate resignation of thirty of its top officials (most of whom had been political appointees of the Reagan administration). He reassured scientists that their views would be taken seriously once again, and pledged himself to "a more sophisticated and accurate view of how to regulate . . . in a credible way."[98]

Yet it soon became clear that what Ruckelshaus had in mind was essentially a reinforcement of the technocratic approach to regulation that economists and scientists had been seeking during the Carter administration and, subsequently, through the Bush task force under President Reagan. Ruckelshaus emphasized in his congressional confirmation hearings that he approved the use of cost-benefit analysis in making regulatory decisions, and he dismissed polls showing that Americans were willing to pay the extra costs of strict pollution controls as an inaccurate gauge of public sentiment on the issue.[99] Furthermore, he made a direct appeal to the scientific community to publicly endorse his efforts to clean up the agency and "recover its equilibrium," suggesting that the regulatory agencies should have a common statutory formula for evaluating the hazards of pollution—the device used by the Carter administration to help centralize regulatory decisions.[100]

This new technocratic approach to regulation was widely welcomed by the private sector, since Ruckelshaus and the others who were falling in line behind him—such as OSHA's Auchter—promised a strategy that would neither present them with a major economic or political threat nor generate a public backlash. Scientists too endorsed the change, since many saw it as an opportunity to place regulation back on a scientific footing. Industry, said one, should recognize that it was in its best interests—as well as in the interests of everyone else—to have a well-funded EPA, "populated by competent scientists confident of keeping their jobs as long as they do them well."[101] There was less enthusiasm among environmentalist and labor groups, however; they pointed out that Ruckelshaus and his policies were still tied to the economic and political coattails of the Reagan administration, and that in substance the EPA had yet to show any significant deviation from its previous negative approach to tougher controls, an impression reinforced later in the year when a White House task force refused to let Ruckelshaus make any concessions to Canadian demands for stricter controls on sulfur dioxide emissions claimed to be the source of acid rain.

The broader significance of Ruckelshaus's appointment, and of its general welcome from both the scientific and the corporate communities, lies in the way it brought environmental disputes back into the realm of technocratic decision-making. Opinion polls showed that strong public sentiment in favor of controls on industrial activity—the same sentiment that had fueled the "silent spring" controversy two decades earlier—was not dead, and had to be responded to. The best way of doing this, the Reagan administration found to its cost, was not to leave it to highly visible political appointees, but to absorb it, as the Oregon survey had suggested, into the administrative techniques of business. The attraction of this shift was that it appeared to make the administration's regulatory decisions more reasonable, particularly when endorsed by leading economists and scientific advisers. But as with the efforts to rationalize regulation during the Carter administration, its political effect was to further reinforce the technocratic over the democratic paradigm as the dominant approach to the social control of technology.

So far we have looked at the conflict between the technocratic and democratic paradigms over the appropriate organization of the government's regulatory activities and the choice of policy-determining methodologies, such as cost-benefit analysis. But the conflict is not confined to procedural issues; indeed, it stretches to the heart of *scientific* disputes over the collection, analysis, and interpretation of the data needed for regulatory decision-making. This conflict feeds on a mismatch confronted by policy-makers in this area—the mismatch between the volume and sensitivity of scientific data on the effects of technology that are now available through increasingly sophisticated detection techniques, and the relative insensitivity of the social mechanisms intended to react to these data and remedy the problems they indicate.

This mismatch creates a situation that is highly susceptible to political manipulation, since a range of cause-effect hypotheses can be put forward, each of which may be perfectly compatible with the available scientific data, but none of which can be shown to be a unique explanation. The identification of a potential hazard—for example, of a new chemical—often becomes largely a function of the results of statistical analysis, such as the increased incidence of a certain type of tumor in mice or rats. Ironically, the more sensitive the detection instruments, the less simple it becomes to interpret the results in a form that can be easily assimilated into public policy. Does the presence at extremely low levels of a chemical known to be toxic at high concentrations—for example, the nitrosamine compounds found as a by-product of the use of nitrites to preserve cooked meats—necessarily imply that the chemical must be considered dangerous at any concentration? How seriously—in policy terms—should an event be treated if it is likely to increase the incidence of a particular cancer by, say, one in a hundred thousand?

When trying to assess the impact of technological products or processes "scientifically," this gap between the scientific knowledge of an event and an understanding of its most likely cause (or prevention) provides scope for a range of different political strategies. In particular, there is a clear difference in the interpretations favored by the democratic and technocratic approaches to the control of technology. Those operating according to the democratic paradigm tend to argue in favor of an inherently conservative approach, planning for worst-case scenarios on the grounds that anticipating less serious possibilities implies courting an unknown danger. "If we wait for scientific proof before taking regulatory action, we will very likely turn out to have waited too long," warned Carter's EPA administrator, Doug Costle, in a paper subtitled "Why Environmental Regulation Cannot Wait for Scientific Certainty." In considering what precautions should be taken against the health hazards of air pollution from automobiles, Costle pointed out that with carbon monoxide there was no "proof" that angina led to permanent heart damage—but there was evidence that it might, and this evidence had to be taken into account. "Given the potential for long-term damage, it seems to me that the case for a policy that emphasizes protecting health where the scientific evidence is inconclusive should be irrefutable," he stated.[102] Bailus Walker, health standards director for OSHA during the Carter administration, described how "we operate with unknowns . . . [and] we must act on the best available evidence because the alternative of waiting for perfect evidence is unacceptable."[103] Such conservatism is justified, supporters of the democratic paradigm maintain, by the need to meet the social and political objectives of the legislation framing the goals of the regulatory agencies.

In contrast, the technocratic approach to such uncertainty is to claim that no action is justified until there is a reasonable amount of "proof" that it is necessary. Keen to maintain profit levels by reducing production costs and to elude external social control over their activities, private corporations adopt the position in public debate over the interpretation of scientific data that no action should be taken on possibly harmful results until they have been "proved." (The tobacoo industry, for example, continues to play up the theoretical weaknesses it says exist in studies that claim to demonstrate the relationship between lung cancer and cigarette smoking.)

It is an argument that has often been heard from regulators under the Reagan administration. In one instance, occupational health officials denied that experimental evidence showing that high doses of formaldehyde caused cancer in rats was sufficient "proof" that formaldehyde should be treated as a human carcinogen (a conclusion disputed by scientists within the National Institutes of Occupational Safety and health).[104]

Similarly, in disputes over the environmental effects of acid rain, U.S. utility companies in Ohio and neighboring states used scientific uncertainties about the precise nature of the chemical transport mechanisms by which pollutants are carried into the upper atmosphere to deny charges that they were the sources of the sulfur and nitrogen oxides that were having such a devastating effect on the lakes and farmlands of New

York State and southern Canada. The Canadians argued that, despite the absence of complete scientific certainty, enough evidence existed to make a plausible case that the Midwestern states were indeed the source of the acid rain (a hypothesis supported by a 1981 report from the National Academy of Sciences' National Research Council). They believed that the hypothesis was already sufficiently strong to warrant strong intervention by the U.S. government. But the Reagan administration for a long time refused to share the same perspective, claiming that the academy report was biased and that since the evidence still appeared inconclusive, no action was called for.[105]

Nor does the difference stop at the interpretation of scientific uncertainties. Even the choice of scientific theories—in the sense of scientific models that seek to explain the relationship between certain causes and effects—is influenced by the same type of distinction. Take, for example, the controversy over whether or not there is a threshold below which a chemical is known to have carcinogenic properties at high levels can be assumed to have no toxic effect. The problem here is that the existence or absence of a threshold cannot be "demonstrated" in a strict scientific sense, since the arguments are essentially statistical. If one is looking at a relatively slight increase in the incidence of a cancer in a large population where the overall incidence tends to be low, it is virtually impossible to state categorically that a particular incidence of such a cancer is in fact due to a particular cause.

The debate over the existence or nonexistence of a threshold again demonstrates a difference in approach between the democratic and the technocratic paradigms, this time at the level of the choice of scientific models to explain the most likely events. The democratic paradigm argues that since there is no evidence to demonstrate that the threshold hypothesis is true, and since there could be serious consequences if it were assumed to be true when it later turned out to be false, then it is prudent for policy-makers to accept a model that assumes a continuous linear relationship down to the lowest levels between exposure to a known carcinogen and the hazardous effects of this exposure. The technocratic approach tends to argue conversely that if there is no scientific evidence that a threshold does not exist, and since the existence of a threshold is compatible with certain scientific studies of the behavior of biological cells, then it is preferable to base policy decisions on the existence of a threshold—or at least on a model where biological effects drop off rapidly at low levels of exposure. To do otherwise, they argue, would result in unnecessary expense to industrial manufacturers.

The political roots of this "scientific" disagreement surfaced in the controversy over the conclusions of a report produced by the Biological Effects of Ionizing Radiation (BEIR) Committee of the National Academy of Sciences in 1979. In revising earlier assessments of the effects of exposure to low levels of ionizing radiation, first published in the early

1970s, the members of the committee found themselves torn between two apparently contradictory positions. At one end of the spectrum, a group headed by the chairman of the BEIR Committee, epidemiologist Edward Radford of the University of Pittsburgh, argued that the lack of evidence in favor of a threshold hypothesis meant that the committee should base its conclusions on the assumption that no such threshold existed. Caution thus required the assumption of a linear dose-response extrapolation from the known effects of high-level radiation as the basis for deciding permissible exposure limits to workers exposed to radiation in the nuclear industry, for instance. In contrast, an opposing faction on the committee, headed by Harold Rossi of New York University Medical School, argued strongly that the lack of evidence applied equally to arguments *against* the threshold hypothesis. What was more likely, this group contended, was a "linear-quadratic" relationship, where the response fell rapidly as the dose reached low levels.[106]

To the embarrassment of the academy, the dispute broke into the public arena. At a press conference held to present the results of the committee's deliberations, Rossi announced his sharp disagreement with what appeared at the time to be the majority view. This was, as the report (and Radford) put it, that the "most prudent assumption" was one that derived "a range of possible human effects at low levels from linear extrapolation of data derived from observations of high-level effects on both humans and experimental animals."[107] When several committee members subsequently shifted their position from Radford's to Rossi's, the report was hurriedly withdrawn from further public dissemination until the dispute could be resolved. Eventually, under pressure from academy president Philip Handler, a compromise formula was put forward, and the report was published with the watered-down conclusion that it "presents a range of risk estimates that reflects the uncertainties involved in interpreting the inconclusive data available òn the induction of human cancer by low-level radiation"—a conclusion from which both Radford and Rossi dissented.[108]

The significance of the dispute between Radford and Rossi is that what appeared to be a professional disagreement over a purely scientific question—namely the most likely shape of the dose-response curve at low levels of radiation—reflected broader philosophical and political differences between the two. Radford was an epidemiologist who made little secret of his sympathies with the U.S. labor movement and his belief that decisions about appropriate safety standards should be as widely discussed as possible by, among others, those exposed to the hazards, with scientific uncertainties made part of the debate and not foreclosed by the subjective judgments and assumptions of "experts." In contrast, Rossi was a biologist whose views were closer to those of the U.S. nuclear industry on the dangers of excessive regulation. Rossi and his supporters made it clear in announcing their disagreement with the BEIR Committee's original conclusions that if the proposed risk assessments were accepted by the general scientific community, their use would help scuttle further attempts to expand the nuclear power industry. One committee member who supported Rossi's position complained to the *New York Times* that "if the guidelines were reduced the way [Radford] wants them there wouldn't be any nuclear industry at all."[109]

Similar disagreements surfaced in discussions about efforts by the Carter administration to develop a "generic" policy for dealing with carcinogens. OSHA officials argued that the urgent need to act against cancer-causing chemicals, even in the absence of detailed knowledge of how they worked, demanded a cautious and conservative approach if the agency was to meet its mandate of creating a "safe and healthy" workplace for all Americans. Furthermore, rather than starting from square one with each suspected chemical individually, OSHA proposed a generic approach that would apply to any suspected carcinogen. On this basis, it suggested that any chemical for which there was evidence of potential carcinogenicity—for example, from tests on laboratory animals —should be treated as a carcinogen, and subject to rigid controls, at least until further data about its effects on humans had been collected. OSHA official Grover Wrenn defended this policy on the grounds that no safe level of exposure should be accepted for potential carcinogens. In his words, the threshold hypothesis (which would imply that the chemical caused cancer only above certain minimum levels of exposure) should be rejected on the grounds that "the likelihood of such evidence [for the existence of a threshold] is so remote that OSHA should not allow itself to waste time and effort arguing the idea in every rule-making procedure."[110]

OSHA's approach was endorsed by several members of the scientific community. Dr. Arthur Upton, director of the National Cancer Institute, claimed that the OSHA proposal "has a sound scientific basis and represents a prudent and justifiable approach to the identification and classification of chemical carcinogens which are likely to be found in the workplace."[111] The chemical industry, however, protested strongly against the economic implications of OSHA's approach, arguing that "cancer prevention policies based on magnified risks inevitably generate magnified expenditures for dealing with such risks."[112] Acting through a lobby group known as the American Industrial Health Council (AIHC), the chemical industry expressed its opposition not merely to the tough controls being proposed by OSHA, but to the whole scientific basis on which the controls were being justified by agency officials. The corporate director for environmental health and environmental affairs for Union Carbide Corporation complained on behalf of the AIHC that the proposed generic carcinogen regulations substituted "inflexible criteria" for "the judgment of scientists."[113]

During the Reagan administration, the issue of whether or not thresholds exist surfaced over the proposal that carcinogens should be categorized according to whether they were genotoxic (directly damaging DNA) or nongenotixic (affecting the genome only indirectly). The suggestion that thresholds be assumed for those falling into the first category, but not those in the second, was included in the first draft of a report on the classification of carcinogens prepared by a committee headed by presidential science adviser George Keyworth. Such a classification was strongly criticized by many scientists as unjustified by the current state of scientific knowledge. But it was supported by the pro-industry officials that Reagan had placed in the EPA. One, previously a public relations officer with a waste disposal company, with no formal scientific qualifications apart from an undergraduate minor in chemistry, wrote a memo openly suggesting the development of a "threshold model risk assessment for nongenotoxic chemicals" which should be given "the blessing of the Science Advisory Board."[114] Attached to the memo was a draft press release suggesting that, using the new methodology, one nongenotoxic chemical, TCE, which had produced toxic effects in laboratory animals, should not be considered a carcinogen, and should instead be regulated as a conventional poison.

The chemical industry, fighting to minimize the economic and political impact of restrictions, argued that they should be introduced only when there is firm scientific evidence of a health hazard. In particular, AIHC lobbied both Congress and the administration hard for the creation of a "panel of top scientists" able to make judgments on whether a particular chemical was to be considered a carcinogen. Such a determination, AIHC claimed, "involves scientific rather than regulatory judgments." In its proposal to Congress, AIHC stated that in the development of chronic health control policies, "scientific determination should be made separate from regulatory considerations, and that such determinations, *assessing the most probable human risk*, should be made by the best scientists available following a review of all relevant data" (italics added).[115] Jackson Browning of Union Carbide told a congressional committee that AIHC's suggestion was based on what he described as a "fundamental deficiency" in the legislation underlying social regulations, namely "a failure to separate the scientific determinations necessary for informed regulations from the governmental or regulatory policy determinations."[116]

Yet in practice, when faced with the need to make such judgments on the nature of the hazards of low-level exposure to toxic substances, scientific panels have consistently failed to reach any straightforward consensus. We have already looked at the disagreements on the BEIR Committee. In the case of an earlier panel established at Congress's request by the National Academy of Sciences to consider the potential carcinogenicity of saccharin, despite the existence of incontrovertible animal data on the effects of exposure to high doses, the panel was unable to decide whether saccharin should be considered to present a "high" or a "moderate" risk of cancer—precisely the type of distinction that the industry had argued should be made "scientifically." Academy president Philip Handler, in his preface to the report, wrote that "the difference of opinion which led to this ambivalent statement is not a differing interpretation of scientific fact or observation; rather, it reflects seriously differing value systems."[117]

Industry, however, was not to be put off. The failure among scientists to reach a neat consensus did not prevent the chemical industry lobbyists from pursuing demands for greater "scientific rigor" in the use of models on which to base regulatory policy. The National Association of Manufacturers and other industry lobby groups lent their support to the AIHC proposal for a panel of scientific "experts" to pronounce on the scientific certainties that should be used as the basis of new regulations.

The debate over the proper control of carcinogens illustrates the central strategic role that concepts of scientific "proof" have come to play in disputes over the measures to protect the health and safety of the community—and how the political dynamics of these disputes can frequently determine the outcome of "scientific" arguments. Research and analysis can indicate the areas of potential need for regulation; yet the value of science as a policy *instrument*—like that of cost-benefit analysis—is both limited and dangerous. Despite the temptation of administrators to believe differently, there is no straightforward dividing line between facts and values; as Costle of Carter's EPA has put it, there comes a point where "the scientific knowledge available can only offer guidance for regulatory decision-makers."[118] Similarly, Judge David Bazelon, of the District of Columbia Court of Appeals, points out that "even where a problem is appropriately characterized as one of scientific fact, consensus and certainty may very often be impossible, even in the scientific community." Referring to the controversy over saccharin, for example, Razelon says that where the debate is couched in terms of the degree of risk, it sounds as though there is a scientific issue, appropriate for resolution by trained scientists: "In fact, however, the terms 'moderate' and 'high' do not conform to any differences in experimental data, but rather correspond to the scientists' view of the appropriate regulatory response."[119]

Such caveats, however, are frequently ignored when science becomes the basis on which regulatory decisions are justified. The temptation is strong to hide behind the aura of scientificity to refrain from unwanted actions, however much these may express democratic desires. Any policy based on the assumption that controls should be placed on products and processes only if it can be shown conclusively that these are dangerous —and not otherwise—conveniently excludes areas of scientific doubt from the need to regulate (as with the case of acid rain). In December

1982 a study published by the staff of a House subcommittee identified several areas where, it claimed, the EPA's Office of Pesticide Programs had reduced the impact of regulation on pesticide manufacturers by redefining the scientific criteria on which the need for regulation was based.[120] A scientists from the Natural Resources Defense Council.con-tended that, with no public debate (or even acknowledgment), the EPA had "raised its acceptance of cancer risks for the U.S. population to at leat 100 times the levels which were sanctioned by previous administrations."[121]

What we find again and again is that apparent differences of opinion over the interpretation of scientific data, differences built into the type of models used to explain biological and medical phenomena, are reflections of the broad assumptions about the political control of technology —indeed of social decisions in general—that we have already characterized as the conflict between the technocratic and the democratic paradigms. The democratic paradigm stresses the uncertainties in the data as requiring action on the basis that it is "better to be safe than sorry." In contrast, the technocratic paradigm uses the same uncertainties as the justification for inaction, using demands for scientific "proof" as a technique for rejecting demands for tighter social controls.

In his comments on recombinant DNA research, for example, Donald Fredrickson, former director of the National Institutes of Health, cast this demand for scientific certainty as the only legitimate ground for direct democratic control on science: "The only valid criterion for interference with laboratory science by small jurisdictional elements (states, provinces, counties, towns) is the presence of *demonstrable* risk. Indeed, a societal taboo must be maintained that resists capricious local interference with scientific or intellectual inquiry on any basis other than imminent hazard to life or property."[122] In contrast, Clifford Grobstein, professor of biological science and public policy at the University of California, San Diego, aruges: "In fundamental science we properly demand incontrovertible evidence, else we would be building on shifting sand. In applied science, however, aggressive application often begins before the requirements for full certainty are satisifed. . . . It would be just as unfortunate for the scientific community to be too late as too early in making people aware of trends that are developing in scientific data. . . . If science is to be used as constructively as it must be, the rigid criteria of fundamental science are often inappropriate."[123]

The political significance of the so-called regulatory reform efforts of both the Carter and the Reagan administrations lay, as we have already seen, in the extent to which they achieved, in the name of a scientific approach to the regulation of technological innovation, a switch from the democratic paradigm (which had characterized much of the social legislation introduced in the early 1970s) to the technocratic paradigm. The latter was necessary to develop *forms* of regulation that would not interfere with the growth and reproduction of U.S. capital. The need was both economic and political—on the one hand being used to justify limits on costly safety procedures, on the other to justify reduced participation in regulatory decisions. Arguing that regulation should be placed on a "scientific" basis allowed companies to demand strict limitations on the role of labor unions, environmental groups, and consumer organizations in regulatory decision-making, on the grounds that the principal decisions were primarily scientific and technical—and therefore required an expertise that existed only within the professional scientific community.

Central to these efforts was the claim that it was necessary to place innovation and regulation policy on a rational basis. "Rationality," drawing directly on the supposedly neutral language of post-Enlightenment science, was frequently invoked by federal officials to justify cutting back on regulations and placing strict limits on democratic participation in regulatory decision-making. In commenting on the conflict between the social objectives of regulations and their economic impact, Barry Bosworth, chairman of the Council on Wage and Price Stability, emphasized the need to make "rational choices" about problems of energy, job safety, and pollution. Congressman Jim Ritter claimed that his new bill would introduce more "rationality" into the way federal regulators did their jobs.[124] Frank Press spoke frequently about the fact that a major goal of the Carter administration's actions in reorganizing the government approach to regulation was "improved care and rationalism, in both substance and process,"[125] just as Alfred Kahn spoke of the same reorganization as bringing "both economic and scientific rationality" to regulatory actions.[126] Dennis Prager, assistant director of OSTP under both Press and his successor, Keyworth, set out the broad strategy: "In the 1980s, it is our view that the primary need is not for new legislated regulatory programs, nor for new regulatory agencies. Rather, the need in the 1980s is to rationalize existing regulatory authorities and agency responsibilities and make the resulting structure more workable."[127]

Reinforcing this pressure for "rational" government, industry representatives spoke with enthusiasm about what they characterized as the dawn of a "new age of reason," a period when the adversary relationship that had, they claimed, dominated the regulatory initiatives of the 1970s could be replaced by a more sympathetic political environment.[128] Many scientists supported the philosophy implicit in this approach. Indeed, the National Association of Manufacturers expressed the hope that a greater input from scientists would bring more "reasoned, rational decision-making."[129] IBM's chief scientist, Lewis Branscomb, went even further, arguing that the development of "more rational decision processes" related to public strategies for generating, introducing, and managing technology was "vital to the survival of democracy itself."[130]

Both the political and business communities made it clear, however, that this new rationality, to which scientific regulation of technological innovation provided an important strategy, was a rationality that obeyed the demands and values of private capital. One scientists involved in testing potentially toxic chemicals wrote to *Science* that he was yet to encounter a regulation that imposed unreasonable demands on manufacturers; "almost without exception, the 'unreasonable' demands are those that prevent the companies from taking dangerous short-cuts."[131] The dominant rationality being demanded was the rationality of the private marketplace and of commercial profit, not the rationality of social need or open, democratic decision-making.

Many industrialists complain that it is the *unpredictability* of regulatory demands forged in the heat of public debate and following the tide of public concerns—rather than the nature of the demands themselves —that poses the greatest burden. The unpredictability of democratic decision-making, it is often argued, reduces the willingness to gamble because of the uncertainty of the regulatory climate. "Technological progress requires an investment environment in which there is a feeling of confidence and reasonable predictability for the long term," explains Thomas Vanderslice of GE, chairman of the CED subcommittee on technology policy.[132]

Policies that appeared to provide the predictable business environment demanded by the private sector were readily legitimized by claims of the need for scientificity in planning and policy measures. In this way, demands that regulatory decisions be placed on a more scientific base came to form part of a broader strategy to reassert capital's hegemony and control over the social dissemination and application of the fruits of scientific research. The increasing injection of demands for scientific rationality in regulatroy decision-making and the support of technological innovation therefore has important political implications. For the desire that decision-making be more "rational" or scientific is linked directly to efforts to limit the scope of political intervention in such decisions. Indeed, scientists, in commenting on the way social policy is made, frequently demonstrate a conviction that society ought to behave according to a neat mathematical model, with any departure from what is seen as a "natural equilibrium" characterized as deviance.

The scientific approach to the regulation of technology is openly offered as an alternative to the democratic process for determining technological choices. Richard Atkinson, chancellor of the University of California, San Diego campus, and formerly director of the National Science Foundation, complained in an editorial in *Science* that implementation of environmental, health, and safety regulations "has become characterized by adversary relationships that inhibit objective use of the best scientific data available and the development of technically optimal solutions." Atkinson suggested that such disruption could be avoided by a "national commission composed of members of Congress, environmental organizations, industry, the scientific community, the EPA administration, and the legal profession"[133]—a formula for the corporatist state (if it worked), but in practice a device for reproduction in the domain of professional experts the same disagreements and political differences that have generated the conflicts in the first place. A survey of the attitudes of scientists and engineers to nuclear energy revealed that while over 80 percent felt that they and their peers should be given substantial influence over nuclear development, only 38 percent felt such influence should be given to political leaders, and 12 percent to the general public.[134]

Frequently scientists and economists writing about regulation and innovation policy display a virtual aversion to political debate. Political struggle is characterized as an essentially anarchic and irrational process that can only undermine efforts at rational decision-making about the allocation and distribution of social resources. Congressman Ritter, in defending his proposed legislation for putting regulation on a neat, quantifiable basis, argued that "maybe the time is coming when 14,000 scientists should march on Washington and say, 'We've had enough,' prompted by 'emotional and political' government regulatory methods."[135] Similar sentiments are revealed by a statement put out by Stanford University, claiming that "overregulation, based upon emotion rather than sound science and logic, can soon become socially unacceptable."[136] Where decisions, often made for political purposes, are defended on the grounds of an appeal to science, the other side of the coin is that, in an equally distorted way, attempts are made to dismiss criticisms of such decisions by disparaging them as being based on emotion—a commentary, if nothing else, on the social and cultural values that dominate the environment in which such decisions are made.

Efforts to deny the impact of external factors on scientific and technological decisions only paper over the extent to which political conflicts within U.S. society remain present, even in what appear to be the most objective of scientific discussions.[137] Decisions about the social control of technology, however much they make use of scientific data and arguments, inevitably form part of this broader canvas, since political conflict and ambiguity are basic realities of almost all technological decisions.[138] Even assessments of acceptable risk depend partly on who is making the assement, whether it is the person at risk, and if so the degree of control he or she has over the potential threat. Those who might tolerate a substantial degree of risk in situations that they have voluntarily entered may simultaneously demand absolute safety in situations where the risk is being imposed on them and is thus outside their control.

Furthermore, attempts to contrast "rational" decision-making to the outcome of explicitly political (or "emotional") debate deny the fact that a rationality is indeed contained within the latter—even if it is not the rationality of science and the scientific method. This is the rationality of the democratic process, which obeys a political rather than an intellectual logic. Ashford of MIT, for example, has suggested that environmental, health, and safety agencies should follow a decision rule based not on economic criteria but on "a concern for equity to workers, consumers, and society—and the desire to minimize the regret of not regulating a particular activity." According to Ashford, this approach to what he calls "minimizing regret" is accomplished by choosing among different hazards to regulate and by choosing a level of protection for a specific hazard that may avoid small probabilities of a large harm: "In general it appears that agencies do consider the distributional and social costs and consequences of regulation. . . . Because health benefits are not maximized or because no unique decision-rule exists does not mean that these decisions are irrational. You may choose to protect 11 workers from an 8 percent chance of death over protecting 10,000 workers or consumers from a 0.1 percent chance of death." [139]

A similar form of rationality was invoked by the Supreme Court in deciding to uphold the cotton dust regulations introduced by OSHA in 1978, rejecting the demand that they should have been subject to strict cost-benefit analysis before being introduced. Justice William Brennan suggested that, despite the lack of requirements for cost-benefit analysis in the original law setting up OSHA, a political rationality still lay behind the decision to establish the basic relationship between costs and benefits. "Congress itself defined the basic relationship between costs and benefits . . . by placing the 'benefit' of workers' health above all other considerations save those making attainment of this 'benefit' unattainable," he wrote. [140]

A different though equally powerful form of rationality is revealed in the numerous surveys that show that the public is prepared to pay a considerable sum to ensure that products do not harm workers or the environment—even in cases where the producers, who see the costs essentially in terms of decreased profits, contend that the resultant burden on the public is unacceptable. According to one survey carried out in 1980, 70 percent of those asked felt occupational health and safety regulations should be tightened up, and 65 percent that regulations designed to protect consumers should also be tightened. Similar survey results produced by a Louis Harris poll in 1982 helped convince the Reagan administration that its anti-environmentalist stance was potentially losing it a lot of voter support. In other words, in contrast to the well-publicized calls for less government regulation, such polls revealed that a majority of the American people still believed in strict regulations in the health, safety, and environmental areas; few, presumably, would dismiss their convictions as irrational.

Such expressions of democratic will, however, pose a direct threat to an economy based on the need to continuously reduce the costs of production—including the external costs demanded by society—and to maintain a strictly hierarchical system for making decisions about the control of technology. Another poll, this time investigating public perceptions about technology, clearly brought out that the difference in attitude depended on one's position on the social ladder and, more fundamentally, on whether technology was experienced primarily through its social effects or through its ability to generate a financial profit. "Most Americans feel strongly that our recent knowledge about the actual risks stemming from modern technology has touched only the tip of the iceberg," the poll concluded. "Corporate leaders flatly disagree, express deep confidence in advanced technology, and see virtually no dangers from decreased government safety regulations." [141]

As these poll results implicitly suggest, many of those in positions of industrial and economic power see public demands for innovation and regulation policies that obey democratic rather than technocratic principles as a basic threat to the stability of modern capitalism. As early as 1971, the report produced by Brooks's committee for the Organization for Economic Cooperation and Development drew attention to what it described as the "instabilities" created by the choices opened up by modern science, stating that "participation and coherence often collide head-on, leading to a paralysis of the decision-making process." [142] Four years later, a report to the Trilateral Commission on *The Crisis of Democracy* took up the same theme. One of the authors, Samuel Huntington, wrote that "the vitality of democracy in the 1960s (as manifested in increased political participation) produced problems for the governability of democracy in the 1970s (as manifested in the decreased public confidence in government)." [143] The main problem with American democracy, it frequently appeared in boardrooms, was that it was working too well. Indeed, at one point Fletcher Byrom, chairman of the Koppers Corporation, business adviser to presidential candidate Reagan, and vice-chairman of the Committee for Economic Development, claimed that "under the conditions of today's technology" democracy had become an anachronism. He called for a constitutional convention to begin restructuring the American political system in the name of modern technology. [144]

The economic and political centrality of decisions about the allocation of scientific and technical resources has created new pressures on the whole of the political process. And these, as we have seen in earlier chapters, are demanding new ground rules for the political conflicts they create. In the battle over these rules, however, the dominant voice being heard is not that of democratic liberalism but that of technocratic corporatism—the political voice of American capital. The widespread use of quantitative decision-making techniques for formulating social policy, the reinstatement of the rule of experts, the exclusion of the public from participation in technological decision-making—each is part of the new ground rules; and each, in its turn, is legitimized by pressure to place political decisions on a more scientific—or rational—basis.

The result is to provide a scientific endorsement for the reinvention of the idea of progress though technological rather than social growth—an idea previously discredited by the mass movements of the early 1970s, which tried to establish the idea that technology should serve, rather than determine, human needs and wishes. Conversely, the new "age of reason" provides a new sense of political power for scientists, who not only feel that their instrumental value to the economy is once again being recognized, but are often keen to promote a greater philosophical and ideological acceptance of scientific rationality as the basis of political decision-making. The desire to place the control of technology through social regulation on a "scientific" basis is the most recent illustration of the way in which, as a source of values and consensus claimed to lie beyond the commands of politics and power, science and science policy are used to legitimate the political procedures of the modern state.

7

TOWARD
A DEMOCRATIC
STRATEGY
FOR SCIENCE

IT IS NOW TIME TO LOOK TOWARD THE FUTURE. THE BULK OF THIS BOOK has addressed two tasks: it has attempted to provide an analytical description of recent changes in the social and economic role played by science in contemporary U.S. society, and at the same time it has tried to develop a critique of this role in terms of its political implications. In this final chapter a synthesis of analysis and critique will be used as the base from which we can begin to outline strategies for achieving a genuine resolution of the current conflicts between science on the one hand and democratic politics on the other. I use the word "strategies" because it would be misleading to pretend that any straightforward policy options lie readily available; rather, it is a question of encouraging progress on a number of fronts, some of which are currently being pursued, while others are relatively ignored. A viable political program for change must be one that relates to opportunities wherever they currently present themselves. So, rather than sketching out a political program for a theoretically conceived movement devoted to the democratization of science, it makes even more sense to describe a mosaic of initiatives and strategies that, taken collectively, offer the possibility of a significant move in this direction.

This does not mean that such diverse activities can afford to ignore the need for a central focus. On the contrary, a focus is essential if they are to develop the coherence that makes political change a realistic possibility rather than a utopian ideal. Indeed, I would suggest further that in the period since the Second World War, the most vital and effective political struggles around scientific issues have been those that have kept in step with the dominant question on the official science policy agenda; and that the same three periods that have appeared frequently in this book as a leitmotif characterizing the evolution of postwar science policy —namely two decades of steady growth, followed by a decade of questioning, since replaced by a new period of growth—can also be used to differentiate three stages through which the broader politics of science have also progressed.

In the immediate postwar period, of course, the single issue that lay heaviest on the conscience and consciousness of the scientific community was its contribution, whether explicit or implicit, to the most horrendous weapon ever conceived, developed, or used by man—the atomic bomb. Few challenged the escalating budget for science at the time, particularly since, coming primarily from public sources, the funds could be justified as social expenditures relatively untainted by the search for private profit. Where protest movements did spring up, as around the Atomic Scientists of Chicago, the Federation of American Scientists, and the journal *Bulletin of Atomic Scientists*, these tended to focus on the moral schizophrenia that the bomb had created within the scientific community—a schizophrenia that was projected onto broader debates about the impact of science and society.[1]

Accepting responsibility for creating the knowledge that had made the bomb possible, these groups tended to characterize critical political questions about science in terms of the balance between the "uses" (such as nuclear power) and the "abuses" (such as nuclear weapons) to which scientific knowledge could be put. Thus the period in which science saw rapidly increased funding, due partly to its contribution to long-term military technology, was also one in which criticism of the implications of this trend, from both within and outside the scientific community, tended to focus on ways of bringing the military uses of science under civilian control. Many of those closely involved in the Manhattan Project, for example, subsequently devoted almost equal efforts to furthering diplomatic initiatives aimed at placing controls on nuclear energy under the Atoms for Peace banner.[2]

In the late 1960s, as we have seen in earlier chapters, the focus and style of the critique shifted. The use during the Vietnam War of a wide variety of new chemical and electronic weapons, as well as scientific experts in fields that ranged from agriculture to sociology, meant that the taint of collaboration with the military was no longer restricted to nuclear scientists, but affected virtually all disciplines of science. Furthermore, growing awareness of the environmental and occupational health problems associated with science-based industrial processes made it impossible to maintain a clear distinction between the military (i.e., "bad") and civilian (i.e., "good") applications of science. A new generation of critics, taking their lead from the civil rights and free speech movements in the U.S., the student revolts in Paris and elsewhere in Europe, and sharp attacks on the political uses of scientific rationality expressed in books such as Herbert Marcuse's *One-Dimensional Man* and Theodore Roszak's *The Making of a Counter-Culture*, foreswore the gentler tactics of their predecessors.[3] Their critique of science took on a more explicitly political content, since it now focused on the ways in which the substance of laboratory practice, and the subsequent results of research were applied to social goals, reflected the broader political values and priorities of U.S. capitalism.

In earlier chapters we have seen how the political edge of these critiques was successfully blunted by a series of legislative and administrative reforms that, while addressing the specific problems—such as the potential hazards of toxic wastes or genetic engineering—identified by these groups, left the political relationships by which science and its applications are governed relatively untouched. Despite this, it can still be argued that the strategies adopted by critics were appropriate to their time, since they challenged the political power expressed through the practice and applications of science at the points where this power was most exposed. Furthermore, an aggressive attack on the substance of science was a necessary antidote to those who had previously argued that, whatever the uses (or abuses) to which it was put, science itself remained above politics and thus essentially neutral. Groups such as Science for the People demonstrated how social and political values saturate the scientific laboratory and even, in cases such as sociobiology and the alleged links between genes and social behavior, the ideas and theories said to belong to science itself.[4]

Despite the importance of both the analytical and political work carried out on such topics, however, the agenda of the radical science movement has frequently remained restricted to those issues which gave it its initial impetus in the late 1960s and early 1970s. The result was a critical approach that had much to say about the need for control of the potential health hazards of recombinant DNA research or chemical carcinogens, but less about the increased private control of scientific knowledge resulting from changes in patent laws, attempts to use controls on the dissemination of scientific knowledge as an instrument of foreign policy and capitalist expansion, the use of scientific arguments to legitimize the molding of the regulation of technology into a form compatible with the political needs of the nation's industrial leaders, or several other key issues in what I have described as the new politics of science.

This is the task that now lies ahead. Building on the work of the two generations of earlier critics,* it is now both possible and necessary to move forward to address the key political issues that are likely to be expressed through science and science policy for the remainder of the decade, if not the century. To put it schematically, the first postwar generation of science critics demonstrated the need to develop a political debate around the applications of science; the second generation shifted focus to the other end of the spectrum, namely the conditions under which sciences is produced. The new task is to integrate these two perspectives into a single critique of the whole spectrum, from the most fundamental science through to its most sophisticated high technology applications. In particular it is necessary to concentrate on ways of politicizing the discussion of the terms and conditions of access to science, the crucial intermediate position between production and application. For it is here, I suggest, that political action is now the most needed, and that the possibilities of opening science to proper democratic control are most in danger of being foreclosed.

One of the main themes of this book has been the degree to which the nation's military and industrial leaders have already grasped the key political significance of this intermediate position. In the first four chapters I showed that, as part of their broader economic and political strategy, such groups have sought to increase their control over the terms and conditions of access to the results of fundamental scientific research at the same time as they have been encouraging greater public support for the funding of basic science itself. The rapidly growing impact of the patent system on university laboratories, particularly in the field of molecular biology and genetic engineering, is one illustration of this trend, since, as we have seen, its function has had as much to do with packaging scientific results in a form in which they can be controlled by private capital as any short-term desire for financial gain by the university concerned. In the case of materials science, software engineering, and other research related to advanced computers, national security arguments have been added to those of commercial viability to justify controls on the public dissemination of basic research results.

Both arguments have been combined to restrict efforts to give developing countries greater control over basic research in these and other strategically important fields, control that the countries argue is an essential component of building up the scientific infrastructures they need to support their development. Nothing better illustrates the growing awareness among all advanced Western nations of the crucial role of access to scientific knowledge than the endorsement of greater cooperation in

---

* A staff report of the Carnegie Institution clarifies the role of such criticism: "Science criticism should identify important trends and changes in the interests, concepts, or values being advanced. It should monitor and comment upon how—and how well—the scientific enterprise sets about achieving its objectives. By its nature, criticism invites more criticism, stimulating controversy as a way of eliciting understanding of what science is and costs."[5]

science made by their heads of state at the Williamsburg summit meeting in May 1983. Beneath the surface, as was argued in Chapter Four, this endorsement was aimed at facilitating access by international capital to the basic science needed for its high technology industries, while tightening the terms and conditions under which this access would be granted to others.

We have also seen how this political awareness of the importance of basic science has been reinforced at the cultural level. Here a major offensive has been launched to restore science to the cultural authority it enjoyed in the 1950s and early 1960s—a direct attempt, I have suggested, to undercut the gains made in the following decade by those who sought to impose broader social values on the scientific enterprise. Where new technological projects previously had to be studied for their environmental impact, the regulations subsequently introduced to mitigate this impact now, in reverse, have to be assessed for *their* economic impact. Similarly, the political initiatives seized in the early 1970s by what opponents labeled the anti-science movement have in turn been taken back by what might now be called the anti-anti-science movement.

One apparent motivation behind current efforts to raise the level of science teaching in the nation's public schools is a desire to limit the disruptive impact of public criticism by reestablishing the authority of science. This was one of the messages of a report on science education commissioned by President Carter from the National Science Foundation and the Department of Education in February 1980.[6] The report was prepared in response to growing concerns that, as part of the liberalization of school curricula during the 1970s, schools were no longer encouraging a positive attitude toward science among their pupils; statistics were waved around Congress and the mass media showing the substantially higher content of mathematics in the education of Soviet schoolchildren (ignoring the question of why, if the teaching of mathematics is so vital to a healthy economy, the Soviet economy continues to behave so badly).

The report to Carter reinforced this message, as did two later reports to the Reagan administration, one prepared by the National Commission on Excellence in Education, the second by a new panel established by the National Science Foundation, and neatly demonstrated the administration's perception of the link between the functional and the ideological roles of science education in schools. As far as the future production of scientists and engineers was concerned, it discovered few problems. In many scientific disciplines, indeed, there was an oversupply of graduates. In those disciplines where there was a shortage, such as computer science and engineering, market forces were already in operation and were expected to provide the necessary remedies; in engineering, for example, the high starting salaries offered to university graduates were creating different difficulties: on the one hand, too many applications for the available university and college places; on the other, reluctance among engineering graduates to remain within the educational system to become teachers or research workers.

Several of the report's recommendations (like those that were subsequently embraced by the Reagan administration in increasing its support for science education in schools) were not on the pragmatic but on the cultural and political level. The report warned of a growing technological illiteracy among U.S. schoolchildren. The decline in both quality and quantity of science teaching in schools was seen as a problem because of the impact on future scientists and engineers and because it removed the legitimacy of the culture of science, considered an essential element for a strategy of reindustrialization. Technological illiteracy, it was claimed, left high school graduates unable to participate in the apparently neutral discourse of high technology in which political decisions are increasingly expressed.

Greater scientific literacy was therefore encouraged not to promote greater questioning of these decisions—a process that many industrial leaders felt had been carried too far in the 1970s—but the reverse: to generate a greater willingness to accept the conclusions of scientific experts. Primarily addressed to the needs of "the overwhelming portion of our population which has no direct involvement in science and technology," the report claimed that "the current trend toward scientific and technological illiteracy, unless reversed, means that important national decisions involving science and technology will be made increasingly on the basis of ignorance and misunderstanding."[7] Little attention was given, however, to the way the rejection of points of view considered by scientists to be "ignorant" could become a useful cloak for stifling political rather than scientific disagreements or, indeed, of the importance of non-scientific disciplines, from economics to psychology, that provide important clues to understanding the time impacts of science on modern society.

The appeal for greater scientific literacy in schools has been matched by similar demands in the university sector. In the early 1980s, appeals came in from many sides for injecting a greater scientific component into the training of all university students, whether they were taking science and engineering courses or not. One might have made the same case about the need for wider training in economics or politics—or even history. Yet the idea was propagated that science, even more than the other subjects, constitutes an essential component of modern education. Donald Kennedy, president of Stanford University, helped launch a campaign to rebridge the two cultures. Kennedy expressed his concern about "a troublesome tendency to regard science as not belonging to the mainstream of intelligent thought" and suggested the need to reinstate "science *as* culture."[8]

Thus, at both the institutional and the cultural levels, the nation's industrial and academic leaders have joined forces to preach the message that the scientific method holds the key to the future international competitiveness of U.S. industry and to the decisions that will make the realization of this competitiveness possible. At the same time, however, they have moved to ensure a tightening of private control over the channels through which research results are transferred from the laboratory to the outside world. The apparent efficiency of the marketplace in achieving this is allowed to obscure the extent to which it is also steadily reinforcing the increased concentration of political power in the hands of private decision-makers. Thus, despite the fact that the application of scientific results to social uses through technology is becoming one of the biggest single issues on the contemporary political agenda, it is an issue that is steadily being removed further and further from the domain of democratic decision-making.

It must also be remembered that this trend is taking place against a specific historical background, namely a period when Western capitalist nations are attempting to restructure their economies, both individually and collectively, to escape the stagnation they entered at the end of the 1970s. The need to emerge from the "crisis" is frequently invoked to justify calls for new attempts at decision-making by consensus—ranging from the Reconstruction Finance Corporation, proposed by New York banker Felix Rohatyn as a way of uniting business and labor,[9] to broader efforts at involving "consumers, small businesses, emerging industries, and nonunion workers," proposed by economist Robert B. Reich.[10] A similar consensus approach to science policy was also advocated by Carter's science adviser, Frank Press, who suggested the need for "a compact between government, industry, and universities for the support of basic science."[11]

The political limits of any such attempt to build a consensus are clear. As Press's comments imply, the consensus is to be reached among government, industry, and university leaders; and the issues to be discussed are those contained within the political goals that tend to be common to these three sectors, with top priority being given to the efficiency of U.S. capital rather than the equitable distribution of its material and financial products. We have already seen how, under both the Carter and the Reagan administrations, "rational" science policies were developed to increase the rate of technological innovation and reduce the restrictions imposed by social regulation, largely at the urging of corporate leaders. Under Carter, the political goal was to counteract the challenge to capital's control of technology coming from environmentalist and labor groups; under Reagan, rational policies were demanded against the protectionist wing of the Republican party, which many high technology companies saw as equally threatening. In both cases, the final result was a postion that primarily reflected the economic and political priorities of these companies. It is an illusion to believe that a future consensus might be harmoniously reached, in isolation from the field of politics, which does not repeat the same experience.

Of course, the ideas of making public policy this way holds many attractions for corporate, military, and academic leaders', since it avoids submitting key topics to "the crucible of public debate" (see page 136). Press himself frequently revealed this preference, as when he stated that science policy must eventually be made "around a table in the Roosevelt Room of the White House," in particular since it was often difficult for outsiders "to see the gaps . . . between public perceptions and the private reality of government decision-making."[12] Indeed, during his term of office under President Carter, this is how the Office of Science and Technology Policy tended to work. Press opposed, for example, the re-creation of the President's Science Advisory Committee partly on the grounds that both the committee and its subcommittee would be required to hold some of their meetings in public.[13] But unless the results of decisions made about science and its applications, as well as the procedures by which these decisions are made, are subject to continuous public scrutiny, the danger remains that the democratic process will have been replaced by negotiations among the members of a relatively small, like-minded elite, justifying the consolidation of their power over important scientific and technological choices by referring to the need for an efficient response to both commercial and military threats, and thus conveniently ignoring the broader political implications of their actions.

The dangers are reinforced if we look briefly at the ways in which science has, during various key periods in the past, been used to reinforce and legitimate the concentration of political power in the hands of those who dominate a nation's economy. During such periods science has often made an important contribution at the material level by helping to open up new techniques that can be exploited as a source of economic or military strength. At the same time, however, a "scientific" way of looking at the world has served as the basis of new patterns of social organization, under the argument that the orderly behavior observed in the natural world can be taken as a model from which orderly behavior can be imposed on the social world, in particular the world of productive labor—that is, the world of work. While defended in the name of increased efficiency, efforts to organize social activity along "scientific" principles are frequently little more than reflections of new techniques by which one group of individuals is able to control and exploit the activities of others. In such situations we find, parallel to the technical contributions made by scientific knowledge, a politically based cultural dimension that is used to reinforce emerging (or in some cases already dominant) patterns in the distribution of political power.

We can look, for example, as far back as the Italian Renaissance of the late fourteenth and early fifteenth centuries to see the complex interrelationships that were beginning to form among economic, scientific, cultural, and political trends. In terms of economics, the cities of the Italian Renaissance were focal points for the first stirrings of the shift, which subsequently swept through Europe, from the medieval feudal economy to one based on the exploits of merchant capitalists.[14] These cities saw the emergence of some of the first efforts at organized workshop production—for example, in the textile and the leather industries, where the tools were collected, owned, and largely controlled by the new class of merchants, rather than, as previously, by the medieval craft guilds. The cities also relied heavily on the contributions of new military technologies, such as the use of gunpowder, in boosting their political power.

The political interests of the merchants and bankers who rose to prominence during the Renaissance were served by the tightly centralized administration of the absolutist state—a device that, acting as a bridge between feudal and capitalist power, effectively challenged the traditional power base of the nobility and the clergy, who had little desire for change. A "scientific" way of looking at the world became expressed through the various art forms that this new class of merchant capitalists enthusiastically supported. Indeed, many years before the explicit recognition of the conceptual basis of the Scientific Revolution, the painters, writers, and sculptors of the Renaissance were implicitly developing ideas about absolute space (represented by the use of perspective in painting), absolute time (represented by narrative in literature), and absolute mass (represented by the breakthroughs in sculpture achieved by the substitution of new bronze casting techniques for wood and stone). Such ideas undoubtedly helped inspire the creation of mechanical devices used as a source of economic and military strength; equally important, however, the way in which many of the humanist philosophers of the Renaissance worked as the clerks and administrators under absolutist leaders such as the Medici of Florence indicates the extent to which the "scientific" philosophy of nature (and man) that they were busy developing can also be seen as the management ideology of the absolutist state.[15]

The same pattern was repeated 200 years later in Northern Europe, this time primarily in England and Holland, the main centers of the Scientific Revolution. The major economic changes during this period focused on the rapid expansion of international trade, an expansion made possible partly by the sophistication of new mechanical instruments such as clocks, telescopes, and sextants. Many of those most closely identified with the Scientific Revolution, such as the Dutch mathematician Christiaan Huygens and his English contemporary Isaac Newton, consciously worked on an agenda that had been set by the technical demands of trade and commerce—a fact that explains much of the significance attached to their activities. Again, however, there was a broad political dimension to the cultural importance awarded to science during this period. Events such as the creation of England's Royal Society in 1662 helped to endorse the social status and political ideas of a new class of capitalist entrepreneurs, represented in such figures as the chemist Robert Boyle and the statistician William Petty, for members of this class made up the bulk of the society's early fellows. To this new class, the ideas about science developed by the English philosopher Francis Bacon (and, in France and Holland, by René Descartes) promised the means for social and economic growth through the exploration of the basic properties of nature; equally important, they provided a blueprint for the scientific method as a form of collective social practice, organized on a hierarchical, fragmented basis that could be carefully orchestrated from the center, and that neatly fit the needs of those who were beginning to organize productive labor in the same way.* [16]

The significance of the Renaissance and the Scientific Revolution to modern debates is that they created the concepts—for example, the distinction between facts and values, or between living organisms and inanimate matter—that continue to dominate the way we look at the natural world and construct theories about how it works. In both cases, it is possible to argue that one incentive for producing this new world view lay in the technical opportunities that were opened up by the prospect, in Bacon's words, of expanding man's "dominion over nature." [18] In both cases, too, the high status given to such ideas within the dominant culture of the time reflected, I suggest, the expression and justification they provided of changing patterns of political control.

We can see the same pattern in events that took place toward the end of the eighteenth century, this time with more direct implications for the U.S., since it was during this period that the Founding Fathers established the basic concepts on which the American political system was built. In Europe this was a period in which the main focus of economic expansion shifted from international trade to domestic manufacture—the origins of the Industrial Revolution. Technologically, the period saw the development of machines—for example, those driven by steam and coal—more suitable for centralized production in factories than for decentralized production in small-scale workshops; the advances of science at this time, ranging from electricity to chemistry, made a direct contribution toward such goals.

But the factory also developed the need for a new form of social discipline, and here again science played a role. Its contribution took the form of a philosophical underpinning to the "new enlightenment," a period in which Newton's ideas of a rational, mechanical universe were expanded into a broad social philosophy by such individuals as John

---

* I have shown elsewhere how the proposals outlined in Bacon's *Novum Organum*, for example, can be treated as a model for the organization of factory labor that was to become the key to the expansion of European industry in the early nineteenth century. [17]

Locke in England and Voltaire in France.[19] The idea that the social world could also be placed on a rational footing greatly influenced the thinking of Thomas Jefferson, Benjamin Franklin, and others among the Founding Fathers; indeed, it provides a crucial key to interpreting the concepts used as a basis for the Declaration of Independence and the U.S. Constitution.[20] The result was that economic, cultural, and political changes —each invoking a scientific philosophy of man and society—joined together in a system that, while successfully overthrowing more dictatorial forms of government (as in the American and French Revolutions), at the same time consolidated power in the hands of a new bourgeois class.

The final historical period to which we can refer is the close of the nineteenth century in the U.S. The Civil War had shown the importance of organization to the operation of large-scale technical systems, such as the military telegraph system set up for the North by a young Scottish engineer, Andrew Carnegie. The social need for mass organization evaporated once the war was over. Yet although the postwar stability provided the basis for a period of spectacular growth, the foundations were fragile. The 1870s and 1880s saw significant growth in the U.S. economy, exploiting major technologies such as the railways, first introduced in the 1840s and integrated into a single nationwide system in the 1880s. The spread of laissez-faire business practices came to an end, however, with the failure of several banks in a major crash in 1893. The following period of depression was one of intense political activity by the representatives of U.S. capital. For they soon realized the need to reorganize—or rationalize—the economic framework of American society if it was to survive the anarchy of cut-throat competition on the one side and heavy monopoly control on the other.[21]

The reorganization of the 1890s took various forms. Under the leadership of East Coast banks, the railways were organized into a more orderly system. Economic regulation of markets was introduced for the first time. Foreign ventures increased the scope for U.S. industry, leading on the one hand to reduced costs and more secure access to raw materials, on the other to new markets for the products of American factories. Out of these changes was forged the modern system of American finance capitalism, with the concentration of control over the economy in the hands of a relatively small number of East Coast bankers. In 1893, as many smaller banks were collapsing, the issue came to a head with the adoption of a single gold standard—a decision that several historians have identified as representing the formal adoption of capitalism as a political as well as an economic system. Henry Adams remarked at the time that "all one's friends, all one's best citizens, reformers, churches, colleges, educated class had joined the banks to force submission to capitalism."[22]

Having learned from the experience of the British and German economies in the mid-nineteenth century, the industrial promoters of this new capitalism began to integrate the latest scientific discoveries into their new machines. Many of the largest companies had set up extensive research laboratories in the 1870s. Out of these emerged a steady string of results, particularly in electricity and chemistry, that fed directly into the most significant technical innovations of the time. On the one hand they produced cost-cutting innovations that helped to compensate for the higher wages paid to skilled labor in the U.S. (e.g., Charles F. Brush's improvements on the dynamo, which Michael Faraday of Britain's Royal Institution had invented in the 1830s). On the other hand, as with the invention and development of the telephone, the research findings helped to create a new technical infrastructure that made it possible to integrate the whole of the U.S. into a single marketplace, so that for the first time the economic and political domains of U.S. capital could become properly coextensive.

As had been the case earlier in Britain, the pressure for technical innovation frequently had an important political function in helping to secure the control of capital over labor. During the nineteenth century, the high cost of labor in the U.S. compared to that in European manufacturing—and the high capital-intensity of the labor process resulting from the higher rate of technical innovation—meant that commodities could only be competitive in the international marketplace if this labor was used more efficiently. This was achieved by stricter work discipline and by speeding up the labor process. One contemporary observer noted that "the American manufacturers can only compete successfully with the British by producing a greater quantity of goods in a given time; hence any machine that admits to being driven at a higher speed . . . will meet with a more favorable reception in this country than in Great Britain."[23]

Inevitably, such trends generated increasingly bitter resentment among those whose labor it exploited—resentment that often could not be contained by higher wages, particularly when the economy started slipping into decline in the early 1890s. Labor unions increased rapidly in both size and militancy to protest the speeding-up and other forms of machine discipline that were being imposed on workers. In reply, industrial leaders did not hesitate to use all the legal powers at their disposal to combat the challenge. Often this was achieved through the direct use of force. But factory owners also began to emulate their European counterparts by introducing technological innovations specifically to break the new power of the unions, particularly those organized by skilled workers. One example was Cyrus McCormick's reaper manufacturing plant in Chicago, where, as Robert Ozane has shown, machines producing inferior castings at greater cost—but using fewer and less-skilled operators—were introduced to destroy the organizing attempts of the short-lived National Union of Iron Molders.[24] It was a similar story with the introduction of ring spinning in the cotton industry, the successor to the mule spinning that had provided the backbone of the British textile industry. Ring spinning had the advantage of employing semiskilled (and hence cheaper) female labor rather than the highly skilled males required by mule spinning. Again factory owners faced an increasingly militant union, this time one that was helping to organize industrial action in other industries as well. And again the desire to break the power of these unions in states such as Massachusetts—where major strikes had occurred in 1870 and 1875—and Maine contributed directly to the introduction of the new technology, despite the higher capital costs that had dissuaded British manufacturers from adopting the same machinery.[25] As a government report, Census of Manufacturers, put it in 1905: "There are reasons, *not unconnected with the labor problem*, which render manufacturers desirous of using frames (i.e., rings) rather than mules whenever it is (technically) practical to do so" (italics added).[26]

To remain effective, however, this control of labor had to be systematized and legitimated. This meant that the managers and administrators responsible for exercising this control had to be provided with a set of ideas about applying it. And here again science came to the rescue. The scientific results produced in the early industrial laboratories had provided the technical basis for the new innovations in manufacturing and distribution. But it was the success of scientists in their own fields of basic research—and in particular the explosive impact of Charles Darwin's hypothesis that natural selection was the cause of evolutionary change, and that the diversity of the animal kingdom was not fashioned in a single stroke by a divine creator—that had the greatest impact at the cultural level. Modern analysis of the social impact of Darwin's concepts usually focuses on the popular ideas of Herbert Spencer, who had already been working on a theory of social evolution through a "survival of the fittest" strategy, and whose philosophy was eagerly espoused by representatives of laissez-faire capitalism. Darwin's demonstration that this process existed in the natural world seemed all the confirmation that Spencer's disciples needed to support their arguments that capitalism was the most effective way of making sure that the fittest did, indeed, survive; conversely, Spencer's ideas have been relatively easy to criticize as an unwarranted extension from natural to social science.[27]

Yet the political stakes cannot be dismissed so straightforwardly. For Darwin's supporters included not only the biologists who accepted his theories, and even the Social Darwinists such as Carnegie, but the intellectual promoters of the new upper and middle classes of the Ivy League universities of the East Coast. Through their control of the banks, which were taking over the railways and the factories, the East Coast elite that these universities catered to was rapidly becoming the key force in U.S. politics. Boston's universities, in particular Harvard, were rapidly becoming what one historian has described as "a major, if not the major, instrument for recruiting a national business and cultural elite."[28] Having distanced itself from the fundamentalist religions that still permeated most of the new regions of the nation, this elite was seeking a new expression and legitimation of its power. It found both in a science whose authority as both a heuristic tool and a philosophical system Darwin had so powerfully shown. This authority provided the new professional classes with a new sense of confidence—for example, by creating trust in scientifically trained experts among the general public.[29] Pushed enthusiastically by university leaders such as John Dewey, and taking their legitimacy from the strictly scientific success of Darwin, ideas about the authority of science formed a central philosophical and educational component of the Progressive Era.[30]

Enthusiasm for the material progress offered by science was understandable. The political use of science as a source of authority was more problematic. As universities such as Harvard made clear, scientific values were to remain subordinate, at the top of the social system, to those of the lawyers and businessmen who were expected to run the country. If science was promoted as an ideology, it was as an ideology of management, not leadership. It was in organizing and controlling the complex technical systems through which capital operated that science was seen as contributing toward logical planning and effective control. Furthermore, placing technological rationality as a link between the capitalists and the workers mediated the conflicts between the two groups in a less destructive way than open confrontation. The role of major educational institutions was to turn out scientists as managers at all levels, one result being an upsurge of interest in the social sciences, through which ideas about the scientific organization of social activity could, in the factory and the bureaucracy it created, be turned into an organizational reality.[31]

The impact of science as a philosophy of social control was equally marked among professional engineers.[32] The successful technological innovation of the last decades of the nineteenth century had given American engineers increasing confidence in their ability to apply science—and the scientific method—to technical problems. If science could solve the most difficult technical tasks that modern industry was able to produce, surely it was the key to social progress in the future. Political circles were unsympathetic, but industrial leaders soon picked up the message. The control that capital needed through the social application of the scientific method and the authority of science was the control of labor in the workplace—not the control of its own influence over political institutions.

The ground was therefore fertile for the development of what rapidly became known as "scientific management." The term was developed by Frederick Taylor, a Harvard Law School dropout turned engineer who set out to bring more rational organization to the labor process through a system that involved breaking the activities of workers down into component steps, allocating a particular time for each step, and then redistributing the now fragmented tasks among different members of a group of workers in a way that substantially increased their overall input.[33] To companies that quickly endorsed and applied Taylor's method, scientific management proved a success in raising output while maintaining strict discipline. To engineers, the effectiveness of Taylor's methods seemed to endorse their ideas about scientific planning of the social world, which, some of their leaders hoped, would lead to the withering of class conflict, since the managerial inefficiencies on which they claimed it was based would rapidly disappear. To the working class, however, scientific management was seen as yet another way of squeezing greater profits out of their labor for capital by subjecting their work even more rigidly to capital's demands.[34]

The significance of scientific management was that it simultaneously provided both a methodology and a legitimation for linking the rationalization of technology to the rationalization of labor. Control of the labor process was concentrated, in both a technical and a managerial sense, in the hands of engineers in the name of efficient factory organization. Perhaps the clearest example of this marriage was the invention by Henry Ford of the assembly line. It was an invention that clearly demonstrated the importance of organizational as well as technical changes in dramatically raising levels of productivity, which in turn proved to be one of the basic reasons for the success of the gasoline engine over its rivals, the steam car and the electric car. Ford's scheme linked together into a single managerial unit the dedicated machine tools developed in the middle of the nineteenth century, the fragmentation and reconstruction on "scientific" lines of production tasks pioneered by Taylor, and the energy-saving possibilities of electric power. It was a powerful—and profitable—combination, achieving both economic goals (high profitability) and political goals (a strictly supervised and controlled labor force) in the name of science, technology, and material progress.

Two conclusions with direct relevance to the modern situation can be drawn from this brief historical survey. The first is that science has frequently helped provide the technical means that have made it possible for capitalist economies to move from one stage of growth to the next, like a snake regularly shedding its skin, a process first described in detail by the economic historian Joseph Schumpeter.[35] The direct contribution can be seen in the new machines and technologies that the results of scientific research made it possible for engineers to develop. Often the research had been consciously carried out for this purpose—as, for example, that of the major industrial laboratories at the end of the nineteenth century.[36] Just as often, however, the results were serendipitous, when research undertaken purely to discover some of the fundamental properties of nature (such as early work on the structure of the atomic nucleus) turned out only later to have broad industrial applications.

Furthermore, not only did science provide technology with the possibility of a steady stream of useful inventions, but it also helped, in the process, to provide the basis needed for a steady evolution in the way that work wa.. organized around machines—an intensification of this work being, at each stage, one of the necessary components enabling capitalism to escape the constraints placed on it by one stage and to break through to the possibilities for expansion offered by the next. If we look at the four major cycles of growth and decline that the capitalist economy has experienced at roughly fifty-year intervals since the end of the eighteenth century—a process first identified by the Russian economist Nikolai Kondratiev—we can identify each one with a set of new, often science-based technologies and at the same time with a new pattern of work organization. The first cycle, from about the 1790s, was built on coal and steam and saw the origins of the factory system. The second, this time predominantly in England and Germany, was based on the sciences of electromagnetism and organic chemistry, accompanied at the level of work organization by the introduction of machine manufacturing into the factories. The third cycle, whose origins were described briefly above, drew strongly on further advances in the understanding of electricity and chemistry, blending them into a set of continuous manufacturing processes that made the assembly line possible. And the last cycle, which started in the early 1940s and has recently been coming to an end, depended for its technological growth on a wide range of discoveries made in the periods immediately before and during the Second World War, from synthetic rubber to solid-state and vacuum physics, this time ushering in an era of automatic manufacturing, where the factory worker became increasingly a machine minder rather than a machine operator.[37]

This pattern holds an optimistic message for the future. For it is possible to speculate that a similar process could repeat itself, namely that the new technologies currently being developed from recent discoveries in fields such as materials science and molecular biology—discoveries that, as we have seen in previous chapters, have been the central focus of the new politics of science—will stimulate a new era of economic growth.[38] The inclusion of robotics in this list, as well as the decentralized organization of work that the microprocessor and advanced telecommunications equipment have made possible, suggest how the new technologies will form the basis of a new form of labor process. Virtually every country in the Western world, and increasing numbers in the less-developed world as well, is drawing up economic development plans in which microelectronics and biotechnology are expected to play a key role. A few years ago, when economic growth seemed to be on an exponential growth curve that directly threatened the availability of future resources, technology and the science that supported it were both pointed to as the villains of the piece. Today it is the downward swing of this curve that has caught economists' and politicians' attention, and technology and science are feted for the promise they undoubtedly hold to help generate a new period of growth.

But we must also look at the other side of the coin. Our brief historical survey has shown how each time the economy has been restructured to create the conditions for a new spurt of growth—a restructuring that some countries have been more successful or fortunate with than others—the process tends to be accompanied by political changes aimed at strengthening the control of capital over labor. This process has taken place both in the workplace (for example, through the development of scientific management) and in the broader political arena, where the new political classes that have come to power have tended to be those associated with positions of management and administrative responsibility within the new division of labor. Rationalization has therefore occurred in two senses. One is a way of describing an economic shakeout, such as that which occurred at the end of the nineteenth century in the U.S. or during the Second World War—in the latter case represented by the close partnership forged between the state, university research laboratories, and the corporate sector, stimulating the development of the new technologies that became the basis of the postwar expansion. The second sense is the rationalization of labor, a tightening up of its control both inside and outside the workplace that has been considered an equally important precondition for capitalist expansion.[39]

This is the broad perspective, I suggest, from which an alternative politics of science must now be approached. We can accept the fact that the new technological opportunities opened up by microelectronics and biotechnology offer new possibilities for social growth. But this does not mean that we have to accept the political conditions under which they are currently being offered, namely that access will be predominantly through the marketplace, and that new technologies in the form of industrial processes or consumer products will be determined primarily by their ability to generate a private profit.

Nor do we have to accept the ideological wrapping in which they are offered—one that expresses social growth in terms of technological growth, rather than broader, nonmaterial values, and uses utopian visions of a science-based future to blind us to the need for an equal effort to create the desirable political institutions and social relations on which this future will just as heavily depend. Indeed, one of the lessons of historical experience is that confidence in science has often been used, either consciously or unconsciously, to help suppress challenges to the concentration of power in the hands of political elites. Arguments that place the need for social efficiency above the need for social equity are often justified, as we have seen, as a more rational and scientific way of organizing people for collective tasks; this is the way I have suggested Francis Bacon's original prescription for science as a social activity provided the blueprint for the factory-based division of labor, Frederick Taylor's scientific management, and ultimately a form of "scientific social management" being elaborated today (see Chapter Six). Each in turn, however, represents a shift from democratic to technocratic *forms* of organization; as such, these techniques become crucial components for reinforcing the concentration of power, despite the fact that the language in which they are expressed appears neutral and apolitical.*

The challenge ahead is relatively clear: How can society exploit the potential offered by the new technologies without once again being cajoled or pressured into accepting the argument that this potential can be achieved only by sacrificing direct democratic control over science and the way it is applied to social objectives? There can be little doubt that the right to such control exists. Virtually all the basic science from which the new technologies have been built was conducted with the use of public funds, and often in public research facilities. In the case of microelectronics, for example, the research that has kept the U.S. in the forefront of international competition since the Second World War was almost entirely financed by the Department of Defense (a fact that often tends to be forgotten by those who claim that the direct subsidies provided by foreign governments to their computer industries represent unfair competition). Similarly, the recent boom in biotechnology has emerged directly from the research sponsored in the 1960s and early 1970s by the Department of Health, Education, and Welfare through the National Institutes of Health; indeed, the commercial applications now being developed for this research are frequently cited as a prime example of the unexpected spin-off that can come from research programs supported primarily because of their scientific quality or promise, rather than devoted to short- or medium-term objectives. In both cases, money raised through taxes and other forms of federal revenue was taken from the public purse to support the research; and it is therefore entirely legitimate to claim that the public has a direct right to determine how the fruits of this research should be used, just as if it had issued a procurement contract, or had employed the scientist under a patronage arrangement.[41]

At present the dominant argument used for the immediate transformation of a public into a private commodity—for example, by allowing the results to be patented, giving the patent rights to the institutions carrying out the research, and allowing these patent rights to be licensed for a substantial commercial fee—is justified on the grounds that the U.S. has chosen the market system as the only way of transferring sci-

---

* Frank Press, President Carter's science adviser, admitted, for example: "I have found it advantageous to be *viewed* primarily as a professional rather than a political appointee, particularly in my dealings with Congress, industry, universities, and professional societies. . . . The credibility of my advice [to the Cabinet] was enhanced by the apolitical and impartial *image* of OSTP" (italics added).[40]

entific results from the laboratory to the world outside (see Chapter Two). Yet other systems are conceivable. The Department of Defense is perhaps one of the best examples of the way new technologies can be stimulated, developed, and applied through public procurement; the Veterans Administration shows how this approach can be applied to the field of health. The land-grant colleges, supported through the U.S. Department of Agriculture, have provided a system that has helped to make American farming the most productive in the world. I am not suggesting that any one of these should be selected as a single model on which all technology transfer should be based, but I am suggesting that there is a wealth of experience from the past to show that public institutions can be an effective channel for bringing research results out of the university or government laboratory, and that the market is not the only mechanism to which this can be entrusted.

The major obstacles are political. Choosing to go through public or private channels for applying science to social goals is not merely a question of effectiveness (however much it may be presented as such); rather, as I have shown at length in earlier chapters, it is a question of whether the channels selected undermine or support the current concentration of economic and political power. Earlier I presented the choice as lying between two mutually exclusive approaches to ways of applying science, the "democratic" and the "technocratic." The first, I suggested, favors control of science through public institutions, with decision-making distributed as widely as possible throughout the community; the second favors private institutions, with decision-making concentrated in the hands of a relatively small elite. It is, of course, a considerable oversimplification to put the choice in such black-and-white terms. Since this is primarily a book about science rather than about politics as such, I have, for example, left out any detailed discussion of the various forms of democracy that exist (including the way a political system labeled democratic by some might be described as technocratic by others). Similarly, it can be argued that science has never properly been under public control, in the sense of the public having a direct input into the choice either of research topics or of problems to be solved, since this control is always mediated by some group (whether scientists, corporate executives, or politicians) that is inevitably pursuing its own agenda at the same time.

But even if one cannot straightforwardly characterize the contents of a democratic, as opposed to a technocratic, science policy, it is still possible to identify trends as lying in one of the two directions. The thrust of the arguments outlined in this book is that during the early 1970s, the major trend was to make science policy more democratic; for the last five years, the trend has been the reverse. The political basis for this reversal has been a broad tightening by U.S. capital of its control of the whole spectrum of social activities associated with science, ranging from its origination in the laboratory to its social use in technological products. To return to a more democratic direction will therefore require not merely specifying how each of the individual points on this spectrum can be made more open to democratic decision-making (the optimal form of which will itself vary along the spectrum), but also showing how these individual challenges must be reinforced by a wider political movement that sees its overall goal as being to confront the growing control of private interests over all spheres of social life.

The substance of a truly democratic strategy for science and science policy would be the reintegration of those needs and aspirations that are steadily being excluded from both by current trends. Within the U.S. this means not merely shifting public research priorities away from destructive ends (such as defense) toward socially constructive goals (such as health and nutrition), long the staple demands of those seeking a "socially responsible" science. Equally important, it means changing the conditions of access to the fruits of publicly funded research so that those social groups that lack the economic or political power currently required to exploit such research are placed in a position to do so. Complementary to this is the need, on an international level, to explore ways in which those countries most in need of the results of this same research to meet their basic requirements for food and energy can also more readily obtain access to it, without being forced to accept the political terms—namely the integration of their economies into a marketplace dominated by the advanced Western nations—on which this research is increasingly being offered.

Achieving these twin goals cannot be done merely by compiling a short list of self-contained political objectives. It requires that a democratic strategy for science be set out in matrix form. One dimension of the matrix lists those points along the research-development-innovation spectrum at which action can be taken to challenge the expression of corporate (or military) power. The second dimension is made up of those groups who are in a position to present such a challenge. Not every hole in this two-dimensional matrix will be covered, since not every group will be able, or have the inclination, to raise a challenge at each separate point on the spectrum. Many of these groups, however, are already addressing certain strategic points. Looking at their current and possible future activities through this matrix approach, I suggest, presents a more optimistic and practical picture of the possibility of generating an alternative science policy than pretending it can be achieved by focusing on one political group or one part of the R&D spectrum alone.

The need to democratize the practice and applications of science can be divided into three principal stages. The first concentrates on the procedures and work practices of the scientific community. Bacon's prescription for the scientific method, with its strict fragmentation of tasks and its rigid hierarchical patterns of control, still rules in the majority of scientific laboratories. One of the first goals of an alternative science policy would be to demonstrate how neither is necessary for a creative and effective research laboratory, yet how these patterns of organization and control of research are frequently imposed as a reflection of broader political relationships that maintain the subservience of science to capital. Democratizing the laboratory does not mean that laboratory technicians, or even members of the outside community, should necessarily be given equal weight with principal investigators in the choice of research directions in fundamental science, or of investigative techniques. But it does mean that the criteria by which priorities and practices are decided should be open to discussion at all levels, that the chances of individual scientists being allowed to build research empires whose top priority becomes economic profitability or institutional survival should be minimized, and that scientists should accept the many ways in which decisions made inside the laboratory have important social dimensions that should not be resolved behind closed doors.[42]

Democratizing the laboratory would be a first step toward creating a science based on new social relations and a new ideology. A second would be democratizing the institutions that decide how research funds should be allocated. Already this is being done to a limited extent. At the National Institutes of Health, for example, each grant request is discussed by two committees, one a scientific committee whose role is to judge the scientific quality of the application, another a committee including nonscientists which decides whether a particular research proposal should be supported on the basis of the prior scientific evaluation as well as other criteria, such as the general availability of research funds and the importance of the research area being pursued. A considerable degree of selectivity in the use of biomedical research funds is also imposed by Congress, where the desires of individual congressmen to be seen securing additional research funds for a particular highly publicized illness have generated what is widely known as the "disease-of-the-month" syndrome. The approach has several weaknesses (many of which are eagerly pointed out by scientists who would like their research funds to come with fewer strings attached, and thus emphasize how cures to a disease may come from completely unexpected areas of research). The extent to which decisions about which diseases shall receive special research treatment are really the result of democratic choices, rather than a vehicle for raising conscience money from the wealthy to be spent on their terms, is also debatable. Nevertheless, as Representative Henry Waxman argued in the summer of 1983 in suggesting that Congress should play a greater role in determining the detailed research programs of the NIH (a suggestion strongly opposed by virtually the whole biomedical research community), the procedures for more direct input into the selection of research priorities exists in embryo form, with enough examples of successful intervention to justify this approach.[43]

At the other end of the spectrum is the need to develop ways of democratizing technological innovation. To give an example: in the middle of the 1970s, workers at the Lucas Aerospace Company in England showed that it was in principle possible to conceive a plan for applying their technical skills as draftsmen, engineers, and computer operators, not toward the military technologies that were at the time their company's chief products, but toward more socially desirable technologies, such as aids for the disabled or novel forms of community transportation. Ideas for the types of machines that were needed, but were not being provided through the market for one reason or another (such as limited production runs), were gathered from a wide number of community groups. As a result, several prototypes—such as a vehicle with two sets of wheels, able to travel either on roads or on railway tracks—have subsequently been developed (although outside the company).[44]

The ideas developed by the Lucas workers into what became known as a "corporate plan" were deliberately devised as a *political* strategy to challenge the Lucas management by confronting it not at the traditional level of wages and working conditions, but at the relatively unusual level of product innovation. This political goal is sometimes ignored by those who have projected the Lucas workers' initiative as merely a *technical* strategy, aimed at finding new uses for high technology production skills. Furthermore, that the effort failed to have a substantial impact on the company was largely because the workers were proposing a process of decision-making that would subject technical innovations to a social rather than an economic imperative, in itself a direct challenge to the way decisions about product choice are conventionally made within a private company. Nevertheless, the Lucas struggle fulfilled an important symbolic function by demonstrating that the choice of products developed from a given set of advanced design and engineering skills was socially and politically determined.* The social control of technological innovation can therefore be suggested as an extension of the Lucas model, where a process of community-controlled decision-making would be used to determine how certain advanced scientific knowledge and technical skills are put to the most socially beneficial use.[45]

In other European countries a different way of experimenting with the application of scientific knowledge to social problems is being explored through what are known as "science shops" (or, in France, as *boutiques de science*). These could, again, form part of an alternative science and technology policy aimed at meeting community needs by offering a channel through which members of the community can gain direct access to scientific and technical expertise. The science shops originated in

---

* Indeed, a scheme of community-based technological centers was drawn up by the Greater London Council in 1983, based directly on the Lucas experience, in an attempt to open up access from the community to scientific and technical expertise existing in research and higher education institutions in the London area.

Holland in the mid-1970s as an outgrowth of the Dutch radical science movement, the first being created at the University of Utrecht in 1973. Their three principal goals are to provide technical information on demand to individuals or the representatives of community groups who come to the shops requesting it; to promote socially relevant research within Dutch universities (in 1986, for example, 15 percent of the research funds of the University of Amsterdam will be devoted to projects that have been identified as socially desirable by the science shop on the university campus); and to explore ways of linking this research directly to those working in the areas where it is needed. An important element in the science shop philosophy is the way access to its services is determined. At the University of Amsterdam, for example, requests for assistance are accepted only from those who have not been able to pay for someone to carry out the research, who promise not to use the results they are given for commercial purposes, and who are able to make productive use of the research results once they are obtained. In this way the science shops are intended to act as a kind of "knowledge broker," mediating between university scientists and members of the outside community, finding ways of connecting university research directly to specific social needs, yet bypassing the conventional commercial channels through which these needs are usually addressed.[46]

So far nothing comparable to the Lucas plan or the science shops has been tried in the United States. There have nevertheless been various attempts to explore ways of making available alternative channels of scientific and technical expertise. In Mountain View, California, the Mid-Peninsula Conversion Project, partly funded by a grant from the Science for Citizens Program of the National Science Foundation, has been exploring ways of making science and technology available to community groups, such as labor unions or disabled veterans, who might not otherwise have access to it.[47] Other groups across the country are exploring ways of applying high technology products to community-based activities. The New Mexico Solar Energy Association has been exploring how microcomputers can help small, self-sufficient farmers make the best use of local resources;[48] in California a small company has developed a technique for linking a personal computer to a hand loom, making it possible to quickly convert new fabric patterns designed on the computer screen into products that are competitive with machine-made fabric. Similarly, the Californian Agrarian Action Project is looking at ways in which biotechnology might be applied to the needs of small-scale organic farmers, for example by improving the overall protein balance in organically-grown foods. Other examples of such "bootstrap community revitalization," exploiting the potential of high technology to help provide an alternative source of livelihood to those displaced by the mainstream economy, are being pursued in groups and collectives across the country.[49]

There is less to report on the third point on the spectrum at which pressure for an alternative science policy needs to be applied, namely the question of maintaining public access to the fruits of publicly funded research. Other countries have shown that it is possible to keep this access open; thus in Britain the National Research Development Corporation, a product of the post-war Labour government, had several major successes to its name in helping to move research results into the community before its rights to patents from government-funded research were ended in 1983 as part of Prime Minister Margaret Thatcher's campaign of privatization. In the U.S. a few Washington-based lobby groups, in particular Ralph Nader's Health Research Group, have vociferously opposed changes in legislation that have steadily eroded the public's right to direct access to the results of the research it has paid for; but these groups have had little impact against the economic and political forces moving, as in Britain, in the opposite direction. On the international front, several developing countries have been pushing for changes in the Paris Convention, the agreement signed initially in 1883, under which countries indicate their willingness to respect a certain common set of rules on patent protection. The developing countries want greater control over the way that outsiders can use patents to manipulate market conditions (for example, by buying up patents merely to keep competitors out, but not using them to produce goods); however, the more the developed countries have realized the economic and political importance of patents, the more opposed they have become to the developing countries' proposals for a change in the rules.

The need and the scope exist for a broad reassessment of the patent system, both domestically and internationally. Would it be possible to grant certain social groups privileged access to patented research results (as currently most scientists are free to use the research results of others, even if they have been patented, on the grounds that they are not put to commercial ends)? Could new public institutions be created responsible for creating links between university scientists and outside groups wishing to use their research, but without going through commercial channels? Are alternatives to patents possible that would provide both an incentive and a limited reward to individual scientists without the need to provide this reward by guaranteeing monopoly control of the market? Should certain areas of science, such as research into various tropical diseases, be acknowledged sufficiently important to humanity that they should be considered unpatentable—or, alternatively, should all patents in these areas be granted to an international agency, such as the World Health Organization?[50] None of these questions, simple as they may sound, is straightforward. Nevertheless, they are the types of questions that must be addressed by anyone seeking to challenge the present system, under which patents are almost universally used to tighten the control of private corporations over the use of scientific knowledge, and thus to restrict the access to this knowledge of others exploring alternative ways of applying it to social needs.

Research, access, application: these, then, are the three fields in which the political values expressed through science lie open to challenge. What about the other dimension in our matrix, those groups in a position to mount such a challenge? The first is the women's movement. Part of the broad critique of the values embedded in science developed in the early 1970s was the demonstration that science is essentially a man's world. The majority of scientists are men, for reasons that range from the way girls are put off the "hard" sciences at school to the competitive pressures that discriminate against a scientist who chooses to put substantial effort into a nonscience activity such as child-rearing. It also tends to be men who select the way science is to be applied, even to women's needs. The liberal response is to argue for more opportunities for women in science, in other words for more women to be given the opportunity to fill the roles currently played by men. The more radical argument is that part of the problem lies in the roles themselves, and that the values expressed through science tend to be male values (illustrated, for example, by the predominance on the White House Science Council—and previously the President's Science Advisory Committee—of members representing the hard sciences such as physics and mathematics over the soft sciences of biology and sociology). "The problem is not one of making women more scientific, but of making science less masculine," says Liz Fee of Johns Hopkins University. "When masculinity is seen as an incomplete and thus distorted form of humanity, the issue of making science and technology less masculine is also the issue of making it more completely human." [51]

The women's movement has already shown how different strategies can be used at different positions on the science-society spectrum. Some, such as Fee, have concentrated on the need to change the conditions within the laboratory, and thus implicitly the form of the knowledge that emerges from laboratory research. Others have focused on the application end, exploring ways that women, either individually or in groups, can control the use of those technologies that most directly affect them, particularly in medicine and childbirth. [52] Women's groups have also been actively engaged in campaigns to protect those in other countries against the side effects of modern medical technologies, such as the contraceptive Depo-Provera. And in Britain women have been among the most militant opponents of the deployment of cruise missiles, symbolized by a year-long, ongoing demonstration outside the Greenham Common Air Force Base. Through such actions the women's movement has already shown that it is likely to remain one of the most consistent and powerful voices demanding changes in the way control over science and its applications is distributed.

A second group is made up of the labor unions. American unions, even less than their European counterparts, do not have a history of deep involvement in political debates about science; it is likely to be a long time before the U.S. sees anything comparable to recent developments in France, where laboratory technicians, nominated through their unions, now sit in some of the policy committees of the principal research-funding agency, the Centre National de la Recherche Scientifique.[53] Nevertheless, there are signs that this involvement is increasing. In the mid-1970s it was generated largely by struggles around occupational health and safety issues, where it was recognized that there was a need to challenge the judgments of scientific experts on, for example, the carcinogenicity of new chemical compounds. During this period officials working with unions such as the Oil, Chemical, and Atomic Workers and the United Steelworkers discovered at first hand how scientific research could be manipulated to provide results that appeared neutral, but in fact represented political and economic, as much as scientific, choices. They also learned the importance of gaining access to the scientific information on which decisions were made, information that companies tried to protect using the argument that it involved trade secrets, but which the unions argued was essential for an informed dialogue on the impact of production techniques on the health of their members.[54]

Other unions, such as the International Association of Machinists, became involved in broader technological issues, such as the safety of nuclear power. Their interest partly reflected a direct interest: those whose members worked as operators in nuclear power plants favored stringent safety requirements, while those employed in power-plant construction were frequently opposed, for they felt the impact of tougher safety standards through higher production costs, expressed in canceled orders and thus lost jobs. Among the more progressive unions, however, there have been signs of a spreading awareness of the broad political challenge to democratic politics being mounted through the control of science and technology.[55] Several prominent union members agreed to serve on a new commission established by Ralph Nader in 1983 to survey the growing impact of private corporations on university research. Others have become active members of the newly-formed Committee for Responsible Genetics. At the grass-roots level, union members have organized around demands for a direct input into decisions about the new technologies they are expected to work with; some have begun to explore variations on the ideas of the Lucas work force for directing technical skills toward the production of socially useful products.[56] And the Reagan administration's attack on occupational health regulations has done as much as anything to demonstrate that scientific issues need to be firmly placed on the political agenda of the labor movement.

The environmental movement is, like the women's movement, already moving firmly in this direction. We have seen in previous chapters how many environmentalist groups, such as Friends of the Earth and the Natural Resources Defense Council, have played key roles in challenging the conventional channels of scientific decision-making. In the laboratory such groups frequently spearheaded campaigns for stricter controls on recombinant DNA research and greater community participation at both the local and national levels in decisions about this research. More broadly, the central focus of the environmental movement has been to find ways of mitigating the social and environmental impact of science-based technologies, from the use of chemical pesticides to the threats of global annihilation raised by the spread of nuclear technologies, in whatever form. While some groups have continued to present nuclear power as one area in which it is necessary to separate rational from irrational choices (e.g., "safe" from "unsafe" working conditions), others, such as the Abalone Alliance in California, have begun to show how the whole nuclear debate is embedded in a politically determined rationality that, like Frederick Taylor's scientific management, expresses political goals within the neutral-sounding language of science. [57]

The frustrations experienced by many environmentalist groups during the Carter administration, together with the frontal attack to which they have been subjected under President Reagan, have demonstrated the increasing need for such groups to think in political as much as single-issue terms. This is partly a question of embracing a broader agenda; those concerned about the way science is used should, I have suggested, be equally concerned about the way it is produced, as well as about the restrictions placed on its dissemination. The experience of the Office of Technology Assessment, or of the National Institutes of Health's Recombinant DNA Advisory Committee, both described in Chapter Five, shows that isolated campaigns that ignore this broader political perspective can quickly lose their effectiveness.

It is also a question of building new alliances around these issues. Already efforts have been made by groups such as Environmentalists for Full Employment to bridge the gaps between environmentalists and the labor movement, showing how apparent conflicts between the two (such as the claim that tougher environmental regulation means fewer jobs) are illusory, and that, as the Reagan administration's attack on regulation in all guises has shown, they have many political needs in common. [58] In the past a major weakness of the alternative technology movement was its failure to address the problems encountered in the lives of the majority of the population, who find themselves locked into a technological system they cannot escape without making a major sacrifice. Many are unprepared to experiment with new technologies if this means giving up the economic security of a full-time job; indeed, for many the fight to retain a job during a period in which modern technology is threatening to create an ever-lengthening unemployment line has inevitably become an issue that takes precedence over any discussion about the conditions under which work is carried out.

The worsening employment situation, however, is making it more important than ever before for political movements to address issues around technology that were already framed by the counterculture movements of the 1970s. At that time new forms of work were proposed as alternatives to the alienation of the assembly line and the destruction of natural resources by science-based technologies; today such work has become an economic necessity for those who find themselves pushed to the margins of the economy. Groups such as the newly formed Intermediate Technology Development Group of North America, based on the "small is beautiful" idea of economist E. F. Schumacher, are now exploring ways of revitalizing communities through self-help schemes that, while drawing on some of the high technology (such as personal computers) offered by the mainstream economy, place it in a context of self-management and self-reliance.[59] The gap between such initiatives and the more conventional political activities of the labor unions and the environmental movement remains wide; but it is a gap that must be bridged if either is to achieve long-term success.

The final set of groups that offer the hope for an alternative science policy are those pressing the demands of the less-developed nations. The scientific needs of these countries demand little elaboration, nor do the barriers that recent experiences (from the United Nations conference in Vienna in 1979 to recent attempts to establish a Biotechnology Center for the Third World) have shown to be formidable. There are a few groups in the U.S., such as the Washington-based Center for Concern, that have begun to address these issues. Nevertheless, it is an area that the Third World countries must themselves develop the technical and political skills to address. Much is already happening on this front. The debates that took place during the Vienna conference itself, as well as those that have taken place within agencies such as the United Nations Conference on Trade and Development (UNCTAD) in Geneva on the economic and political consequences of patent laws, indicate the height of current awareness about how much needs to be done and where. Furthermore, over the past ten years even the once radical ideas of Schumacher have now gained broad endorsement through bodies such as the Organization for Economic Cooperation and Development.

The danger here remains that development will be portrayed as a technical problem—even if the technology is "intermediate" or "appropriate"—rather than one that also has deep political roots.[60] It is not up to those from the developed world to prescribe which technological strategies are the most appropriate for these countries; nevertheless, it is up to us to help ensure that important opportunities are not foreclosed. This means confronting the various ways that policies created by the advanced industrialized nations to exploit their leadership in science can undermine the efforts by developing countries to enjoy the benefits of science without at the same time sacrificing their newfound political independence.

It is relatively easy to identify, as I have tried to do above, the miscellaneous groups already engaged at one level or another in the struggle to create a more democratic politics of science. Expressing this strategy as a matrix also indicates the current gaps in this strategy, such as the lack of labor union activity around the democratization of scientific work (made all the more difficult by the relative weakness of labor unions within universities, as well as the highly competitive conditions in most laboratories, which act against any chance of collective action). The more difficult task is to see how these different groups will be able to weld themselves into a single political movement sufficiently powerful to mount a direct challenge to undemocratic policies introduced in the name of national efficiency. Given the common political nature of the issues each group is addressing—the concentration of power over science and its applications in the hands of a relatively small elite—coordinated action is necessary for the highest chance of success.

Some encouragement can perhaps be reaped from an unexpected quarter, namely the success of the creationist movement in developing a nationwide challenge to dominant ideas about science based on a detailed critique of both the values it contains and its social implications. It is not necessary to support the content of creationist ideas—often based on a highly selective reading of the Bible, a distortion of Darwin's ideas, a misinterpretation of the scientific method, and a reactionary political program that seeks to reimpose the moral values of the nineteenth century. Yet one can take heart from the relative effectiveness of a campaign that used the creationist doctrine as a vehicle for promoting a political program that included a vision of an alternative science.[61] The creationists have shown how it is possible to live with the fruits of modern science without at the same time awarding to science the moral and cultural authority it is frequently given. The creationists have succeeded in injecting their values and ideas about science into a remarkably high proportion of the American population, given the way many of these ideas fly directly in the face of modern scientific research. The prospects for an alternative strategy that does not try to contradict science, but still challenges its values and its implications, must therefore remain high.

The broader political strategy that needs to be adopted, however, is a subject that goes beyond the boundaries of this book. I have presented in earlier chapters an analysis and critique of the current situation, and in this chapter a brief outline of how a political strategy designed to create an alternative approach to science might be achieved. It is up to others, more deeply involved in political campaigns, to work out how this strategy might be turned into practice. Some might argue that it can be developed within the more radical wing of the Democratic party, aligned with groups such as the California-based Campaign for Economic Democracy, and offering an alternative to the search for an "industrial policy" that other Democrats are now advocating as a replacement for Reaganomics.[62] Others may feel sufficiently disillusioned with the Tweedledum-Tweedledee of conventional electoral politics to suggest that the same ideas can be developed only in a setting that is independent of the main political parties. My analysis does not lead directly to the one or the other; but it does suggest that a properly democratic science policy will be achieved only by a political program that directly challenges the current distribution of wealth and power in U.S. society, given the extent to which this is now being served by a science policy that seems to be moving sharply in the opposite direction.

It would be wrong to pretend that there are any easy solutions. Equally, it would be wrong to adopt a fatalistic stance, accepting the advance of science and technology as inevitable, and the social destruction and authoritarian practices that they bring in their wake as the necessary by-products of progress. Science is one of the greatest cultural and intellectual achievements of the modern age. But its social significance must be placed in its proper perspective; it must not be seen as a key to utopia, a blueprint to a perfect future, or even the ultimate expression of human reason. Rather, science must remain firmly identified as a powerful tool that can help us understand the natural universe in potentially useful ways, but at the same time carries the seeds of human exploitation. How to tap the one without falling victim to the other is the key challenge of the decades ahead. Creating the individuals and the political institutions through which this can be successfully achieved is the principal task now facing all those engaged in struggles over the new politics of science.

SOURCE NOTES

INTRODUCTION

1. Business-Higher Education Forum, *America's Competitive Challenge: The Need for a National Response* (Washington, D.C.: American Council on Education, April 1983).
2. Anne Keatley, "Knowledge as Real Estate," *Science*, vol. 222 (November 18, 1983).

CHAPTER ONE

1. Frank Press, "Annual Report of the President" (address to National Academy of Sciences, Washington, D.C., April 26, 1983 [mimeographed]).
2. William D. Carey, "1984: Science's Multicolored Coat," *Science*, vol. 220 (April 15, 1983).
3. "America Rushes to High Tech for Growth," *Business Week* (March 28, 1983). See also Warren Kalbacker, "How to Profit from Progress," *Science Digest* (October 1981). Kalbacker writes: "These are exciting times for science—space, computers, recombinant DNA—and the stock market is proof. Investors in high tech could reap enormous profits."
4. Quoted in "Are High-Tech Stocks Flying Too High?," *Business Week* (March 21, 1983).
5. Quoted ibid.
6. Margaret Loeb, "Computers May Widen Gap in School Quality between Rich and Poor," *Wall Street Journal* (May 26, 1983).
7. For analysis of this budget, see Willis H. Shapley et al., *Research and Development: AAAS Report VI* (Washington, D.C.: American Association for the Advancement of Science, 1981).
8. See, for example, Representative John M. Ashbrook, "Basic Research or Biased Research," *Conservative Digest* (May/June 1980). After criticizing the use of the results of research funded by the National Science Foundation to justify government welfare programs, Ashbrook suggested that Congress should consider "phasing out social science funding altogether." For earlier criticism of NSF programs, see John Walsh, "NSF: How Much Responsibility for Course Content, Implementation?," *Science*, vol. 190 (November 14, 1975).
9. Office of Management and Budget, "Revised Special Analysis of the R&D Component of the 1981 and 1982 Budgets of the U.S. Government" (Washington, D.C.: OMB, April 1981 [mimeographed]).
10. "Next to Godliness," *The Economist* (February 5, 1983).
11. Daniel S. Greenberg, *The Politics of Pure Science.* (New York: New American Library, 1967). During the 1980 election campaign, Reagan's supporters did little to encourage either scientists or technologists to support the

Republican cause; *Science* editor Philip Abelson described the material submitted by the Reagan camp to the October 1980 issue of the engineering journal *Spectrum* as "an insult to the profession" (see "President Reagan, Science, and Engineering," *Science*, vol. 212 [May 29, 1981]).

12. Conference on Federal Research and Development Budget for 1982 and Future Years, "Consensus Statement" (Washington, D.C.: National Academy of Sciences, October 26–27, 1981). See also Robert Reinhold, "Reagan Aides Fail to Mollify Worried Scientists," *New York Times* (October 27, 1981); "Latest Budget Cuts Arouse Concern and Recommendations," *Physics Today* (December 1981).

13. Edward E. David, "To Prune, Promote, and Preserve," *Science*, vol. 217 (August 13, 1982).

14. Quoted in "Steady Gains in R&D Spending," *Business Week* (January 12, 1981).

15. Willis H. Shapley et al., *Research and Development: AAAS Report VII, Federal Budget—FY1983* (Washington, D.C.: American Association for Advancement of Science, 1982), p. 14.

16. George A. Keyworth, "Federal R&D: Not an Entitlement," *Science*, vol. 219 (February 18, 1983).

17. See Frank Press, "New Cuts in Agency Budgets," *Science*, vol. 214 (October 16, 1981). According to Press: "All sectors of the scientific community must be prepared to set aside the shibboleths of the past and perhaps propose new modes of research just as effective yet less costly. . . . Out of this time of trial may emerge a totally new environment for science in the United States, perhaps even a better one."

18. Quoted in Daniel Greenberg, "Science's New Friend in the White House," *New Scientist* (February 24, 1983).

19. Quoted in "Science Is Suddenly a White House Priority," *Business Week* (December 27, 1982).

20. George A. Keyworth, "The Need for New Partnerships in American R&D" (speech to Council for Chemical Research, Houston, Tex., September 29, 1982 [mimeographed]).

21. George A. Keyworth, "Revitalizing the American Economy: The Essential Role of Basic Research" (speech to American Physical Society, Baltimore, Md., April 18, 1983 [mimeographed]).

22. David, "To Prune, Promote, Preserve" (cit. 13).

23. C. Wright Mills, *The Power Elite* (New York: Oxford University Press, 1970).

24. National Science Foundation, *Science and Engineering Employment: 1970–1980*, Special Report 81-310. (Washington, D.C.: NSF, 1981).

25. Ibid.

26. "A Research Spending Surge Defies Recession," *Business Week* (July 5, 1982).

27. Figures taken from National Science Foundation, *National Patterns of Science and Technology Resources, 1983* (Washington, D.C.: NSF, in press).

28. D. Bruce Merrifield, "Forces of Change Affecting High Technology Industries," *National Journal* (January 29, 1983).

29. National Science Board, *Science Indicators 1980* (Washington, D.C.: National Science Board, 1981), p. 72.

30. Figures taken from Office of Management and Budget, "OMB Data for Special Analysis K" (Washington, D.C.: OMB, January 1983 [mimeographed]).

31. For a full description of the budget process through which proposals for federal support of science must pass, see Shapley et al., *AAAS Report VII* (cit. 15), chap. 6 ("The Budget Process and R&D").

32. Ibid.

33. See, for example, the descriptions in Greenberg, *The Politics of Pure Science* (cit. 11), and in Don K. Price, *The Scientific Estate* (Cambridge, Mass.: Harvard University Press, 1956).

34. See Greenberg, *The Politics of Pure Science* (cit. 11), chaps. 4 and 5; and Daniel Kevles, "The National Science Foundation and the Debate over Postwar Research Policy," *ISIS*, vol. 68 (1977), pp. 5–26.

35. See David Noble, *Forces of Production* (New York: Knopf, 1984). For a history of the legislation which eventually led to the creation of the National Science Foundation, see J. Merton England, *A Patron for Pure Science: The National Science Foundation's Formative Years, 1945–57* (Washington, D.C.: NSF, 1982).

36. Evidence in U.S. Congress, Senate Committee on Military Affairs, subcommittee, *Hearings on Science Legislation* 79th Cong., 1st sess. (1945), p. 203.

37. Vannevar Bush, *Science: The Endless Frontier* (Washington, D.C.: U.S. Government Printing Office, 1945; reprinted Washington, D.C.: National Science Foundation, 1960).

38. Quoted in Greenberg, *Politics of Pure Science* (cit. 11).

39. See England, *Patron for Pure Science* (cit. 35).

40. Charles J. V. Murphy, "The White House Since Sputnik," *Fortune* (January 1958).

41. Meg Greenfield, "Science Goes to Washington," *The Reporter* (September 26, 1963).

42. Philip H. Abelson, "The President's Science Advisers," *Minerva*, vol. 3 (Winter 1965).

43. Quoted in Godfrey Hodgson, *In Our Time: America from World War II to Nixon* (London: Macmillan, 1976). "U.S. Scientists," *Time* (January 2, 1961). The magazine wrote that "statesmen and savants, builders and even priests are their servants: at a time when science is at the apogee of its power for good or evil, they are the Men of the Year 1960."

44. White House, press release, quoted in *Science*, vol. 153 (July 6, 1966). Johnson's comments were reinforced by the publication of a study commissioned by the Department of Defense, known as "Project Hindsight," which appeared to show that the contributions of university research to the development of twenty weapons systems had been minimal, and that most contributions had come from mission-oriented research programs. See C. W. Sherwin and R. S. Isenson, *First Interim Report on Project Hindsight* (Washington, D.C.: Office of Director of Defense Research and Engineering, June 30, 1966).

45. For a description of science policy-making during the Nixon era, see Edward J. Burger, *Science at the White House: A Political Liability* (Baltimore: Johns Hopkins University Press, 1980).

46. For a discussion of these trends, see National Science Board, *Science Indi-*

cators 1980 (cit. 29), chap. 4 ("Industrial R&D and Technological Progress").

47. Quoted in "The Painful Struggle for Relevancy," *Business Week* (January 2, 1971).

48. See Greenberg, *Politics of Pure Science* (cit. 11), chap. 12 ("The New Politics of Science").

49. Roger Brinner and Miriam Alexander, *The Role of High Technology Industries in Economic Growth* (Cambridge, Mass.: Data Resources, Inc., March 15, 1977).

50. National Science Board, *Science Indicators 1980* (cit. 29), p. 236.

51. Edwin Mansfield, paper to National Science Foundation, Washington, D.C., May 21, 1977 (mimeographed).

52. Carl P. Gerstacker, "Chemistry in the 1980s," *Chemical and Engineering News* (November 26, 1979).

53. Organization for Economic Cooperation and Development, *Technical Change and Economic Policy* (Paris: OECD, 1980), p. 20.

54. "The unfortunate fact is that few of our policy-makers have recognized how much of today's necessary expenditures for growth are in the area of 'knowledge-capital,' " said Arthur M. Bueche in a speech to the Middle Atlantic Regional Meeting of the American Chemical Society, April 5, 1978. According to George A. Keyworth, President Reagan's science adviser: "New scientific knowledge and technological know-how represent our most productive capital today. . . . It is very much a part of the administration's economic recovery plan" ("Science and Technology Policy—What's Ahead," address to Sixth Annual AAAS R&D Colloquium, Washington, D.C., June 25, 1981).

55. George N. Carlson, "Tax Policy toward Research and Development," *Technology in Society*, vol. 3, nos. 1/2 (1981), p. 69.

56. Organization for Economic Cooperation and Development, *Science, Growth, and Society: A New Perspective* (Paris: OECD, 1971).

57. National Academy of Sciences, *Science and Technology in Presidential Policy-Making: A Proposal* (Washington, D.C.: NAS, 1974).

58. White House, press release (May 11, 1976).

59. Ibid.

60. White House, press release (November 12, 1975).

61. A detailed description of Carter's links—and debts—to the Trilateral Commission is provided in Laurence H. Schoup, *The Carter Presidency and Beyond* (Palo Alto: Ramparts Press, 1980).

62. National Science Board, *Science Indicators 1980* (cit. 29), p. 263).

63. Willis H. Shapley et al., *AAAS Report VIII: Research and Development, FY 1984* (Washington, D.C.: American Association for the Advancement of Science, 1983).

64. See John Walsh, "Executive Office Reorganization: OSTP and CEQ Are Still In," *Science*, vol. 197 (July 29, 1977).

65. President Jimmy Carter, "The Science and Technology Message to the Congress," White House (March 27, 1979), p. 3.

66. Quoted in Nicholas Wade, "Why the Government Should Not Fund Science," *Science*, vol. 210 (October 3, 1980).

67. Milton Friedman, "An Open Letter on Grants," *Newsweek* (May 18, 1981).

68. Richard Speier, "General Science, Space, and Technology," in Eugene J. McAllister, ed., *Agenda for Progress* (Washington, D.C.: Heritage Foundation, 1981), p. 63. See also the description of the Heritage Foundation's new interest in science in Wil Lepkowski, "Debate over Federal Science Policy Sharpens," *Chemical and Engineering News* (April 6, 1981).
69. Speier, "Science, Space, Technology" (cit. 68), p. 80.
70. Simon Ramo, *America's Technology Slip* (New York: Wiley, 1980), pp. 4, 7, 90–91.
71. Quoted in Daniel Greenberg, "Keyworth Thriving as Reagan's Science Aide," *Science and Government Report* (May 15, 1983).
72. See Keyworth, "Science and Technology Policy" (cit. 54). Keyworth said: "It is no longer within our economic capability, nor perhaps even desirable, to aspire to primacy across the spectrum of scientific discipline." The *Washington Star* headlined a story on Keyworth's speech: "U.S. Can't Afford First Place in Research, Reagan Science Adviser Tells Experts" (June 26, 1981).
73. Quoted in "Science Advisers on Science Adviser," *SIPIscope* (July/August 1981).
74. In making such appointments, the Reagan administration was continuing a tradition of using primarily male, white physical scientists as the chief source of scientific advice, a tradition that has existed since the Truman administration. For a list of those who served between 1951 and 1973 on the President's Science Advisory Committee and its predecessor (the Science Advisory Committee of the Office of Defense Mobilization), see William T. Golden, ed., *Science Advice to the President* (New York: Pergamon Press, 1980), pp. viii–ix. Of the eighty-seven names listed, all are male and forty are physicists, compared with five biologists (and one sociologist).
75. Quoted in Robert Reinhold, "Can Science and Politics Safely Mix?," *New York Times* (June 13, 1982).
76. Quoted in *Business Week*, "Science Is Suddenly a White House Priority," December 27, 1982. See also "New Broom Sweeps Clean at NSF," *Science*, vol. 218 (December 24, 1982). For a reply to these charges, see Daniel Greenberg, " 'Perhaps a Little Naive' Says New NSF Chief," *Science and Government Report* (January 15, 1983).
77. *Washington Post* (October 9, 1981).
78. Dale Russakoff, "Adviser to Watt Blackballed by GOP Committee," *Washington Post* (March 27, 1983).
79. Eliot Marshall, "USDA Official Defends Loyalty Checks," *Science*, vol. 216 (June 25, 1982).
80. Bush, *Science* (cit. 37).
81. *New York Times* (May 9, 1982; May 21, 1982).
82. George B. Kistiakowsky, *A Scientist at the White House* (Cambridge, Mass.: Harvard University Press, 1976), p. 379.
83. Reinhold, "Can Science and Politics Mix?" (cit. 75).
84. Press, "Annual Report" (cit. 1).
85. Quoted in Kim Macdonald, "After 18 Months of Confrontation, Keyworth Talks about His Role as Science Adviser," *Chronicle of Higher Education* (November 10, 1982).
86. Quoted ibid.

89. Ibid.
88. OMB, "Special Analysis K" (cit. 30).
89. George A. Keyworth, "The Role of Science in a New Era of Competition," *Science*, vol. 217 (August 13, 1982), p. 607.
90. Evidence in U.S. Congress, House Committee on Science and Technology, Subcommittee on Energy Research and Production, National Laboratory Relationships with Industry and the University Community, 97th Cong., 1st sess. (July 29, 1981), p. 41.
91. John Walsh, "Panel Pans DoE Management of Labs," *Science*, vol. 217 (September 10, 1982), p. 1015.
92. Herbert I. Fusfeld et al., *The Changing Tide: Federal Support of Civilian Sector R&D* (New York: Center for Science and Technology Policy, New York University, November 1, 1981).
93. Keyworth, "Revitalizing American Economy" (cit. 21).
94. Ibid. See also Keyworth's remarks to AAAS symposium on R&D policy, Washington, D.C., March 24, 1983 (reprinted as "Federal R&D and Industrial Policy," *Science*, vol. 220 [June 10, 1983]).
95. Colin Norman, "Committee Axes NACM," *Science*, vol. 220 (June 10, 1983).
96. Keyworth, "Federal R&D and Industrial Policy" (cit. 94).
97. Don K. Price, "The Scientific Establishment," in Robert Gilpin and Christopher Wright, eds., *Scientists and National Policy-Making* (New York: Columbia University Press, 1964).
98. Philip Handler, "When Science Becomes a Public Venture, to Whom Is the Scientist Accountable?," *Chronicle of Higher Education* (March 3, 1980). (Excerpt from an address at City University of New York.)
99. See, for example, Richard Atkinson (former director of the National Science Foundation), "Reinvigorating the Contract between Science and Society," *Chronicle of Higher Education* (March 19, 1979); also other contributions in Gerald Holton and Robert S. Morison, eds., *The Limits of Scientific Inquiry* (New York: Norton, 1979).
100. Bush, *Science* (cit. 37).
101. Russell Long, "Dear Colleague" letter, U.S. Senate (February 21, 1980).
102. Joseph Pechman, remarks to AAAS symposium, June 1980; reprinted in *AAAS R&D Colloquium, 1980* (Washington, D.C.: American Association for Advancement of Science, 1980), pp. 48, 55–56.
103. "Tax Aide Urges More Benefits for Research," *Washington Post* (May 28, 1983).
104. Reprinted as Edwin Mansfield, "Tax Policy and Innovation," *Science*, vol. 215 (March 12, 1982).
105. "Painful Struggle" (cit. 47).
106. OMB, "Special Analysis K" (cit. 30).
107. See OECD, *Technical Change and Economic Policy* (cit. 53).
108. Quoted in *Business Week* (March 8, 1982).
109. William Greider, "The Education of David Stockman," *Atlantic Monthly* (December 1981).
110. Greenberg, "Keyworth Thriving" (cit. 71).
111. Mitchell Waldrop, "Keyworth Calls for Bold Push in Space," *Science*, vol. 221 (July 8, 1983).

112. David Joravsky, "Scientists as Servants," *New York Review of Books* (June 28, 1979).
113. Quoted in "After Affluence, Americans Are Not Prepared to Go Back," *U.S. News and World Report* (August 11, 1980).
114. National Research Council, *International Competition in Advanced Technology: Decisions for America* (Washington, D.C.: National Academy Press, 1983).
115. Press, "Annual Report" (cit. 1).
116. Ramo, *America's Technology Slip* (cit. 70).
117. William Winpisinger, "A Labor View of Technological Innovation," *Technology Review* (April 1981).
118. Quoted in "Trade Unionist Speaks Out," *Genewatch*, Newsletter of the Committee for Responsible Genetics (November/December 1983).

CHAPTER TWO

1. Evidence in U.S. Congress, House Committee on Science and Technology, Subcommittee on Investigations and Oversight and Subcommittee on Science, Research, and Technology, *Commercialization of Academic Biomedical Research*. Hearings, 97th Cong., 1st sess. (June 8–9, 1981), p. 8.
2. "Commercialization and University Research" (background paper prepared for Pajaro Dunes meeting, Stanford University, August 27, 1981 [mimeographed]).
3. Evidence in *Commercialization of Research* (cit. 1), p. 20.
4. Quoted in Jeffrey L. Fox, "Can Academia Adapt to Biotechnology's Lure?" *Chemical and Engineering News* (October 12, 1981).
5. Quoted in Barbara J. Culliton, "Pajaro Dunes, the Search for Consensus," *Science*, vol. 216 (April 9, 1982).
6. Dwight D. Eisenhower, "Farewell Address to the Nation" (January 17, 1961). Reprinted in Stephen E. Ambrose and James Alden Barber, Jr., *The Military and American Society* (New York: The Free Press, 1972).
7. Quoted in Ann Crittenden, "Industry's Role in Academia," *New York Times* (July 22, 1981).
8. Organization for Economic Cooperation and Development, *The Research System*, vol. 1 (Paris: OECD, 1972), p. 249. A 1970 report of a UK working party similarly praised "the tradition of close collaboration between universities and industry" in the U.S.: United Kingdom Working Party on Universities and Industrial Research, *Industry, Science, and the Universities* (London: Confederation of British Industry, 1970).
9. National Science Board, *University-Industry Research Relationships: Myths, Realities, and Potentials*, Fourteenth Annual Report (Washington, D.C.: National Science Board, 1982), p. 1.
10. Leon Wofsy, "Biology and the University in the Marketplace: What's for Sale" (lecture at University of California, Berkeley, March 16, 1982).
11. Quoted in Margie Ploch, "Industry Invests in Research Centers," *High Technology* (May 1983), p. 15.
12. See, for example, David Landes, *The Unbound Prometheus* (Cambridge,

Eng.: Cambridge University Press, 1969), chap. 3 ("Continental Emulation").

13. Evidence in U.S. Congress, House Committee on Science and Technology, Subcommittee on Science, Research and Technology, *Government and Innovation: University-Industry Relations* (Hearings), 96th Cong., 1st sess. (July 31, August 1–2, 1979), p. 287.

14. See *Commercialization of Research* (cit. 1), pp. 33.

15. David F. Noble, *America by Design: Science, Technology, and the Rise of Corporate Capitalism* (New York: Knopf, 1977).

16. Elihu Root, "The Need for Organization in Scientific Research," *National Research Council Bulletin*, vol. 1 (October 1919), p. 8. Quoted in Noble, *America by Design* (cit. 15), p. 110.

17. Henry S. Pritchett, "The Function of Science in a Modern State," *National Research Council Bulletin*, vol. 1 (1918) p. 11. Quoted in Noble, *America by Design* (cit. 15), p. 157.

18. William Wickenden, "The Place of the Engineer in Modern America" (speech of March 20, 1936). Quoted in Noble, *America by Design* (cit. 15), p. 128.

19. Don K. Price, "Endless Frontier or Bureaucratic Mass?," in Gerald Holton and Robert S. Morison, eds., *The Limits of Scientific Inquiry* (New York: Norton, 1979).

20. Lewis E. Auerbach, "Scientists in the New Deal: A Pre-war Episode in Relations between Science and Government in the United States," *Minerva*, vol. 3, no. 4 Summer 1965). See also Daniel S. Greenberg, *The Politics of Pure Science* (New York: New American Library, 1967), chap. 3 ("When Science Was an Orphan").

21. Vannevar Bush, *Science: The Endless Frontier* (Washington, D.C.: U.S. Government Printing Office, 1945; reprinted Washington, D.C.: National Science Foundation, 1960).

22. National Science Board, *University-Industry Research Relationships* (cit. 9), p. 4.

23. Bruce L. R. Smith and Joseph J. Karlesky, *The State of Academic Science* (New York: Change Magazine Press, 1977). See also Walter S. Baer, "The Changing Relationship: Universities and Other R&D Performers," in Bruce L. R. Smith and Joseph J. Karlesky, eds., *The State of Academic Science: Background Papers* (New York: Change Magazine Press, 1978).

24. Baer, "The Changing Relationship" (cit. 23), pp. 85–86.

25. National Science Board, *Science Indicators 1980* (Washington, D.C.: National Science Board, 1981).

26. See Committee for Economic Development, Research and Policy Committee, *Stimulating Technological Progress* (New York: CED, January 18, 1980), and Industrial Research Institute, *Annual Report 1980* (New York: IRI, 1980).

27. Edward E. David, Jr., presidential address to American Association for Advancement of Science, Washington, D.C., January 6, 1979. Published as "Science Futures: The Industrial Connection," *Science*, vol. 203 (March 2, 1979).

28. The arrangement is described in Barbara J. Culliton, "Harvard and Monsanto: The $23-Million Alliance," *Science*, vol. 195 (February 25, 1977).

29. Massachusetts Institute of Technology, press release (April 28, 1980).
30. White House, press release (October 31, 1979).
31. Denis J. Prager and Gilbert S. Omenn, "Research, Innovation, and University-Industry Linkages," *Science*, vol. 207 (January 25, 1980).
32. George A. Keyworth, Brunswick Lecture to American Society for Microbiology, Atlanta, Ga., March 10, 1982.
33. National Science Board, statement of January 31, 1978.
34. Evidence in *Government and Innovation* (cit. 13), p. 76.
35. Ibid., p. 72.
36. See Colin Norman, "Electronics Firms Plug into the Universities," *Science*, vol. 217 (August 6, 1982).
37. Quoted in "Colleges and Industry Join to Counter Japan," *Business Week* (September 7, 1981).
38. "Business and Universities: A New Partnership," *Business Week* (December 20, 1982).
39. National Science Board, *University-Industry Research Relationships*, (cit. 9).
40. Quoted by R. E. Lyon of Exxon Research and Engineering Company, in "A Bridge Reconnecting Academic and Industry through Basic Research" (address delivered at Georgetown University, Washington, D.C.: March 1981).
41. Quoted in "Colleges and Business Counter Japan" (cit. 37).
42. National Science Board, *Science Indicators 1980* (cit. 25), p. 108.
43. Quoted in Rochelle L. Stanfield, "Campuses and Corporations: Industry Offers Money, But Not Without Strings," *National Journal* (November 29, 1980).
44. Herbert I. Fusfeld et al., *The Changing Tide* (New York: Center for Science and Technology Policy, New York University, November 1, 1981).
45. Quoted in "Industry's Role in Academia," *New York Times* (July 22, 1981).
46. Quoted in Stanfield, "Campuses and Corporations" (cit. 43).
47. Evidence in *Government and Innovation* (cit. 13), p. 73.
48. Ibid., p. 151.
49. Ibid., p. 77.
50. Christopher Freeman, "The Determinants of Innovation," *Futures* (June 1979).
51. Evidence in *Commercialization of Research* (cit. 1), p. 91.
52. Quoted in National Commission on Research, *Industry and the Universities: Developing Cooperative Research Relationships in the National Interest* (Washington, D.C.: NCR, August 1980), p. 21.
53. Stanford University, press release (November 18, 1981).
54. Quoted in Hal Lancaster, "Nonprofit Researchers Seeking Corporate Cash," *Wall Street Journal* (June 30, 1981).
55. Stanford University Press Office, report on Committee on Research meeting of March 11, 1981.
56. The term has, for example, recently become popular in describing common research projects among member countries of the European Economic Community. See "New Push for European Science Cooperation," *Science*, vol. 220 (June 10, 1983).

57. Quoted in David E. Sanger, "Business Rents a Lab Coat and Academe Hopes for the Best," *New York Times* (October 9, 1981).
58. Quoted in Stanford University, press release (March 30, 1981).
59. Quoted in Sanger, "Business Rents Lab Coat" (cit. 57).
60. Evidence in *Commercialization of Academic Biomedical Research* (cit. 1).
61. Philip J. Hilts, *Scientific Temperaments* (New York: Simon & Schuster, 1982).
62. Nicholas Wade, "Midas in Academe" (report for Twentieth Century Fund, New York, 1983 [mimeographed]).
63. Quoted in "Industry Is Taking a Renewed Interest in College Research," *Christian Science Monitor* (July 28, 1981).
64. Quoted in Stanford University report (cit. 55).
65. Evidence in *Commercialization of Research* (cit. 1), p. 76.
66. Quoted in Stanford University report (cit. 55).
67. Quoted in "A Campus Brain Drain," *New York Times* (June 28, 1981).
68. Ibid.
69. See Barbara J. Culliton, "Drug Firm and UC Settle Interferon Suit," *Science*, vol. 219 (January 28, 1983).
70. Quoted in Barbara J. Culliton, "Biomedical Research Enters the Marketplace," *New England Journal of Medicine*, vol. 304 (May 14, 1981), pp. 1195–1201.
71. Fox, "Can Academia Adapt?" (cit. 4).
72. See "Conflict of Interest on American Campus," *The Economist* (May 22, 1982).
73. Letter from Robert L. Rudd, professor of zoology, to Alan G. Marr, Dean of Graduate Studies and Research, University of California, Davis, November 10, 1981.
74. "Harvard Drafts Rules on Conflicts of Interest," *New York Times* (October 4, 1981).
75. Evidence in *Commercialization of Research* (cit. 1), p. 118.
76. Ibid., pp. 98–99.
77. Quoted in "Harvard Considers Commercial Role in DNA Research," *New York Times* (October 27, 1980).
78. Quoted in Nicholas Wade, "Gene Goldrush Splits Harvard, Worries Brokers," *Science*, vol. 210 (November 21, 1980).
79. Quoted in Mitchell C. Lynch, "Harvard's Plan for Gene-Splicing Meets with Scorn from Other Institutions," *Wall Street Journal* (November 12, 1980).
80. Derek Bok, *The President's Report 1979–80* (Cambridge, Mass.: Harvard University Press, 1981).
81. *Commercialization in Research* (cit. 1), p. 52.
82. Quoted in Culliton, "Pajaro Dunes" (cit. 5).
83. Quoted in Sanger, "Business Rents Lab Coat" (cit. 57).
84. Anne C. Roark, "UC Failure to Bare Business Ties Charged," *Los Angeles Times* (September 7, 1981); and Alan Hammond, "Methanol at MIT: Industry Influence Charged in Project Cancellation," *Science*, vol. 190 (November 21, 1975). See also Crittenden, "Industry's Role in Academia" (cit. 6).
85. Faculty members of University of California, Davis, letter to Dean Charles E. Hess (May 21, 1981).

86. See, for example, Mike Castro, "U.S. Professor Backs Off from Genetic Contract," *Sacramento Bee* (September 16, 1981).
87. Dean Charles E. Hess, memorandum (July 23, 1981).
88. "Harvard Adopts Guidelines on Sponsored Research," *New York Times* (May 22, 1983).
89. See "Making Private Interests Public," *Nature*, vol. 295 (February 4, 1982).
90. "Keeping Hands Clean," *Nature*, vol. 304 (July 7, 1983).
91. Quoted in Sanger, "Business Rents Lab Coat" (cit. 57).
92. National Commission on Research, *Industry and Universities* (cit. 52).
93. Ibid., p. 1.
94. Jerome B. Wiesner, "Universities and the Federal Government: A Troubled Relationship" (speech to National Council of University Research Administrators); reprinted in *Chemical and Engineering News* (December 11, 1978).
95. Quoted in "Business and Universities: A New Partnership," *Business Week* (December 20, 1982).
96. John Ziman, *Public Knowledge: The Social Dimension of Science* (Cambridge, Eng.: Cambridge University Press, 1968).
97. Quoted in Suzanne Perry, "Professors Can Land Corporate Sponsors for Research—If They Follow the Rules," *Chronicle of Higher Education* (April 20, 1983).
98. Quoted ibid.
99. Quoted in *The Research News*, vol. 31 (Ann Arbor: University of Michigan, June 1980).
100. Quoted ibid.
101. Quoted in "America Rushes to High Tech for Growth," *Business Week* (March 28, 1983).
102. Ibid.
103. Richard W. Lyman, "Federal Regulation and Institutional Autonomy: A University President's View," in Paul Seabury, ed., *Bureaucrats and Brainpower* (San Francisco: Institute for Contemporary Studies, 1979).
104. National Commission on Research, *Industry and the Universities* (cit. 52).
105. "Corporate Aid to Universities at Record High," *New York Times* (June 10, 1980).
106. Lyman, "Federal Regulation and Institutional Autonomy" (cit. 103).
107. Quoted in Jack Magarell, "Academe and Industry Weigh a New Alliance," *Chronicle of Higher Education* (February 5, 1979).
108. Quoted in ibid.
109. See "Business-Higher Ed Forum Opposes 'Intrusive' Federal Regulations," *Higher Education and National Affairs*, vol. 3. (March 27, 1981).
110. Quoted in Stanfield, "Campuses and Corporations" (cit. 43).
111. National Commission on Research, *Accountability: Restoring the Quality of Partnership* (Washington, D.C.: National Commission on Research, March 1980).
112. Tom Moss, "New Partnerships a Bargain for Industry, a Boon for Colleges and Universities," *Chronicle of Higher Education* (April 6, 1983).
113. Quoted in "The Colleges Discover a Profit in Patents," *Business Week* (January 12, 1981).
114. Quoted in Culliton, "Biomedical Research" (cit. 69).

115. Robert Merton, "The Normative Structure of Science," in *The Sociology of Science* (Chicago: University of Chicago Press, 1973).
116. "Memo Spells Out Technology Transfer Policies," *Harvard Gazette* (October 31, 1980).
117. Derek Bok, *The President's Report* (cit. 80).
118. See Barry Fox, "Decision Due in Million-Dollar Patent Row," *New Scientist* (June 30, 1983).
119. Moss, "New Partnerships" (cit. 112).
120. Evidence in U.S. Congress, Senate Select Committee on Small Business, Subcommittee on Monopoly and Anti-competitive Practices, *Government Patent Policies: Institutional Patent Agreements* (Hearings), 96th Cong., 1st sess. (May 22–23, June 20–21, 26, 1979), p. 339.
121. "Patents Called a 'Must' for Companies Sponsoring Research," *Chronicle of Higher Education* (November 17, 1982).
122. U.S. Congress, Senate, *Congressional Record*, vol. 126 (February 6, 1980), S1034.
123. Ralph Nader, letter to Jay Solomon (March 20, 1978).
124. Quoted ibid.
125. Russell Long, "Dear Colleague" letter, U.S. Senate (February 21, 1980).
126. Joshua Lederberg, letter to Senator Gaylord Nelson (May 22, 1978).
127. Wiesner, "Universities and Federal Government" (cit. 94).
128. Robert Hatfield, Introduction to Seabury, ed., *Bureaucrats and Brainpower* (cit. 103).
129. Wiesner, "Universities and Federal Government" (cit. 94).
130. Caspar Weinberger, "Regulating the Universities," in Seabury, ed., *Bureaucrats and Brainpower* (cit. 103).
131. U.S. Congress, House Committee on Government Operations, Subcommittee, *Accountability of Educational Institutions for Federal Funds and the Effectiveness of Federal Audits* (Hearings), 96th Cong., 1st sess. (July 17, 19, 1979), p. 196.
132. Dael Wolfle, "The Changing Relationship" in Smith and Karlesky, eds., *Background Papers* (cit. 23).
133. Greenberg, *Politics of Pure Science* (cit. 20).
134. See *Accountability of Educational Institutions* (cit. 131), pp. 28–90.
135. Evidence of Clifford Melby, Audit Manager, General Accounting Office, ibid., p. 20.
136. "The Colleges' Big Con Game with U.S. Grants," *Business Week* (December 17, 1979).
137. Wiesner, "Universities and Federal Government" (cit. 94).
138. Sloan Commission on Government and Higher Education, "A Program for Renewed Partnership" (March 1980 report).
139. National Commission on Research, *Accountability: Restoring the Quality of Partnership* (cit. 111) (Washington, D.C.: NCR, March 1980).
140. A. Bartlett Giamatti, "Science and the University," *Science*, vol. 210 (November 28, 1980).
141. Business–Higher Education Forum, *Statement on Federal Regulatory Reform* (Washington, D.C.: American Council on Education, March 1981).
142. Quoted in Timothy B. Clark, "Universities Give Administration a 'C' in Its Campaign Against Regulation," *National Journal* (August 29, 1981).

143. Quoted ibid.
144. Joseph S. Warner, "The Third Stage of Research: Auditing," *Science*, vol. 220 (June 10, 1983).
145. Colin Norman, "Audit May Cost UC Millions," *Science*, vol. 216 (April 16, 1982).
146. See Anne C. Roark, "Academic Ties Face Challenge," *Los Angeles Times* (September 26, 1981).
147. Bruce Owen and Ronald Brautigan, *The Regulation Game* (Cambridge, Mass.: Ballinger, 1978).
148. National Commission on Research, *Industry and Universities* (cit. 52), p. 21.
149. Michael Heylin, "Industry-Academic Ties in Chemistry Probed," *Chemical and Engineering News* (October 29, 1979).
150. Edward Kane, "The Environment for R&D," *Chemical and Engineering News* (December 4, 1978).
151. "New President Is Chosen at MIT; He Warns of U.S. Technology Lag," *New York Times* (October 6, 1980).
152. *New York Times* (July 22, 1980).
153. Wiesner, "Universities and Federal Government" (cit. 94).
154. Christopher DeMuth, "Harvard's Policy Analysis Component," in "Joint MIT-Harvard Program on the Impact of Chemicals on Human Health and the Environment" (Cambridge, Mass.: John F. Kennedy School of Government, April 30, 1979 [mimeographed]).
155. See statement by Samuel A. Goldblith, MIT vice-president of resource development, in *Government and Innovation* (cit. 13).
156. Business–Higher Education Forum, *America's Competitive Challenge: The Need for a National Response* (Washington, D.C.: American Council on Education, April 1983).
157. Quoted in Seabury, ed., *Bureaucrats and Brainpower* (cit. 103), p. 21.
158. Wolfle, "The Changing Relationship" (cit. 132), p. 33.
159. Evidence in *Commercialization of Research* (cit. 1), p. 93.
160. Moss, "New Partnerships" (cit. 112).
161. David Noble and Nancy Pfund, "Business Goes Back to College," *The Nation* (September 19, 1980). Harvard's president Derek Bok, not surprisingly, claimed that this charge, directed primarily at the university's arrangement with Monsanto, gave a "distorted" picture, since "the company involved will not have special access to an entire school or department but only a working relationship with the scientists who receive financial support" (see Bok, *President's Report* [cit. 80]).
162. Quoted in "University Links with Industry" (cit. 99).
163. "Government Scrutinizes Links between Genetics Industry and Universities," *New York Times* (June 16, 1981).
164. National Commission on Research, *Industry and Universities* (cit. 52), p. 15.
165. Business–Higher Education Forum, *America's Competitive Challenge* (cit. 156), p. 5.
166. Karl Marx, preface to "A Contribution to the Critique of Political Economy," in Karl Marx, *Early Writings*. (Harmondsworth: Penguin Books, 1975).

167. Quoted in "Business and Universities" (cit. 95).
168. Quoted in Robert Marshak, "Focusing Applied Research on Global Problems," *Physics Today* (November 1979).
169. Carnegie Foundation for the Advancement of Teaching, *Higher Learning in the Nation's Service* (Washington, D.C.: Carnegie Foundation, November 1981).
170. Quoted in "Business and Universities" (cit. 95).
171. Quoted ibid.
172. Quoted in "MIT Favoring Offer on Biomedical Institute," *New York Times* (October 1, 1981).
173. Quoted in "Business and Universities" (cit. 195).
174. David Noble, "The Selling of the University," *The Nation* (February 6, 1982).

CHAPTER THREE

1. Colin Norman, "Knowledge and Power: The Global Research and Development Budget," *Worldwatch Paper 31* (Washington, D.C.: Worldwatch Institute, July 1979).
2. Ruth Szilard, *World Military and Social Expenditures 1981* (Leesburg, Va.: World Priorities, 1981).
3. Based on figures taken from Office of Management and Budget, "OMB Data for Special Analysis K" (Washington, D.C.: OMB, 1983); and Willis H. Shapley et al., *AAAS Report VIII: Research and Development, FY 1984* (Washington, D.C.: American Association for the Advancement of Science, 1983).
4. Evidence in U.S. Congress, House Committee on Science and Technology, *U.S. Science and Technology under Budget Stress* (Hearings), 97th Cong., 1st and 2d sess. (December 10, 1981; February 2–4, 1982).
5. Figures based on OMB, "Special Analysis K" (cit. 3). An article in *Business Week* stated: "America's universities are swinging back into a Pentagon orbit after twelve years of self-imposed freedom from military research" ("The Reenlistment of the Campus," *Business Week* [June 14, 1982]).
6. Quoted in Jennifer Bingham Hull, "Defense Contracts Stir Some Student Protests on College Campuses," *Wall Street Journal* (May 20, 1983), p. 1.
7. Quoted in "Good Links Reported between DoD, Universities," *Science and Government Report* (May 1, 1983), p. 3.
8. Quoted in "Defense Department Boosts Research Spending," *Chemical and Engineering News* (April 27, 1981).
9. Science for the People, "Scientists and the Military" (mimeographed pamphlet, January 1982).
10. "Signs of Doubt," *Nature*, vol. 295 (February 11, 1982). See also Hull, "Defense Contracts" (cit. 6).
11. Norman, "Knowledge and Power" (cit. 1).
12. Science for the People, "Scientists and Military" (cit. 9).
13. Colin Norman, "Downsizing at the University of Michigan," *Science*, vol. 220 (April 15, 1983).

14. Robert A. Rosenbaum et al., "Federal Restrictions on Research: Academic Freedom and National Security," *Academe: Bulletin of the American Association of University Professors*, vol. 68 (September–October 1982).

15. For a general discussion of these issues, see Dorothy Nelkin, "Intellectual Property: The Control of Scientific Information," *Science*, vol. 216 (May 14, 1982); James R. Ferguson, "Scientific Freedom, National Security, and the First Amendment," *Science*, vol. 221 (August 12, 1983).

16. National Academy of Sciences, Committee on Science, Engineering, and Public Policy, Panel on Scientific Communication and National Security, *Scientific Communication and National Security* (Washington, D.C.: National Academy Press, 1982), p. 5 (hereafter cited as *Corson Report*).

17. Ibid., p. 5.

18. Department of Defense–University Forum, statement endorsed at meeting of April 19, 1983.

19. Colin Norman, "Administration Grapples with Export Controls," *Science*, vol. 220 (June 3, 1983).

20. "An Ominous Shift to Secrecy," *Business Week* (October 18, 1982), p. 142.

21. Harvey M. Sapolsky, "Academic Science and the Military: The Years Since the Second World War," in Nathan Reingold, ed., *The Sciences in the American Context: New Perspectives* (Washington, D.C.: Smithsonian Institution, 1979).

22. "Defense Department to Encourage Industry-University Ties," *Chronicle of Higher Education* (May 4, 1983). This proposal had initially been made by William J. Perry under the Carter administration; see "DoD Encourages Industry to Subcontract Research," *Physics Today* (December 1980).

23. "Soviet Lag in Key Weapons Technology," *Science*, vol. 219 (March 18, 1983).

24. Szilard, *World Military and Social Expenditures 1981* (cit. 2).

25. See R. Jeffrey Smith, "Reagan Plans New ABM Effort," *Science*, vol. 220 (April 8, 1983).

26. Marek Thee, "The Arms Race, Armaments Dynamics, Military Research, and Development and Disarmament," *Bulletin of Peace Proposals*, vol. 9, no. 2 (1978). Richard Barnett of the Institute of Policy Studies in Washington, D.C., suggests that "the very existence of research and development programs is destabilizing for they create an edgy military environment in which military planners think seriously about hair-trigger responses" ("Challenging the Myths of National Security," *New York Times Magazine* [April 1, 1979]).

27. See David F. Noble, *America by Design: Science, Technology, and the Rise of Corporate Capitalism* (New York: Knopf, 1977), p. 150.

28. Evidence in *U.S. Science and Technology* (cit. 4).

29. Don K. Price, *The Scientific Estate* (Cambridge, Mass.: Harvard University Press, 1965).

30. Hunter Dupree, *Science in the Federal Government: A History of Policies and Activities to 1940* (Cambridge, Mass.: Harvard University Press, 1957).

31. Daniel J. Kevles, "Scientists, the Military, and the Control of Postwar Defense Research: The Case of the Research Board for National Security," *Technology and Culture*, vol. 16 (1975) pp. 20–47.

32. See Carroll Pursell, "Science Agencies in World War II: The OSRD and Its Challenges," in Reingold, ed., *Sciences in American Context* (cit. 21).

33. Quoted in Michael Klare, *The University-Military-Police Complex* (North American Congress on Latin America, 1970).

34. Daniel S. Greenberg, *The Politics of Pure Science* (New York: New American Library, 1967).

35. Quoted in Kevles, "Scientists, Military" (cit. 31).

36. Quoted ibid.

37. Ibid.

38. See Charles J. V. Murphy, "The White House Since Sputnik," *Fortune* (January 1958).

39. Ibid.

40. James Fallows, *The National Defense* (Garden City, N.Y.: Doubleday, 1981).

41. Klare, *University-Military-Police Complex* (cit. 32).

42. Quoted ibid.

43. See Jonathan Allen, ed., *March 4: Scientists, Students, Society* (Cambridge, Mass.: MIT Press, 1970).

44. U.S. Congress, Senate, *Congressional Record*, vol. 113 (December 13, 1967), S18485.

45. Walter S. Baer, "The Changing Relationship: Universities and Other R&D Performers," in Bruce L. R. Smith and Joseph J. Karlesky, eds., *The State of Academic Science: Background Papers* (New York: Change Magazine Press, 1978).

46. Quoted in Allen, ed., *March 4* (cit. 43).

47. John Walsh, "NIH: Demand Increases for Applications of Research," *Science*, vol. 153 (July 8, 1966).

48. See C. W. Sherwin and R. S. Isenson, "Project Hindsight," *Science*, vol. 156 (June 23, 1967), p. 1571–77. For a critique of the methodology used, together with political background, see K. Krielkamp, "Hindsight and the Real World of Science Policy," *Science Studies* (1971), pp. 43–66.

49. Public Law 91–121, Section 203.

50. Evidence in U.S. Congress, House Committee on Armed Services, Subcommittee on Research and Development, *Capability of the Academic Community to Respond to R&D Needs* (Hearings), 97th Cong., 2d sess. (April 3, 1981).

51. Quoted in Rodney Nichols, "Mission-Oriented R&D," *Science*, vol. 172 (April 2, 1971).

52. Quoted ibid.

53. See Allen, ed., *March 4* (cit. 43), in which one scientist is quoted as saying during the March 7 demonstration at MIT that "one often has to do some incredible stretching of an idea to convince some military agency of the military connection."

54. Lord Rothschild, *Framework for Government Research and Development* (London: HMSO, Cmnd 5046, 1972).

55. Nichols, "Mission-Oriented R&D" (cit. 51).

56. National Science Board, *Science Indicators 1978* (Washington, D.C.: National Science Board, 1979), p. 194.

57. Ibid.

58. Organization for Economic Cooperation and Development, *Science, Growth, and Society: A New Perspective* (Paris: OECD, 1971).

59. John Foster, "The Defense Role of U.S. Colleges," *New York Times* (January 12, 1970).

60. See, for example, Deborah Shapley, "Air Force R&D Policy: More for Basic Research, Universities," *Science*, vol. 187 (January 24, 1975).

61. Herbert F. York and G. Allen Greb, "Military Research and Development: A Post-War History," *Bulletin of Atomic Scientists* (January 1977).

62. "DoD Basic Research: An Uphill Climb," *Physics Today* (January 1980).

63. Quoted in *Business Week* (August 11, 1980).

64. For a summary of Perry's philosophy, see "William Perry and the Weapons Gamble," *Science*, vol. 211 (February 13, 1981). Also William Perry and Cynthia Roberts, "Winning Through Sophistication: How to Meet the Soviet Military Challenge," *Technology Review* (July 1982).

65. Quoted in "Perry and Weapons Gamble" (cit. 64).

66. Quoted in "Cruise Missiles: U.S. Heavily Reliant on New Technology," *Washington Post* (June 30, 1980).

67. Science Advisor's Panel on Basic Research in Department of Defense, *Basic Research in the Department of Defense* (Washington, D.C.: Office of Science and Technology Policy, June 22, 1978).

68. Ibid.

69. Ibid.

70. Quoted in "DoD Basic Research" (cit. 62).

71. Science Adviser's Panel, *Basic Research in Department of Defense*, (cit. 67).

72. Ibid.

73. Evidence in *Capability of Academic Community to Respond* (cit. 50).

74. Ibid.

75. Robert Reinhold, "Pentagon Renews Ties with Colleges," *New York Times* (May 13, 1980).

76. Quoted ibid.

77. Jacques Gansler, *The Defense Industry* (Cambridge, Mass.: MIT Press, 1980).

78. "TRW Leads a Revolution in Managing Technology," *Business Week* (November 15, 1982).

79. Quoted in *The Economist* (July 17, 1982). The same magazine reported seven months later that "the American defense business could hardly be doing better if the country were at war" ("Resurrection in the Death Business," *The Economist* [February 12, 1983]).

80. "Military Technology Is America's Gold," advertisement, *New York Times* (April 12, 1981).

81. "Brains vs. Bucks," *Wall Street Journal* (September 3, 1981).

82. Quoted in "Weinberger Asks War Readiness for Many Fronts," *Wall Street Journal* (May 6, 1981).

83. Evidence in *Capability of Academic Community to Respond* (cit. 50).

84. Ibid. The President of the National Defense University has similarly, recently claimed that the lack of adequate science and technology teaching in schools is a "risk to military preparedness." Quoted in "Notes on Computers," *Chronicle of Higher Education* (October 12, 1983).

85. See the remarks in the National Commission of Research, *Funding Mech-*

anisms: Balancing Objectives and Resources in University Research (Washington, D.C.: NCR, May 1980): "One of the most commonly perceived weaknesses in the present system [of federal support for university research] is the lack of continuity. For maximum effectiveness, research projects must operate for a period long enough for serious accomplishment. . . . In many basic research fields annual or biannual renewal cycles are simply too short to permit acquisition of equipment and supplies, staffing for research activity, and implementing the research strategy."

86. Association of American Universities, *The Scientific Instrumentation Needs of Research Universities* (Washington, D.C.: AAU, June 1980).

87. Department of Defense, *Department of Defense Budget for Fiscal Year 1983* (Washington, D.C.: DoD, 1982).

88. "Pentagon Plan Aims at Luring Students into Military-Related Doctoral Programs," *Chronicle of Higher Education* (September 7, 1981).

89. Norman, "Downsizing" (cit. 13).

90. Evidence to hearing before U.S. Congress Senate Committee on Commerce, Subcommittee on Science, Technology, and Space (March 7, 1979).

91. Evidence in *Capability of Academic Community to Respond* (cit. 50). See also Robert Sproull, "Federal Regulation and the Natural Sciences," in Paul Seabury, ed., *Bureaucrats and Brainpower* (San Francisco: Institute for Contemporary Studies, 1979).

92. Kim McDonald, "Defense: A Booming Bankroll for Basic Science," *Science and Government Report* (September 15, 1981).

93. U.S. House of Representatives, *Congressional Record* (July 10, 1981), H4209.

94. For a general discussion of the congressional difficulties raised by the defense budget, see Willis H. Shapley et al., *Research and Development: AAAS Report VI, 1982* (Washington, D.C.: American Association for the Advancement of Science, 1981), chap. 6 ("R&D for National Defense").

95. See Samuel H. Day, Jr., "The Nuclear Weapons Labs," *Bulletin of the Atomic Scientists*, vol. 33, April 1977.

96. Faculty Members of University of California, "Faculty Call for UC Severance from Nuclear Weapons Laboratory," press release (July 17, 1979).

97. Charles Schwartz, "The Berkeley Weapons Controversy," *Bulletin of Atomic Scientists* (September 1978).

98. Los Alamos Scientific Laboratory, office memorandum (July 18, 1977). Quoted ibid.

99. Report of committee chaired by Paul Zinner, professor of political science. Quoted ibid.

100. William Geberding et al., *Report of the Committee to Examine the University's Relationship with the Los Alamos and Lawrence Livermore Laboratories* (Berkeley: University of California, October 2, 1978).

101. Quoted in "U.S. Questions UC Plan for Weapon Labs," *Los Angeles Times* (November 1980).

102. "Statement of Reservations" issued by six members of the Energy Research Advisory Board (Thomas Cochran, John Gibbons, Denis Hayes, John Holdren, Margaret Kivelson, David Pimentel).

103. "California Panel Wants Study of Nuclear Labs," *Chronicle of Higher Education* (May 25, 1983).
104. Quoted in Richard G. Hewlett, "Born Classified in the AEC: A Historian's View," *Bulletin of Atomic Scientists* (December 1981).
105. Quoted ibid.
106. See P. V. Dankwerts, "The Fire at Windscale," *New Scientist* (November 18, 1982).
107. Hewlett, "Born Classified" (cit. 104).
108. James Newman and Byron Miller, *The Control of Atomic Energy* (New York: McGraw-Hill, 1948).
109. Harold P. Green, "Where the Balance Has Been Struck: Information Control under the Atomic Energy Act" (paper to AAAS meeting, January 7, 1982).
110. See *Scientific American* (May 1950), p. 26.
111. See "Military in Clash over U.S. Nuclear Fusion Research," *Nature*, vol. 281 (October 11, 1979).
112. Quoted in "Should Inertial Confinement Fusion Be Classified?," *Physics Today* (August 1980).
113. Quoted ibid.
114. Quoted ibid.
115. William D. Metz, "Thermonuclear Fusion: U.S. Puts Wraps on Latest Soviet Work," *Science*, vol. 194 (October 8, 1976).
116. For a discussion of the *Progressive* case and its implications, see Mary M. Cheh, "The *Progressive* Case and the Atomic Energy Act: Waking to the Dangers of Government Information Controls," *George Washington Law Review*, vol. 48, no. 2 (January 1980). See also Mary M. Cheh, "Government Control of Private Ideas," and Paul M. McCloskey, "*Progressive* Case and the Need to Amend the Atomic Energy Act" (papers to meeting organized by American Association for Advancement of Science, Washington, D.C., January 7, 1982).
117. *United States v. Progressive, Inc.*, 467 F Supp. 990 (W. D. Wis. 1979) at 996.
118. Cheh, "*Progressive* Case" (cit. 116).
119. David Kahn, *The Code Breakers* (New York: Macmillan, 1967).
120. Evidence in U.S. Congress, House Committee on Government Operations, Subcommittee, *The Classification of Private Ideas* (Hearings) 96th Cong., 2d sess. (February 28, March 20, August 21, 1980).
121. Bobby Inman, "The NSA Perspective on Telecommunications Protection in the Nongovernment Sector," reprinted in *Classification Hearings* (cit. 120).
122. For a description of the Davida case, see David Kahn, "Cryptology Goes Public," *Foreign Affairs* (Fall 1979).
123. "Federal Agency Drops Order Imposing Secrecy on Research Projects at University of Wisconsin," *Chronicle of Higher Education* (June 19, 1978).
124. See Deborah Shapley and Gina Bari Kolata, "Cryptology: Scientists Puzzle over Threat to Open Research," *Science*, vol. 197 (September 30, 1977).
125. International Traffic in Arms Regulations (22 C.F.R. Sections 120.01–130.33).

126. Quoted in Deborah Shapley, "Intelligence Agency Chief Seeks 'Dialogue' with Academics," *Science*, vol. 202 (October 27, 1978).

127. Fred W. Weingarten, NSF memorandum (May 2, 1977). Reprinted in *Classification Hearings* (cit. 120).

128. Richard Atkinson, letter to Admiral Bobby Inman (September 7, 1978). Reprinted in *Classification Hearings* (cit. 120).

129. Quoted in Gina Bari Kolata, "Cryptography: A New Clash Between Academic Freedom and National Security," *Science*, vol. 209 (August 29, 1980).

130. Quoted ibid.

131. U.S. Congress, House Committee on Government Operations, *The Classification of Private Ideas*, Report No. 96-1540 (December 22, 1980).

132. Shapley, "Intelligence Agency Chief" (cit. 126).

133. Weingarten, memo (cit. 127).

134. Donald Langenberg, deputy director of National Science Foundation, letter to William B. Robinson, State Department (March 11, 1981).

135. "The Pentagon's Push for Superfast ICs," *Business Week* (November 27, 1978).

136. William J. Perry, testimony to U.S. Congress, Senate Committee on Armed Services, *Hearings on Department of Defense Authorization for Appropriations for Fiscal Year 1980*, 96th Cong., 1st sess. (date n.a.).

137. Robert Reinhold, "Pentagon Renews Ties with Colleges," *New York Times* (May 13, 1980).

138. "Controls Sought on Technology Exports," *Aviation Week* (February 16, 1981).

139. Betac Corporation, "Final Report: Phase 2 of the United States Technology Transfer Export Controls Project" (Arlington, Va.: Betac, January 1980). Quoted in *Classification Report* (cit. 131).

140. *Classification Report* (cit. 131).

141. "New Pentagon Rules on Overseas Students," *Nature*, vol. 289 (February 26, 1981).

142. Donald Kennedy et al., letter to Secretary of Commerce Malcolm Baldridge et al. (February 27, 1981). See "Universities Complain at Pentagon Policy," *Nature*, vol. 290 (April 9, 1981).

143. James Buckley, letter to Donald Kennedy (July 3, 1981). See also "U.S. Tries to Allay Universities' Fears on Security Rules," *Chronicle of Higher Education* (January 20, 1982).

144. John Walsh, "DoD Funds More Research in Universities," *Science*, vol. 212 (May 29, 1981).

145. See Office of Secretary of Defense, "Initial Military Critical Technologies List," *Federal Register*, 45:192 (October 1, 1980).

146. Admiral Bobby Inman, "National Security and Technical Information" (speech to AAAS annual meeting, Washington, D.C., January 7, 1982). For summary of the debate leading up to Inman's speech, see Christopher Paine, "Admiral Inman's Tidal Wave," *Bulletin of Atomic Scientists* (March 1982).

147. See draft report by U.S. Government Interagency Working Group on Competitive and Transfer Aspects of Biotechnology, published as *Biobusiness World Data Base* (New York: McGraw-Hill, 1983). The report claims: "Bio-

technology can enhance the military capabilities of potential United States adversaries. Therefore controls to monitor and restrict biotechnology exports are warranted." See also letter from State Department to the National Academy of Sciences (November 6, 1981), forbidding a Soviet scientist visiting the U.S. from access to any genetic engineering research at MIT (in *Corson Report* [cit. 16], Appendix J).

148. See "Scientists Protest at Exclusion of Russians from Conferences," *Nature*, vol. 283 (February 28, 1980). Quoted in Gina Kolata, *Science*, vol. 197 (July 29, 1977).
149. Ibid.
150. See Rosemary Chalk, "Security and Scientific Communications," *Bulletin of the Atomic Scientists*, vol. 37 (August–September 1983).
151. Gerald J. Liebermann, Stanford University, letter to Diana B. Bieliauskas, National Academy of Sciences (Janaury 13, 1982).
152. Stanford University, press release (January 14, 1982).
153. *Corson Report* (cit. 16).
154. U.S. Congress, House Committee on Foreign Affairs, *Export Administration Amendments Act of 1981*, Report No. 97-57, 97th Cong., 1st sess., 1981.
155. "Reagan Signs Order on Classification," *Science*, vol. 216 (April 16, 1982).
156. Evidence in *Capability of Academic Community to Respond* (cit. 50).
157. Rosenbaum et al., "Federal Restrictions" (cit. 14).
158. *United States* v. *Edler Industries Inc.*, 579 F 2nd 516 (9th Circuit 1978).
159. John M. Harmon, Assistant Attorney General, memorandum to Frank Press, director of Office of Science and Technology Policy (May 11, 1978). Reprinted in *Classification Hearings* (cit. 120).
160. *Corson Report* (cit. 16), p. 112.
161. Quoted in "An Ominous Shift to Secrecy," *Business Week* (October 12, 1982), p. 138.
162. Quoted in Defense Science Board Task Force, *An Analysis of Export Control of U.S. Technology: A DoD Perspective* (Washington, D.C.: U.S. Department of Defense, 1976).
163. *Corson Report* (cit. 16), p. 42.
164. Quoted in "Federal Agency Imposing Secrecy" (cit. 123).
165. See Norman, "Administration/Export Controls" (cit. 19).
166. "More Secrecy on Cryptography Research," *Nature*, vol. 289 (February 19, 1981).
167. Inman, "National Security and Technical Information" (cit. 146).
168. Gina Bari Kolata, "Bills Proposed to Curb Export of Technology," *Science*, vol. 217 (September 10, 1982).
169. All quoted in Philip J. Hilts, "Scientists Call Research Censorship a 'Nightmare,' " *Washington Post* (January 7, 1982).
170. Inman, "National Security and Technical Information" (cit. 146).
171. Lawrence Brady, "Taking Back the Rope: Technology Transfer and U.S. Security" (speech to Association of Former Intelligence Officers, Washington, D.C., March 29, 1982). Quoted in *Corson Report* (cit. 16), p. 10.
172. Donald Kennedy, address to Stanford conference, Los Angeles, March 7, 1982. Quoted in Stanford University, press release (March 5, 1982).

173. Evidence in *Capability of Academic Community to Respond* (cit. 50).
174. Edward Teller, "Secrecy, the Road to Nowhere," *Technology Review* (October 1981).
175. Rosenbaum et al., "Federal Restrictions" (cit. 14).
176. Cheh, "Government Control of Private Ideas" (cit. 116).
177. See George Davida, "Safety in Numbers," *The Sciences* (July/August 1981). Davida wrote: "I think the academic community has made an important and quite dangerous, concession to the NSA, one which could easily damage research in this field for some time, and which in the long run could undermine the civil liberties of the entire country."
178. *Corson Report* (cit. 16).
179. Richard Mandelbaum, letter to *Science*, vol. 210 (November 28, 1980).
180. See "U.S. Security Worries—No Compromise," *Nature*, vol. 291 (June 4, 1981). The mathematical and computer sciences advisory committee said that the ACE proposal for voluntary prepublication review was "a direct and serious threat to NSF's charter of furthering basic scientific research."
181. Corson Report (cit. 16).
182. Department of Defense–University Forum statement (cit. 18).
183. "Computer Encryption and the NSA Connection," *Science*, vol. 197 (July 29, 1977).
184. Walter Sullivan, "U.S. Seeks Links to Industry on Computer Defenses," *New York Times* (August 12, 1981).
185. See discussion on patents in *Classification Report* (cit. 131).
186. Green, "Where Balance Has Been Struck" (cit. 109).
187. See "Padlocking the Laboratory," *Business Week* (April 4, 1983). *Business Week* quotes a DoD official as claiming that "defense contractors are going to roll over and accept these restrictions" because the market is so important to them. The magazine adds: "That seems to be what is happening. Companies involved in the big government efforts to develop VHSICs have all gone mum about their work."
188. Daniel C. Schwartz, "Scientific Freedom and National Security" (paper to AAAS meeting, Washington, D.C., January 7, 1982).
189. Cheh, *The Progressive Case* (cit. 116).
190. Quoted in "U.S. Questions UC Plan" (cit. 101).
191. Paul N. McCloskey, "*Progressive* Case" (cit. 116).
192. Quoted in Allen, ed., *March 4* (cit. 43).
193. Quoted in "A Role for Universities in Ending the Arms Race," *Chronicle of Higher Education* (July 6, 1981).
194. Quoted in "White House Scorns Anti-nuclear Scientists," *New Scientist*, (May 26, 1983).
195. Quoted in Janet Stobart, "Pope Asks Scientists to Shun Military Work," *Chronicle of Higher Education*, (November 23, 1983).
196. Quoted in Colin Norman, "Nuclear Vote Threatens Draper Lab,", *Science*, vol. 222 (October 7, 1983).
197. See "Cambridge Votes Non-nuclear," *Nature*, vol. 306 (November 24, 1983).
198. See Ben H. Bagdikian, "A Most Insidious Case," *The Quill* (June 1979).
199. See Alice Kimball Smith, *A Peril and a Hope* (Chicago: University of Chicago Press. 1965). Edward Teller later wrote that Oppenheimer "thought it

improper for a scientist to use his prestige as a platform for political pronouncements. . . . I was happy to accept his word and his authority. I did not circulate Szilard's petition. Today I regret that I did not" (Edward Teller with Allen Brown, *The Legacy of Hiroshima* [Garden City, N.Y.: Doubleday, 1962]).

CHAPTER FOUR

1. For a concise expression of the Reagan administration's concerns about Soviet access to U.S. science and technology, see Richard Perle, "The Soviet Connection," *Defense 82* (February 1982), pp. 10–15.
2. See "Scientific Cooperation Endorsed at Summit," *Science*, vol. 220 (June 17, 1983).
3. National Science Board, "Statement on Science in the International Setting" (adopted at meeting of September 16–17, 1982).
4. These, for example, are the main themes of Eugene B. Skolnikoff, *Science, Technology, and American Foreign Policy* (Cambridge, Mass.: MIT Press, 1967). They are also the focus of the three volumes of the Congressional Research Service, *Science, Technology, and Diplomacy in an Age of Interdependence* (report for U.S. Congress, House Committee on International Relations, Subcommittee on International Security and Scientific Affairs, June 1976). For a good review of the literature, see Brigitte Schroeder-Gudehus, "Science, Technology, and Foreign Policy," in Ina Spiegel-Rösing and Derek de Solla Price, eds., *Science Technology and Society: A Cross-Disciplinary Perspective* (Berkeley/London: Sage, 1977).
5. Evidence to U.S. Congress, Senate Committee on Commerce, Subcommittee on Science, Technology, and Space, *U.S. Policies and Initiatives for the U.N. Conference on Science and Technology for Development* (July 17, 1979), 96th Cong., 1st sess., p. 9.
6. Organization for Economic Cooperation and Development, *Technical Change and Economic Policy* (Paris: OECD, 1980).
7. Thomas Pickering, presentation to AAAS colloquium on R&D policy, June 20, 1979. Published in Don I. Phillips et al., eds., *Colloquium Proceedings 19–20 June 1979* (Washington, D.C.: AAAS Report No. 79-R-14, October 1979).
8. Henry Nau, *National Politics and International Technology: Nuclear Reactor Development in Western Europe* (Baltimore: Johns Hopkins University Press, 1974).
9. National Science Board, *Science Indicators 1980* (Washington, D.C.: National Science Board, 1981), Appendix tables 1–24, 1–26, 1–19.
10. Edwin Mansfield, paper to National Science Foundation, May 21, 1977 (mimeographed).
11. Edwin Mansfield, Anthony Romeo, and Samuel Wigner, "Foreign Trade and U.S. Research and Development," *Review of Economics and Statistics* (February 1979), p. 55.
12. Meryl L. Kroner, "U.S. Transactions in Royalties and Fees, 1967–78," *Survey of Current Business*, vol. 60 (January 1980).

13. Organization for Economic Cooperation and Development, *North-South Technology Transfer: The Adjustments Ahead* (Paris: OECD, February 1981).

14. Defense Science Board Task Force, *An Analysis of Export Controls of U.S. Technology: A DoD Perspective* (Washington, D.C.: U.S. Department of Defense, 1976).

15. For a detailed analysis of the way that multinational corporations control access to the scientific knowledge required for the development of microelectronics production, see Dieter Ernst, *The Global Race in Microelectronics* (Frankfurt: Campus Verlag, 1983).

16. See, for example, Philip J. Hilts, "U.S. Science Losing Its Magic as Rivals Excel," *Washington Post* (May 24, 1983).

17. See Alan T. Bull et al., *Biotechnology: International Trends and Perspectives* (Paris: OECD, 1982). The OECD report states: "Present indications are that a significant brain drain is taking place." In a press release on September 28, 1982, the British Science and Engineering Council announced that it had awarded a contract to the Institute of Manpower Studies to carry out a pilot study into "the scale of the brain death of biotechnologists leaving the U.K.", and to establish "the impact of this loss to biotechnology and to the U.K. economy."

18. Harold E. Fitzgibbons, "A European Perspective on U.S. High Technology Competition," *National Journal* (January 22, 1983).

19. Ibid.

20. See, for example, "Open Row about Joint Space Project," *Nature*, vol. 290 (March 5, 1981).

21. See "How Washington Put the Squeeze on Austria," *Business Week* (April 4, 1983).

22. See Shroeder-Gudehus, "Science, Technology, Foreign Policy" (cit. 4). She comments: "Scientific and technical superiority usually enables a dominant nation further to consolidate and extend its already powerful position, be it only by setting the standards of international competition in military and civilian technology."

23. Colin Norman, "Knowledge and Power: The Global Research and Development Budget," *Worldwatch Paper 31* (Washington, D.C.: Worldwatch Institute, July 1979).

24. Ibid.

25. Thomas N. Gladwin and Ingo Walter, *Multinationals Under Fire* (New York: John Wiley, 1980), p. 484.

26. George A. Keyworth, remarks at 41st Annual Science Talent Search Banquet, Washington, D.C. (March 1, 1982).

27. See, for example, the essays in Dieter Ernst, ed., *The New International Division of Labor, Technology, and Underdevelopment* (Frankfurt: Campus Verlag, 1980).

28. See "New Push for European Science Cooperation," *Science*, vol. 220 (June 10, 1983).

29. For a history of the involvement of scientists in debates over the control of nuclear technology, see Alice Kimball Smith, *A Peril and a Hope: The Scientists' Movement in America, 1945–47* (Chicago: University of Chicago Press, 1965).

30. See Leneice N. Lu, *The Baruch Plan: U.S. Diplomacy Enters the Nuclear Age* (Washington, D.C.: Library of Congress, 1972). The implications of the events are discussed fully in Congressional Research Service, *Science, Technology, Diplomacy* (cit. 4).

31. Lu, *Baruch Plan* (cit. 30), p. 24.

32. Warren Donnelly, *Commercial Nuclear Power in Europe: The Interaction of American Diplomacy with a New Technology* (Washington, D.C.: Congressional Research Service, 1972).

33. See P. V. Dankwerts, "The Fire at Windscale," *New Scientist* (November 18, 1982).

34. Donnelly, *Commercial Nuclear Power* (cit. 32).

35. Lloyd V. Berkner, *Science and Foreign Relations: Report to the State Department* (Washington, D.C.: Department of State, 1950).

36. See Walter R. Schilling, "Scientists, Foreign Policy, and Politics," in Robert Gilpin and Christopher Wright, eds., *Scientists and National Policy-Making* (New York: Columbia University Press, 1964).

37. James R. Killian, "Making Science a Vital Force in Foreign Policy," excerpt from address delivered December 13, 1960, *Science*, vol. 131 (January 6, 1961).

38. See Eugene B. Skolnikoff, "Birth and Death of an Idea: Research in AID," *Bulletin of Atomic Scientists* (September 1967).

39. See James B. Killian, "Science in the State Department: A Practical Imperative," *Bulletin of Atomic Scientists* (May 1965).

40. See Klaus-Heinrich Standke, "Science and Technology in the United Nations System," *United Nations*, vol. 24, no. 1 (1976).

41. Ibid.

42. Jean-Jacques Servan-Schreiber, *The American Challenge*, trans. Ronald Steel (New York: Atheneum, 1976).

43. Elliot Richardson, address to AAAS colloquium, June 20, 1979.

44. For a full description of the Trilateral Commission's activities, see Holly Sklar, *Trilateralism: The Trilateral Commission and Elite Planning for World Management* (Boston: South End Press, 1980).

45. Commission on the Organization of the Government for the Conduct of Foreign Policy Report (Washington, D.C.: U.S. Government Printing Office, 1975).

46. Congressional Research Service, *Science, Technology, Diplomacy* (cit. 4).

47. The legislation was incorporated as Title V of the Foreign Relations Authorization Act of 1978.

48. See, for example, Henry A. Kissinger, *Nuclear Weapons and Foreign Policy* (New York: Harper & Brothers for Council on Foreign Relations, 1957).

49. "U.S.-Soviet Summit: Make Science, Not War," *Science*, vol. 185 (July 19, 1974), p. 237. For a review, see Linda L. Lubrano, "National and International Politics in U.S.-USSR Scientific Cooperation," *Social Studies of Science*, vol. 11 (1981), pp. 451–480.

50. Henry Kissinger, address to Sixth Special Session of United Nations General Assembly, New York, April 15, 1974.

51. Henry Kissinger, address to Seventh Special Session of United Nations General Assembly, New York, September 1, 1975.

52. Nicholas Wade, "Kissinger on Science: Making the Linkage with Diplomacy," *Science*, vol. 184 (May 12, 1974).
53. Robert Gillette, "A Conversation with Dixy Lee Ray," *Science*, vol. 189 (July 11, 1975).
54. Dixy Lee Ray, letter to President Gerald Ford (June 20, 1975).
55. See, for example, comments in T. Keith Glennan, *Technology and Foreign Affairs*, report to Deputy Secretary of State Charles W. Robinson (Washington, D.C.: Department of State, December 1976), Appendix E ("Summary of Discussion with Invited Industry Representatives," New York, June 1, 1976).
56. William Casey, "Science, Technology, and World Economic Affairs" (speech to Industrial Research Institute, Chicago, October 1973).
57. Glennan, *Technology and Foreign Affairs* (cit. 55).
58. Ibid., Appendix E.
59. John Walsh, "Science and Technology at State: Recognizing the Problem," *Science*, vol. 196 (April 8, 1977).
60. For a discussion of this letter, see William Carey, evidence in U.S. Congress, Senate Committee on Commerce, Subcommittee on Science, Technology, and Space, *U.S. Preparation for the 1979 UN Conference on Science and Technology for Development* (Hearings), Report No. 95-59, 95th Cong., 1st sess. (December 15, 1977).
61. See Laurence Shoup, *The Carter Presidency and Beyond* (Palo Alto: Ramparts Press, 1980).
62. Zbigniew Brzezinski, *Between Two Ages: America's Role in the Technetronic Era* (New York: Viking Press, 1970). See also Nicholas Wade, "Brzezinski: Role of Science in Society and Foreign Policy," *Science*, vol. 195 (March 11, 1977).
63. Brzezinski, *Between Two Ages* (cit. 62), p. 288.
64. Frank Press, "Science and Technology in the White House, 1977–1980, Part 2," *Science*, vol. 211 (January 16, 1981), p. 249.
65. President Jimmy Carter, "The Science and Technology Message to the Congress," White House (March 27, 1979).
66. See Zbigniew Brzezinski, *Power and Principle: Memories of the National Security Adviser* (New York: Farrar, Straus, and Giroux, 1983).
67. John Deutch, director of the Department of Energy's Office of Energy Research, admitted candidly: "By no means should the balance sheet on science and technology cooperation [with China] be evaluated on science and technology grounds alone" (quoted in *Physics Today* [November 1980).
68. White House, "Agency for Technological Cooperation," internal memorandum (March 1978).
69. See, for example, James R. Killian, "An International Institute of Science and Technology," in Norman Kaplan, ed., *Science and Society* (Chicago: Rand McNally, 1965).
70. George Hammond and Murray Todd, "Technical Assistance and Foreign Policy," *Science*, vol. 189 (September 26, 1975).
71. U.S. Chamber of Commerce Task Force, *Technology Transfer and the Developing Countries* (Washington, D.C.: U.S. Chamber of Commerce, April 1977).
72. Brzezinski, *Between Two Ages* (cit. 62).

73. Lester E. Gordon, *Interim Report: An Assessment of Development Assistance Strategies* (Washington, D.C.: Brookings Institution, October 6, 1977).

74. Henry Owen, "The White House in Touch with Science," letter to *New York Times* (May 15, 1980).

75. Frank Press, director of Office of Science and Technology Policy, memorandum to Henry Owen (February 23, 1978).

76. "Foundation for International Technological Development: Planning Office Status Report" (Washington, D.C.: Office of Science and Technology Policy/AID, January 17, 1979).

77. See William Colglazier and Paul Doty, "U.S. Debates a New Agency," *Bulletin of Atomic Scientists* (May 1980).

78. Press, memo (cit. 75).

79. "Foundation for International Technological Cooperation: Plans and Concepts" (Washington, D.C.: Office of Science and Technology Policy, June 14, 1978).

80. Quoted in Jim Gudaitis, "Review, Reservations, and Recommendations on the Institute for Scientific and Technological Cooperation," *UNCSTD Memorandum #7* (Washington, D.C.: Center of Concern, June 5, 1979).

81. Ibid.

82. See, for example, conclusions of workshop on "Planning for Science and Technology in Development," Aspen, Colo., August 13–16, 1978.

83. Evidence in U.S. Congress, House Committee on Science and Technology, and House Task Force on Industrial Innovation, *Technology Trade* (Hearings), 96th Cong., 2d sess. (June 24–26, 1980).

84. Theodore Hesburgh, address to U.N. Conference on Science and Technology for Development, Vienna, Austria, August 20, 1979 (mimeographed).

85. See Gordon, *Interim Report* (cit. 73). Also Colglazier and Doty, "U.S. Debates Agency" (cit. 77).

86. Donald R. Finberg, "The Brookings Institution's Proposals for an 'International Development Foundation' " (information memorandum for administrator of U.S.-AID, November 29, 1977). The memorandum is prefaced with a cartoon of a man returning home to tell his wife, "Well, today I dreamed the impossible dream, and it was impossible, all right."

87. U.S. Congress, Senate Committee on Appropriations, Investigation Staff, *Report on Questionable Use of Appropriated Funds to Lobby for the Authorization and Funding of a Proposed Institute for Scientific and Technological Cooperation*, Report No. 79-8, submitted to Subcommittee on Foreign Operations, 96th Cong., 1st sess. (October 1979).

88. Ibid.

89. Quoted in Colglazier and Doty, "U.S. Debates Agency" (cit. 77).

90. Ibid.

91. Gudaitis, "Review" (cit. 81).

92. "Multinationals: Comfortable Code," *The Economist* (September 12, 1981).

93. U.S. Department of State, "Preparations for 1979 UN Conference on Science and Technology for Development" (edited transcript of meeting of November 17, 1976).

94. Ibid.

95. Carey, in *U.S. Preparation for UNCSTD* (cit. 60).
96. Frederick Seitz, president of Rockefeller University, letter to Frank Press (October 31, 1977). Reprinted in *U.S. Preparation for UNCSTD* (cit. 60).
97. National Research Council, Board on Science and Technology for International Development, *U.S. Science and Technology for Development* (Washington, D.C.: National Academy of Sciences, 1978).
98. Seitz, letter (cit. 96).
99. Schilling, "Scientists, Foreign Policy, Politics" (cit. 36).
100. Carey, in *U.S. Preparation for UNCSTD* (cit. 60).
101. Frank Press, "Science and Technology in International Affairs" (address to Council on Foreign Relations, New York, February 21, 1978).
102. Jean Wilkowski, evidence in U.S. Congress, Senate Committee on Commerce and House Committee on Science and Technology, Subcommittees, *U.S. Policies and Initiatives for the UN Conference on Science and Technology for Development* (Hearings), Report No. 96-43, 96th Cong., 1st sess. (July 17, 1979).
103. See "Putting Science in Its Place," *Nature*, vol. 274 (July 20, 1978).
104. *African Goals and Aspirations* (report of symposium, Arusha, Tanzania, January 30 to February 4, 1978). See also *Science and Technology and the Future: Nairobi Declaration* (adopted at African Regional Symposium, Nairobi, Kenya, July 10–12, 1979).
105. Nat C. Robertson, evidence in *U.S. Policies and Initiatives for UNCSTD* (cit. 102).
106. Industrial Sector Advisory Group, *The Contribution of Transnational Enterprise to Future World Development* (report to Secretary General of UNCSTD, May 1979).
107. James D. Grant, evidence in *U.S. Policies and Initiatives for UNCSTD* (cit. 102).
108. For a discussion of the major events leading up to and following the conference, see Klaus-Heinrich Standke, "The Prospects and Retrospects of the United Nations Conference on Science and Technology for Development," *Technology in Society*, vol. 1 (1979), pp. 353–386. See also "Dependence or Autonomy: UNCSTD's Hidden Agenda," *Nature*, vol. 280 (August 16, 1979); Volker Rittberger, "Global Conference Diplomacy in the Service of Development?," *Law and State*, vol. 1980 (1980).
109. Hesburgh, address to UNCSTD (cit. 84).
110. Ibid.
111. Theodore Hesburgh, evidence in *U.S. Preparation for UNCSTD* (cit. 60).
112. Genevieve J. Knezo, *UNCSTD: U.S. Participation—Issue Brief No. IB78034* (Washington, D.C.: Congressional Research Service, 1979).
113. U.S. Congress, House, *Report of a Congressional Delegation*, submitted to Committee on Foreign Affairs and Committee on Science and Technology, 96th Cong., 1st sess. (December 1979).
114. J. Brian Atwood, State Department, letter to Senator Adlai Stevenson, Jr. (August 17, 1979).
115. John Walsh, "U.S. Planning for UNCSTD Problems of Development," *Science*, vol. 200 (June 16, 1978).
116. Press, "Science and Technology" (cit. 64).

117. *R&D Mexico*, vol. 1, no. 9 (June 1981). Volker Rittberger has written that for developing countries "what was offered by the program of action is but the all too familiar raindrop in the desert" ("Global Conference Diplomacy" [cit. 108]).

118. Ward Morehouse, "The Vienna Syndrome," *New York Times* (September 6, 1979).

119. David R. Francis, "Vienna Talks Open Technology Door for Developing Nations," *Christian Science Monitor* (September 6, 1979). In contrast, another newspaper report of the meeting carried the headline: "To Many, the United States Was the Biggest Culprit at the UN's Conference on Science and Technology" (*Chronicle of Higher Education* [September 10, 1979]).

120. Stephanie Yanchinski, "UNCSTD and After," *New Scientist* (September 6, 1979).

121. Alexander Haig, "A Strategic Approach to American Foreign Policy" (address to American Bar Association, New Orleans, August 11, 1981).

122. Ronald Reagan, address to World Affairs Council of Philadelphia, October 15, 1981.

123. Haig, "Strategic Approach" (cit. 121).

124. Richard Allen, interview with Marvin Kalb, *Today Show*. White House, press release (October 22, 1981).

125. Colin Norman, "Science Helps Break the Ice," *Science*, vol. 217 (August 13, 1982).

126. Nathaniel H. Leff, "Technology Transfer and U.S. Foreign Policy: The Developing Countries," *Orbis* (Spring 1979).

127. Ibid.

128. Evidence in *Technology Trade* (cit. 83), p. 69.

129. Statement of July 13, 1966. Quoted in Elliot L. Richardson, address to 75th Anniversary Convocation of American Society of International Law, Washington, D.C., March 25, 1981.

130. Henry Kissinger, "The Law of the Sea: A Test of International Collaboration," *Department of State Bulletin*, vol. 74 (April 26, 1976).

131. See, for example, William R. Hawkins, "Rethinking the Law of the Sea," *Washington Inquirer* (September 4, 1981); Northcutt Ely, "One OPEC Is Enough," *Regulation* (November/December 1981). For a description of the political roots of opposition to the treaty, see David Dickson, "Scuttling the Sea-Law Treaty," *The Nation* (May 30, 1981); William Wertenbaker, "The Law of the Sea," *New Yorker* (August 15, 1983).

132. James Arnold Miller, Daniel I. Fine, and R. Daniel McMichael, eds., *The Resource War in 3-D: Dependency, Diplomacy, Defense* (report to 18th World Affairs Forum sponsored by World Affairs Council of Pittsburgh, June 17, 1980).

133. Daniel James, letter to *Washington Post* (April 27, 1981).

134. Alexander Haig, president of United Technologies Corp., letter to Robert B. Owen, legal adviser, Department of State (June 4, 1980).

135. White House, press release (January 29, 1982).

136. James L. Malone, statement before House Committee on Merchant Marine and Fisheries (February 23, 1982).

137. Elliot L. Richardson, "Factless and Feckless: Safire's 'Triumph of Yahooism,'" *Washington Star* (March 1981).

138. Ibid.

139. "North and South Battle over Sea Law," *New Scientist* (December 2, 1982).

140. Quoted ibid.

141. Malone, statement (cit. 136).

142. *Priorities in Biotechnology Research for International Development* proceedings of workshop organized by Board on Science and Technology for International Development, Office of International Affairs, National Research Council, National Academy of Sciences, Washington, D.C., July 26–30, 1982).

143. David Baltimore, "Priorities in Biotechnology," ibid., p. 35; "IPRI: Tasting Better," *The Economist* (November 5, 1983).

144. Abd-El Rahman Khane, speech of February 4, 1981, *UNIDO/IS.259* (November 26, 1981), p. 3.

145. Dermot A. O'Sullivan, "Global Biotechnology Center to Aid Developing Countries Planned," *Chemical and Engineering News* (January 10, 1983), p. 18. A report prepared by a State Department advisory committee—subsequently suppressed by the Reagan administration, apparently for not going far enough in suggesting tough controls on the export of biotechnology data—made clear U.S. thinking on the UNIDO proposal. It claimed that the center "could prove overly ambitious in the light of the operating budget," and stated that the center "is unlikely to produce world-class research" (draft report by U.S. Government Interagency Working Group on Competitive and Transfer Aspects of Biotechnology, published as *Biobusiness World Data Base* [New York: McGraw-Hill, 1983]). See also "UNIDO Hopes for Biotechnology Center," *Science*, vol. 221 (September 30, 1983).

146. "Progress and Competitive Pressures in Fighting Malaria," *The Economist* (March 26, 1983), p. 93.

147. Tam Dalyell, "Too Big for Their Boots?," *New Scientist* (September 2, 1982), p. 644. See also Ernst, ed., *New International Division of Labor* (cit. 27).

148. Brzezinski, *Between Two Ages* (cit. 62). Bobby Inman, president and chief executive officer of the newly formed Microelectronics and Computer Technology Company, which pools some of the long-term research of twelve high technology U.S. companies, suggests that eventually European and Japanese companies may be included as well, since economic competition "is going to fray the alliance structure," and sharing technological leadership "encourages them to want to keep their economic relationship with the U.S." Quoted in John Walsh, "MCC Moves Out of the Ideas Stage," *Science*, vol. 220 (June 17, 1983).

149. National Research Council, Office of International Affairs, Panel on Advanced Technology Competition and Industrialized Allies, *International Competition in Advanced Technology: Decisions for America*, consensus statement (Washington, D.C.: NRC, 1983).

150. *Technology, Growth, and Employment*, report of Working Group set up by Economic Summit Meeting of 1982 (London: HMSO, Cmnd. 8818, March 1983).

151. "Text of the Williamsburg Declaration on Economic Recovery," *New York Times* (May 31, 1983).

152. *Technology, Growth, Employment* (cit. 150).
153. See *The Role of the Patent System in the Transfer of Technology to Developing Countries* (New York: United Nations, 1975).
154. See, for example, Francisco Sagasti, "Toward an Endogenous Scientific and Technological Development for the Third World," in Ward Morehouse, ed., *Science Technology and the Social Order* (New Brunswick, N.J.: Transaction Books, 1979).
155. Quoted in Jeff Frieden, "The Coming Trade War at Home," *The Nation* (April 1, 1981).
156. Economic Policy Council of UNA-USA, Technology Transfer Panel, *The Growth of the U.S. and World Economics Through Technological Innovation and Transfer* (New York, 1980).
157. Business–Higher Education Forum, *America's Competitive Challenge*, report to U.S. President (Washington, D.C.: American Council on Education, April 1983).
158. Committee for Economic Development, Committee on Research and Policy, "Memoranda of Dissent," in *Transnational Corporations and Developing Countries* (New York: CED, 1981).
159. *Pugwash Guidelines for International Scientific Cooperation for Development* (submitted to UNCSTD, Vienna, August 1979).
160. Anil Agarwal, "Indian Scientists Object to Solar Imports," *New Scientist* (March 6, 1980). For an alternative approach, see *State of India's Environment—1982: A Citizen's Report* (New Delhi: Center for Science and Environment, 1982). Also further discussion in Chapter Seven.
161. Paulo D'Arrigo Vellinho, president of Springer-Admiral Refrigeracao SA, address to seminar organized by Council of the Americas with support from U.S. State Department, Rio de Janeiro, May 10–11, 1979.
162. See Samir Amin, "Crisis, Nationalism, and Socialism," in S. Amin et al., *Dynamics of Global Crisis* (New York: Monthly Review Press, 1982). According to Amin: "A reduction in external relations [would be desirable] because the technology that would be imported, were these relations to be maintained, is not neutral and is in fact a hindrance to social transformation."
163. *Draft Report of International Forum on Technological Advances and Development* (Tbilisi, USSR, April 12–16, 1983).
164. Surendra Patel, Postface to Jacques Richardson, ed., *Integrated Technology Transfer* (Mt. Airy, Md.: Lomond Publications, 1979).

CHAPTER FIVE

1. Deborah Shapley, "NSF Promotes Ex-SE-Asia Expert," *Science*, vol. 180 (June 1, 1973).
2. See, for example, Barry Commoner, *Science and Survival* (New York: Viking Press, 1972); Jacques Ellul, *The Technological Society* (New York: Knopf, 1964); Herbert Marcuse, *One-Dimensional Man: The Ideology of Industrial Society* (London: Routledge & Kegan Paul, 1964); Theodore Roszak, *The Making of a Counter-Culture* (London: Faber, 1970).

3. See Barbara Culliton, "Kennedy: Pushing for More Public Input in Research," *Science*, vol. 188 (June 20, 1975). For a review of these pressures, see Organization for Economic Cooperation and Development, Secretary General's Ad Hoc Group on New Concepts of Science Policy, *Science, Growth, and Society: A New Perspective* (Paris: OECD, 1971).

4. Hugh DeWitt Stetten, "Freedom of Inquiry," *Science*, vol. 189 (September 19, 1975).

5. David Baltimore, "The New Biology Becomes the New Politics" (speech at University of Missouri, Columbia, May 6, 1977). During congressional hearings, Ray Thornton, chairman of the science, research and technology subcommittee of the House Science and Technology Committee, compared the DNA issue to the dilemmas that had faced Galileo; subcommittee member Mike McCormack claimed that suggested legislation "sets a dangerous precedent for the regulation of scientific research" (U.S. Congress, House, *Hearings on Recombinant DNA Technology*, 95th Cong., 1st sess. [March 29, 1977]).

6. Rachel Carson, *Silent Spring* (Boston: Houghton Mifflin, 1962).

7. For a complete history of the DDT controversy, see Thomas R. Dunlap, *DDT: Scientists, Citizens, and Public Policy* (Princeton, N.J.: Princeton University Press, 1981).

8. I. L. Baldwin, "Chemicals and Pests, *Science*, vol. 137 (September 28, 1962), p. 1042. William Darby, "Silence, Miss Carson," *Chemical and Engineering News* (October 1, 1962). Quoted in Joel Primack and Frank von Hippel, *Advice and Dissent: Scientists in the Political Arena* (New York: Basic Books, 1974).

9. See Frank Graham, Jr., *Since Silent Spring* (Boston: Houghton Mifflin, 1970).

10. President's Science Advisory Committee, *Use of Pesticides* (Washington, D.C.: White House, May 15, 1963).

11. For a general review of the tactics used, see William A. Shurcliff, *SST/Sonic Boom Handbook* (New York: Ballantine, 1970).

12. U.S. Congress, House Committee on Appropriations, Hearing on the Department of Transportation and Related Agencies Appropriations for 1971, 92nd Cong., 1st sess. (April 23, 1970). The report prepared by Garwin's committee to President Nixon had concluded that all government support should be withdrawn from the SST prototype program.

13. See Mel Horwitch, *Clipped Wings: The American SST Conflict* (Cambridge, Mass.: MIT Press, 1982). Also Primack and von Hippel, *Advice and Dissent* (cit. 8), chap. 2 ("The Supersonic Transport: A Case History in the Politics of Technology").

14. Quoted in Primack and von Hippel, *Advice and Dissent* (cit. 8).

15. Robert A. McCaughey, "American University Teachers and Opposition to the Vietnam War," *Minerva*, vol. 14, no. 3 (Autumn 1976).

16. See, for example, copies of the magazine *Science for the People* from 1969; also collection of articles from this magazine and elsewhere in Rita Arditti et al., eds., *Science and Liberation* (Boston: South End Press, 1980).

17. Alex Capron, book review, *Southern California Law Review*, vol. 48 (1974).

18. Editorial, *Fortune* (January 1971).

19. Quoted in *Boston Globe* (May 5, 1972). Cited in "Technology Assessment and Social Control," *Science*, vol. 180 (May 4, 1973).

20. Michael Polyani, "The Republic of Science: Its Political and Economic Theory," *Minerva*, vol. 1 (1962).
21. *New York Times* (October 24, 1971).
22. National Science Foundation, Ethical Values in Science and Technology Program: Fiscal Year 1981 Grants (Washington, D.C.: NSF, November 1981).
23. William D. McElroy, memorandum to members of National Science Board (December 15, 1971).
24. Harvey Brooks, Harvard University, letter to William D. McElroy, National Science Foundation (January 23, 1972).
25. Louis Leven, National Science Foundation, letter to Harvey Brooks (March 1, 1972).
26. Mary Ames, *Outcome Uncertain: Science and the Political Process* (Washington, D.C.: Communication Press, 1978).
27. Primack and von Hippel, *Advice and Dissent* (cit. 8).
28. Ralph Nader, "Professional Responsibility Revisited," in Samuel Epstein et al., eds., *Science, Technology, and the Public Interest: Information Communications and Organizational Patterns* (report of conference held in 1973) (Jeannette, Penn.: Mounsour Medical Foundation, 1977).
29. For a description of Kennedy's views, see Culliton, "Kennedy" (cit. 3).
30. Quoted in Ken Hechler, *Toward the Endless Frontier: History of the Committee on Science and Technology, 1959–79* (Washington, D.C.: U.S. House of Representatives, Committee Print, 1980).
31. Barbara Culliton, "NSF: Trying to Cope with Congressional Pressure for Public Participation," *Science*, vol. 191 (January 23, 1976).
32. See, for example, McCormack's comments to hearings of House Science and Technology Committee (March 2, 1977), quoted in Hechler, *Toward the Endless Frontier* (cit. 30). Also Philip M. Boffey, "NSF: New Program Criticized as 'Appalling' Subsidy to Activists," *Science*, vol. 94 (October 15, 1976).
33. Culliton, "NSF" (cit. 31).
34. McCormack, comments to hearings (cit. 32).
35. Tom Harkin, evidence to hearings (cit. 32).
36. See Mary E. Ames, *Outcome Uncertain: Science and the Political Process* (Washington, D.C.: Communication Press Inc., 1978).
37. Michael S. Baram, "Technology Assessment and Social Control," *Science*, vol. 180 (May 4, 1973).
38. See Gary Werskey, *The Visible College* (London: Allen Lane, 1978).
39. David Dickson, "Science and Political Hegemony in the Seventeenth Century," *Radical Science Journal*, no. 8 (1979).
40. Jerome Wiesner, *Where Science and Politics Meet* (New York: McGraw-Hill, 1965).
41. National Academy of Engineering, Committee on Public Engineering Policy, report for House Committee on Science and Engineering (Washington, D.C.: NAE, July 1969).
42. National Academy of Sciences, Ad Hoc Committee, *Applied Science and Technological Progress*, report for House Committee on Science and Aeronautics (Washington, D.C.: NAS, June 1967). An official history of the Science and Technology Committee states that the idea of technology assessment had one of its principal early roots in "discussions with represen-

tatives of the scientific community" (Hechler, *Toward the Endless Frontier* [cit. 32]).

43. National Academy of Sciences, Committee on Science and Public Policy, Ad Hoc Panel, *Technology: Processes of Assessment and Choice,* report to House Committee on Science and Astronautics (Washington, D.C.: NAS, 91st Cong., 1st sess., 1969), pp. 12, 83.

44. Ibid., pp. 14, 70, 84.

45. Ibid., p. 78.

46. See, for example, Barry M. Casper, "The Rhetoric and the Reality of Congressional Technology Assessment," *Bulletin of Atomic Scientists* (February 1978).

47. U.S. Congress, House Committee on Science and Astronautics, Subcommittee on Science, Research, and Development, *Inquiries, Legislation, Policy Studies: Re Science and Technology—Review and Forecast,* 89th Cong., 2nd sess. (1966).

48. Quoted in Hechler, *Toward the Endless Frontier* (cit. 32).

49. U.S. Congress, Senate, *Congressional Record,* vol. 117 (1971), S6334.

50. Ibid.

51. Report of the Climate Impact Assessment Program mounted by the Department of Transportation in 1971. See Luther J. Carter, "Deception Charged in Presentation of SST Study," *Science,* vol. 190 (November 28, 1975).

52. U.S. Congress, House, *Congressional Record,* vol. 118 (1972), H3202.

53. U.S. Congress, Senate, *Congressional Record,* vol. 116 (1970), S41594.

54. Jude Wanniski, "Teddy Kennedy's Shadow Government," *Wall Street Journal* (March 27, 1973).

55. U.S. Congress, House Committee on Science and Technology, press release (November 20, 1978). See also Wil Lepkowski, "OTA Gets Encouraging Nod from House Report," *Chemical and Engineering News* (November 27, 1978).

56. National Academy of Engineering, *Technology Assessment* (cit. 41).

57. National Academy of Sciences, *Technology* (cit. 43).

58. *Congressional Record* (cit. 49).

59. Quoted in "OTA: An Idea That Will Have to Wait," *Business Week* (June 24, 1972). The Office of Management and Budget is said to have told executive agencies to withhold information from the OTA on the grounds that it would be used to shoot down the administration's projects, such as the supersonic transport ("Looking In on a 'Far-Sighted' Agency," *Business Week* [April 6, 1974]).

60. "OTA" (cit. 59).

61. Quoted in "Congress Gears Up to Assess Technology," *Business Week* (January 13, 1973).

62. Hechler, *Toward the Endless Frontier* (cit. 32), p. 560.

63. See Casper, "Rhetoric and Reality" (cit. 46).

64. For a description of the House Debate, see Hechler, *Toward the Endless Frontier* (cit. 30), pp. 558–9.

65. Quoted in Philip M. Boffey, "Office of Technology Assessment: Bad Marks on Its First Report Cards," *Science,* vol. 193 (July 16, 1976).

66. Technology Assessment Board and Technology Assessment Advisory

Council, minutes of joint meeting of February 25, 1975. Quoted in Casper, "Rhetoric and Reality" (cit. 46).

67. Boffey, "OTA" (cit. 65).
68. Casper, "Rhetoric and Reality" (cit. 46).
69. Quoted in Constance Holden, "OTA—Daddario's Exit Heightens Strife over Kennedy Role," *Science*, vol. 197 (July 1, 1977).
70. Russell Peterson, "Science and the Quality of Life" (speech to AAAS annual meeting, Washington, D.C., February 16, 1978). Daniel Greenberg commented that "it was assumed—obviously erroneously—that he would recede into the quiet anonymity that is usually expected of Congress's hired hands" ("OTA Head Spouts 100-Proof Environmentalism," *Science and Government Report* [March 1, 1978]).
71. See Dickson, "Science and Political Hegemony" (cit. 38).
72. Office of Technology Assessment, press release (September 18, 1978).
73. Quoted in Don K. Price, *The Scientific Estate* (Cambridge, Mass.: Harvard University Press, 1965).
74. Quoted in "Congress Troubled about Course of OTA," *Science*, vol. 203 (February 23, 1979).
75. Quoted in "Technology Assessment Wins New Friends," *Nature*, vol. 293 (October 8, 1981). For a general description of Gibbon's approach, see "A Narrower Focus on Technology Assessment," *Business Week* (August 27, 1979).
76. Jack Gibbons, interview, Washington, D.C. (September 30, 1981).
77. Office of Technology Assessment, *Impacts of Applied Genetics: Micro-Organisms, Plants, and Animals* (Washington, D.C.: OTA, April 1981).
78. OTA staff, memorandum to Jack Gibbons (November 19, 1980).
79. See, for example, the general attitudes of scientists quoted by Harold Schmeck, "Scientists Seek to Influence Legislation on Gene Research," *New York Times* (July 6, 1977).
80. Letter to *Science*, vol. 185 (July 24, 1974).
81. Quoted in "DNA Folly Continues," *New Republic* (January 13, 1979).
82. For a full description of the origins of the recombinant DNA debate, see Nicholas Wade, *The Ultimate Experiment* (New York: Walker, rev. 1979).
83. Quoted ibid., p. 49.
84. Quoted ibid., p. 50.
85. Evidence in U.S. Congress, Senate Committee on Labor and Public Welfare, Subcommittee on Health, *Genetic Engineering: Examination of the Relationship of a Free Society and its Scientific Community* (Hearings), 94th Cong., 1st sess. (April 22, 1975). Brown later claimed the existence of an implicit social contract, under which the average citizen had given up the democratic right to control science—delegating this responsibility to scientific experts, in return for the material benefits science promised ("Quality and Relevance," *The Hastings Center Report* [Hastings-on-Hudson, New York: June 1975]).
86. Evidence in *Genetic Engineering* (cit. 85).
87. Ibid.
88. Donald Fredrickson, "Science and the Cultural Warp: rDNA as a Case Study" (paper to AAAS annual meeting, Washington, D.C., January 7, 1982).

89. Sheldon Krimsky, *The Social History of the Recombinant DNA Controversy* (Cambridge: MIT Press, 1982).

90. See, for example, Nicholas Wade, "Recombinant DNA: NIH Group Stirs Storm by Drafting Laxer Rules," *Science*, vol. 188 (June 6, 1975).

91. See, for example, "Statement by Ray Thornton to September 10–11, 1981, NIH-RAC Meeting" (mimeographed) (Bethesda: National Institutes of Health, September 1981).

92. Wallace Rowe, letter to *Science*, vol. 198 (November 11, 1977).

93. Professor Roy Curtiss, University of Alabama, letter to Donald Fredrickson, National Institutes of Health (October 4, 1979).

94. For a description of these local initiatives, see Wade, *Ultimate Experiment* (cit. 82), chap. 11 ("From Campus to Congress via City Hall").

95. Fredrickson, "Science and Cultural Warp" (cit. 88). The *Higher Education Daily* reported that "there is a growing realization that federal legislation is needed, if only to keep states and local governments from imposing more stringent barriers" (vol. 5 [October 31, 1977]).

96. Quoted in Nicholas Wade, "Gene-Splicing Preemption Rejected," *Science*, vol. 196 (April 22, 1977).

97. See Harlyn O. Halvorson, letter to *Science*, vol. 196 (June 10, 1977). Also Harlyn O. Halvorson, "Recombinant DNA Legislation—What's Next?," *Science*, vol. 198 (October 28, 1977).

98. Nicholas Wade, "Gene-Splicing: Senate Bill Draws Charges of Lysenkoism," *Science*, vol. 197 (July 22, 1977).

99. Philip Abelson, "Recombinant DNA," *Science*, vol. 197 (August 19, 1977).

100. Baltimore, "New Biology" (cit. 5).

101. Quoted in Halvorson, "Recombinant DNA Legislation" (cit. 97).

102. For a description of these lobbying tactics, see Harlyn O. Halvorson, "The Impact of the Recombinant DNA Controversy on a Professional Scientific Society" (paper to AAAS meeting, Washington, D.C., January 7, 1982 [mimeographed]). Also Barbara Culliton, "Recombinant DNA Bills Derailed: Congress Still Trying to Pass a Law," *Science*, vol. 199 (January 20, 1978).

103. A memorandum from Donald Moulton et al. to "Friends of DNA" (dated November 17, 1977) supports a bill written by staff members for Representative Harley Staggers which would preempt all federal agencies except OSHA and "all state and local governments." See Susan D. Chira, "Harvard Officials Lobby for Federal DNA Control," *Harvard Crimson* (March 2, 1978); "Friends of DNA Strike Back," *Nature*, vol. 272 (April 20, 1978).

104. Evidence to U.S. Congress, House Committee on Science and Technology, Subcommittee on Science, Research, and Technology, 95th Cong., 2nd sess. (April 11, 1978).

105. Evidence in U.S. Congress, Senate Committee on Commerce, Subcommittee on Science, Technology, and Space, *Regulation of Recombinant DNA Research* (Hearings), Report No. 95-52, 95th Cong., 1st sess. (November 2, 8, 10, 1977).

106. "Statement by Thornton" (cit. 91).

107. Sherwood Gorbach, letter to Dr. Donald Fredrickson, National Institutes of Health, quoted in Friends of the Earth, press release (October 4, 1977).

108. N.J. Department of Public Advocate, "Technical Basis of Public Advocate

Determination Not to Modify the Position Outlined in the Petition," statement of September 23, 1977. See also Friends of Earth/Environmental Defense Fund, "Scientists and Environmentalists Accuse Pro-DNA Forces of Deception and Urge Strong Regulatory Decision" (press release accompanied by letter signed by "over 100 scientists and concerned citizens," Washington, D.C., October 4, 1977).

109. Fredrickson, "Science and Cultural Warp" (cit. 88).
110. Paul Berg, Stanford University, letter to William Gartland, National Institutes of Health (January 22, 1982).
111. Michael Ross, Genentech, letter to William Gartland, National Institutes of Health (February 1, 1982).
112. Harvey S. Price, executive director of Industrial Biotechnology Association, letter to William Gartland, National Institutes of Health (February 1, 1982).
113. Thomas O'Brien, Brigham and Women's Hospital, letter to William Gartland, National Institutes of Health (January 28, 1982).
114. See record of meeting of NIH Recombinant DNA Advisory Committee, Bethesda, Md., February 8, 1982.
115. Ibid.
116. Don Fuqua et al., House Science and Technology Committee, letter to Ray Thornton, chairman of Recombinant DNA Advisory Committee (November 20, 1981).
117. Fredrickson, "Science and Cultural Warp" (cit. 88).
118. Susan Wright, "Molecular Politics in Great Britain and the United States: The Development of Policy for Recombinant DNA Technology," *California Law Review*, vol. 51 (September 1978).
119. Nancy E. Abrams and Joel R. Primack, "The Public and Technological Decisions," *Bulletin of Atomic Scientists* (June 1980).
120. For a contemporary review of the various forms of these demands, see James D. Carroll, "Participatory Democracy," *Science*, vol. 171 (February 19, 1971).
121. See Dorothy Nelkin, *Technological Decisions and Democracy* (Beverly Hills, Cal.: Sage Publications, 1977), esp. chap. 1 ("Participation as an Ideology").
122. National Academy of Sciences, *Technology* (cit. 43).
123. See Krimsky, *Genetic Alchemy* (cit. 89).
124. See Susan Wright and Robert L. Sinsheimer, "The Fourth Horseman: Recombinant DNA Technology and Biological Warfare," *Bulletin of Atomic Scientists*, vol. 39, no. 9 (November 1983). According to Wright, some scientists claimed, in correspondence with the National Institutes of Health, that the data the experiments would provide could be obtained by other means, thus heightening concern about the reasons the experiment was being planned.
125. Quoted in Colin Norman, "Clerics Urge Ban on Altering Germ-line Cells," *Science*, vol. 220 (June 24, 1983).
126. D. W. Schindler, "The Impact Statement Boondoggle," *Science*, vol. 192 (May 7, 1976). For a reply, see Russell Peterson, "The Impact Statement: Part II," *Science*, vol. 193 (July 16, 1976).
127. Sally Fairfax, "A Disaster for the Environmental Movement," *Science*, vol. 199 (February 17, 1978).

128. For a description of some European experiences, see Nelkin, *Technological Decisions* (cit. 121).
129. See Wright, "Molecular Politics" (cit. 118).

CHAPTER SIX

1. William Ruckelshaus, "Science, Risk, and Public Policy" (address to National Academy of Sciences, Washington, D.C., June 22, 1983). Published in *Science*, vol. 221 (September 9, 1983).
2. James C. Miller, "Defining Consumer Deception," letter to *Science*, vol. 219 (March 18, 1983).
3. R. Jeffrey Smith, "FTC Seeks a Little Less Honesty," *Science*, vol. 218 (December 24, 1982).
4. White House, memorandum of February 10, 1981. Reprinted in U.S. Congress, House Committee on Science and Technology, Subcommittee on Natural Resources and Agricultural Research and Environment, *Hearings on Environmental Protection Agency Research and Development Authorization for Fiscal Years 1983 and 1984*, 97th Cong., 2d sess. (February 24, March 2, 19, 1982), Appendix C.
5. Environmental Protection Agency, press release (May 8, 1981). See also Joanne Omang, "White House Seeks to Loosen Standards under Clean Air Act," *Washington Post* (August 6, 1981). Compare with David Stockman's 1979 statement (while still a congressman) that "air pollution control is a public policy art and not a science" (quoted in *Air Waves: Bulletin of National Commission on Air Quality* [December 1981]).
6. Quoted in Eliot Marshall, "Revisions in Cancer Policy," *Science*, vol. 220 (April 1, 1983).
7. Evidence to U.S. Congress, House Committee on Energy and Commerce, Subcommittee on Commerce, Transportation, and Tourism, 98th Cong., 1st sess. (March 17, 1983).
8. For a discussion of the problems facing regulators in this situation, see a speech to Stanford University by its recently appointed president, Donald Kennedy, previously head of the Food and Drug Administration. Reprinted as "The Politics of Preventive Health," *Technology Review* (November/December 1981).
9. Quoted in Jean-Jacques Salomon, *Prométhée empêtré: la résistance au changement technique* (Paris: Pergamon Press, 1981).
10. Donald E. Kash, evidence in *Hearings on EPA* (cit. 4).
11. Julius E. Johnson, evidence in *Hearings on EPA* (cit. 4).
12. Frederick M. Taylor, *The Principles of Scientific Management* (New York: Harper & Brothers, 1911). For a critique of Taylor's ideas and an analysis of their political implications, see Harry Braverman, *Labor and Monopoly Capital: The Degradation of Work in the Twentieth Century* (New York: Monthly Review Press, 1974); Andrew Zimbalist, ed., *Case Studies on the Labor Process* (New York: Monthly Review Press, 1979); Les Levidow and Bob Young, eds., *Science, Technology, and the Labor Process* (London: CSE Books, 1981).
13. Ralph Lapp, *The New Priesthood* (New York: Harper & Row, 1965).

14. Arnold Schlesinger, Jr., *A Thousand Days* (London: Andrew Deutsch, 1975).

15. See full description in Joel Primack and Frank von Hippel, *Advice and Dissent: Scientists in the Political Arena* (New York: New American Library, 1974), Part II, chap. 4 ("Not the Whole Truth: The Advisory Reports on the Supersonic Transport").

16. Quoted ibid.

17. For full description of the cyclamate story, see James S. Turner, *The Chemical Feast*, report of Ralph Nader Study Group on Food Protection and the Food and Drug Administration (New York: Grossman Publishers, 1970).

18. Primack and von Hippel, *Advice and Dissent* (cit. 15).

19. Organization for Economic Cooperation and Development, Secretary General's Ad Hoc Group on New Concepts of Science Policy, *Science, Growth, and Society: A New Perspective* (Paris, OECD, 1971).

20. Ibid.

21. National Academy of Sciences, *Technology, Trade, and the U.S. Economy*, report of workshop in Woods Hole, Mass. (Washington, D.C.: NAS, 1978).

22. Quoted in Edwin McDowell, "OSHA, EPA: The Heyday Is Over," *New York Times* (January 4, 1981).

23. See, for example, the statement by the Pittsburgh Area Committee for Occupational Safety and Health: "Unless we begin to fight for the right to control our own working conditions, we will never be able to make our workplaces healthy and safe" (quoted in Dan Berman, *Death on the Job* [New York: Monthly Review Press, 1978]).

24. Paul G. Rogers, address to Third Annual Conference on Health Policy sponsored by *National Journal*, Washington, D.C., May 22, 1978.

25. Quoted in "Industry-Government Tensions Spotlighted Again," *Chemical and Engineering News* (November 3, 1980).

26. John L. Paluszek, *Will the Corporation Survive?* (Reston, Va.: Reston Publishing, 1977).

27. Quoted ibid.

28. Murray Weidenbaum, *Business, Government and the Public* (Englewood Cliffs, N.J.: Prentice-Hall, 1981).

29. Industrial Research Institute, *Impact of Regulation on Innovation*, position statement (New York: IRI, July 18, 1979).

30. Committee for Economic Development, *Stimulating Technological Progress* (New York: CED January 1980). See also CED, *Redefining the Government's Role in the Market System* (New York: CED, July 1979).

32. Jordan Baruch, address to AAAS colloquium on R&D policy, Washington, D.C., June 19, 1979. Published in Don I. Phillips et al., eds., *Colloquium Proceedings, 19–20 June 1979* (Washington, D.C.: AAAS Report No. 79-R-14, October 1979).

33. See "Vanishing Innovation," *Business Week* (July 3, 1978). *Business Week* reported: "Following months of informal but intense lobbying led by such executives as N. Bruce Hannay, vice-president for research and patents at Bell Telephone Laboratories, and Arthur M. Bueche, vice-president for research and development at General Electric, the White House has ordered up a 28-agency review."

34. Quoted in Claude E. Barfield, *Science Policy from Ford to Reagan: Change and Continuity* (Washington, D.C.: American Enterprise Institute, 1982).
35. Frank Press, "Science and Technology in the White House," *Science*, vol. 211 (January 9, 1981).
36. Jules Blake, "OSTP: The Last Four Years," *Science*, vol. 2 (December 12, 1980).
37. Press, "Science and Technology" (cit. 35).
38. Frank Press, "The Importance of American Industrial Innovation (remarks to symposium on innovation at MIT, Cambridge, Mass., May 18, 1978 [mimeographed]).
39. Quoted in "Digging a Spur into Innovation," *Business Week* (Februrary 12, 1979).
40. Stuart E. Eizenstat, White House, "Issue Definition Memorandum: Federal Policy on Industrial Innovation," memorandum to U.S. Secretary of Treasury et al. (n.d.).
41. "Draft Report: Review and Recommendations on Policy Alternatives of the Public Interest Advisory Subcommittee" (draft report for U.S. Secretary of Commerce, Washington, D.C., December 28, 1978).
42. White House, press release (October 31, 1979).
43. See National Science Foundation, *Science and Technology Report: 1978* (Washington, D.C.: NSD, 1978). According to the NSF: "With regard to technology output and international earnings from R&D intensive activities, available data indicate little or no erosion in U.S. technological capabilities. The data on both inputs to and outputs from innovative activity thus suggest that the relationships between science and technology and economic and trade performance are not direct or simple. Neither the available economic nor technical indicators provide hard evidence of negative economic consequences." Ironically, while government officials were complaining of a slowdown in research spending by industry, *Business Week* was reporting a "record year" ("R&D Spending at 683 Companies: Another Record Year," *Business Week* [July 2, 1979]).
44. Congressional Research Service, *Technology and Trade: Some Indicators of the State of U.S. Industrial Innovation* (report for House Committee on Ways and Means, Subcommittee on Trade, April 21, 1980).
45. Edwin Mansfield, "Long Waves and Technological Innovation" (address to American Economics Association, New York, December 1982 [mimeographed]); Jean-Jacques Salomon, "Science as a Commodity," paper delivered in Stockholm, May, 2–3, 1983.
46. Baruch, address to AAAS (cit. 32).
47. W. N. Smith and Charles F. Larson, eds., *Innovation and U.S. Research*, Symposium Series No. 129 (Washington, D.C.: ACS, 1980).
48. Robert H. Hayes and William J. Abernathy, "Managing Our Way to Economic Decline," *Harvard Business Review* (July/August 1980).
49. Quoted in Ruth Ruttenberg, "Regulation Is the Mother of Invention," *Working Papers* (May/June 1980).
50. See "Textiles Reel Off the Ropes," *The Economist* (December 6, 1980). *The Economist* reported: "Tougher government regulations on workers' health have, unexpectedly, given the industry a leg up. Tighter dust control rules for cotton plants caused firms to throw out tons of old, inefficient, ma-

chinery and replace it with the latest available from the world's leading textile machinery firms in Switzerland and West Germany."

51. *Wall Street Journal* (November 22, 1978). The advertisement portrayed the Statue of Liberty with a rope around its neck and claimed that "the noose of regulation" threatened "ultimately to stifle progress." See Charles Roberts, "Rhetoric Against Regulation," letter to *Washington Post* (January 1979).

52. Robert F. Dee, "Musical Glasses and the Milky Way" (speech to Fourth Franklin Conference, Franklin Institute, Philadelphia, November 29, 1979).

53. Quoted in "Innovation—Has America Lost Its Edge?," *Newsweek* (June 4, 1979).

54. National Agricultural Chemicals Association, Washington, D.C., press release (October 31, 1980).

55. See the remarks of Rita Lavelle, who resigned as assistant administrator for solid waste from the Environmental Protection Agency over allegations of the political use of funds to clean up chemical dumps. She was alleged to have described the business community in a memorandum as "the primary constituents of this administration" ("Toxic Agency," *The Economist* [February 19, 1983]). In a memorandum of October 5, 1982, she suggested that controversial plans for imposing threshold model risk assessment techniques should be announced in a press release as a "first step" in "an expeditious, well-conceived, planned and executed communication to the scientific and regulated communities of our plans for application of 'good science' " (quoted in Marshall, "Revisions in Cancer Policy" [cit. 6]).

56. Quoted in "Vanishing Innovation" (cit. 33). One industry-sponsored group that specialized in producing critiques of environmental, health, and safety regulation under the veil of scientific objectivity was the American Council on Science and Health; for a description and critique of the council's activities, see Peter Harnik, *Voodoo Science, Twisted Consumerism: The Golden Assurances of the American Council on Science and Health* (Washington, D.C.: Center for Science in Public Interest, 1982).

57. "Vanishing Innovation" (cit. 33). In a similar vein, one company executive complained: "Industry has been compelled to spend more and more of its research dollars to comply with environmental, health, and safety regulations—and to move away from longer-term efforts aimed at major scientific advance" (Rawleigh Warner, Jr., quoted in "Innovation" [cit. 53]).

58. "America's Technology Lag," *New York Times* (April 24, 1979).

59. "The Innovation Recession," *Time* (October 2, 1978).

60. Amitai Etzioni, "Why U.S. Industry Needs Help," *Forbes* (August 18, 1980).

61. For discussion, see Sidney Lens, "Reindustrialization: Panacea or Threat?," *The Progressive* (November 1980).

62. See Richard Kazis and Richard L. Grossman, *Fear at Work: Job Blackmail, Labor, and the Environment* (New York: Environmentalists for Full Employment/Pilgrim Press, 1982).

63. Richard Kazis, "Fighting Job Blackmail: Forging a Political Movement for Jobs *and* the Environment" (paper to conference of Les Amis de la Terre, Paris, April 23–24, 1983 [mimeographed]).

64. Quoted in Barfield, *Science Policy* (cit. 34).

65. Quoted in "Digging a Spur" (cit. 39).
66. Frank Press, address to AAAS colloquium on R&D policy, Washington, D.C., June 19, 1979. Printed in Phillips et al., *Colloquium Proceedings* (cit. 32).
67. Ibid.
68. Ibid.
69. Quoted in *A Conversation with Alfred E. Kahn*, report of meeting of April 3, 1980 (Washington, D.C.: American Enterprise Institute for Public Policy Research, 1980).
70. Office of Science and Technology Policy, "Identification, Characterization, and Control of Potential Human Carcinogens: A Framework for Federal Decision-Making" (Washington, D.C.: OSTP, February 1979 [mimeographed]).
71. Nicholas Ashford, "The Limits of Cost-Benefit Analysis in Regulatory Decision-Making," *Technology Review* (May 1980). In later congressional testimony, Ashford added: "The location of a centralized entity for performing comparative risk assessments within OSTP undermines the basic consideration that risk management decisions are social policy decisions which are based only partly on hard science. Attempts to separate the scientific basis for these decisions from other considerations relevant to social policy design are as misguided as earlier attempts to establish a science court to aid in technological decision-making" (evidence to House Committee on Science and Technology, Subcommittee on Science, Research, and Technology, 96th. Cong., 1st sess. [May 14, 1980]).
72. Quoted in "Vanishing Innovation" (cit. 33).
73. Justice William J. Brennan, delivering the verdict for the majority, argued that when it created OSHA in 1970, Congress has chosen "to place preeminent value on assuring employees a safe and healthful working environment." See Linda Greenhouse, "Justices Decide U.S. Must Protect Worker's Safety Despite High Cost," *New York Times* (June 18, 1981), p. 60.
74. Press, address to AAAS (cit. 66).
75. Quoted in "Agencies May Increase Use of Risk Analysis," *Chemical and Engineering News* (October 12, 1981).
76. Statement before House Committee on Science and Technology, Subcommittee on Science, Research, and Technology, 96th Cong., 1st sess. [May 14, 1980]). See also Steven Kelman, "Cost-Benefit Analysis: An Ethical Critique," *Regulation* (January/February 1981); David F. Noble, "Cost-Benefit Analysis," *Health PAC Bulletin* (July/August 1980); Ashford, "Limits of Cost-Benefit Analysis" (cit. 71).
77. Kazis and Grossman, *Fear at Work* (cit. 62).
78. Quoted in Philip Shabecoff, "Reagan Order on Cost-Benefit Analysis Stirs Economic and Political Debate," *New York Times* (November 7, 1981). Judge David Bazelon, of the U.S. Court of Appeals for the District of Columbia, warns similarly that "the growing use of analytic tools such as cost-benefit analysis magnifies the chance that unrecognized value judgments will creep into apparently objective assessments" ("Risk and Responsibility" [address to National Institute on Law, Science, and Technology in Health Risk Regulations of American Bar Association]; published as an "occasional paper" by Hoffman-La Roche, New York, 1979).

79. William K. Tabb, "Government Regulation: Two Sides to the Story," *Challenge*, no. 48 (November/December 1980).
80. Quoted in Shabecoff, "Reagan Order" (cit. 78).
81. William D. Carey, "Science Policy: New Directions?," *Science*, vol. 210 (November 21, 1980).
82. Ashford, "Limits of Cost-Benefit Analysis" (cit. 71).
83. The claim that regulations have caused major job losses is convincingly rebutted by Kazis and Grossman, *Fear at Work* (cit. 62).
84. Quoted in Bill Peterson, "Reagan Is Finally Picking up Support in the Boardrooms," *Washington Post* (May 16, 1980).
85. Quoted in Shabecoff, "Reagan Order" (cit. 78).
86. Christopher C. DeMuth, "A Strong Beginning on Reform," *Regulation* (January/February 1982).
87. George A. Keyworth, "Science and Technology Policy—What's Ahead?" (remarks at Sixth Annual AAAS R&D Colloquium, Washington, D.C., June 25, 1981).
88. George A. Keyworth, "Issues at the Interface of Science/Technology and the United States Government" (address to annual luncheon of Parliamentary and Scientific Committee, London, February 16, 1982).
89. George A. Keyworth, remarks at Annual Monsanto Science and Technical Awards Dinner, St. Louis, January 21, 1982.
90. Quoted in R. Jeffrey Smith, "Gorsuch Strikes Back at EPA Critics," *Science*, vol. 217 (July 16, 1982).
91. Dale Russakoff, "Watt Acknowledges Consulting RNC," *Washington Post* (March 28, 1983).
92. "Carcinogen Regulations: Cleansing Solution," *Nature*, vol. 292 (July 23, 1981).
93. See, for example, the cross-examination of Gorsuch on March 19, 1982, in *Hearings on EPA* (cit. 4).
94. Quoted in administration documents in U.S. Congress, House Committee on Science and Technology, Subcommittee on Investigation and Oversight, *Formaldehyde: Review of Scientific Basis of EPA's Carcinogenic Risk Assessment* (Hearings), 97th Cong., 2d sess. (May 20, 1982), Appendix.
95. Quoted in Robert W. Crandall, "The Environment," *Regulation* (January/February 1982).
96. Richard W. Lindblom, quoted in "What Price Regulation?," *Business Week* (March 30, 1981).
97. See, for example, "A Partisan Swing Back to More Regulation," *Business Week* (May 30, 1983); Michael Wines, "The Pendulum Swings," *National Journal* (May 5, 1983).
98. Quoted in "Welcome Back, Bill Ruckelshaus," *Business Week* (April 4, 1983).
99. Cass Peterson, "Ruckelshaus Finds Issues Unchanged," *Washington Post* (May 28, 1983).
100. Ruckelshaus, "Science, Risk, Public Policy" (cit. 1).
101. Robert E. Seivers, "Revitalizing EPA," *Science*, vol. 220 (April 22, 1983).
102. Doug Costle, "Pollution's 'Invisible' Victims: Why Environmental Regulation Cannot Wait for Scientific Certainty" (address to National Coalition

on Disease Prevention and Environmental Health, Washington, D.C., April 28, 1980).

103. Quoted in Arlen Large, "The Risk-Benefit Debate," *Wall Street Journal* (June 11, 1980). Large adds: "There's obviously growing demand for a push-button objectivity machine that would reduce the 'unknowns' faced by OSHA and other agencies and make their rules seem more reasonable and acceptable."

104. See, for example, administration documents in *Formaldehyde* (cit. 94). For a full discussion, see Nicholas A. Ashford et al., "Law and Science in Federal Regulation of Formaldehyde," *Science*, vol. 222 (November 25, 1983).

105. See, for example, Philip Shabecoff, "Acid Rain Debate Tells as Much about Washington as Science," *New York Times* (February 9, 1982); Eliot Marshall, "Air Pollution Clouds U.S.-Canadian Relations," *Science*, vol. 217 (September 17, 1982); "The Bitter Politics of Acid Rain," *Newsweek* (April 5, 1983).

106. See "U.S. Academy Denies Threshold for Radiation Damage," *Nature*, vol. 279 (May 10, 1979); Richard D. Lyons, "Two Reports See Risks in Nuclear Future," *New York Times* (April 30, 1979).

107. National Academy of Sciences, press release (May 3, 1979).

108. National Academy of Sciences, press release (July 29, 1980): "Dr. Radford . . . holds that the linear model, which estimated a higher level of risk, is the only appropriate dose-response model. Dr. Rossi contends that the pure quadratic model, with a lower estimate of risk, should be preferred." See Victor Cohn, "New Study Downgrades Low-Level Radiation Risks," *Washington Post* (July 30, 1980).

109. Quoted in Lyons, "Two Reports" (cit. 106). At a National Academy of Sciences press conference, Rossi claimed that he feared the report "would contribute to excessive, and potentially detrimental, apprehension over radiation hazards" (quoted in "U.S. Academy Denies Threshold" [cit. 106]).

110. Quoted in "OSHA Hearings on Generic Cancer Policy Begin," *Chemical and Engineering News* (May 29, 1978).

111. Quoted ibid.

112. American Industrial Health Council, New York, press release (May 18, 1979).

113. Jackson Browning, evidence to Senate Committee on Environmental Affairs. Quoted ibid.

114. Quoted in Marshall, "Revisions in Cancer Policy" (cit. 6).

115. American Industrial Health Council, "AIHC Proposal for a Science Panel" (New York: AIHC, March 26, 1980 [mimeographed]).

116. Quoted in AIHC, press release (cit. 113).

117. Institute of Medicine and National Research Council, *Saccharin: Technical Assessment of Risks and Benefits* (Washington, D.C.: National Academy of Sciences, 1978).

118. Costle, "Pollution's 'Invisible' Victims" (cit. 102).

119. Bazelon, "Risk and Responsibility" (cit. 78).

120. "Regulatory Procedures and Public Health Issues in the EPA's Office of Pesticide Programs" (staff report for House Committee on Agriculture,

Subcommittee on Department Operations, Research, and Foreign Agriculture, December 1982). See Eliot Marshall, "EPA's High-Risk Cancer Policy," *Science*, vol. 218 (December 3, 1982); Christopher Joyce, "U.S. Takes Pot Luck on Cancer Risks," *New Scientist* (March 10, 1983).

121. Karim Ahmed, quoted in Eliot Marshall, "House Reviews EPA's Record on Pesticides," *Science*, vol. 219 (March 11, 1982).

122. Donald Fredrickson, "A Scientist's View of Priorities and Control in the Organization of Research," in T. Segerstedt, ed., *Ethics for Science Policy*, report from Nobel Symposium (Stockholm: Pergamon Press for Royal Swedish Academy of Sciences, 1979).

123. Clifford Grobstein, "Should Imperfect Data Be Used to Guide Public Policy?," *Science 83* [December 1983].

124. Quoted in "Risk-Benefit Debate" (cit. 103).

125. Press, address to AAAS (cit. 66). See also "U.S. Seeks to 'Rationalize' Health and Safety Regulation in the Interest of Profits," *Nature*, vol. 279 (June 28, 1979).

126. *Kahn* (cit. 69). In a similar vein, in late 1980 David Stockman (then a congressman from Michigan, later appointed director of the Office of Management and Budget by President Reagan) claimed: "You don't need to dial back on the original public health protection . . . but we need to recalibrate all the standards and the control machinery to a scientifically and economically sensible concept of public health" (quoted in "Reagan's Big Cleanup Fight," *Newsweek* [December 8, 1980]).

127. Denis Prager, evidence to House Committee on Science and Technology, Subcommittee on Science, Research, and Technology, 96th Cong., 2nd sess. (May 15, 1980). Keyworth himself spoke of the need "to improve, through science, the rational basis for establishing regulatory priorities" (George A. Keyworth, statement before House Committee on Science and Technology, 97th Cong., 1st sess. [December 10, 1981]). Similarly, William Ruckelshaus, soon after his appointment as the new administrator of the Environmental Protection Agency, described his goal as being "the rationalization of the regulatory process" (quoted in "Interview with William Ruckelshaus," *Business Week* [August 22, 1983]).

128. Joseph Williams, "1980s: The New Age of Reason," *Chemical and Engineering News* (November 19, 1979).

129. See statement by James P. Carty, on behalf of National Association of Manufacturers, to House Committee on Science and Technology, Subcommittee on Science, Research, and Technology, 96th Cong., 2nd sess. (May 14, 1980).

130. Lewis Branscomb, "Science Policy Issues in the 1980s," evidence in U.S. Congress, House Committee on Science and Technology, *National Science and Technology Policy Issues 1979: Part 1*, 96th Cong., 1st sess., p. 122

131. Donald J. House, *Science*, vol. 202 (December 22, 1978).

132. General Electric, Albany, press release (September 10, 1979).

133. Richard C. Atkinson, "Environmental Regulation," *Science*, vol. 209 (August 29, 1980).

134. S. Robert Lichter and Stanley Rothman, "Scientists' Attitudes toward Nuclear Energy," *Nature*, vol. 305 (September 8, 1983).

135. Quoted in Large, "Risk-Benefit Debate" (cit. 103).

136. Stanford University, press release (no date).
137. Sociologist Yaron Ezrahi describes the same phenomenon when he writes: "It is . . . often the prestige of scientific knowledge rather than scientific knowledge itself that politicians and others draw upon to justify their positions and to discredit their adversaries. . . . The increasing prominence and influence of scientists in the making of policy [does] not necessarily indicate a corresponding increase in the assimilation of scientific knowledge into the handling of problems of policy. It may very well mean, particularly when there is disagreement about the objectives of policy, that science is utilized for its political rather than its intellectual value." Yaron Ezrahi, "Utopian and Pragmatic Rationalism: The Political Context of Scientific Advice," *Minerva*, vol. 17, no. 1 (Spring 1980).
138. See, for example, Dorothy Nelkin, *Technological Decisions and Democracy* (Beverly Hills/London: Sage Publications, 1977); Organization for Economic Cooperation and Development, *Technology on Trial* (Paris, OECD, 1979).
139. Ashford, "Limits of Cost-Benefit Analysis" (cit. 71).
140. Quoted in Greenhouse, "Justices Decide" (cit. 73).
141. Peter J. Schuyten, "Scientific Gains and Risks," *New York Times* (May 22, 1980).
142. OECD, *Science, Growth, Society* (cit. 19).
143. Michel J. Crozier et al., *The Crisis of Democracy* (New York: New York University Press, 1975).
144. Quoted in Leonard Silk and David Vogel, *Ethics and Profits* (New York: Simon & Schuster, 1976).

CHAPTER SEVEN

1. For a detailed history of this period, see Alice Kimball Smith, *A Peril and a Hope: The Scientists' Movement in America* (Chicago: University of Chicago Press, 1965); and Robert Jungk, *Brighter Than a Thousand Suns: The Moral and Political History of the Atomic Scientists* (London: Gollancz, 1958).
2. See James R. Newman and Byron S. Miller, *The Control of Atomic Energy* (New York: McGraw-Hill, 1948); Robert Gilpin, *American Scientists and Nuclear Weapons Policy* (Princeton, N.J.: Princeton University Press, 1962).
3. See the collection of articles reprinted from *Science for the People* and other journals in Rita Arditti et al., eds., *Science and Liberation* (Boston: South End Press, 1980).
4. See, for example, Ann Arbor Science for the People Editorial Collective, *Biology as a Social Weapon* (Minneapolis: Burgess, 1977).
5. Christopher Wright and Anne C. Kalicki, "Annual Report of the Staff: Program in Science and Society," *Carnegie Institution of Washington Yearbook, 1980* (Washington, D.C.: Carnegie Institution, December 1981).
6. National Science Foundation and Department of Education, *Science and Engineering Education for the 1980s and Beyond* (Washington, D.C.: NSF/Department of Education, October 1980).

7. Ibid. For a critical comment, see Bruce A. Beatie, "The Need for 'Literacy' Goes Beyond Science," *Chronicle of Higher Education* (June 8, 1983).

8. Donald Kennedy, 1982 Convocation Address at University of Oregon, Eugene. Printed in *New York Times Higher Education Supplement* (December 17, 1982).

9. Felix Rohatyn, "Time for Change," *New York Review of Books* (August 18, 1983).

10. Robert B. Reich, "The True Road to Industrial Renewal," *The Nation* (March 7, 1981). See also Robert B. Reich, *The Next American Frontier* (New York: N.Y. Times Books, 1983).
   Frank Press, testimony to House Committee on Science and Technology 97th Cong., 1st sess. (December 10, 1981).

12. Frank Press, "Rethinking Science Policy," *Science*, vol. 218 (October 1, 1982).

13. See, for example, Press's reply to a report from the General Accounting Office criticizing, among other things, the lack of a formal mechanism to provide a detailed review of the agenda of the Office of Science and Technology Policy. Press contended: "I have consciously hesitated to establish a more formal mechanism because of the need for confidentiality at critical junctures in the review process" (Comptroller General of U.S., *The Office of Science and Technology Policy: Adaptation to a President's Operating Style May Conflict with Congressionally Mandated Assignments* [Washington, D.C., General Accounting Office, September 3, 1980]). No such reservations, however, seem to have been felt by the Reagan administration in creating the White House Science Council.

14. See, for example, Robert S. Lopez, *The Commercial Revolution of the Middle Ages, 950–1350* (Englewood Cliffs, N.J.: Prentice-Hall, 1971).

15. The political basis of the new naturalistic ideology of Renaissance painting is described in Frederick Antal, *Florentine Painting and Its Social Background* (London: Kegan Paul, 1947); and Lauro Martines, *Power and Imagination: City States in Renaissance Italy* (New York: Knopf, 1979), chap. 13 ("Art: An Alliance with Power").

16. See Charles Webster, *The Great Instauration* (London: Duckworth, 1975). According to Webster: "The fragmentary philosophical system bequeathed by Bacon became for Puritan intellectuals both the basis for the conception of material progress and the framework for their social planning."

17. David Dickson, "Science and Political Hegemony in the 17th Century," *Radical Science Journal*, no. 8 (1979).

18. Francis Bacon, *Novum Organum: or True Directions for the Interpretation of Nature* (London: Ward, Locke & Bowden, 1894).

19. The spread of scientific rationality as a key component of political thinking during the Enlightenment is described in Peter Gay, *The Enlightenment: An Interpretation* (New York: Knopf, 1969). For a survey of the main ideas of this period and their roots in the Scientific Revolution of the seventeenth century, see Isaiah Berlin, ed., *The Age of Enlightenment* (New York: New American Library, 1956).

20. A detailed analysis of Thomas Jefferson's intellectual debts to Bacon and Newton is provided by Gary Wills in *Inventing America: Jefferson's Declaration of Independence* (Garden City, N.Y.: Doubleday, 1978). See also

Henry Steele Commager, *The Empire of Reason: How Europe Imagined and America Realized the Enlightenment* (Garden City, N.Y.: Anchor Press/Doubleday, 1977).

21. One story of the opposition to this process of rationalization is told in Lawrence Goodwin, *Democratic Promise: The Populist Moment in America* (Oxford: Oxford University Press, 1976).

22. Quoted in Peter Dobkin Hall, *The Organization of American Culture 1700–1900* (New York: New York University Press, 1982).

23. J. Montgomery, *The Cotton Manufacture of the United States Contrasted and Compared with That of Great Britain.* Quoted in H. J. Habakkuk, *America and British Technology in the Nineteenth Century* (Cambridge, Eng.: Cambridge University Press, 1962).

24. Robert Ozane, *A Century of Labor-Management Relations at McCormick and International Harvester* (Madison: University of Wisconsin Press, 1967).

25. Lars G. Sandberg, "American Rings and English Mules: The Role of Economic Rationality," *Quarterly Journal of Economics* (February 1969).

26. U.S. Bureau of Census, *Census of Manufacturers, 1905*, vol. 3 (Washington, D.C.: Bureau of Census, 1909), p. 42. Quoted ibid.

27. See, for example, Kennedy, Convocation Address (cit. 8).

28. Hall, *Organization of American Culture* (cit. 22).

29. See Burton J. Bledstein, *The Culture of Professionalism: The Middle Class and the Development of Higher Education in America* (New York: Norton, 1976).

30. See Hall, *Organization of American Culture* (cit. 22). In his words: "Thanks to the war and their social reading of Darwin [intellectual and cultural leaders] could redefine their ideas about the locus of authority, shifting it from politics and religion to science, the world of matter in which the voice of God expressed itself far more authoritatively than through the voice of the people. In concrete social and political terms, this shift altered the public perception of the relation between wealth, ideas, and power."

31. See Loren Baritz, *The Servants of Power: A History of the Use of Social Science in American Industry* (Middletown, Conn.: Wesleyan University Press, 1960).

32. For a description of the attraction of science as a political ideology to professional engineers, see William E. Akin, *Technocracy and The American Dream: The Technocratic Movement, 1900–1941* (Berkeley: University of California Press, 1977).

33. Frederick M. Taylor, *The Principles of Scientific Management* (New York: Harper & Brothers, 1911).

34. See Richard Edwards, *Contested Terrain: The Transformation of the Workplace in the Twentieth Century* (New York: Basic Books, 1979). Edwards writes: "The Ford [assembly] line resolved technologically the essential first control system task: it provided unambiguous direction as to what operation each worker was to perform next, and it established the pace at which the worker was forced to work. Henry Ford himself emphasized this aspect of the line by stating as one of his three principles of progressive manufacture, 'the delivery of work instead of leaving it to the workman's initiative to find it.' Ford might well have added that the line's 'delivery of work' also relieved his foreman of having to push work on to the worker, as was necessary with simple control."

35. See Joseph A. Schumpeter, as in his *Business Cycles: A Theoretical, Historical, and Statistical Analysis of the Capitalist Process* (New York: McGraw-Hill, 1939).

36. See David F. Noble, *America by Design: Science, Technology, and the Rise of Corporate Capitalism* (New York: Knopf, 1977), esp. chap. 1 ("The Rise of Science-Based Industry").

37. For a detailed discussion of the application of Kondratiev's and Schumpeter's ideas to current thinking about the role of science and technology in economic growth, see Christopher Freeman et al., *Unemployment and Technical Innovation: A Study of Long Waves and Economic Development* (London: Pinter, 1982). See also the papers by Freeman and other authors in *Futures* (August 1981).

38. See, for example, Bruce Merrifield (Assistant Secretary of Commerce for Science and Technology), "Forces of Change Affecting High Technology Industries," *National Journal* (January 29, 1983). Merrifield writes that "a tremendous buildup of underutilized technology is already fueling the next cycle—in electronics, communications, engineering, plastics, biogenetics, specialty chemicals, pharmaceuticals, and so forth." The most positive statement of the possibilities offered by the new science-based technologies is in Gerhard Mensch, *Stalemate in Technology: Innovations Overcome the Depression* (New York: Ballinger, 1979); for a critique of Mensch's theoretical perspective, however, see Freeman et al., *Unemployment and Technical Innovation* (cit. 37).

39. See the remarks of economist Ernest Mandel in *Long Waves of Capitalist Development: The Marxist Interpretation* (Cambridge, Eng.: Cambridge University Press, 1980). He suggests that "toward the end of an expansionist long wave and during a large part of the subsequent depressive long wave, the decline in the rate of profit is pronounced, and that rate remains generally in a trough much lower than during the preceding expansionist long wave. There is then a growing and powerful incentive for capital to radically increase the rate of surplus value, which cannot be achieved through increases in the work load, speed-ups, intensification of the existing labor process, etc., but demands profound change in that process."

40. Frank Press, "Science and Technology in the White House," *Science*, vol. 211 (January 9, 1981).

41. See, for example, the press release of September 19, 1983, of the newly formed Committee for Responsible Genetics, a group of scientists and labor unionists. Their statement argued: "The new developments in genetics are the product of forty years of taxpayers' financing through the NIH and the NSF. Presently major developments that should remain in the public sector are being transferred to the private sector. As a result the public is being forced to buy back what it itself has financed. One of the activities of the committee will be to protect the public's substantial investment in this essential technology."

42. See Barbara Culliton, "House Battles over NIH Legislation," *Science*, vol. 221 (August 19, 1983).

43. A description of one attempt to put such ideals into practice can be found in the Thimann Laboratory Group, "Toward a Liberatory Research Environment," in Arditti et al., eds., *Science and Liberation* (cit. 3). In the article, "a group of scientists and science students at the University of

California, Santa Cruz, describe their efforts to develop a more human, creative, and liberating work environment by restructuring their work life along lines of cooperative support." Other information from: Science for the People, 897 Main Street, Cambridge, Mass. 02139.

44. Hilary Wainwright and David Elliott, *The Lucas Plan: A New Trade Unionism in the Making* (London: Allison & Busby, 1982). The principles on which the Lucas campaign was based are outlined in Mike Cooley, *Architect or Bee?* (Boston: South End Press, 1980).

45. See the press release of September 29, 1983, from the Committee for Responsible Genetics, which states: "Society has learned a great deal from witnessing developments in nuclear and chemical technologies over the past several decades. One important lesson is that it is crucial to inform the public on ways that technologies can affect their lives. Another lesson is that it is critical to involve diverse groups of people in the formulation of policies before a technology has been fully integrated into the industrial sector." Further information from: Committee for Responsible Genetics, PO Box 759, Cambridge, Mass. 02238.

46. See Dorothy Nelkin and Arie Rip, "Distributing Expertise: A Dutch Experiment in Public Interest Science," *Bulletin of Atomic Scientists* (May 1979); Jon Turney, "What Do Science Shops Offer to Their Customers?," *Times Higher Education Supplement* (December 10, 1982). The Dutch science shops found limitations in a strategy based primarily on answering individual queries, so they have recently developed a system of working through "project centers" (one for women, one for environmental problems, one for labor unions, and one for Third World questions). This approach is similar to the "matrix strategy" described in this chapter. See Peter Groenewegen and Paul Swuste, "Science Shops in the Netherlands" (paper for conference at Nijmegen, Netherlands, May 2, 1983). More information can be obtained from: Wetenschapswinkel, University of Amsterdam, Herengracht 530, Amsterdam, Netherlands.

47. See, for example, Joel S. Yudken et al., "Knowhere: A Community-Based Information Utility for the Disabled Using Microcomputers," available (with other information) from: Mid-Peninsula Conversion Project, Inc., 86 West Dana Street #203, Mountain View, Cal. 94041. The group's work is described in Robert Howard, "Engineers Take the Knowledge and Run," *In These Times* (September 2–8, 1981).

48. New Mexico Solar Energy Association, PO Box 2004, Santa Fe, N.M. 87501.

49. See "Bootstrap Community Revitalization in North America: An Account of the First Seminar on Tools for Community Economic Transformation," organized by E. F. Schumacher Society in Great Barrington, Mass., May 18–25, 1982.

50. See, for example, *Draft Report of International Forum on Technological Advances and Development* (Tbilisi, USSR, April 12–16, 1983). It proposed that "a new form of international cooperation be considered with the designation of a limited number of new advanced technologies to meet needs of a clear and urgent character to the human community as 'technologies for humanity.' These technologies should be developed as disseminated in the public domain."

51. Liz Fee, "A Feminist Critique of Scientific Objectivity," *Science for the People* (July/August 1982). Also Women's Group from Science for the People, "Declaration: Equality for Women in Science," in Arditti et al., eds., *Science and Liberation* (cit. 3).

52. See Boston Women's Health Book Collective, *Our Bodies, Ourselves: A Book by and for Women* (New York: Touchstone/Simon & Schuster, 1975).

53. See David Dickson, "France Sets Out to Democratize Science," *Science*, vol. 218 (October 29, 1982).

54. For a full account of the growth of political awareness in labor unions around health and safety issues, see Daniel M. Berman, *Death on the Job: Occupational Health and Safety Struggles in the United States* (New York: Monthly Review Press, 1978).

55. See, for example, William Winpisinger, "A Labor View of Technological Innovation," *Technology Review* (April 1981).

56. Karl Frieden, *Workplace Democracy and Productivity* (Washington, D.C.: National Center for Economic Alternatives, 1980).

57. For a discussion of the "scientization" of the debate over the safety of nuclear energy, see David Rosenfeld, "Don't Just Reduce Risk—Transform It," in *No Clear Reason: Nuclear Power Politics* (London: Free Association Books, 1984). Further information from: Abalone Alliance, c/o American Friends Service Committee, 944 Market Street, Room 307, San Francisco, Cal. 94102.

58. See "Environmentalists Dig In, Form Coalitions," *Chemical and Engineering News* (November 24, 1980); OSHA/Environmental Network "Connecticut Unionists and Environmentalists Protest Reagan Administration Attacks on OSHA and Clean Air Act," press release (October 5, 1981). Details of the growing cooperation between the labor and environmental movements are given in Richard Kazis and Richard L. Grossman, *Fear at Work: Job Blackmail and the Environment* (New York: Environmentalists for Full Employment) Pilgrim Press, 1982). Further information from Environmentalists for Full Employment, 1536 16th Street NW, Washington, D.C. 20036.

59. Information available from: The Intermediate Technology Development Group of North America, Inc., 777 United Nations Plaza, New York, N.Y. 10017.

60. These issues are discussed in David Dickson, *The Politics of Alternative Technology* (New York: Universe Books, 1975).

61. For a description of the strategies of the creationist movement, see Dorothy Nelkin, *The Science-Text Book Controversies* (Cambridge, Mass.: MIT Press, 1976); Joel Guerin, "The Creationist Revival," *The Sciences* (April 1981); John Skow, "The Genesis of Equal Time: Creationism as Social Movement," *Science 81* (December 1981); George M. Marsden, "Creation versus Evolution: No Middle Way," *Nature*, vol. 305 (October 13, 1983).

62. An outline of a possible alternative strategy is provided in Martin Carnoy and Derek Shearer, *Economic Democracy: The Challenge of the 1980s* (White Plains, N.Y.: Sharpe, 1980).

GLOSSARY
of ACRONYMS

AAAS—American Association for the Advancement of Science
AAU—Association of American Universities
AAUP—American Association of University Professors
ABM—anti-ballistic missile
ACE—American Council on Education
AEC—Atomic Energy Commission
AFL-CIO—American Federation of Labor–Congress of Industrial Organizations
AID—Agency for International Development
AIHC—American Industrial Health Council
ARPA—(DARPA)—Advanced Research Projects Agency
ASM—American Society of Microbiology
AT&T—American Telephone and Telegraph

BEIR—(Committee)—Biological Effects of Ionizing Radiation

CBA—cost-benefit assessment
CDC—Center for Disease Control
CED—Committee for Economic Development
COGENT—Center for Generic Technology
COWPS—Council on Wage and Price Stability

DARPA—see ARPA
DDR&E—Director of Defense Research and Engineering
DIB—defense industrial base
DoD—Department of Defense
DoE—Department of Energy
DSB—Defense Science Board

EAR—Export Administration Regulations
EPA—Environmental Protection Agency
ERAB—Energy Research Advisory Board
ERDA—Energy Research and Development Agency
ESPRIT—European Strategic Research Program on Information Technology
EVIST—Ethics and Values in Science Technology

FFRDC—federally funded research and development center
FPPC—Fair Political Practices Commission
FTC—Federal Trade Commission

GE—General Electric

HEW—(Department of) Health, Education, and Welfare

IAEA—International Atomic Energy Agency
IBCs—Institutional Biosafety Committees
IBM—International Business Machines
ICBM—intercontinental ballistic missile
ICF—inertial confinement fusion
IDF—International Development Foundation
IEEE—Institute of Electrical and Electronic Engineers
IPA—institutional patent agreement
IRLG—Interagency Regulatory Liaison Group
ISTC—Institute for Scientific and Technical Collaboration
ITAR—International Traffic in Arms Regulations
ITEK—a high-technology company known only by this acronym

LDCs—less-developed countries

MIT—Massachusetts Institute of Technology
MNC—multinational corporation

NAE—National Academy of Engineering
NAS—National Academy of Sciences
NASA—National Aeronautics and Space Administration
NATO—North Atlantic Treaty Organization
NDRC—National Defense Research Committee
NEA—Nuclear Energy Agency
NEPA—National Environmental Policy Act
NIH—National Institutes of Health
NRC—National Research Council
NRDC—Natural Resources Defense Council
NSA—National Security Agency
NSF—National Science Foundation

OECD—Organization for Economic Cooperation and Development
OES—Bureau of Oceans and International Environmental and
        Scientific Affairs
OMB—Office of Management and Budget
ONR—Office of Naval Research
OPEC—Organization of Petroleum Exporting Countries
OSHA—Occupational Safety and Health Administration
OSRD—Office of Scientific Research and Development
OSTP—Office of Science and Technology Policy
OTA—Office of Technology Assessment

PCSG—Public Cryptography Study Group
PSAC—President's Science Advisory Committee
PVC—polyvinyl chloride

RAC—Recombinant DNA Advisory Committee
RARG—Regulatory Analysis Review Group
RBNS—Research Board for National Security

R&D—research and development
rDNA—recombinant DNA
RIAs—regulatory impact analyses

SESPA—Scientists and Engineers for Social and Political Action
SST—supersonic transport

TRW—a company known only by this acronym

UC—University of California
UN—United Nations
UNCSTD—United Nations Conference on Science and Technology for
Development
UNCTAD—United Nations Conference on Trade and Development
UNDP—United Nations Development Program
UNIDO—United Nations Industrial Development Organization

VHSIC—very high speed integrated circuits
VLSI—very large-scale integration

WHO—World Health Organization

INDEX